POPULAR CHILDREN'S LITERATURE IN BRITAIN

This book is dedicated to the memory of Professor Julia Briggs

Popular Children's Literature in Britain

Edited by

JULIA BRIGGS†

DENNIS BUTTS

M. O. GRENBY

ASHGATE

Julia Briggs, Dennis Butts and Matthew Grenby have asserted their moral right under the Copyright, Designs and Patents Act, 1988, to be identified as the editors of this work.

Published by
Ashgate Publishing Limited
Gower House
Croft Road
Aldershot
Hampshire GU11 3HR
England

Ashgate Publishing Company
Suite 420
101 Cherry Street
Burlington, VT 05401-4405
USA

Ashgate website: http://www.ashgate.com

British Library Cataloguing in Publication Data
Popular children's literature in Britain
  1. Children's literature, English – History and criticism 2. Children – Books and reading – Great Britain 3. Popular literature – Great Britain – History and criticism 4. Literature and society – Great Britain – History
  I. Briggs, Julia II. Butts, Dennis, 1932–
  III. Grenby, M. O. (Matthew Orville), 1970–
  820.9'9282

Library of Congress Cataloging-in-Publication Data
Briggs, Julia.
  Popular children's literature in Britain / Julia Briggs, Dennis Butts, and M.O. Grenby.
     p. cm.
  Includes bibliographical references.
  ISBN 978-1-84014-242-6 (alk. paper)
  1. Children's literature, English–History and criticism. 2. Children–Books and reading–Great Britain. 3. Popular literature–Great Britain–History and criticism. 4. Literature and society–Great Britain–History. I. Butts, Dennis, 1932– II. Grenby, M. O. (Matthew Orville), 1970– III. Title.

PR990.B69 2007
820.9'9282–dc22
                                                                                2007030557

ISBN 978-1-84014-242-6

Printed and bound in Great Britain by TJ International Ltd, Padstow, Cornwall.

Contents

List of Illustrations

Notes on Contributors

Brian Alderson has been an author, editor, translator and reviewer of children's literature. He has lectured and published widely on the subject, revising F.J. Harvey Darton's *Children's Books in England* (1982) and, most recently, producing *Edward Ardizzone: A Bibliographic Commentary* (2003) and (with Felix de Marez Oyens) *Be Merry and Wise: Origins of Children's Book Publishing in England, 1650–1850* (2006).

Gillian Avery is the author of many children's books and won the *Guardian* award for children's fiction for *A Likely Lad* (1971). Her critical books include *Nineteenth-Century Children* (1965), *Childhood's Pattern* (1975), *Behold the Child: American Children and Their Books* (1995) and (edited with Kimberly Reynolds) *Representations of Childhood Death* (2000).

David Blamires, formerly Professor of German at Manchester University, has written on many aspects of children's literature, especially fairy tales, Heinrich Hoffmann's *Struwwelpeter*, and the reception of nineteenth-century German children's books in English.

Julia Briggs OBE was Professor of English Literature and Women's Studies at De Montfort University. She has published extensively in several fields, her books including *A Woman of Passion: The Life of E. Nesbit* (1987), *This Stage-play World: Texts and Contexts, 1580–1625* (revised edition 1997) and *Virginia Woolf: An Inner Life* (2006). Julia Briggs died in 2007.

Dennis Butts taught on the MA course in children's literature at Reading University. He has written widely on various aspects of nineteenth-century children's literature, and edited several children's books in the World's Classics series for Oxford University Press. His most recent publication was a collection of unpublished short stories by G.A. Henty entitled *Six Dusty Diamonds* (2005).

Kevin Carpenter taught English at the University of Oldenburg. He is the author of a number of studies of British popular literature, including *Penny Dreadfuls and Comics: English Periodicals for Children from Victorian Times to the Present Day* (1983) and *Robin Hood: The Many Faces of that Celebrated English Outlaw* (1995).

Julia Eccleshare has been an author and editor of children's books and is now children's books editor for the *Guardian.* She is the author of *A Guide to the Harry Potter Novels* (2002), co-author (with Anne Fine) of *Beatrix Potter to Harry Potter: Portraits of Children's Writers (2002)* and co-editor (with Nicholas Tucker) of *The Rough Guide to Books for Teenagers* (2003).

Aileen Fyfe is Lecturer in the History of Science at the National University of Ireland, Galway. She is the author of *Science and Salvation: Evangelicals and Popular Science Publishing in Victorian Britain* (2004) and editor of *Science for Children* (2003).

Stacy Gillis is Lecturer in Modern and Contemporary Literature at Newcastle University, UK. She has published widely on contemporary feminist theory, cybertheory, cyberpunk and popular fictions.

M. O. Grenby is Reader in Children's Literature in the School of English at Newcastle University. He works on eighteenth-century culture, especially the early history of children's literature. His publications include *The Anti-Jacobin Novel* (2001), an edition of Sarah Trimmer's *Guardian of Education* (2002), *The Edinburgh Critical Guide to Children's Literature* (2002) and the Hockliffe Project, an online resource containing hundreds of digitised early children's books plus contextualising essays, <http://www.cts.dmu.ac.uk/hockliffe>.

Peter Hollindale was formerly Reader in English and Educational Studies at the University of York. His publications include *Choosing Books for Children* (1974), *Ideology and the Children's Book* (1988) and *Signs of Childness in Children's Books* (1997), as well as the Oxford University Press World's Classics edition of *Peter Pan in Kensington Gardens and Peter and Wendy* (1991).

Elaine Lomax gained her PhD from De Montfort University for 'A Study of the Writings of Hesba Stretton in their Social and Cultural Context'. Her monograph, *The Writings of Hesba Stretton: Reclaiming the Outcast*, will be published by Ashgate in 2009.

Kimberley Reynolds is Professor of Children's Literature in the School of English at Newcastle University. She founded the National Centre for Research in Children's Literature and was President of the International Research Society for Children's Literature from 2003–7. Her most recent publication is *Radical Children's Literature: Future Visions and Aesthetic Transformations in Children's Literature* (2007).

David Rudd is Professor of Children's Literature in the Department of Cultural and Creative Studies at the University of Bolton. He has published over a hundred articles as well as two books, *A Communication Studies Approach to Children's Literature* (1992) and *Enid Blyton and the Mystery of Children's Literature* (2000).

Judy Simons is Professor of English and Pro Vice Chancellor at De Montfort University, Leicester. She has written widely on nineteenth and twentieth-century literature. Her books include *Diaries and Journals of Literary Women from Fanny Burney to Virginia Woolf* (1990), *Rosamond Lehmann* (1992), *What Katy Read: Feminist Re-readings of 'Classic' Stories for Girls* (1995) co-authored with Shirley Foster, and *The Contexts of English Literature* (2001), edited with Rick Rylance.

George Speaight was smitten by toy theatres when a young boy, just after the First World War. The performances he gave to customers when he worked at Bumpus's bookshop in London in the early 1930s quickly became legendary, enticing even Queen Mary to visit. He remained the most celebrated exponent of the toy theatre throughout his life, as well as becoming a distinguished puppeteer. He published widely on the history of these forgotten art forms. *Juvenile Drama: The History of the English Toy Theatre* appeared in 1946 (revised 1969), *The History of the English Puppet Theatre* in 1955, *Bawdy Songs of the Early Music Hall* in 1975, and *Punch and Judy: A History* in 1970. George Speaight died in 2005.

Acknowledgements

This book has been a long time in the making. It was conceived in the mid 1990s, before the arrival of the first Harry Potter book, and the new relevance that J.K. Rowling's extraordinary success gave to a study of popularity and children's literature. Since its inception, the volume has gone through a number of incarnations, and its roster of contributors has changed many times. Thanks are due to those who were commissioned to contribute chapters as much as a decade ago and who have revised and resubmitted their chapters several times since so that they appear here in an evolved and up-to-date form. This patience, and willingness to revise, has been testament to the enduring scholarly values of the contributors in an age when institutional and personal deadlines and assessment exercise cut-off dates often put pressure on academics to research, publish and move on in as short a time as possible. Thanks are also due to those who wrote chapters for the volume but subsequently, and for a variety of different and compelling reasons, withdrew them: notably Valerie Alderson, Sue Dipple, Pat Garrett, Selwyn Goodacre, Andrea Immel and Chris Routh. These contributions helped to shape the volume as it grew, and their trace clearly remains in the make-up of the book and the approach that the editors have adopted.

Enormous patience and tolerance has been shown by our editors at Ashgate Press, most particularly Ann Donahue and Erika Gaffney. But above all, this book has benefited from careful scrutiny by two of the most distinguished scholars of children's literature, Peter Hunt and Brian Alderson. Both very kindly agreed to read a full draft, and their corrections and suggestions for revision have made both the individual chapters and the volume as a whole very much stronger. The full typescript was read by two anonymous readers for Ashgate Press, and their careful criticism has also improved the book significantly. Those mistakes and omissions that remain are, of course, the responsibility of the authors and editors alone.

We would also like to thank those who have provided illustrations, or given permission for their use. Most of the illustrations reproduced here have been taken from the personal collections of the contributors and editors (full details can be found in the List of Illustrations). But we are very grateful for the enthusiastic cooperation, and willingness to grant permissions, shown by Diana Saulsbury, Library Services Manager at the Polhill Library of the University of Bedfordshire, home to the Hockliffe Collection (for an illustration in Chapter 2); Colin Lattimore, Chairman of the Bookplate Society (for the illustrations in Chapter 10); Tony Summerfield of the Enid Blyton Society (for an illustration in Chapter 13); and Romily Must of the Christopher Little Literary Agency and Kate Harvey, Rights Executive at

Bloomsbury Publishing (for the illustrations in Chapter 15). In all cases, every effort has been made to trace copyright holders, but if any have inadvertently been overlooked we will be pleased to make any necessary arrangements at the first opportunity.

Julia Briggs, Dennis Butts and Matthew Grenby
Newcastle upon Tyne, 31 May 2007

Professor Julia Briggs died suddenly on 16 August 2007, while this book was in press. The initial idea for the book was Julia's, and it was she who established the book's philosophy and set it on its way to publication. Presenting the idea to an initially sceptical publisher in the mid 1990s (for academic studies of children's literature were then much rarer than they are now), Julia secured a contract with a typically brilliant and utterly convincing account of what the book was to be about and why it was important. This is one small instance of the great work that Julia performed in the service of neglected literature of many kinds, especially in establishing scholarly research into children's books. This book is gratefully and affectionately dedicated to her memory.

Chapter 1

General Introduction

M. O. Grenby

The recent astonishing success of certain children's books makes a study of popularity and children's literature a very timely undertaking. J.K. Rowling's 'Harry Potter' books are, of course, the most prominent example. *Harry Potter and the Order of the Phoenix* (2003) was the fastest selling book in UK history (5 million copies in one day); *Harry Potter and the Half-Blood Prince* (2005) had a larger print-run than any previous title in the USA (10 million copies). The spontaneity and universality of this acclaim and appeal, but equally its contrivance and pervasiveness, provides the impetus for a fresh investigation into the complex interplay of forces that come to bear on literary popularity. Such phenomenal success calls for a reassessment of our understanding and interpretation of the workings of popularity within children's culture. It has certainly reminded us, if we needed reminding, of just how passionately children care about their books, and just how potent a force the popularity of children's books can be.

Above all, such success demands a careful consideration of the historical perspective. The apparent step-change in the possibilities of popularity of children's books requires us to ask whether the Harry Potter phenomenon is unique and unprecedented, or simply part of a repeated cycle of success and decline within the publishing industry. Perhaps it might even be the inevitable consequence of children's reading habits – a tendency to surfeit on particular kinds of texts, to consume, almost fanatically, works by one particular author, or of one distinct genre. Critical discussion of the Harry Potter series has often asked whether it was the imaginative quality of Rowling's work, or simply their shrewd marketing that has made these books so successful. The chapters in this volume begin to answer these questions, not simply on behalf of the Harry Potter books, but on behalf of successful children's literature over the last two or three centuries. Taken individually, these chapters provide a series of case studies exploring the popularity of particular books, or particular types of books. Taken together, they explore how and why popularity in children's literature can be – and has been – created, sustained and lost, and whether the same processes which have made a cultural icon of Harry Potter have also been at work for as long as children's books have been published, read and loved.

The first step must be to define what constitutes popular children's literature, for the term 'popular' is peculiarly slippery. Dictionaries provide a web of related but potentially contradictory definitions. To complicate things further, the term is liable to be appropriated in the service of competing ideological interests. For some, the popular (popular music, popular literature, popular practices and beliefs) can threaten the highest achievements of a society – its art, its manners, its values and laws – and therefore should be curbed or reformed. For others, the popular is itself an expression of cultural identity – the spirit of the people – and as such must be protected and fostered.[1] For our purposes, there are two main ways of understanding popular literature. The first defines it as that which is suited to ordinary tastes, and to ordinary means: the quotidian and the 'low', the inexpensive and the ephemeral, or, as Victor Neuburg put it in his path-breaking study of popular literature, 'what the unsophisticated reader has chosen for pleasure'.[2] A quick glance through the contents page of this volume shows that some of the chapters seem to conform to this definition: the chapter on chapbooks, for instance. Alongside it, other chapters in the 'Old Tales Retold' section of this book chart the enduring popularity of traditional folk and fairy tales.

But several other chapters in this volume are predicated on an altogether different definition of the popular. Those in the Part II, for instance, that examine once celebrated but now neglected authors, or those in Part IV, that investigate the reasons for the appeal of particular bestsellers, define popular literature as that which has been well-liked or commercially successful, or both. Nor do we find in Arthur Mee's *Children's Encyclopedia* (discussed by Gillian Avery) that crude, unrefined and subversive quality so often associated with the literature of the street. Yet although these two basic definitions of popular literature seem in some ways to compete, in actual fact they have seldom been mutually exclusive. The 'vulgar' is often commercially successful; the quotidian could certainly be well-loved and enduring.

Slippery at the best of times, both these definitions of the popular become more problematic when we consider popular literature written specifically for children. For one thing, it is notoriously difficult to be sure who were the intended readers of the street literature, traditional tales, chapbooks and broadsides that constitute 'popular literature' according to our initial definition. In his survey, Victor Neuburg did not risk an attempt to separate material addressed to children from that which was intended for adults.[3] Is it possible, then, to talk of a distinct 'popular children's literature' in this sense? Yet, methodologically speaking, our second definition is no easier. For adult literature, popularity (in the sense of those books that were well-liked) can be estimated convincingly on the basis of sales. Since Sir Walter Scott's *Waverley* went through four editions within a year of publication, and *Betty Crocker's Cookbook* sold 20 million copies between 1969 and 1982, it may reasonably be argued that they were popular.[4] But with children's books, sales figures (generated by the decisions of the adults who buy the books) do not necessarily correspond to

---

1   These competing definitions, and others, are discussed in the first chapter ('A History of Changing Definitions of "The Popular"') of Morag Shiach's *Discourse on Popular Culture: Class, Gender and History in Cultural Analysis, 1730 to the Present* (Cambridge: Polity Press, 1989), pp. 19–34.

2   Victor Neuburg, *Popular Literature: A History and Guide* (London: Woburn Press, 1977), p. 12.

3   Ibid.

4   Walter Scott, *Waverley*, ed. Claire Lamont (1814, repr. Oxford: Oxford University Press, 1986), p. xxii; D. Maryles, 'All-Time Hardcover Bestsellers, Adult and Children's Books', pp. 69–71, in *Publishers Weekly Yearbook: News, Analyses and Trends in the Book Industry* (New York and London: R.R. Bowker 1983), p. 69.

the actual appeal of the text to its end-users (the children who read it), and who may have had little say as to which books were bought or borrowed for them.

On the other hand, if we discount sales figures, how are we to ascertain children's reading preferences at all? Records of children's opinions are scarce, especially before the twentieth century, and where they do exist they are scarcely reliable. Diaries, journals and letters purporting to reveal children's reading habits are prone to embellishment and a tendency to conform to what their authors think is expected of them or to how they would like to appear. Childhood memoirs, written many years later, are even less trustworthy. Like diaries, they often follow established rhetorical conventions, and include predictable and audience-pleasing lists of reading. They are further distorted by lapses of memory and the almost irresistible urge to edit autobiography. By and large, they tend to be produced by a self-selecting section of the population – writers, politicians, clergymen and so on: high-achievers in their adult lives, and thus hardly representative of the general run of children of that generation. The surveys of children's reading preferences, conducted from the late nineteenth century to the present, demonstrate comparable problems. For example, Edward Salmon included a survey of a thousand 'young ladies' in an article on 'What Girls Read' which he published in 1886, but having pondered the results, he could not 'help thinking that the list far from adequately represents what girls read'. Salmon surmised that the interviewees probably 'considered it proper to vote for such names as Scott and Dickens' (who easily top the list). Or perhaps, he suggested, they could not remember the names of those writers whose work they enjoyed more, so that they were forced to fall back on well-known authors whose names came instantly to mind.[5] Surveys of juvenile reading habits conducted and published in the USA in the 1920s, by A.J. Jenkinson in Britain in 1940, by Frank Whitehead and his team in 1972 and Martin Coles and Christine Hall in 1994–95, not to mention the newspaper, broadcasting and bookshop-sponsored lists of favourite books which appear so often today, are all prone to exactly the same objections that Salmon identified more than a century ago.[6]

On the other hand, we should not dismiss these surveys just because they throw up results that look, at first sight, somewhat unlikely. Salmon, for example, thought

---

5   Edward. G. Salmon, 'What Girls Read', *Nineteenth Century* 20 (1886), 515–29 (p. 528).

6   A.M. Jordan, *Children's Interests in Reading* (Chapel Hill and London: University of North Carolina Press, 1921, rev. 1926); L.M. Terman, and M. Lima, *Children's Reading* (New York: Appleton, 1925); C. Washburn and M. Vogel, *Winnetka Graded Book List* (Chicago: American Library Association, 1926); A.J. Jenkinson, *What Do Boys and Girls Read?* (London: Methuen, 1940). The methodological problems of such surveys, and consideration of how they may be overcome, are explored in the opening chapter of the final report by Frank Whitehead [*et al.*], *Children and their Books*, Schools Council Research Studies (London: Macmillan, 1977). Brief analysis of the Hall and Coles survey is online at <http://www.nottingham.ac.uk/education/centres/clr/wh-smith-report.pdf> (accessed 18 April 2007). For a more recent survey of children's favourite books, conducted after the advent of J.K. Rowling's Harry Potter books, see a report in the *Guardian*, 23 September 2002, <http://books.guardian.co.uk/news/table/0,6109,797541,00.html> (accessed 18 April 2007) or 'The Big Read' survey conducted in the UK by the BBC during 2003, <http://www.bbc.co.uk/arts/bigread/> (accessed 18 April 2007).

it 'absurd' to imagine that Thomas Carlyle was more popular with girls than, say, *Black Beauty*, as his raw data seemed to show. But as he himself pointed out, the availability of a book is just as important a factor in its popularity as its literary merits or its appeal for children. Dickens, Scott and Carlyle were 'probably in the school or home library, and hence easily get-at-able', he wrote.[7] This observation further complicates any attempt to define popularity in terms of what children apparently enjoy. They are not, after all, typical consumers, and their preferences are not based on unlimited access to literature, but have to be constructed from what is obtainable, where and when they live, what they are given by others, or what they can afford. To a large extent, access to children's books has been determined by publishers, who decide what to keep in print and what prices to charge, and by parents, teachers and librarians, who regularly attempt to supervise distribution. Any attempt to define popularity in terms of children's preferences thus necessarily runs up against these external controls. Was Dickens really 55 times better liked by children than Lewis Carroll, as the Salmon survey indicated? Or was it because the only edition of *Alice's Adventures in Wonderland* then available cost the princely sum of six shillings? Macmillan did not issue their 'People's Edition' (without the gilt edges and fancy binding, and costing less than half the price of the standard edition) until 1887 – a year after Salmon's article was published. Similarly, does the fact that J.K. Rowling has not been among the top ten of the most-borrowed children's authors from British libraries suggest that she was less popular than Nick Butterworth, Dick King-Smith, Jacqueline Wilson, R.L. Stine, Enid Blyton and other writers whose books were lent out more often? Or was it simply that children possessed their own copies of the 'Harry Potter' books, so that they did not have to borrow them? Or even that library policies restricted the availability of Rowling's work?[8]

Since children's actual opinions are so difficult to ascertain, and their preferences so circumscribed by external factors, perhaps the most useful way to define popularity may, after all, be in terms of sales. Many of the chapters in this book provide information on the subject, either in the form of estimates of the number of copies sold in Britain and throughout the world, the size of print runs, the numbers of editions, or the sheer length of publication history. Further problems are, of course, inherent in the gathering and interpretation of this kind of information. Figures are not always available, and title pages claiming that 200,000 copies have been sold, or that one holds in one's hands the 'twenty-second edition', must be treated with a degree of scepticism. In the eighteenth and nineteenth centuries, for instance, new 'editions' were often really only new issues of old stock, with fresh title pages. But apart from such false claims, sales figures are also problematic as a dependable index of popularity because they bear so little relation to the degree of pleasure a child actually derives from a book. A favourite book may only be bought once, yet re-read

---

7   Salmon, 'What Girls Read', p. 528.

8   The findings of the Public Lending Right report are summarised in the *Times Educational Supplement*, 1 February 2002. In fact, Rowling's Harry Potter books top the list of the most borrowed individual titles. It is largely because librarians seldom chose to stock multiple copies of individual titles that other authors, who had published numerous books all of which were separately available for borrowing, were thus able to eclipse Rowling.

daily, or nightly – until it is loved to death.[9] How can mere sales figures register this kind of popularity? Likewise, a book may sell in vast numbers, but its readers may loathe it – a Latin textbook or a list of historical facts to be learned by heart, say, or an overly moral, or pious, or edifying story. Once again, this is a factor that sales figures cannot register. Such books may have been popular with purchasers rather than end-users. Above all, they have been popular with those who stand to gain from sales rather than user-approval: publishers, printers, booksellers and authors.

An example of a more structural kind of distortion of the sales-equals-popularity equation occurs in Aileen Fyfe's chapter on children's science books in this volume, where she discusses the role of the Religious Tract Society in bringing certain kinds of publications to vast audiences in the early and mid-nineteenth century. Estimates of sales for the most popular of the Society's children's tracts run comfortably into six figures – arguing that these short, didactic pamphlets (including those that mixed the traditionally unpopular subjects of science and religion), sold better than almost any other contemporary children's text. Were they actually as popular as, say, Hans Christian Andersen or Captain Marryat, or even Charlotte Yonge or Mary Louisa Charlesworth? Surely not, for in large part the tracts owed their huge print-runs to the Society's practice of pricing their publications at two or three shillings per hundred, the idea being that they could be bought in bulk, and then given away to children. What was true of Religious Tract Society publications was also true of many other kinds of children's literature – of Hannah More's 'Cheap Repository Tracts' (1795–98) which were also distributed in bulk to children and adults alike, and of many primers, catechisms and textbooks, designed for school and church. Heavily discounted and efficiently distributed, such books were printed in their hundreds of thousands. But it is also true in a more general sense that price and distribution networks have always played a large part in determining sales. In this way, publishers, together with those who bought tracts by the hundred to give away gratis, may be said to have imposed popularity on children.

Indeed, it might be argued that almost all children's books have been imposed on their end-users. It is a commonplace that children seldom choose their own books, but have them selected on their behalf by parents, relatives, teachers and other adults (though today this may be becoming less true). This process, benign though it often is, further problematises attempts to determine popularity from sales figures. It is dramatised most clearly in Kim Reynolds's chapter on reward books – that is, books given by schools or religious organisations to some or all of the children who attended. These were titles clearly imposed on their end-users, texts chosen, in many cases, not to please the recipients, but to improve them or bind them to the organisation that awarded the prize, or to demonstrate the generosity of the donors. But, though less overt, exactly the same process was at work whenever adults selected books for children. It has often been observed, for example, that the popularity of children's texts is affected by a time-lag. Adults buy for their children the books they themselves had enjoyed a generation before. Even though the next generation may

---

9 In the survey carried out by Hall and Coles in 1994–95, 33.2 per cent of children questioned had re-read one or more books within the month prior to the survey: Christine Hall and Martin Coles, *Children's Reading Choices* (London and New York: Routledge, 1999), p. 9.

also enjoy the books their parents had been so pleased with, the difficulty of equating commercial success with genuine enjoyment is only too evident.

Further evidence of the frequent disjunction between books liked by children and books liked by their elders comes from the chapters on Enid Blyton and Roald Dahl in this volume. David Rudd points out how often parents, teachers, reviewers and librarians have disapproved of the dullness and repetitiveness of Blyton's books (two-thirds of the primary schools surveyed by Whitehead in 1971 refused to stock them).[10] With Dahl, Peter Hollindale notes, it was the irreverence, darkness and even sadism of the text that adults disapproved of (though Dahl, as Hollindale shows, deliberately cultivated an appearance of subversion). In such cases, an alliance was forged between those who published the texts and those who read them, leaving parents, teachers and librarians, the intermediate, self-appointed arbiters of children's literature, out of the loop. Interestingly, the popularity of Blyton and Dahl has been sustained after their initial publication by a second generation of readers. By this time, the original readers of Blyton's and Dahl's books had themselves become parents, teachers and librarians, and they happily recommended the books they had enjoyed themselves to their own children, untroubled by earlier misgivings.

Popularity can thus be imposed on children in various ways, yet this is certainly not to say that they do not enjoy the texts that others select for them. Even highly didactic texts, valued by adults for their improving qualities, have been relished by children, as Gillian Avery observes in her chapter on Arthur Mee's *Children's Encyclopedia*. Similarly, the reward books discussed by Kim Reynolds may seem appallingly moralistic and pious in the twenty-first century, but they were nevertheless loved and valued by many of their first readers, often, as Reynolds documents, being taken abroad amongst an emigrant's few most-prized possessions. Elaine Lomax enlarges on this point in her account of Hesba Stretton (whose books were often given out as rewards). The pleasure might derive from the books' own strengths, for they were often genuinely well-crafted and engaging. Alternatively, a different form of pleasure could be created by reading against the text, so that dramatic accounts of bad behaviour and its inevitable consequences, intended to shock and deter the reader or to lay the foundation for a tale of repentance and redemption, became its chief source of attraction.

Some sense of the way that superficially dry or improving children's books could be appropriated for purposes very different from those originally intended, can be gathered from E. Nesbit's accounts of the Bastable children's literature-inspired games. In *The Wouldbegoods* (1901), for example, they play at being the children from Mrs Charlesworth's exhaustingly pious *Ministering Children* (1854), but they make it fun by emphasising the secret society element of the earlier text, and ignoring its religious content. The point is clarified when the children disagree about the appeal of Charlotte Yonge's *Daisy Chain*: 'it's about a family of poor motherless children who tried so hard to be good, and they were confirmed, and had a bazaar, and went to church at the Minster, and one of them got married and wore black watered silk and silver ornaments. So her baby died, and then she was sorry she had not been a good mother to it', Daisy Foulkes reports. Although she picked up on

---

10 Whitehead, *Children and their Books*, p. 232.

the book's piety, she was equally interested in Yonge's descriptions of dresses. For Dickie Bastable, however, *The Daisy Chain* was 'not a bit like that really' – it was a 'ripping book', in which 'one of the boys dresses up like a lady and comes to call, and another tries to hit his little sister with a hoe'.[11] The particular pleasure a child might take in a book does not necessarily derive from any qualities which an adult might perceive in it. And the delight to be gained from books as physical objects – their pictures and typefaces, their bindings and gilt edges – may exist irrespective of textual content. So too does the simple pleasure of ownership which, when children possess very little of their own, may well compensate for any disappointment caused by its actual content. Kim Reynolds's chapter certainly gives the impression that reward books were enjoyed partly as trophies rather than as books to be read, as property rather than as text.

As if all these problems in defining popularity were not enough, we must also take into account the fact that popularity is never stable. Variations have always existed, for example between what is popular in one region and another (and this holds good even in an age of globalisation). Likewise, different books have been popular with different sexes, age groups and socio-economic classes. In the absence of firm data on children's reading habits, it is difficult to be sure what form these variations take. Salmon's 1886 attempt to determine 'What Girls Read' may be compared with another article from the same year entitled 'What Boys Read', but the principal conclusions to be drawn are merely that boys preferred adventure stories while girls were generally provided with much duller tales celebrating domestic virtue (though who is to say if they actually liked them?), and that there was probably more crossover of girls reading boys' stories than one might think.[12] On the other hand, as the opening of Judy Simons's chapter on Angela Brazil reminds us, girls' stories were also surreptitiously enjoyed by boys. The findings of surveys, often based as much on supposition as on empirical research, are themselves open to question.

A number of late twentieth-century surveys into reading and book-borrowing habits certainly have undertaken a great deal of empirical research, but their conclusions tend to expose the complexity of the situation, rather than to solve questions as to why certain texts are popular with certain groups. On the question of the impact of gender on popularity, for instance, one of the most striking findings in Frank Whitehead's 1971 survey was that more than three times more boys than girls said they had read non-narrative works in the month before the survey was carried out (23.2 per cent and 6.9 per cent).[13] This finding is supported by I.J. Leng's 1968 report on children's public library borrowing habits: 23 per cent of ten-year-old boys borrowed non-fiction titles, compared with only 5 per cent of ten-year-old girls.[14]

---

11 E. Nesbit, *The Wouldbegoods: Being the Further Adventures of the Treasure Seekers* (1901, repr. Harmondsworth: Puffin, 1981), pp. 189–90.

12 Salmon, 'What Girls Read', Edward G. Salmon, 'What Boys Read', *Fortnightly Review* n.s. 39 (1886), 248–59.

13 These figures are derived from Whitehead's 'Table 54', and exclude annuals and some books which were unclassifiable (*Children and their Books*, p. 115).

14 I.J. Leng, *Children in the Library: A Study of Children's Leisure-Reading Tastes and Habits* (Cardiff: University of Wales Press, 1968), pp. 209–10.

Hall and Coles, on the other hand, found that neither boys nor girls read significant amounts of non-fiction, and, under scrutiny, Leng's figures reveal anomalies, for example, that seven-year-old girls borrowed more non-fiction than their male equivalents.[15] Again, a case could be argued that children's reading preferences have become steadily less gendered, but only if the detail is ignored. According to Whitehead's survey, the nation's favourite children's author in the early 1970s was Enid Blyton, and Whitehead shows that she was enjoyed far more by girls than boys; in the early 1990s survey, the nation's favourite children's author was Roald Dahl, and Hall and Coles discovered that he was almost equally read by children of both sexes.[16] But their conclusion was undermined by the very noticeable differences they themselves spotted between the individual titles favoured by boys and girls. Ten-year-old boys put Dahl's *The Twits* at the head of their list, whereas no ten-year-old girls even mentioned it as amongst their favourites, preferring *Matilda*, which topped their list. Other 1990s favourites also owed their place at the top of Hall and Coles's lists to the support of either one sex or the other: the 'Point Horror' series came second almost wholly due to girls' preferences, and Blyton came third overall only because she was the favourite of 15 per cent of ten-year-old girls.[17]

The variations in children's reading preferences across socio-economic and age groupings are, if anything, even more difficult to ascertain than those across gender. Leng predictably found that boys borrowed increasingly more adventure stories as they grew older (from 1 per cent at age six to around 50 per cent at twelve), and fewer puppet, animal and fairy tales (a pattern also followed by girls, who largely switched to mysteries, rather than to adventures). Not only are these figures suspicious since levels of book-borrowing as a whole shift dramatically across age bands, but they are contradicted by Whitehead's figures for the popularity of *Treasure Island*. He arrived at a 'liking score' for each book, charted on a scale of one to five, and though *Treasure Island* was one of the favourite books in his survey, its 'liking score' diminished as children grew older, from 4.1 at age ten, to 3.9 at twelve, and 3.4 at fourteen (below the overall average for all books, which was 3.75).[18] Though he tried, Leng could not discover any connections between social class and reading preferences, except that the 'Gang Story' appealed largely to children from non-working class backgrounds

---

15 Hall and Coles, *Children's Reading Choices*, pp. 32–3; Leng, *Children in the Library*, pp. 209–10.

16 In Whitehead's 1971 survey, 50.1 per cent of ten and eleven-year-old girls named Blyton as their favourite, but only 19.5 per cent of similarly aged boys. For twelve and thirteen year olds the figures were 31.2 and 10.3 per cent, and for fourteen and fifteen year olds, they were 9.0 and 3.1 per cent (*Children and their Books*, p. 152). In Hall and Coles's survey, 24 per cent of boys and 21 per cent of girls named Dahl as their favourite writer (*Children's Reading Choices*, p. 45).

17 Hall and Coles, *Children's Reading Choices*, pp. 33–40.

18 Whitehead, *Children and their Books*, p. 229. Whitehead derived his 'liking score' by asking his sample to rate each book they mentioned by placing a tick in one of five columns, labelled: 1. I did not like it at all; 2. I did not like it much; 3. I quite liked it; 4. I liked it very much; and 5. It was one of the best I have ever read (p. 141).

(a preference which he was tempted to attribute to 'an unconscious rejection of middle-class standards' by 'the less intelligent of the middle-class boys').[19]

Interestingly, Coles and Hall found that the appeal of both Blyton and Dahl tended to increase 'as one moves down the social scale'.[20] It was also noticeable that the tendency to name Dahl as favourite author declined as children grew older (as Whitehead had found in the case of Blyton), from 30 per cent of ten year olds to 26 per cent of twelve year olds and 12 per cent of fourteen year olds. Fascinating as such data is, it would be foolhardy to draw from it any general conclusions as to what kind of reading different classes of children preferred.[21]

The shifts in popularity that take place over time are slightly easier to investigate. Comparisons between the Coles and Hall survey and Whitehead's work from 20 years before are illuminating in themselves. A sharp decline in Enid Blyton's popularity is apparent, for instance: in the 1971 survey, she was named as favourite author by 1,604 children, but only by 498 (from a similar sized sample) in 1994–95. It is tempting to suggest that her popularity in the 1970s was due to the fact that the generation which had first grown up with Blyton in the 1940s and 1950s, was then exposing its own offspring to her work, and that 20 years or so after that, in the 1990s, the link with the original Blyton generation was becoming increasingly attenuated. Such an argument looks persuasive until we note that many other authors also suffered a dramatic decline in popularity between the Whitehead and the Hall and Coles surveys. Robert Louis Stevenson was named as favourite by 120 children in 1971, but only 3 in 1994–95. Charles Dickens dropped from 158 to 28, Arthur Conan Doyle from 45 to 9, and Louisa May Alcott dropped from 43 to zero. Of all those in Whitehead's list of favourite authors, only C.S. Lewis had retained his place, being mentioned by 54 children in the 1970s and 53 in the 1990s.[22] Swings in popularity, then, do not depend merely on the distance from a text's first publication. The production of television and film adaptations is also important, and the popularity of the Narnia books has certainly been buoyed by a late 1980s television series and the series of Hollywood films begun in 2005. More generally, reading habits as a whole also change. In the 1970s, the number of children's periodicals read declined as they grew older. In the 1990s, the reverse was true. Of course, the nature of the periodicals available had also changed.

In the perspective of the last two or three centuries, rather than the last two or three decades, such changes look even more dramatic. The inclusion of almost forgotten names such as Barbara Hofland, G.A. Henty, Hesba Stretton and Angela Brazil in a book on popular children's literature is itself a reflection on the transience

---

19 Leng, *Children in the Library*, pp. 156–7 and 209–10.

20 Hall and Coles, *Children's Reading Choices*, p. 46. Edward Salmon also attempted to discover 'What the Working Classes Read' (*Nineteenth Century* 20 (1886), 108–17), but this essay concluded little more than that they generally read very few books indeed, but 'wasted' their time on cheap journalism.

21 Other interesting findings from the Hall and Coles survey include these: that girls claimed to prefer series fiction, whilst boys said they liked books which might also appeal to adults (Terry Pratchett, Alistair Maclean, John Le Carré, Stephen King and so on); and that ethnicity seems to have affected reading choices very little (*Children's Reading Choices*, p. 47).

22 Ibid., p. 45.

of fame: they stand in Part II of this volume like the ruined statue of Ozymandias in the desert.[23] Yet it is hardly surprising that many once-famous children's authors have fallen into obscurity, when the same thing has happened to so many writers for adults. And it might be argued that since cultural constructions of childhood, and perhaps the nature of childhood itself, have changed so much since the seventeenth and eighteenth centuries, writers for children will have been far more likely to go out of fashion. These cultural shifts, linked with demographic change and technological developments, have also wrought a transformation in the economics of publishing for children. All the writers in the 'Forgotten Favourites' section of this volume have one thing at least in common, namely their extraordinary productivity. Hofland, Henty, Stretton and Brazil all wrote dozens of books for children, either repeating a winning formula over and over again, or turning their hands to different kinds of texts, or both. Barbara Hofland, for instance, produced over 60 titles (though not all were expressly aimed solely at children). She wrote poetry, guide books, books teaching geography, an *Illustrated Alphabet* and *Little Dramas for Young People*, as well as the stories that Dennis Butts discusses in his account. Many more recent authors have been extremely productive too. Enid Blyton published an astonishing 700 books for children. Anne Fine and Geraldine McCaughrean, to take just two contemporary British examples, average over a book per year, and they have written in a variety of genres. The very bestselling authors, though, are not compelled to publish at such a furious rate. Roald Dahl published around 18 major titles. J.K. Rowling has pledged to write just seven Harry Potter books (although these have appeared in fairly regular succession, and are exceptionally long). This may reflect the increased profits that it is possible to make from writing children's books, even if there are just as many children's writers who struggle to support themselves at the turn of the twenty-first century as there were at the turn of the nineteenth. The point is that today the popular children's authors with whom we are here concerned are not compelled to publish incessantly nor continually to repeat a winning formula.

In the earliest days of children's literature, as we can see from the Part I of this collection, the majority of authors were content to remain anonymous. This would be all but impossible now, publishers having recognised children's preference for books by an author they already know: to 'travel in the company of reliable friends', as Gabrielle Cliff Hodges puts it.[24] The author most adept at marketing her name

---

23 Henty was still borrowed by two boys in the late 1960s, as Leng reveals in *Children in the Library*, p. 211, and is apparently becoming popular once again among some constituencies in the USA. Several websites offer new editions of his books for sale, such as <http://www.robinsonbooks.com> (accessed 17 April 2007), based in Oregon, which boasts that 99 Henty books are available (in print and on CD-Rom). Henty's work is suitable for 'home, church or school', the website claims, arguing that they will also improve the vocabulary of modern children.

24 Gabrielle Cliff Hodges, 'Encountering the Different', pp. 264–77, in Morag Styles, Eve Bearne and Victor Watson (eds), *Voices Off. Texts, Contexts and their Readers* (London: Cassell, 1996), pp. 266–7. Evidence of this tendency to seek out the familiar is to be found in some of the case studies included in Leng's *Children in the Library* (along with a good examples of the anti-Blyton prejudices of many involved in children's literature and education in the post-war years). One boy, Leng reports (p. 183), 'begins the year by borrowing Enid

was Blyton, whose autograph is still used as a logo to identify and sell her books a generation after her death (as David Rudd observes). Other chapters in this volume suggest that the use of an author's name as a brand mark has had a much longer history. According to Dennis Butts, Blackie and Son marketed G.A. Henty, using carefully placed advertisements to guide readers towards his other books. Over a century earlier, the same had been true of John Newbery, the first great publisher for children. His tendency to 'puff' other works he had published (and perhaps also written) within his own covers was designed to create a 'virtuous circle' of popularity, carrying the child forward from one book to the next along a path determined by the publisher.

Another surprising continuity is to be found in the connections between children's books and other media. Hall and Coles note in the 1990s that 'one in seven of the books read in the month before the survey had an obvious media tie-in.'[25] They were referring to recent television or cinematic adaptations of these books. Stacy Gillis notes that with Harry Potter, the strategic marketing of related products in different media has reached a new level and sophistication. But this is no new phenomenon: A.J. Jenkinson in his 1940 survey *What do Boys and Girls Read* also noted that 'film companies often produce versions of well-known books' and 'Publishers and booksellers quite often try to improve the opportunity by special advertisements, by displays, or by new or cheaper editions.' 'It seems feasible', he wrote, that the presence of Mary Shelley's *Frankenstein* amongst the children's favourites in his 1938 survey, was due 'largely to the film'.[26] In fact, several chapters in this volume show that cross-media tie-ins of this kind long pre-date the invention of cinema, let alone television. Kevin Carpenter reports that nineteenth-century Robin Hood tales, particularly those by Pierce Egan, were indebted to the popular theatre. Earlier still, a major factor in the reintroduction of fairy tales in the first years of the nineteenth century was their successful representation on the London stage. Such links between stage and book are explored in George Speaight and Brian Alderson's chapter on the systematic appropriation of theatrical successes by publishers of children's literature.

David Rudd congratulates Enid Blyton on creating and exploiting cross-media connections, pointing to her shrewd deployment and management of dramatic and television adaptations, as well as to clever merchandising, which colonised the toy market, and even breakfast cereals, with her characters. This kind of cross-media marketing (to accompany initial publication, rather than after a book's popularity has already been firmly established), has sometimes been used to explain the success of

---

Blyton's *Mystery of the Hidden House*. Three months later, he is reading Enid Blyton's *Lucky Story Book*; three months later still, it is Blyton's *Sunny Story Book*, and at the end of the year, he is back where he began, with Enid Blyton's *Mystery of the Hidden House*. In all he borrowed 74 books in the year, 38 of them by Blyton. In the following year, he borrowed none at all. It need not be doubted that he enjoyed his reading, but it got him nowhere, and so he gave it up. And this, perhaps, is not to be regretted; others, less wise or less fortunate, fail to break the habit, but obsessively continue looking for they know not what, reading ever more futilely until at last they become incurably addicted to reading-matter of the most ephemeral kind.'

25 Hall and Coles, *Children's Reading Choices*, p. 48.
26 A.J. Jenkinson, *What do Boys and Girls Read?* p. 94.

J.K. Rowling. Julia Eccleshare, however, argues in her chapter that the Harry Potter phenomenon is not driven either by the cinematic adaptations, the media 'hype', or the creation of a range of Harry Potter consumer products. Rowling's books have succeeded, claims Eccleshare, because children actually read and enjoy them, not because they are somehow tricked into doing so either by clever marketing or an externally imposed cultural currency. The same was probably true of Newbery's publications, Tabart and Harris's early nineteenth-century fairy tales, Egan's *Robin Hood and Little John*, Blyton's Noddy books, and indeed most of the texts discussed in this volume.

One evident *dis*continuity to emerge from these accounts of popular children's literature is that only in recent times have a few individual children's authors dominated the market, achieving almost monopolistic positions. In terms of sales, Rowling currently bestrides the world of children's literature, and publishers (other than her own) and public bodies such as the Arts Council complain that sales of the Harry Potter books may have broken records for children's books, but the children's books market as a whole has been simultaneously depressed.[27] Before her Roald Dahl was a dominant figure, although not quite to the same extent (in Christine Hall and Martin Coles's 1994–95 survey over three times as many children named Dahl as their favourite author as the next most popular author or series, the 'Point Horror' books).[28] And for a previous generation, Enid Blyton was pre-eminent. This volume includes chapters on each of these three giants, and together they create a sort of 'apostolic succession', not merely because the sequence is so clear, but also because each evidently drew inspiration from his or her predecessor. Julia Eccleshare shows that the first Harry Potter book was immediately compared to some of Dahl's, and several critics congratulated Rowling on the similarities. Others have criticised Rowling for what A.S. Byatt has termed her 'intelligently patchworked derivative

---

27 Between 1997 and 2002 the British children's book market grew by 8 per cent, which was less that the 14 per cent growth in the market for books as a whole. The extent to which this growth in the children's books market was powered by Harry Potter alone is indicated by the 11 per cent slump in 2002, a year in which no Harry Potter book appeared. This has led to speculation that children have been transferring their allegiance from other books to Harry Potter and not returning, that the high price of the Harry Potter books, especially in the hardback editions which have sold so unprecedentedly well, is reducing the amount of money which children and their parents are willing or able to spend on children's literature, and even that the amount of time spent reading (and re-reading) Rowling's books cuts into time which could be devoted to other children's books. Stephen Bohme of Book Marketing Limited, which independently surveys the book industry, has summarised these trends succinctly: 'The received wisdom is that the Potter trend has done amazing things for the children's market. But the truth is that Harry Potter did amazing things for Harry Potter only … The reality is that sales of Potter books have done nothing to increase the volume of books sold to their target audience, children aged seven to 14.' See *From Looking Glass to Spyglass: A Consultation Paper on Children's Literature* (London: Arts Council England, 2003), <http://www.artscouncil.org.uk/documents/publications/495.pdf > (accessed 17 April 2007), especially pp. 21–2, and the *Observer*, 5 May 2002, <http://books.guardian.co.uk/news/articles/0,6109,710189,00.html> (accessed 17 April 2007).

28 Hall and Coles, *Children's Reading Choices*, p. 43.

motifs', taken from Dahl in particular.[29] While the relationship between Dahl and Blyton includes as many differences as similarities, Peter Hollindale's chapter shows how much the two had in common, as well as how the inevitable comparisons have worked to disadvantage Dahl. As for Blyton, David Rudd identifies Arthur Mee as her greatest influence, especially in the matter of the personal branding of her work, thus forging a further link in the chain of succession.

The criterion most often used by critics and academics for determining which texts should be analysed and taught is whether they advanced the history of children's literature. Thus children's literature courses commonly concentrate on those texts that first began to amuse rather than educate children, and those that developed new ways of addressing or entertaining their readers. In this way, a canon of children's literature has been built – a 'Great Tradition'. A few of the texts which mark milestones along this teleology are discussed in this volume, but most of the usual breakthrough-texts are not, their places having been taken by lesser-known titles. In a deliberate attempt to interrogate the 'Great Tradition', the criterion of popularity alone has been used to determine the contents of this collection.

Of course, many other texts might still have been included under this rule: those by James Janeway, John Newbery, Eleanor Fenn or Mary Martha Sherwood, to take a few examples from early British children's literature, by Lewis Carroll, Robert Louis Stevenson or C.S. Lewis more recently, or by Philip Pullman and Jacqueline Wilson today. Those texts which are discussed in this volume were published across four centuries, written for all ages and both sexes, directed at very different sections of society and published in very different shapes and sizes, and for very different purposes. It is intended that these chapters should act as case studies, raising important questions of wide relevance. What actually constitutes popularity within the field of children's literature? How and why did certain texts become popular, and how was their popularity sustained (or not, as the case may be)? Which children's books were genuinely popular and are they the same books that usually feature in accounts of the history of children's literature? This volume suggests that there may be a different narrative to be told, a history of children's literature based on the principle of popularity.

In order to do this, it has been necessary to examine texts that, far from 'advancing' children's literature along the traditional axis of 'progress' – that is to say away from instruction and towards delight – might be accused of doing just the reverse. The science books discussed by Aileen Fyfe were primarily intended to teach, and only secondarily, if at all, to entertain. The Amalgamated Press factual books investigated by Gillian Avery were also primarily didactic in intent, though they could employ elements of fiction to enhance their purpose. Children may not want to read non-fiction – the surveys of Jenkinson, Ling, Whitehead and Hall and Coles suggest that this is (increasingly) the case – but non-fiction books are certainly popular according to sales figures, and have always been popular with publishers and purchasers, if not with end-users. It is doubtful whether the children's publishing industry could have survived without them, at least in its early stages. All sorts of textbooks, grammars,

---

29 A.S. Byatt, 'Harry Potter and the Childish Adult', *New York Times*, 7 July 2003.

primers, guidebooks and religious works, and more recently, *inter alia*, sports books, hobby books, technical books and biographies, must play their part in any account of the development of children's literature. Only a few varieties of this sort of literature are here investigated, but they provide stepping stones on the journey towards a wider understanding of children's print culture.

Didactic books such as ABCs, or religious catechisms, have always been popular because they are considered essential for a child's spiritual or temporal welfare. Vast numbers of these were printed, bought and (probably) read, because teachers and parents, those who had control of reading practice, commissioned and imposed them on children. But how did works of fiction or verse, or any texts not regarded as essential to education, gain popularity? There is no straightforward answer to this question. If publishers knew what would make an appealing children's book, they would never bring out a failure, nor would publishing houses go out of business. Part of the difficulty of predicting success is that there are so many different kinds of successful books – and children's reasons for preferring certain books are quite inscrutable. As Whitehead lamented when trying to account for the results of his survey, 'The young reader seldom finds it possible to be articulate in any specific way about what he has liked or valued in his reading.'[30] This difficulty has not prevented various commentators from trying to discover the secret of popular children's literature – nor has it inhibited this enquiry. After all, the Romantic myth that writers stumble across success as if by accident, not because they were searching for it, becomes less convincing when applied to children's books. It may have applied to Lewis Carroll or J.R.R. Tolkien, perhaps, but others deliberately set out to appeal to a mass readership. Enid Blyton, as David Rudd points out, specifically intended to manufacture a product which would rival Disney. Through a careful assessment of what was needed, and the ability to provide it, she succeeded in this ambition.

The possible reasons for the popularity of children's books might usefully be divided into three basic categories: the textual, the contextual and what might be called the paratextual. The commonest theories advanced to explain popularity fall into the first of these categories, that is to say they hold that there is some special quality present in any successful text that accounts for its appeal. A good example of this occurs in Frank Whitehead's early, very empirical study, 'The Attitudes of Grammar School Pupils towards some Novels Commonly Read in School.'[31] Whitehead took ten novels frequently found on school curricula and asked children to rank them in terms of preference.[32] The same novels were then read by a panel of qualified adults who also ranked them according to five criteria: simplicity of language, ease of identification with the hero or heroine, the degree of emotional

---

30 Whitehead, *Children and their Books*, p. 206.

31 Frank Whitehead, 'The Attitudes of Grammar School Pupils towards some Novels Commonly Read in School', *British Journal of Educational Psychology* 26 (1956), 104–11.

32 The novels were *Pride and Prejudice* (Jane Austen), *Jane Eyre* (Charlotte Brontë), *Prester John* (John Buchan), *Pilgrim's Progress* (John Bunyan), *A Christmas Carol* and *A Tale of Two Cities* (Charles Dickens), *Silas Marner* (George Eliot), *The Trumpet Major* (Thomas Hardy), *The Cloister and the Hearth* (Charles Reade), *Kidnapped* and *Treasure Island* (Robert Louis Stevenson) and *Gulliver's Travels* (Jonathan Swift).

immaturity of the main themes, the openness of the wish-fulfilment element and, last, the degree of coherence between narrative, character, motives and so on. The results of both rankings were then correlated. Whitehead was evidently searching for some connection between qualities supposed to be present in the texts, and the children's approval. And of course he found it: there was a strong correlation for all but the fifth criterion. In other words, 'imaginary coherence' made little difference to the reader's enjoyment, but children preferred books 'in which they find it easy to identify themselves with the hero or heroine, and in which the element of wish-fulfilment is comparatively open and undisguised; it is an added recommendation if these novels also deal with themes that are relatively immature emotionally, and are written in comparatively simple language'.[33]

These conclusions were endorsed in the lengthy consideration of preferences appended to Whitehead's 1977 *Children and their Books*, where he argued that the principal motive for children's taste in books was the extent to which 'vicarious imaginative satisfaction of a wish-fulfilment kind' was available from a text. In other words, it was of no importance whether a particular book was naturalistic or fantastic, or was set in the present or the past, as long as the text allowed its readers to identify with characters whom they would like to be. He grudgingly accepted that this must also be the root of Enid Blyton's popularity, in addition to sheer 'readability at the simplest level', though he professed himself saddened by the kinds of children the reader was invited to identify with ('stereotypes of character', 'cardboard ... Janets and Johns'), and the types of materialistic, unimproving, 'philistine' wishes that readers were being encouraged to fulfil.[34]

By the 1990s, Hall and Coles were more optimisitic. They too sought textual explanations for popularity, alighting on the child-centred nature of Blyton and Dahl's writings as the key to their success. Giving children 'the freedom to go off and have their own adventures free from adult interference', and to 'do good in a world where adults are often badly behaved' was what made these books appealing. Indeed, it was their very exclusion of adult values, their closedness to adults (as demonstrated by Whitehead's attack on Blyton, and the later adult hostility to Dahl) that was 'bound to appeal to children'. This begins to sound more convincing when we apply it to other works here discussed. Child protagonists from Jack (of Beanstalk fame) to James (of the Giant Peach), Alice to Harry Potter, Jim Hawkins to the Famous Five, Barbara Hofland's Ludovico Lewis (*The Son of a Genius*) to G.A. Henty's Charlie Marryat (*With Clive in India*), all go out into the world, freed from normal parental constraint, to test their mettle in the face of adult depravity and deceit. In such tales, as Hall and Coles argue, 'readers can safely indulge their fears and fantasies of life without adult control'.[35] The difficulty is that thousands of other texts have used the same narrative strategies as Dahl and Blyton, Henty, Brazil, Carroll, Rowling and the rest, without achieving anything like the same success, if they were accepted by publishers at all. There must be another factor that causes some works employing this theme to succeed where other and similar texts have failed.

---

33 This summary is from Whitehead, *Children and their Books*, p. 214.
34 Ibid., pp. 208, 234–5 and 233.
35 Hall and Coles, *Children's Reading Choices*, p. 53.

This type of criticism can also be levelled at the psychoanalytical approach to explaining popularity. Kate Friedlaender, for example, in a 1942 essay entitled 'Children's Books and their Function in Latency and Prepuberty', suggested that successful children's books tended to correspond to conflicts that occurred during a particular phase of a child's psychological development. For instance, Friedlaender read the recurrent motif of the child taken away from his or her home and deposited in a new and unfamiliar environment (as in *Kidnapped* or *Little Lord Fauntleroy*), as a dramatisation of the psychological conflicts Sigmund Freud had located during the 'latency period', just prior to the onset of puberty. At this stage in their psychic development, Freud had argued, children grew disillusioned with their parents, whom they had formerly regarded as omnipotent and infallible. Narratives of displacement followed by a revelation of true identity would appeal to these children, argued Friedlaender, since they enacted at a safe distance Freud's 'family romance', the fantasy that the child actually belongs to much more distinguished parents, who do not share the weaknesses so recently discovered in the reader's own mother and father (evidently, the Harry Potter novels fit neatly into Friedlaender's theory).[36]

Other Freudian motifs have been considered equally important in determining the appeal of children's literature. *Jane Eyre* has been continually popular with girls, claims Friedlaender, because it fulfils their Oedipal fantasies when the heroine, a neglected Cinderella-figure, wins the affection of a father-figure, Rochester. Bruno Bettelheim in *The Uses of Enchantment* (1977) advanced a similar argument in relation to fairy tales. Other psychoanalytical explanations have drawn on theories of cognitive development. J.A. Appleyard, for example, has suggested that adventure series such as Blyton's 'Famous Five' and 'Secret Seven', though extremely repetitive, reproducing the same adventures over and over again in slightly different settings, are popular with seven to twelve year olds because the chief task of children at that age is to 'gather and organise information about the new world they have been launched into' by simultaneously discovering what is new, and 'learning the rules that prevent facts from just being random and confusing data'. Thus they particularly relish the combination of the exciting and the familiar.[37]

Once again, this kind of analysis can be compelling, yet it fails to address the objection that only some of the texts that dramatise these psychological developments, or meet the needs of these cognitive stages, acquire popularity. Why not all? One way of answering this might be to fall back on literary quality as the factor that distinguishes one text from another. Few would doubt that the narrative skills of, let us say, Stevenson were largely responsible for the appeal of *Treasure Island*. On the other hand, the history of children's literature is studded with examples of authors who have been hugely popular but whose work has been condemned as devoid of literary merit, Blyton, Dahl and Rowling being only the most conspicuous recent examples. In Whitehead's 1956 experiment, the one factor he found to be

---

36 Friedlaender's position is concisely summarised in Whitehead, *Children and their Books*, pp. 208–9 and 250. See also J.A. Appleyard, *Becoming a Reader: The Experience of Fiction from Childhood to Adulthood* (Cambridge: Cambridge University Press, 1990), especially pp. 38–42.

37 Appleyard, *Becoming a Reader*, pp. 62–3.

*un*important in determining a book's popularity with its child readers was literary coherence. The very category of literary merit is so subjective: what one generation admires, another derides – which is why so many of the contributors to this book emphasise contextual as well as textual reasons for literary success.

For Julia Eccleshare, the textual satisfactions of J.K. Rowling's *Harry Potter and the Philosopher's Stone* were the deciding factor in securing its success. The panel of children who read and enjoyed it, and awarded it the important Smarties Prize, did more to secure its triumph than any marketing campaign could have done (the role of marketing in maintaining the success of Harry Potter, for the sequels and associated products, is discussed by Stacy Gillis). But Eccleshare also points out that a key consideration in the book's success was that it appeared at a moment when the children's book market was torpid, almost stagnant, when no single writer had grabbed children's imagination as Dahl had done during the 1970s and 1980s. It might be argued, then, that the market was ready and waiting for a new hero or heroine, smoothing Rowling's path to success. A similar argument about the importance of the initial context in securing literary success might be made with almost any of the texts here discussed: Roald Dahl filled the post-Blyton vacuum, and two centuries earlier, John Newbery's publications flourished because a market for new consumer products had developed which no-one else was supplying. In a similar way, Dennis Butts and Kevin Carpenter emphasise how Henty's adventure stories, and the tales of Robin Hood, thrived in the particular ideological and cultural climate in which they first appeared. Success with children's books is, it might be argued, as much a matter of good timing as anything else.

Both text and context are evidently important, then, but other factors can also mediate between the text and the reader, and as many of the chapters in this volume illustrate, these can be equally effective in establishing the popularity of a particular book. Gérard Genette uses the term 'paratext' for all the ways in which a text turns itself into a book and presents itself to its readers, and though he was mostly concerned with title, prefatory material, chapter headings and the like ('peritext'), and with reviews, authorial interviews and letters and so on ('epitext'), other critics have included typeface, binding, paper, illustrations and the other characteristics of a book's physical format.[38] Whatever terminology we use, it is clear that the reading experience can be significantly affected by such factors. Illustration, for example, is clearly important. Peter Hollindale argues that a significant part of Roald Dahl's success is due to the unique partnership he developed with Quentin Blake. The same point could be made about John Tenniel's illustrations of Lewis Carroll's work or Thomas Taylor's influential image for the cover of the British edition of *Harry Potter and the Philosopher's Stone*. With the chapbooks, Robin Hood tales, and pantomime books discussed in this volume, the texts are fully integrated with graphic images.

---

38 The term 'paratext' was originally coined by Gérard Genette in his book *Seuils* (1987), appearing in English as *Paratexts: Thresholds of Interpretation*, trans. Jane E. Lewin (Cambridge: Cambridge University Press, 1997). Important redraftings of its definition are to be found in Samuel Kinser, *Rabelais's Carnival: Text, Context, Metatext* (Berkeley: University of California Press, 1990) and Peter Shillingsburg, *Scholarly Editing in the Computer Age* (Ann Arbor: University of Michigan Press, 1996).

More difficult to assess is the significance of the idiosyncratic images used for Angela Brazil's books, especially on the covers. If nothing else, those images identified the texts as part of a series, thus contributing to their appeal. Dennis Butts argues that the repeated format and appearance of G.A. Henty's books was an important part of their attraction, with children often wanting to collect the set. Their formulaic titles helped, and so did their uniform size: Henty produced enough text to fill precisely the same number of pages in each volume. The instinct to collect was also exploited by the *Children's Encyclopedia* and most proficiently of all by Enid Blyton. As David Rudd shows, Blyton exerted as much control over the physical appearance of her books as she did over the text. She was convinced that children's books sold on looks quite as much as on literary merit. The publishers of reward books knew this too, as Kim Reynolds demonstrates. They decorated their texts with gilt edges, fancy bindings and ornate illustrations. Publishers quickly recognised that the more expensive the book looked, the more conspicuous would seem the generosity of those giving it away, and in meeting this demand for ostentatious display, they heightened their sales. Even today, a shelf of nineteenth-century reward books in a second-hand bookshop can look bright and inviting.

Another factor contributing to the relationship between text and reader is the biography of the author, often carefully devised, cultivated and disseminated. In the work of John Newbery or Barbara Hofland, Angela Brazil or Arthur Mee, a consciously constructed authorial persona guides the reader through the text. In more recent times, the 'epitextual' construction of an authorial personality through memoirs, autobiographies, print and broadcast interviews, meet-the-author events and so on, has played an increasing part in shaping a book's reception. Eccleshare on Rowling, and Hollindale on Dahl, both stress the importance of the biographical 'myths' that have been generated – Rowling as an impoverished single parent, writing in a café where she and her baby could keep warm, and Dahl as a fighter-pilot whose life was punctuated by personal tragedy. A century earlier, Henty's publishers had also sought to influence the market with references to his career as a war correspondent in the Crimea, Italy, France, Spain, Abyssinia, Ashanti and India. Just as the details of musicians' lives have become essential to rock and pop music sales, so children's books also sell on the basis of a (largely imaginary) rapport between author and reader.

It is one thing to sustain popularity over the course of a career and another to sustain it in perpetuity, or something approaching it. The circumstances required for initial success may be quite different from those required for abiding popularity. Part of the secret of Barbara Hofland's success was her versatility, it seems, for she was able to turn her hand to anything the contemporary market demanded. But the very disparate nature of her output has counted against her in the long run, since most of the authors whose success has endured have been valued for one particular kind of writing. One possible means of achieving popularity, it has been suggested, is the discovery of a successful formula and a dogged faithfulness to it. Blyton might often have been labelled 'a donkey on a treadmill, knowing or desiring no other kind of mill', but the repetitiveness of her work was highly remunerative.[39] The same

39 Whitehead, *Children and their Books*, p. 233.

is true of Henty, Brazil and Stretton, but their failure to endure shows that Blyton may be the anomaly, and that formulaic writing may bring transient success but often militates against immortality. In fact, one secret of abiding popularity seems to be the ability to evolve. What differentiates *Alice's Adventures in Wonderland* or *Treasure Island*, for example, from the novels of Henty or Brazil has been their adaptability, the continual reinvention of the text. Abridged and illustrated editions, animated, radio and cinematic versions, games and websites, have all kept them at the forefront of children's culture. With Harry Potter, the adaptation and remediation is happening at the same time as the texts themselves appear, and even before, the publisher producing websites to trail the new books and films. But even before this, it had been the decisions of television and film producers, and publishers anxious to pioneer new markets, quite as much as the quality of the text itself, that has been responsible for a title remaining a popular classic, rather than following Henty, Hofland, Stretton and a multitude of other once-popular authors into obscurity.

Other chapters also link popularity with the ability to evolve. David Blamires charts the ways in which fairy tales have changed to suit particular publishing agendas or shifting audience tastes. Kevin Carpenter also shows how the tales of Robin Hood were kept in constant circulation by subtle alterations to suit new tastes. Aileen Fyfe's case study of John Aikin and Anna Laetitia Barbauld's *Evenings at Home*, first published in the 1790s but kept in print for over a century despite its rapidly outdated scientific writing, shows just how wily publishers could be. Rather than lose a once-profitable title from their lists, successive generations of publishers commissioned revised editions, and then deliberately rebranded the text as a 'classic', which no home should be without. The shift from cutting-edge science textbook to 'timeless masterwork' took only 50 years. Perhaps the classic example of a text's constant evolution is Daniel Defoe's *Robinson Crusoe*. Once re-presented as a book for children, *Robinson Crusoe*, or at least the many 'robinsonnades' of which it was the source, became the most frequently retold formula of all. The publishers' willingness to modify *Robinson Crusoe* to enable it to open new markets contributed to its apotheosis as one of the central myths of western culture.

The chapbook tales discussed in Chapter 2 have also been subject to substantial revisions over the course of time. These evolved orally, and then changed again with the proliferation of cheap, ephemeral printed editions in the seventeenth, eighteenth and nineteenth centuries. It is their fluidity, the way they have been created and recreated by those who told, and then sometimes printed them, that invites us to see them as the kind of popular literature that is 'of the people', rather than merely a bestseller. We might also see texts such as *Alice* or *Robinson Crusoe* as popular literature in this same sense, since they too have so often been retold, across so many different media, that at times they have lost their links with their originals. Although their ur-texts are still in print, through their constant repetition in a range of forms, these stories have become as much part of popular culture as Jack the Giant-Killer or the Seven Champions of Christendom once were. And this process of mythologisation draws the various different strands and definitions of popular literature together. Texts like *Alice* or *The Lord of the Rings*, Blyton's Noddy books or Madame d'Aulnoy's 'The White Cat', are popular both in the sense that they have sold well and have been loved by their readers. This combination of cultural penetration and affection has given them a rare longevity and ensured their reincarnation in a variety of forms. Thus, they were absorbed into popular culture. Once a text has been thus absorbed, it becomes almost impossible to dislodge.

PART I
Old Tales Retold

Introduction

M. O. Grenby

Several definitions of popular literature – that which sold well, that which was well-liked, and that which was somehow 'of the people' – come together in the four chapters in this section. The fairy stories, the myths and legends, the accounts of heroes and heroines, which are all to be encountered here, had for centuries constituted a core of popular culture. In fact, they go a long way to defining it. As for their enduring appeal, and the delight that readers continued to take in them, these are evident from the sheer length of their publishing history and their perpetual re-publication in new forms. It is doubtless true that there is something inherently satisfying about these resilient texts – *Jack the Giant Killer*, say, or *Sleeping Beauty in the Wood*, or the history of Robin Hood – and that it was at least partly the particular qualities of these narratives, settings and characters which kept them popular for so long. But what also emerges very strongly from these four chapters is that it was the ability to adapt that was the secret of their success. Chapbook tales and fairy stories were reinvented over and over again in the eighteenth and nineteenth centuries, and as David Blamires shows with particular reference to the story of *The White Cat*, they are still evolving today. Kevin Carpenter and George Speaight have surveyed this process in detail, the former tracing the ways in which the Robin Hood story was deliberately refashioned to appeal to new audiences, and the latter (in collaboration with Brian Alderson) examining the ways in which chapbook and fairy tales were adapted to the specific demands of the pantomime and the moveable book.

What it was about the chapbook and fairy stories discussed here that rendered them so eminently adaptable is a difficult question, but several possible answers suggest themselves. First, the fact that so many of these tales have no obviously traceable source has surely encouraged adaptation (even those which were influentially 'captured' by Charles Perrault or the Brothers Grimm were often advertised as deriving from much older folk traditions). This might be partly for practical reasons – there is no copyright to worry about – but also, with no 'ur-text', no fixed source, it seems that authors have had fewer qualms about amending, or even wholly reworking, such tales. Second, from the eighteenth century to the present there has clearly been a strong sense among readers, writers and publishers that chapbook and fairy tales somehow represent a 'national', or to use a more expressive, if more loaded, term, 'völkisch' culture. Given such a sense, it has been thought especially fitting that these stories should be continually made available to each succeeding generation, at least from the early nineteenth century onwards when an indigenous, colloquial, national culture had come to be regarded as something desirable, to be cherished and fostered. It is also perhaps the case that the supposedly 'national' status of this kind of text encouraged more of a cross-generational audience for such tales than existed for other forms of children's literature. It is true that fairy tales, after Hans Christian Andersen, were largely addressed to children (on the page at least: George Speaight points out the continuing cross-over appeal of fairy tales on stage, as pantomime).

But the stories of Robin Hood, or Dick Turpin or Sweeny Todd could, like the dime novels of the American West (a comparison Kevin Carpenter makes), be regarded as a legitimate branch of literature for adults and children alike. Given the prospect of this kind of cross-reading, the 'old tales' probably seemed highly attractive propositions to publishers working on the margins of profitability in the precarious world of children's book production. Such tales offered them a relatively low-risk route to commercial success and so were frequently reworked (although, as these chapters reveal, their publishers often tried to disguise reproductions of old texts behind new titles or formats).

One cannot help noticing that the same somewhat shadowy individuals and publishing houses recur in each of these chapters: Clucr Dicey, Richard Marshall, Dean and Co., Warne, Carvalho and Benjamin Tabart, as well as the more celebrated John Newbery and his heirs. Some of these firms flourished over decades, while others were more transient, or disreputable, and could be rather furtive, using deliberately misleading imprints, for instance, to bolster respectability and deceive the public into thinking that their enterprise was flourishing. This murky world of children's publishing in the eighteenth and (probably murkier still) nineteenth century has never been fully explored. All four chapters here shed new light on this world. What little further information is available is to be found in the bibliographies and catalogues listed in the 'Further Reading' section at the end of this book. What stands out, though, is that, before the twentieth century, it was publishers and printers who were primarily responsible for creating and shaping the majority of the literature that children were consuming, not authors, illustrators or educationalists. As Brian Alderson and Felix de Marez Oyens have put it, 'tradesmen were at the heart of the establishment of English children's literature', and it was these publishers whose shrewd assessment of what the market could bear took children's literature 'into areas of new and different possibility' and thereby did much to define the emerging genre.[1]

---

1   Brian Alderson and Felix de Marez Oyens, *Be Merry and Wise: Origins of Children's Book Publishing in England, 1650–1850* (London: The British Library; New Castle, DE: Oak Knoll Press, 2006), pp. xi–xii.

Chapter 2

Before Children's Literature: Children, Chapbooks and Popular Culture in Early Modern Britain

M. O. Grenby

Beginning in the later seventeenth century, and increasingly in the eighteenth, new kinds of literature especially designed for children began to appear in Britain. Previously there had certainly been religious and educational books intended for children's use. But the new books, even if they were still pious and didactic to a greater or lesser extent, were also designed to engage children's attention by offering them a robust narrative, strong child characters, attractive illustrations, rhymes or riddles, or a text which took the child's point of view. But were children also reading for fun before the arrival of this new children's literature? It has generally been assumed that they were. After all, in the Middle Ages and during the Renaissance and Reformation there was a wealth of entertaining books available, not targeted at children in particular, but very possibly read by them. In his recent survey of the history of childhood in Britain, for instance, Hugh Cunningham writes that 'There was no clear dividing line in the Middle Ages between adult and children's literature'.[1] Before modern children's literature, in other words, there would certainly have been a literature exclusively for adults: serious and scholarly works requiring high levels of literacy and erudition (although no doubt some precocious children read these too). But, it seems likely, there would also have been a tradition of popular literature read both by adults and children. This consumption of popular literature by children, both before and during the development of a new literature exclusively for children, is what this chapter will investigate.

So what was the popular literature of early modern Britain? Its boundaries are blurred, but at its core were romances, like *The Seven Champions of Christendom* and *Valentine and Orson*, and ballads, such as *The Children in the Wood* or *A Weeks Loving, Wooing, and Wedding: or, Happy is That Wooing that is Not Long a Doing*. Fables and 'jestbooks' were also common, as well as what we might now loosely call fairy tales, such as *Jack the Giant-Killer*. Didactic and factual, or pseudo-factual, texts should also be included: almanacs, biographies, histories, hagiographies and some political and religious matter.[2] Popular literature was not all riotous and bawdy, but could be earnest and instructive. It was in prose and verse. No doubt it

---

1   Hugh Cunningham, *The Invention of Childhood* (London: BBC Books, 2006), p. 57.

2   Probably the best short summary remains Victor E. Neuburg's *Popular Literature: A History and Guide: From the Beginning of Printing to the Year 1897* (London: Woburn Press, 1977).

was connected with an oral tradition of story-telling and lesson-giving, although of course this is difficult to corroborate. It circulated in manuscript before the advent of printing, but what is striking is that almost as soon as the printing press was brought to England it was this kind of popular literature that was selected for publication, with William Caxton and his successors realising its commercial viability. One of the first books Caxton printed, in 1483, was *The Golden Legend*, a collection of lives of the saints featuring far-fetched accounts of their miracles and martyrdoms. He followed it with French romances such as *The History of Paris and Vienne* (1485). Caxton's successor, Wynkyn de Worde, continued in the same vein, printing the scurrilous *The Friar and the Boy* in around 1512 and, at around the same time, the *Gesta Romanorum* ('Acts of the Romans'), a very miscellaneous collection of secular stories with religious morals applied. Both remained popular throughout the sixteenth, seventeenth and even into the eighteenth centuries.

Much of this kind of material is fairly coarse – not smutty necessarily (although it often was), but unsophisticated in terms of style and content. *Scogin's Jests*, for example, probably first published in the late sixteenth century and remaining in print until at least the 1790s, is a compilation of anecdotes, jokes, witticisms and misunderstandings centring on the eponymous hero, Oxford-educated but crude and iconoclastic. A typical episode is 'How *Scogin* and his wife made an Heire'. Consulting a lawyer about some property he has purchased, Scogins is told he needs to make an heir. He takes his wife to bed and he 'pulled the sheet & the clothes ouer his own head and his wiues, and did let a great fart … so long they lay together, that with stink they were almost choked.' Returning to the lawyer, Scogins is indignant: 'you bad me make an heire, and I and my wife made such an heir in our beds yesternight, that she & I were almost poysoned'. Scogins has misunderstood the legal meaning of making someone his heir, and had misheard 'heir' for 'air'. There is a token moral – 'whereby it appeares that mis-hearing of a tale, maketh mis-understanding' – but all that really matters is the double-pronged joke, mixing the sexual and the scatological.[3] The suitability of this kind of material to children is open to question. An anecdote such as this is not exactly pornographic. Scogin's assumption that he should fart rather than fornicate is actually rather childlike, and one can imagine a joke like this, based on ludicrous misapprehension, appealing to young as well as old. But it is unsafe to make any assumptions about audience responses. Hugh Cunningham suggests that *The Friar and the Boy*, also a story largely concerned with farting, would appeal especially to children, since it tells of a boy's revenge against his cruel stepmother by magically making her break wind in public (its title page describes the text as 'Very delectable, though unpleasant to all Step-mothers').[4] This is, as Cunningham says, the kind of situation that Roald Dahl might have created, and which late twentieth-century children have delighted in. But based only on a perceived similarly between the subversive, coarse, child-versus-adult humour of texts separated by almost 500 years, it does seem a leap to describe

---

3   *The First and Best Part of Scoggins Iests Full of Witty Mirth and Pleasant Shifts, Done by Him in France, and Other Places: Being a Preseruatiue Against Melancholy. Gathered by Andrew Boord, Doctor of Physicke* (London: Francis Williams, 1626), pp. 34–6.

4   *The Friar and the Boy* (Glasgow, 1668).

The Friar and the Boy as 'the beginning of what we now call children's literature'.[5] Certainly there is no unbroken tradition between *Scogin's Jests* or *The Friar and the Boy* and *James and the Giant Peach* (1961), *The Twits* (1980) or *The BFG* (1982). The development of a new, much more respectable children's literature intervened in the mid to late eighteenth, and early nineteenth, centuries.

In fact, if a point of origin for modern children's literature is being sought, the *Gesta Romanorum* is a much more likely candidate. Its publishers do not explicitly claim that the book was intended for children, even in later, eighteenth-century editions. But it does share many of the characteristics of those texts which were being deliberately designed for children from the late seventeenth century. In its usual full title, for instance, there are claims for historical authenticity which, although erroneous, represent a striving for respectability, and the promise of moral and religious instruction is foregrounded: *Gesta Romanorum: Containing Fifty Eight Remarkable Histories, Collected Originally from the Best and Most Ancient Roman Records. With morals and Applications, Tending to the Suppressing of Vice and the Encouragement of Virtue, and the Love of God.* As another concession to readers who might struggle with the text, some editions promise 'a new Set of Cuts, proper to Illustrate and Explain the Respective Stories'. There are also hints of the famous 'Instruction with Delight' mantra endorsed by John Locke and taken up by the great pioneer of children's literature, John Newbery:

The Story's pleasant, and the Moral good,
If read with Care, and rightly understood.[6]

Much of this might have been publishers' flannel, but it does raise the question of whether children had become a distinct part of the audience for these texts, as projected by those who wrote and marketed them.

But the form of popular literature most often regarded as being a staple of early modern children's reading, and as the forerunner of children's literature, is the chapbook. Broadly speaking, the chapbook was a short, cheap book produced in large numbers from the sixteenth to the nineteenth centuries – a vehicle, in other words, for the sort of text which we have already been looking at. But there is a great deal of confusion about what the chapbook actually is. Indeed, the word has been used to describe such a diverse range of texts that it has become more of a hindrance than a help. The term is, as one of the most authoritative scholars of the form has noted, not much more than 'a bibliographic conceit'.[7]

Defining the Chapbook

It used to be thought that the term 'chapbook' was first used only after the form it describes had fallen out of use, from about the 1820s onwards. Much earlier

---

5   Cunningham, *Invention of Childhood*, p. 58.

6   *Gesta Romanorum: Containing Fifty Eight Remarkable Histories ... By A.B.* (London: T. Norris and A. Bettesworth, 1722).

7   Barry McKay, *An Introduction to Chapbooks* (Oldham: Incline Press, 2003), p. 5.

occurrences have now been discovered. Barry McKay has unearthed an advertisement for 'New Chap Books' in the *Cumberland Pacquet* for 1774, placed by the London publisher Richard Snagg.[8] There were 12 titles on offer but, McKay warns, these were productions 'which now we might hesitate to call chapbooks'. They were abridged versions of novels: *The Comical Adventures of Roderick Random* and *The Pleasing History of Pamela, or Virtue Rewarded*, for example, though also included among the 12 was *The Entertaining History of the Fortunate Country Maid, Who from a Cottage through a Great Variety of Diverting Adventures, Became a Lady of the First Quality in the Court of France*. Moreover, they cost ninepence each, and, according to McKay, were all 64 pages long including a copper-engraved frontispiece.[9] McKay speculates that these abridgements may have been designed for children. Going still further back, Jan Fergus has discovered that the archives of the Clays, booksellers in Daventry, Rugby, Lutterworth and Warwick, contain references to chapbooks from as early as 1747. It is possible, Fergus notes, that John Clay might have been abbreviating 'chapmen's books' – the ledgers speak of orders for '25 Chap: Books' (1747). But his son, Thomas, did not use any punctuation to abbreviate the term, writing in 1773, for instance, that he had been paid for 'Art of Destruction a chap Book'.[10] Most commonly, the Clays seem to have labelled traditional tales costing eight-pence as 'chapbooks', a commodity which sold very well to the boys at Rugby School. The important point behind all this bibliographical detail is that the term 'chapbook' has always been used loosely, designating an amorphous and fluid literary form; as much a concept as an actual group of texts. Nor has the full range of chapbooks survived; we draw our conclusions from what we find in a small number of collections, mostly assembled in the nineteenth or twentieth centuries. Naturally, these collections were shaped by the priorities of the collectors, and their pre-existing notions of what chapbooks should be.

---

8   Ibid., p. 33. The advertisement is repeated in facsimile on p. 34. The *Oxford English Dictionary* records 1824 as the earliest usage of the term, by Thomas Dibdin in *The Library Companion; or, The Young Man's Guide and Old Man's Comfort, in the Choice of a Library* (London: Harding, Triphook and Lepard), p. 238.

9   McKay, *An Introduction to Chapbooks*, pp. 33–4. Closer inspection of the extant volumes from this series in the British Library reveals a little more variety. *The History of Sir Charles Grandison and the Hon. Miss Byron; In Which is Included Memoirs of a Noble Italian Family* (London: R. Snagg, n.d.) is fully 82 pages long and contains three full page engravings. A book-list at the end, listing the same 12 titles as the advertisement, also suggests that Snagg's venture was not a success: 'Price only 9d. each bound' is printed at the head of the list, but '9d.' has been crossed through, and '6d.' carefully written in above (British Library 1607/4667).

10   I am grateful for Jan Fergus's willingness to let me see material from her study of the book-buying habits of the boys of Rugby School and for providing much supplemental information by private correspondence. Fergus provides an introduction to the data in 'Solace in Books: Reading Trifling Adventures at Rugby School', in Andrea Immel and Michael Witmore (eds), *Childhood and Children's Literature in Early Modern Europe 1550–1800* (New York and London: Routledge, 2006), pp. 243–59. See also her *Provincial Readers in Eighteenth-Century England* (Oxford: Oxford University Press, 2007) and (with Ruth Portner) 'Provincial Bookselling in Eighteenth-Century England', *Studies in Bibliography* 40 (1987), 147–63.

This said, because chapbooks are so central to the question of what children read before children's literature, a more precise working definition of the term will be required. The word 'chapbook' derives from the much older word 'chapman', meaning an itinerant trader. 'Chapbook', therefore, has come to mean (as Harry B. Weiss put it) 'anything from a broadside to a good-sized book – anything printed – that was carried for sale by a chapman into villages, hamlets, towns'.[11] Others have preferred to concentrate on the form's physical characteristics. For John Simons, a chapbook is best defined, 'strictly and briefly', as 'a single sheet of paper printed on both sides and then folded so as to make a book of twelve leaves or twenty-four pages'.[12] Victor Neuburg combines these two criteria, but adds further defining characteristics to the checklist: they 'measured about six inches by four inches', were usually issued unbound, with the title page also acting as a wrapper, 'nearly always with a woodcut illustration', and they generally cost just 'a copper or two'.[13] Here, then, are three principal constituent parts of the chapbook's technical definition – its distribution by 'chapmen', or pedlars, its small size and short length and its low price. We can perhaps best get to grips with the multiple strands by constructing a Venn diagram, a schematic representation of the chapbook's overlapping characteristics (see Figure 2.1).

Figure 2.1 can be used to solidify our thinking on what is and is not a chapbook. It is possible, for instance, to hypothesise about a set of encyclopaedias sold by a hawker, which being neither cheap, nor short and small, would fit into Figure 2.1 at point 'a', and certainly ought not to be considered a chapbook. Similarly, a short but well-printed manual on irrigation techniques could be placed at point 'b', and a newspaper, catalogue or a subsidised bible might figure at 'c'. A pamphlet lampooning Members of Parliament and intended for the political cognoscenti, or a periodical such as Ned Ward's *London Spy* (1698–1700), might feature at 'd', and religious treatises or spiritual autobiographies, when sold by chapmen, could be placed at 'e'. None of these should be considered as chapbooks. Indeed, some texts might fulfil all three of Neuburg's criteria ('f') but are still not usually thought of as chapbooks: almanacs, broadsides, primers, alphabets, recipe books, Papal Bulls, some sermons or religious tracts, for example. As for the children's books which started to be produced in the middle of the eighteenth century, the pioneering titles published by John Newbery, Mary Cooper and others, these generally possessed some of the characteristics of chapbooks – they were short and small – but they were distributed from shops instead of by hawkers, and could range in cost from a penny to more than a shilling. They would feature on the diagram at either 'b' or 'd'.

---

11 Harry B. Weiss, *A Catalogue of the Chapbooks in the New York Public Library* (New York: New York Public Library, 1936), p. 3.

12 John Simons (ed.), *Guy of Warwick and Other Chapbook Romances: Six Tales from the Popular Literature of Pre-Industrial England* (Exeter: University of Exeter Press, 1998), p. 4. Simons admits that chapbooks could sometimes be a little shorter or longer than the standard 24 pages.

13 Victor Neuburg, *The Penny Histories: A Study of Chapbooks for Young Readers Over Two Centuries* (London: Oxford University Press, 1968), pp. 3–6.

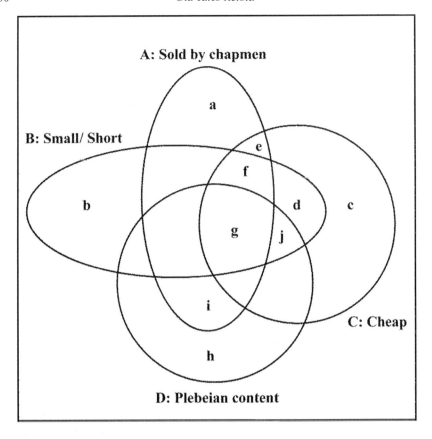

Figure 2.1   Chapbooks: possible defining characteristics.

One retort to these rather arcane demarcation difficulties might be to adhere to the most serviceable definition of the chapbook: that is, any small, cheap, widely distributed book which is not already known by another name. Certainly chapbooks cannot easily be delimited generically: they could contain prose or verse, fiction or fact, old or new material. Perhaps the 'classic' chapbooks contained popular songs and myths, legends and highly abridged chivalric romances, which later morphed into the 'penny dreadfuls' and 'shilling shockers' of the nineteenth century. But a chapbook might also contain anything from fairy tales to biographies, jests to true crime, ABCs to last testaments, recipes to abridged novels (sometimes called 'bluebooks').[14] Indeed, probably the majority of chapbooks contained religious matter. The sermons, prayers, catechisms, hymns and tales issued as chapbooks

---

14 See Roger Davis, *Kendrew of York and his Chapbooks for Children with a Checklist* (Wetherby: Elmete Press, 1988), p. 6, for a concise summary of the variety available, and for a fuller account see Bernard Capp, 'Popular Literature', in B. Reay (ed.), *Popular Culture in Seventeenth-Century England* (London: Croom Helm, 1985), pp. 198–243. On the 'bluebooks' see William W. Watt, *Shillings Shockers of the Gothic School: A Study of Chapbook Gothic Romances* (Cambridge, MA, 1932, repr. New York, 1967).

by the Society for the Propagation of Christian Knowledge (SPCK) and more particularly the Religious Tract Society (RTS) were produced in vast numbers.[15] And even before the RTS, according to one account of lowland Scotland at least, the chapbook meant not romances like *Valentine and Orson* or *Jack the Giant-Killer*, but 'usually pamphlets, or religious tracts' which were 'purchased from travelling chapmen at a cheap rate,' and which were regularly read, at least one memoir insists, by children to their parents on Sabbath afternoons.[16]

Yet even if chapbooks cannot be identified from their subject matter, it might still be argued that it is their tone, their associations and their readership which form the most important part of their definition. The term chapbook has always been largely synonymous with what might be called popular or street literature. When the term 'chapbook' came into common use in the nineteenth century, it was supposed to convey notions of ephemerality, of tawdriness, of a connection with the traditional literature of the rural or urban working classes. This suggests another set to add to the Venn diagram in Figure 2.1 – plebeian content or associations. This new criterion does not solve all problems of definition, but it can further focus thinking. The intersection of all four sets ('g') is the location of what might be termed the classic chapbook. But we can also think about which texts have plebeian associations, through their content, tone or physical properties, but which do not necessarily fall into one or more of the other sets. For instance, the 'Chap Books' advertised by Snagg were certainly neither particularly small and short nor particularly cheap. Presumably, then, they were advertised as chapbooks at least in part because of their content: condensed, popularised novels (they could be located, therefore, at 'h' or 'i'). The same is apparently true of the chapbooks sold by the Clays to Rugby schoolboys. What they called 'chapbooks' were neither cheap (they were usually eight pence) nor sold by chapmen, and they were probably not small either. They must have been so designated according to content and associations. The most popular were *Guy of Warwick*, *The Seven Champions of Christendom* and *Valentine and Orson*. Such chivalric romances, like the fairy tales written for the French court by Madame d'Aulnoy and Charles Perrault, had been part of elite culture, but in an abridged and amended form were quickly amalgamated into popular culture, and it is this slide from gentility to popularity which seems to identify them, once they became a little more widely available, as chapbooks (presumably to be placed, in Figure 2.1, at 'h').

The association of chapbooks with the lower classes is not straightforward. Even if they cost only a penny or so, they were probably beyond the financial reach of many. There are also difficulties in cleanly dividing lower-class and elite culture. In

---

15 Astonishing figures are given by J.S. Bratton in her account of the RTS chapbook distribution – for instance the 5,084,958 copies of certain heavily edited fairy tales which were distributed, often free, between 1824 and 1847 (*The Impact of Victorian Children's Fiction* (London: Croom Helm, 1981), p. 39).

16 George Robertson, *Rural Recollections* (1829), quoted in Margaret Spufford, *Small Books and Pleasant Histories: Popular Fiction and its Readership in Seventeenth-Century England* (London: Methuen and Co., 1981), p. 47. Robertson was remembering his childhood in the later eighteenth century.

his important revisionist book *Popular Culture in Early Modern Europe*, Peter Burke argued that the elite often participated in 'low' culture. They played parts in all the festivities and rituals of the community, and they consumed popular literature too. It was the lower classes who could not, in general, cross out of their cultural boundaries by participating in elite culture.[17] Some who have studied chapbook readership have found that the rich certainly did enjoy them. Tessa Watt has found records of chapbooks being left in the wills of the affluent.[18] John Mullan and Christopher Reid have noted that George Woodward, a rector in Berkshire, contemplated borrowing chapbooks from his servants. So desperate was he for reading matter, he wrote, that had a friend not sent him Samuel Richardson's refined novel *Sir Charles Grandison*, 'we sh^d. have degraded our Taste so far, as to have borrow'd Valentine & Orson from ye Gentry in ye Kitchen, where he is Conn'd over every Night with wonderful Pleasure.'[19] He may have been sneering at his servants' literary tastes, but he clearly knew what they were reading, and is there perhaps a hint of envy in his admission, or at least something suspicious in his determination to protest that he would never stoop so low as a chapbook? Even taken at face value, such comments as this suggest that the affluent and educated read chapbooks, but regarded themselves as trespassers in the literary domain of their social inferiors when they did so. It could have been largely acknowledged, in other words, that the chapbook was a plebeian form, irrespective of who was actually reading it – and irrespective of content too. A small, cheap book, even if it contained a poem, narrative or sermon which had, in other contexts, been the cultural property of the elite, would still have plebeian associations stemming from its physical form. After all, chapbooks looked very different from the books of the middle and upper classes. They were generally small and short, as we have seen, and often but not always poorly printed on cheap paper, using often fairly rudimentary woodcuts, and, at least before the eighteenth century, were often printed in black letter type.[20]

Ultimately, then, it was probably the relationship between the various components of a chapbook's definition which caused contemporary readers to understand a text as a chapbook (irrespective of whether they used the term itself). Size, length, type, price, content, cultural associations and tone, and the mode by which it was sold were

---

17 Burke, *Popular Culture in Early Modern Europe* (1978, repr. Aldershot: Scolar Press, 1994), p. 28.

18 Tessa Watt, *Cheap Print and Popular Piety 1550–1640* (Cambridge: Cambridge University Press, 1991), pp. 1–2.

19 George Woodward to George London, February 1754. Quoted in John Mullan and Christopher Reid (eds), *Eighteenth-Century Popular Culture: A Selection* (Oxford: Oxford University Press, 2000), p. 1.

20 Keith Thomas has argued that the black letter type generally used for early chapbooks, although we think of these 'gothic' letters as much more difficult to read than roman or italic type, was actually the most legible kind of script for inexpert readers in the eighteenth century. After all, Thomas says, most children's hornbooks, catechisms and primers were printed in black letter. 'The Meaning of Literacy in Early Modern England', pp. 97–31 in Gerd Baumann (ed.), *The Written Word: Literacy in Transition* (Oxford: Oxford University Press, 1986), p. 99. On the other hand, black letter type was often used for extremely respectable documents, such as Acts of Parliament.

all important, but none of these characteristics were in themselves the determining factor. It was the combination which was important. The precise combination of these ingredients which was necessary to form the chapbook changed over time. In the two centuries after the arrival of printing it seems likely that the most important element of the chapbook was that it was sold by hawkers. By the later eighteenth century, with better communication networks allowing more people access to fixed retail facilities, and with those retailers having expanded into material and markets which were previously the domain of the pedlars, it seems likely that it was the plebeian associations of the texts which were more important in their designation as chapbooks.

Did Children Read Popular Literature?

To establish a working definition of the chapbook, while acknowledging its complications and instability, is important because the term has so often been used so loosely in studies of early children's literature. Texts generally called chapbooks were still appearing in the nineteenth century – these will be discussed later – and it is only by understanding the characteristics of the seventeenth- and eighteenth-century chapbook that we can understand whether and how the form changed following the appearance of a literature that was especially designed for children. However, in early modern Britain, the chapbook was only one part of a larger body of popular literature, including, *inter alia*, the ballads, jest-books and semi-factual material that were mentioned earlier. The complaint of one early seventeenth-century critic that children were gaining access to 'sweete songs and wanton tales' as various as 'the Court of *Venus*, the Pallace of Pleasure, *Guy of Warwicke, Libbius* and *Arthur*, *Bevis of Hampton*, the wise men of *Goatam*, *Scogins* Jeasts, *Fortunatus*, and those new delights that have succeeded these, and are now extant, too tedious to recken up' gives a sense of the range of popular literature that children might have been reading.[21] Accounts such as this also raise, and go someway to answering, the crucial question of whether children read popular literature, and chapbooks in particular.

Certainly to modern eyes, many chapbooks, bearing titles such as *The Wanton Wife of Bath, and the Quaker's Courtship* or *A Cup of Good Whisky*,[22] can seem rather unsuitable for children. Yet the general supposition has been that chapbooks were intended for a wide audience, comprised of people with a rudimentary literacy, whether adults denied a formal education or children who were learning to read – as well as those who could not read themselves, but could find someone to read

---

21 Henry Crosse, *Vertues Common-wealth: or The High-way to Honour. Wherein is Discovered, that although by the Disguised Craft of this Age, Vice and Hypocrisie may be Concealed: Yet by Tyme (the Triall of Truth) it is Most Plainly Revealed* (London: John Newbery, 1603), unpaginated but pp. 102–3.

22 From the Robert White collection of chapbooks held in the Robinson Library of Newcastle University. See Desmond Sparling Bland, *Chapbooks and Garlands in the Robert White Collection in the Library of King's College* (Newcastle: University of Newcastle upon Tyne Press, 1956).

to them.[23] It has further been claimed that before children's literature, chapbooks very often provided the texts used to teach children, even affluent children, to read. John Simons, for instance, has argued that chapbooks were read by 'the children of the gentry'.[24] And Gary Kelly has asserted that chapbooks were 'commonly used by middle- and upper-class families as their children's first books'.[25] Such claims are very difficult to substantiate, and neither Simons nor Kelly provide proof. There is a wealth of evidence, but much of it is circumstantial, subjective and tendentious. To establish the use of chapbooks in educational programmes for children, for example, one might point to a claim made by Edward Synge in 1742 that Roman Catholic children were trained to read at school using *The Seven Wise Masters*, the *Gesta Romanorum*, *Fortunatus*, *Valentine and Orson*, *The Seven Champions of Christendom* and other such chapbook titles. The evidence is less persuasive, though, when we take into account that this accusation appeared in an account of a conversion from Catholicism in which Synge was intent on ridiculing the Catholic Church for preventing the laity from reading the Scriptures for themselves.[26] Another indication that chapbooks were used to teach affluent children comes from *The Art of Teaching in Sport* (1785), in which the author, 'Mrs Lovechild', tells of a boy being given a copy of *The Seven Champions of Christendom* to teach him to read the black letter alphabet in preparation for his entry into the priesthood. The author repeats this claim more as a comic anecdote than anything else though, relating that the serious and scholarly boy who was given the chapbook became unexpectedly captivated by the text, running off to read it sitting astride a beam in a barn.[27] Similarly equivocal is the evidence provided by surviving marginalia. Nicholas Orme has suggested that two boys probably used an early sixteenth-century copy of *Bevis of Hampton* in their school. But this version of the chapbook tale was in fact a very substantial edition, and in any case, there is no certainty about when or in what circumstances the marginal marks were added.[28]

Evidence of children reading popular literature for pleasure, rather than as part of a curriculum, is more plentiful. Describing his late sixteenth-century childhood, Robert Ashley remembered delighting in 'Bevis of Hampton', 'Guy of Warwick', 'The History of Valentine and Orson' and the 'Life of King Arthur of Britain'.[29] In his semi-autobiographical *A Few Sighs from Hell, or The Groans of a Damned*

---

23 Davis, *Kendrew of York*, p. 8; Neuburg, *Penny Histories*, p. 18.

24 Simons (ed.), *Guy of Warwick*, p. 7;

25 Gary Kelly, 'Introduction' to 'Street Gothic: Female Gothic Chapbooks', vol. 2 of *Varieties of Female Gothic*, gen. ed. Gary Kelly (6 vols, London: Pickering and Chatto, 2002), p. xi.

26 Edward Synge, *A Sincere Christian and Convert from the Church of Rome, Exemplified in the Life of Daniel Herly, a Poor Irish Peasant* (London: Thomas Trye, 1742), p. 7.

27 'Mrs Lovechild' [Ellinor Fenn], *The Art of Teaching in Sport; Designed as a Prelude to a Set of Toys, for Enabling Ladies to Instill the Rudiments of Spelling Reading, Grammar, and Arithmetic, under the Idea of Amusement* (London: John Marshall and Co., 1785), p. 28.

28 Nicholas Orme, *Medieval Children* (New Haven, CT: Yale University Press, 2001), pp. 298–302. The annotated copy is in the Bodleian Library (Douce B. subt.234).

29 Ronald S. Crane, 'The Reading of an Elizabethan Youth', *Modern Philology* 11 (1913–14), 269–71.

Soul (1658), John Bunyan recalled that, to the exclusion of the Scriptures, his childhood reading was dominated by ballads, 'news-books' and titles like *Bevis of Southampton*.[30] Half a century later, Richard Steele, writing in the *Tatler*, has his Mr. Bickerstaff describe an eight-year-old boy who had read 'Lives and Adventures of Don *Bellianis* of *Greece*, *Guy* of *Warwick*, the *Seven Champions*' and many other chapbooks, and knew them well enough to subject them to some precocious literary criticism.[31] Samuel Johnson, or James Boswell, according to their own accounts, were not unlike this boy. Johnson recalled having been delighted by tales like *St George and the Dragon*.[32] Boswell recounted that he had 'when a boy, been much entertained with *Jack the Giant-Killer* and such little story-books'.[33] Several accounts of fictional boys repeat these autobiographical descriptions of childhood devotion to chapbooks. In Laurence Sterne's *Tristram Shandy* (1759–67), for example, Uncle Toby recalls that 'When Guy, Earl of Warwick, and Parismus and Parismenus, and Valentine and Orson, and the Seven Champions of England, were handed round the school, – were they not all purchased with my own pocket money?'[34]

But the evidence is difficult to interpret, especially since it seems so often to serve particular purposes. Bunyan, like other Puritans, mentions chapbook reading as an indication of youthful debauchery, showing how distant the child was from the chance of salvation. As early as 1528, William Tyndale had complained that the minds of the young were being corrupted by 'Robin Hood and Bevis of Hampton, Hercules, Hector, and Troylus, with a thousand histories and fables of love and wantons and of ribaldry', and that the clergy was not doing enough to stop it.[35] Just as polemical was the blast from 'R.H.' against those parents who preferred 'a *Tom Thumb*, *Guy of Warwick*, *Valentine and Orson*, or some such foolish Book, before the Book of Life!'[36] Tendentious in a different way is evidence available from the *Newgate Calendar*, accounts of convicted criminals which often focused on the

---

30 John Bunyan *A Few Sighs from Hell, or The Groans of a Damned Soul* (London: Ralph Wood, 1658), pp. 156–7.

31 Richard Steele, *Tatler* 95 (17 November 1709), repr., ed. Donald F. Boyd (3 vols, Oxford: Clarendon Press, 1987), vol. 2, pp. 92–3.

32 Hester Lynch Piozzi, *Anecdotes of the Late Samuel Johnson, LL.D. During the Last Twenty Years of his Life* (London: T. Cadell, 1786), p. 15.

33 James Boswell, *Boswell's London Journal, 1762–63*, ed. F.A. Pottle (London: Heinemann, 1950), p. 299 n. 6.

34 Lawrence Sterne, *The Life and Opinions of Tristram Shandy, Gentleman* (1759–67, repr., ed. Graham Petrie, Harmondsworth: Penguin, 1985), p. 443 (vol. VI, ch. 32).

35 William Tyndale, *The Obedience of a Christian Man*, (Antwerp, 1528, fol. 20r), quoted in Orme, *Medieval Children*, p. 288.

36 R.H., *The History of Genesis. Being an Account of the Holy Lives and Actions of the Patriarchs; Explained with Pious and Edifying Explications, and Illustrated with Near Forty Figures. Fitted for the Use of Schools, and Recommended to Teachers of Children, as a Book Very Proper for the Learning Them to Read English; and Instructing Them in the Right Understanding of these Divine Histories*, 2nd edn (London: J. Darby, 1702), pp. vi–vii. A more substantial discussion of this kind of evidence of children's chapbook use, and problems with interpreting it, is available in M.O. Grenby, 'Chapbooks, Children and Children's Literature', *The Library: Transactions of the Bibliographical Society* 8 (2007), 277–303.

youthful conduct which brought them to the gallows. The history of Mary Carleton, for example, executed in 1673, stresses her childhood reading of popular tales like '*Parismus and Parismenus, Don Belianis of Greece*, and *Amadis de Gaul*'. This is apparently because it explains her later bigamy and imposture, crimes committed because she had become convinced that she belonged in higher station than that into which she was actually born.[37] The class dimension to responses to children's reading of popular literature is also evident in a letter purportedly written to the editor of the *Reflector* (1788). It describes a twelve-year-old's fascination with 'Jack the merry piper, and that great champion Jack the giant-killer', which he 'is always reading when he has time from driving the plough' and knows 'off by heart'. Seeking to take his education further, his father has bought him 'two fine bound books called the Seven Champions, and the Seven Wise Masters'. But this account was doubtless fabricated simply to introduce the long response from the magazine's editor which follows, detailing what is actually proper for children 'in the lower ranks of life' to read: the Scriptures, polite miscellanies, history, geography, natural history, but certainly neither Latin nor chapbooks.[38]

Several other accounts of children's chapbook reading are more playful, and clearly satirical in intent. Should we trust Henry Fielding in *Joseph Andrews* (1742), for instance, when his narrator praises several chapbooks tales as 'of excellent use and instruction, finely calculated to sow the seeds of virtue in youth, and very easy to be comprehended by persons of moderate capacity'. His sardonic descriptions are, after all, surely meant to deride the usefulness to youth of such texts:

> the history of John the Great, who, by his brave and heroic actions against men of large and athletic bodies, obtained the glorious appellation of the Giant-killer; that of an Earl of Warwick, whose Christian name was Guy; the lives of Argalus and Parthenia, and above all, the History of those seven worthy personages, the Champions of Christendom.

After such burlesque descriptions, is he being ironic when he concludes by saying that 'In all these, delight is mixed with instruction, and the reader is almost as much improved as entertained'? Or is he mocking anyone who would actually make the claim that these chapbook tales could be useful to the young – which would nevertheless confirm that there were some who did so?[39]

Similarly resistant to easy interpretation is the account is to be found in *The Columbian Orator*, a celebrated collection of short pieces designed by Caleb Bingham to teach reading and oratory to American children. In an address intended to demonstrate the folly of conceitedness, Charles Chatterbox, a 'Very Small Boy', boasts of his extensive reading. Yet the list of titles he mentions is presumably

---

37 *The Complete Newgate Calendar*, ed. J.L. Rayner and G.T. Crook (6 vols, London: Navarre Society, 1926), vol. 1, p. 249.

38 *The Reflector: A Selection of Essays on Various Subjects of Common Life. From Original Papers. Illustrated with Entertaining Anecdotes* (London: W. Lane, 1788), pp. 69–75.

39 Henry Fielding, *Joseph Andrews*, ed. R.F. Brissenden (1742; London: Penguin, 1985), pp. 39–40. One cannot help but notice that it would be only another two years before John Newbery used the 'delight ... mixed with instruction' formula in another context: his pioneering children's book *A Little Pretty Pocket-Book* (1744).

supposed to be credible, and perhaps gives an indication how totally a late eighteenth-century American boy might be immersed in popular literature. His list begins with 'the Arabian Tales', then 'Tom Thumb's Folio', 'Winter Evening Tales', 'Seven Champions', 'Parismus and Parismenus', 'Valentine and Orson', 'Mother Bunch', 'Seven Wise Masters' and 'a curious book, entitled, Think well on't'. Besides these chapbooks, he claims to have consumed longer texts too, although these may well have been in abridged chapbook versions:

> I have also read Robinson Crusoe, and Raynard the fox, and Moll Flanders; and I have read twelve delightful novels, and Irish Rogues, and Life of Saint Patrick, and Philip Quarle, and Conjurer Crop, and Æsop's Fables, and Laugh and be fat, and Toby Lumpkins' Elegy on the Birth of a Child, and a Comedy on the Death of his Brother, and an Acrostic, occasioned by a mortal sickness of his dear wife, of which she recovered.

Some texts he mentions in more detail, giving what appears to be an insight into the unsuitability of the texts children were reading. He seems to have relished such books despite their bawdiness and coarseness, violence and transvestism – or perhaps because of it:

> Then there is another wonderful book, containing fifty reasons why an old bachelor was not married. The first was, that nobody would have him; and the second was, he declared to every body, that he would not marry; and so it went on stronger and stronger. Then, at the close of the book, it gives an account of his marvellous death and burial. And in the appendix, it tells about his being ground over, and coming out as young, and as fresh, and as fair as ever. Then, every few pages, is a picture of him to the life … Then, I have read this history of a man who married for money, and of a woman that would wear her husband's small-clothes in spite of him; and I have read four books of riddles and rubuses; and all that is not half a quarter.[40]

Charles Chatterbox's account has a ring of realism to it, but its intention is both didactic and satirical. It must remain an open question how genuine this log of a child's reading history might be.

Reading some of the reports of children's reading of popular literature from the later eighteenth and early nineteenth centuries a different problem is confronted: the accounts seem almost conventional. The poetical description of his early reading given by Robert Alves, born in 1745 in Elgin in the north-east of Scotland, is typical. 'The Weeping Bard' (1789) is his autobiographical poem, and it begins by describing a solitary, melancholy childhood, enlivened only

---

40 Caleb Bingham, 'Self-conceit', in *The Columbian Orator: Containing a Variety of Original and Selected Pieces; Together with Rules; Calculated to Improve Youth and Others in the Ornamental and Useful Art of Eloquence* (Boston: for the author, 1797), pp. 70–72.

With fairy tales of old; each mighty feat
Of *Valentine*, or *Orson*, or *St George*,
That with the dragon made a bloody fray!
Of the *Seven Champions*, all as brave as they!
Of *Fortunatus* with his *Wishing-Hat*!
Even to the *doughty deeds of Tommy Thumb*!
How happy, happy then,
With the dear present of a sixpence gay,
On Christmas-time or other holy-day,
To run to wandering pedlar at his stall,
Then buy a choice of learned books withal,
For tedious winter-eve by ruddy-beaming fire![41]

William Wordsworth's more famous account in *The Prelude* of 1805 is in some respects identical:

Oh! give us once again the Wishing-Cap
Of Fortunatus, and the invisible Coat
Of Jack the Giant-Killer, Robin Hood,
And Sabra in the forest with St. George![42]

But in fact, this nostalgic delight in the memory of childhood chapbook reading is echoed by almost all the Romantic poets. Samuel Taylor Coleridge wrote fondly of his childhood love of *Tom Hickathrift, Jack the Giant-Killer*, 'Belisarius, Robinson Crusoe, and Philip Quarles; and … the Arabian Nights' Entertainments'.[43] John Clare remembered reading the booklets sold by 'every doorcalling hawker & found on every bookstall at fairs & market', naming '*Valentine & Orson, Jack & the Giant, Long Tom the Carrier, The King & the Cobbler, Tawney Bear, The Seven Sleepers, Tom Hickathrift, Johnny Armstrong, Idle Laurence*' and many others.[44]

Chapbooks, Children's Literature and Popular Culture

There is, of course, a good deal more evidence of children's use of popular literature in early modern Britain than has been presented here, but most of it is similar in terms of the texts mentioned, the attitudes displayed towards them, and the motivations for

41 Robert Alves, 'The Weeping Bard', canto III, ll. 37–48, in *Edinburgh: A Poem, in Two Parts* (Edinburgh: for the author, 1789), p. 59.

42 William Wordsworth, *The Prelude* (1805), bk. 5, lines 364–7, in *William Wordsworth*, ed. Stephen Gill (Oxford: Oxford University Press, The Oxford Authors, 1989), p. 443.

43 Samuel Taylor Coleridge, *Letters of Samuel Taylor Coleridge*, ed. Ernest Hartley Coleridge (2 vols, London: William Heinemann, 1895), vol. 1, pp. 11–12.

44 John Clare, 'Autobiography, 1793–1824', in J.W. and Anne Tibble (eds), *The Prose of John Clare* (London: Routledge and Kegan Paul, 1951), p. 19. A full analysis of Clare's chapbook reading, and his references to them in his poetry and prose, is available in David Blamires, 'Chapbook, Fairytales and Children's Books in the Writings of John Clare', parts I and II, *John Clare Society Journal* 15 (1996), 27–53, and 16 (1997), 43–70.

the accounts. There is certainly enough data to build a case that children were a substantial part of the audience, and probably therefore the target market, for popular literature of several kinds, and especially chapbooks. What is striking is the length of time for which many chapbook titles were in common currency – from the sixteenth to the nineteenth centuries – although it is noticeable that by the later eighteenth century, other forms of popular literature – ballads, jests, bawdy tales such as *The Friar and the Boy* – were no longer being mentioned so frequently alongside the chapbooks. What is also conspicuous is that the seventeenth-century Puritan disgust at children's reading of popular literature was no longer much in evidence by the later eighteenth century. Oddly, though, it had been replaced by another complaint: that children, regrettably, were no longer reading chapbook tales as much as they once had been. Wordsworth had asked for chapbook tales to be 'give[n] us once again' – as if they had died out. He clearly preferred them to the new literature, designed especially for children, that had emerged in the second half of the eighteenth century. Coleridge, Clare, Dickens, William Godwin, Charles Lamb and others concurred. The new children's literature, they argued, deadened its readers, teaching them dry science and formulaic morality. But the 'wild tales' of chapbooks, as Lamb put it, inspired a 'beautiful interest ... which made the child a man, while all the time he suspected himself to be no bigger than a child'.[45] And for Godwin too, although himself an author and publisher of serious didactic books for children, *Fortunatus*, *Valentine and Orson*, *The Seven Champions of Christendom* and other such tales were the texts most likely to produce in the reader 'an active mind and a warm heart'.[46]

These laments give the clear impression that the rise of a literature specifically for children in the later eighteenth and early nineteenth centuries displaced children's reading of popular literature. This is certainly a persuasive argument – that the new children's literature meant that children no longer used chapbooks either for education or pleasure – and it has been made by a number of critics. Andrew O'Malley has taken this case furthest, arguing that the pioneers of the new children's literature, notably John Newbery, constructed their books in opposition to chapbook values. Whereas the chapbooks purveyed a 'lottery mentality', he argues, in which worldly success was dependent on good fortune, the new children's literature retailed more solidly middle-class values, notably education and industry.[47]

This argument, though, is open to question. Firstly, even if some early nineteenth-century commentators, such as Wordsworth and Lamb, were of the opinion that 'Mrs. Barbauld's stuff has banished all the old classics of the nursery' (meaning that the

---

45 Charles Lamb to Samuel Taylor Coleridge, 23 October 1802, in Charles and Mary Lamb, *Letters of Charles and Mary Lamb*, ed. E.V. Lucas (London: Dent and Methuen, 1935), p. 326.

46 William Godwin to William Cole, 2 March 1802, in C. Kegan Paul, *William Godwin: His Friends and Contemporaries* (2 vols, London: Henry S. King and Co., 1876), vol. 2, pp. 118–20.

47 Andrew O'Malley, *The Making of the Modern Child: Children's Literature and Childhood in the Late Eighteenth Century* (New York and London: Routledge, 2003), especially ch. 1: 'The Coach and Six: Chapbook Residue in Late Eighteenth-Century Children's Literature'. A lengthier consideration of this argument is available in Grenby, 'Chapbooks, Children and Children's Literature'.

'new' children's literature of rational, moral authors such as Barbauld had supplanted chapbook tales), this was evidently not the case for all children.[48] Perhaps the parents or teachers of the affluent could afford to purchase books specifically designed for children, which would lead to a diminished reliance on chapbooks. But it is clear that poorer children were still delighting in popular literature even at the very time that their obsolescence was being lamented. John Clare, for instance, was born in 1793 into rural poverty, but still read chapbooks in his early nineteenth-century childhood, later recalling that he 'savd all the pence I got to buy them'.[49] Samuel Bamford, born into a slightly more comfortable urban family in 1788, likewise remembered that 'every farthing' he could 'scrape together was ... spent in purchasing histories of "Jack the Giant Killer", "Saint George and the Dragon", "Tom Hickathrift", "Jack and the Beanstalk", "The Seven Champions of Christendom", the tale of "Fair Rosamond" ... and such like romances'.[50] Charles Dickens, born in 1812, much of whose early life was marked by hardship, remembered similar childhood reading in his childhood too: 'Faust', 'the Norwood Fortune Teller', 'Fairburn's Comic Songsters', 'Tom Thumb', 'Fair Rosamond', 'Fortunatus', 'The Seven Champions', 'Mother Bunch's Wonders' – all, he wrote, 'infinite delights to me'.[51]

The second reason why it does seem entirely convincing to claim that children's use of popular literature was smoothly eclipsed by the modern children's literature is that, in the early nineteenth century, a new kind of chapbook had emerged. Although they had much in common with the earlier forms of chapbook, this new generation of texts was different because it was designed especially for children. What is confusing is that these two different species are almost always elided under the same term, even though, as Sue Dipple insists, 'The name chapbook really describes two different kinds of book.' The first, 'the old fashioned variety,' cheap and sold by chapmen, I have already tried at some length to define. Dipple defines the second variety thus: 'cheap little books printed in large quantities, in the late 18th and early 19th centuries, usually for children, which were often sold directly by their publishers and printers'. She gives more detail:

> These little books were quite different to the early kind. Frequently formed from one folded sheet or half-sheet, they were mostly quite short, of 8, 12 or 16 pages. They were cheap, costing a halfpenny or a penny, and often had a small woodcut on every page to make them more attractive to children. Sometimes covered with Dutch flowered papers wrappers, plain or printed coloured paper or card wrappers, they often had no wrappers at all. They were smaller than the earlier chapbooks, usually 3 to 4 in[che]s by 2 to 3 in[che]s and were intended exclusively for children. Often quite carefully printed in consideration of the age of the reader, they contained stories more suitable for the nursery, and, in the nineteenth century, the illustrations may have been dab-coloured or stencil-coloured. The

---

48 Charles Lamb to Samuel Taylor Coleridge, 23 October 1802, in *Letters of Charles and Mary Lamb*, p. 326.

49 Clare, 'Autobiography', p. 19.

50 Samuel Bamford, *Passages in the Life of a Radical and Early Days*, ed. Henry Dunckley (2 vols, London, 1893), vol. 1, p. 87.

51 Harry Stone, 'Dickens's Reading', (2 vols, PhD dissertation, University of California at Los Angeles, 1955), vol. 1, pp. 75–82.

two kinds have little in common other than their inexpensive price, crude cuts and cheap method of printing.[52]

They were produced by firms like J.G. Rusher of Banbury, Mozley of Gainsborough, Houlston of Wellington, James Lumsden of Glasgow, George Ross of Edinburgh, James Kendrew of York, and William Davison of Alnwick (see Figure 2.2). London firms also published them. John Newbery himself, the pioneer of more respectable children's literature, could perhaps be included in this list since he published at least four penny books for children in the 1750s and 1760s.[53] Indeed, Cluer Dicey, perhaps the principal mid-eighteenth-century publisher of chapbooks, might be regarded as the pioneer of what would later emerge as children's chapbooks. He produced titles such as *The Child's New Year's Gift; A Collection of Riddles* and *The House that Jack Built; A Diverting Story for Children of all Ages* in about 1750: just 16 pages long, extensively illustrated, and evidently intended for children.[54]

In some ways, then, there are clear continuities between the classic chapbook for the early modern period and the children's variety of the nineteenth century. What divides the two forms is that the latter were apparently not distributed by itinerant hawkers. After all, except in remote areas, the age of the chapman was drawing to a close by the early nineteenth century, with better transport links to convey books from publisher to retailer to consumer, and with every town, and many villages, acquiring its own bookshops, circulating libraries and sometimes even printers. That most of these children's chapbooks very obviously bear the name and location of their publisher, in a way that few earlier chapbooks had done, also indicates that they were no longer peddled from place to place. In many cases, imprints like 'Printed for the Running Stationers' had been replaced by formulations such as 'Otley: printed by and for W. Walker, at the Wharfdale Stanhope Press' or 'London: Printed for J. Brambles, A. Meggitt, and J. Walters by H. Mozley, Market-place, Gainsborough'. (As it happens, only the Mozley half of this imprint was genuine – the London details were wholly fabricated, added to enhance the standing of a small, Lincolnshire business.)[55] In terms of the Venn diagram in Figure 2.1 the nineteenth-century

---

52 Sue Dipple, *Chapbooks: How They Be Collected by Sondrie Madde Persons, and Something of their Trew Historie* (Hoddesdon, Herts.: Children's Books History Society, 1996), p. 4. Brian Alderson and Felix de Marez Oyens, however, note that some of these children's chapbooks could be of quite high quality, often with bespoke wood engravings, and might be made extremely attractive, with 'covers coloured in sugar-paper or brushed with a colored wash' for instance (*Be Merry and Wise: Origins of Children's Book Publishing in England, 1650–1850* (London: The British Library, and New Castle, DE: Oak Knoll Press, 2006), p. 200).

53 Dipple, *Chapbooks: How They Be Collected*, p. 14. See Sydney Roscoe, *John Newbery and his Successors 1740–1814: A Bibliography* (Wormley, Herts.: Five Owls Press, 1973), cat. nos, J.103, J.267, J.269 and J.356.

54 These are in the collection of Birmingham City Library. Other similar titles published by Dicey include *Cock Robin; A Pretty Gilded Toy for either Boy or Girl* and *The Tragical Death of A. Apple Pye*, both in the British Library, but the earliest extant copies of these date from after 1753.

55 The names used in this fake imprint give the game away: 'Brambles', 'Meggitt' and 'Waters' were the maiden names of Henry Mozley's wife, mother and mother-in-law respectively. I am grateful to Sue Dipple for drawing this to my attention in an unpublished essay.

Figure 2.2   *The History of Robin Hood, Captain of the Merry Outlaws of Sherwood Forest* (Alnwick: W. Davison, no date but *c*.1820). Hockliffe Collection, Polhill Library, University of Bedfordshire, Bedford.

children's chapbooks, being cheap and small and short, but not sold by chapmen, should be placed either at 'd' or 'j'.

Their exact location on the diagram is dependent on their content. Traditional chapbook tales, such as *Jack the Giant-Killer*, *The Seven Champions of Christendom* or very heavily abridged versions of *Robinson Crusoe*, along with fairy tales and nursery rhymes, were staples of the form, maintaining the links with plebeian culture which had been a feature of earlier chapbooks. But children's chapbooks could also contain elaborate alphabets, or short histories, or verses by Isaac Watts, as well as much other religious or didactic material. They also frequently displayed the influence of the much more respectable children's literature which had developed since the middle of the eighteenth century. They might be pirated and abridged editions of moral tales produced by the established and respectable publishers of children's literature like Elizabeth Newbery, John Marshall or William Darton.

Alongside chapbook staples such as *The House that Jack Built*, *The Cries of London* and an abridged *Robinson Crusoe*, for instance, Kendrew of York published concise fairy tales, an abridged version of John Newbery's classic *The History of Giles Gingerbread, a Little Boy, who lived upon Learning* and a 31-page imitation of the new kind of rational, child-centred books called *Mrs. Lovechild's Golden Present for all Good Little Boys and Girls*. All cost only one penny. Others imitated the sort of moral tales for children being written by Dorothy Kilner, Maria Edgeworth and Maria Budden. These were condensed into 24 or 36 pages, and cost only two or three pence. Typical is *The Bad Boy Reformed by Kindness; To Which is Added, The Little Miser*, published in the 1810s by Whitrow and Co. in London. Here were two moral tales, crammed into the form of a well-illustrated, 32-page chapbook, and retailing for only three-pence. In the first, Philip has been given a new cane, but knocks over a bucket of water being carried by a poor boy. Angrily, the boy breaks the cane, but Philip is prevailed upon not to seek revenge, but instead to help the less privileged boy – reforming him by his kindness. The second tale is even simpler, telling of a boy who cannot bear to part with his sweets and apples but who comes to realise that his schoolfellows bully him because of his stinginess. Both tales were evidently directed at affluent readers, indicating that despite the physical form of the book, these are texts without strong plebeian associations ('d' in Figure 2.1).[56]

More research might usefully be conducted into the phenomenon of the children's chapbook.[57] For the purposes of this chapter though, the key point about the form is that it indicates the continuing engagement of children, even affluent children, with popular literature even after the emergence of a distinct literature for children. Some of the children's chapbooks may have been essentially moral tales in miniature, but many included material which had for many decades been a staple of the popular literature tradition – titles like *Jack the Giant-Killer*, *The Cries of London*, *The World Turned Upside Down*, *Robin Hood*, *Guy of Warwick* and so on. The new children's literature, in other words, did not immediately supplant popular literature in children's lives, nor suddenly sever children's connections with chapbook literature. Rather, what seems to have happened is that the commercial success of the new children's literature with an upper- and middle-class consumer base encouraged some enterprising publishers, largely but not exclusively working in the provinces, to venture a literature especially designed for poorer families who could not afford the products of major children's publishers. These had to be cheap, and so were small and short, although they could certainly be made to look attractive. And as for their content, it made no economic sense to commission authors to produce new texts, nor (in general) illustrators to produce new images. Pirating recent children's books was one possibility, but another was to reuse the traditional texts and familiar cuts that had been in circulation, and enjoyed by children, for decades. The children's chapbook

---

56 Anon., *The Bad Boy Reformed by Kindness; To Which is Added, The Little Miser. Embellished with 14 Fine Engravings on Wood* (London: Whitrow and Co., n.d. but *c.*1815). In the Hockliffe Collection, Polhill Library, University of Bedfordshire, Bedford, cat. no. 0059. Full page images are online at <http://www.cts.dmu.ac.uk/hockliffe/> (accessed 20 December 2007).

57 The most detailed and recent consideration is to be found in Alderson and Oyens, *Be Merry and Wise*, ch. 13.

was the result – a response to the new, more respectable children's literature which did not efface the engagement of children in popular literature, but rather maintained it.

The purpose of this chapter has been to explore the relationship between children's literature and popular literature, and especially the ways in which the chapbook stands at the intersection of these two types of text, or more correctly, concepts. What has emerged is a complicated picture, which changes substantially over time, particularly in the later eighteenth and early nineteenth centuries, when a new children's literature emerged and established itself. This can be simplified in another Venn diagram, Figure 2.3.

Clearly, there are forms of popular literature which were neither chapbooks nor children's books – almanacs and broadsides for example – and these would feature on the diagram at 't'. Equally clearly, most chapbooks should be regarded as a form of popular literature, and so a great many would feature in the segment labelled 'u'. Considering children's reading complicates the picture. There had long been books published for children which did not fulfil any of the characteristics of chapbooks, and which were too substantial, too expensive and perhaps too weighty to be considered as belonging to popular culture. Examples range from late seventeenth-century Puritan texts to the moral tales of the early nineteenth century, and on to the canonical children's books of the Victorian era ('v'). But as we have seen, many chapbooks, perhaps the majority, were read by children, irrespective of whether they were intended to be so by their producers or those children's elders, a finding that shifts many chapbooks from 'u' to 'w'. It is also easy to think of texts which were read by children and were part of popular literature, yet were not chapbooks ('x'). These might include ABCs and battledores, as well as jest books, certain picture

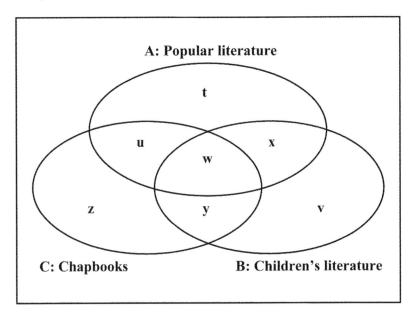

Figure 2.3   Chapbooks, children's literature and popular culture.

books, and perhaps some narratives not published in chapbook format (fables, fairy tales and so on). Perhaps more surprising was the development of titles which could populate the segment labelled 'y' – chapbooks read by children, but which cannot be thought of as popular literature. These were the 'children's chapbooks' which proliferated in early nineteenth century. Their low cost, and the poor quality of some of these publications, would ensure a bleed into 'w', but others were probably isolated from popular culture by the self-consciously educational content. The 16-page *Historical Anecdotes Connected with the Ancient Castles of Great Britain, for the Improvement and Entertainment of Youth* published by Joseph Toller of Kettering in the 1840s, for instance, is probably too didactic and too aware of its young audience to be properly considered as popular literature. This leaves the curious question of whether a chapbook could exist which could be considered neither part of children's literature nor of popular literature ('z'). Certain short religious texts might fulfil these criteria, the tracts published by the Religious Tract Society or Hannah More's 1790s propagandistic Cheap Repository Tract scheme for instance, which imitated popular literature without necessarily becoming part of it. On the other hand, arguments might be made for their identity as either (or both) children's or popular literature.

Where the diagram becomes most useful is in thinking about the placement of individual titles and charting their shifts across boundaries. The fairy tales of Charles Perrault and Madame d'Aulnoy, for instance, began their textual history outside all three sets, appearing in Britain first as expensively published translations marketed for adults. They were quickly absorbed within children's literature, both as texts to be read for enjoyment and to help teach French ('v'). There they were joined by other fairy tales, such as *Beauty and the Beast*, written specifically for children by Madame Le Prince de Beaumont in 1756. By the early nineteenth century, all of these were being published as chapbooks, although probably always directed primarily at children ('y'). Undeniably they soon became part of popular literature too ('w' or 'x'). Yet unlike *Jack the Giant-Killer*, say, or even *Jack and the Bean-Stalk*, with which they would come to be associated, they did not emerge from popular culture. *The History of Goody Two-Shoes* followed, to some extent, the same path. Beginning as a text intended exclusively for children ('v'), even if it was first published in a format which owed something to the chapbook, Goody subsequently made her regular appearances in chapbooks ('y') and became a familiar part of popular culture ('w'). Throughout the history of children's literature there have been a great many texts which have followed a similar trajectory, from 'v' to 'x', or 'w'. *Alice's Adventures in Wonderland*, *Peter Pan* and *Harry Potter*, to name only some of the most prominent examples, have all followed in the footsteps of *Cinderella*, *Beauty and the Beast* and *Goody Two-Shoes*.

The idea that the recognisably 'modern' children's literature, beginning in the later eighteenth century and coming to maturity in the nineteenth, could be regarded as having developed out of popular literature traditions has also been briefly touched upon in this chapter. The most common formulation of this idea is that the new, respectable children's literature was designed to wean children from a popular literature that was becoming increasingly unpalatable to affluent and socially-ambitious parents. As Humphrey Carpenter and Mari Prichard, writing in the *Oxford Companion to Children's Literature*, put it, 'The work of the writers of moral tales for the young in the late 18th and early 19th centuries was largely a reaction against chapbook literature.'[58]   In the fullness of time, books specifically for children certainly did come to replace chapbooks, designed for a general audience, as the principal reading matter of children. And it is convenient to regard the proponents of the new, respectable children's literature as developing their books in response to growing anxieties concerning children's reading of profane, unprofitable and distinctly plebeian chapbooks. Yet the migration of texts the other way – from children's culture to popular culture – which has been charted here, compromises this view. The cultural traffic evidently travelled both ways. It would continue to do so. Elements of popular culture, whether Robin Hood or Superman, would migrate into children's literature, just as elements of children's literature, like Goody Two-Shoes, the Famous Five, or Harry Potter, would enter popular culture. Such cross-pollination decisively demonstrates that, despite the claims to the contrary made by contemporary commentators and modern critics, no final rupture has ever occurred between children's literature and popular culture.

---

58   Humphrey Carpenter and Mari Prichard, *The Oxford Companion to Children's Literature* (Oxford: Oxford University Press, 1984), p. 106.

Chapter 3

Robin Hood in Boys' Weeklies to 1914[1]

Kevin Carpenter

Bearing in mind the huge popularity of the Robin Hood legend over several centuries, the number of books presenting his life and adventures for young readers in the nineteenth century is surprisingly low.[2] At the beginning of the century, there was little apart from prose renderings of the old ballads in chapbook form. In 1804 Benjamin Tabart brought out a 40-page prose version, followed by William Darton's children's story in 1818.[3] The popularity of Scott's *Ivanhoe* (1819) prompted Longman to issue a new edition of Joseph Ritson's great late eighteenth-century collection of the Robin Hood ballads in 1820, specifically designed as 'a book which could with propriety be put into the hands of young persons'.[4] More than 60 years later Routledge was to revive Ritson for the 'reward' and 'prize' market.[5] The first children's novel seems to have been *Robin Hood and His Merry Foresters* (1841), appearing under the pseudonym 'Stephen Percy' (i.e. Joseph Cundall), a book that saw numerous reprints in England and America up to the end of the century.[6] It was a fairly short book, intended for young children. The first substantial novel for boy readers, written by John B. Marsh, came out a quarter of a century later, in

---

1 I am using the term 'boys' weeklies' to designate penny-parts novels, magazines and similar published for boy readers on a regular basis, usually weekly, although not necessarily so.

2 On Robin Hood in children's literature, see David Blamires, *Robin Hood: A Hero For All Times* (Manchester: John Rylands Library, 1998), pp. 16–20, 45–6, 53–6 and 59–63; Bennett A. Brockman, 'Robin Hood and the Invention of Children's Literature', *Children's Literature* 10 (1982), 1–17, and 'Children and the Audiences of Robin Hood', *South Atlantic Review* 48 (1983), 67–83; Kevin Carpenter (ed.), *Robin Hood: The Many Faces of that Celebrated English Outlaw* (Oldenburg: BIS Universität Oldenburg, 1995), pp. 65–86, 97–8 and 218–57; Kevin Carpenter, 'A Note on Robin Hood in Victorian Boys' Books', *The Henty Society Bulletin* 12 (1999–2000), 9–11; R. B. Dobson, and J. Taylor, *Rymes of Robyn Hood: An Introduction to the English Outlaw*, (1976, repr. London: Alan Sutton, 1997), pp. 58–62; and Stephen Knight, *Robin Hood: A Complete Study of the English Outlaw* (Oxford: Blackwell, 1994), pp. 186–96 and 201–17.

3 *The History of Robin Hood*, item 65 in Marjorie Moon, *Benjamin Tabart's Juvenile Library* (Winchester: St Paul's Bibliographies, 1990); *Robin Hood* (London: William Darton, 1818, reprinted with new illustrations in 1822).

4 Preface to *Robin Hood: A Collection of All the Ancient Poems, Songs and Ballads*, (London: Longman, 1820), p. [vii].

5 Published in 1884 and thereafter in various binding cloths and styles up to the end of the century, with illustrations by adventure story artist Gordon Browne (son of 'Phiz').

6 J. Harris Gable, *A Bibliography of Robin Hood* (Lincoln: University of Nebraska Press, 1939), p. 27, has a dubious 1840 edition.

1865.[7] And in 1883 an innovative American version of the legend by Howard Pyle was published in London in a limited edition.[8] Apart from these publications, Robin Hood books for juvenile readers prior to the Edwardian era are puzzlingly few and far between.

It seems reasonable to assume that Robin Hood was regarded with some suspicion by such prolific Victorian boys' writers as W.H.G. Kingston, Thomas Mayne Reid, R.M. Ballantyne, G.A. Henty, Gordon Stables and many others, who opted not to write novels about the greenwood outlaws. Robin Hood appeared as a very minor figure in a Henty novel, while G.M. Fenn's *Young Robin Hood* was an insipid tale for young children about a friendship between two Robins, the outlaw himself and the sheriff's son.[9] Such up-market boys' magazines as Routledge's *Every Boy's Magazine* and the Religious Tract Society's *Boy's Own Paper* also ignored the legend.[10] Robin Hood evidently made many Victorian children's writers feel uncomfortable. He may have been an English hero, a patriotic fighter, but he was also an outlaw, a robber, a resister, and as such not necessarily a model for the impressionable young. One children's writer who dared to approach the topic felt he had to preface his book with a warning: 'Here is the story of Robin Hood, the bold English archer ... I hope you will like it, and that you will not misunderstand it.'[11] Some late-Victorian versions recommended themselves to potential buyers (parents) by emphasising their compilers' credentials on the title page, one being penned by 'Rev. E. Gilliat, M.A., Assistant Master in Harrow School', while another announced its author was 'Late Professor and University Examiner in Moscow', who consulted many books and manuscripts in the British Museum (the preface adds) before composing his novel.[12] Most Victorian children's books adhered closely to the old ballads, a procedure which had to be selective, one writer points out, since he felt he should paraphrase only the 'finest and most rational ballads', ignoring those that were 'discreditable'.[13] The old legend was evidently dangerous if not properly filtered. J.F. Hodgetts (our man in Moscow) expressed his hope that 'this attempt at placing Robin Hood in his true light will ... not be confounded with the morbid feeling which seeks to deify a

---

7   John B. Marsh, *The Life and Adventures of Robin Hood*, (London: Routledge, *c.*1865). Gable's *Bibliography of Robin Hood* has eight pre-1914 editions (p. 73). There was at least one more: Routledge, 1903.

8   *The Merry Adventures of Robin Hood of Great Renown, in Nottinghamshire* (London, 1883). Sampson and Low imported 510 copies into Britain in 1883, pricing Pyle's novel at 15 shillings, about three times the usual price for a boys' book. The British Library has only the first edition; Gable's *Bibliography of Robin Hood* records only two later British editions, in 1893 and 1904 (pp. 92–3).

9   See G.A. Henty, *Winning His Spurs: A Tale of the Crusades* (London: Sampson Low & Co., 1882) and G.M. Fenn, *Young Robin Hood* (London: Ernest Nister; New York: E.P. Dutton, [1899]).

10   *Every Boy's Magazine* printed a children's play, 'Robin Hood & His Merrye Men' by W. R. Snow in 1871. Beeton's *Boy's Own Magazine* published an essay on the old ballads in 1865.

11   *Robin Hood and His Merry Men* (London, [1906]), p. 5.

12   Title pages of E. Gilliat, *In Lincoln Green* (1897) and J.F. Hodgetts, *Edwin, the Boy Outlaw* [1887].

13   Preface to F.C. Tilney, *Robin Hood and His Merry Outlaws* (1913), pp. 5–6.

scoundrel like Claude Duval, or a still greater villain like Jack Sheppard'.[14] This is a revealing comment, for if we go looking for Robin Hood in children's literature of the nineteenth century, we will soon have to set aside the books issued by the respectable publishing houses to seek him in the company of those scoundrels and villains mentioned by Hodgetts – in the cheap magazines and serialised novels put out by the Victorian penny press.

The starting point for such a search has to be the popular fiction produced for working-class readers between 1830 and 1850.[15] Penny-part novels of this period regularly dealt with crime and 'low life' in London, the adventures of pirates, smugglers and highwaymen, and the doings of vampires and other creatures of the night. The characters peopling this fiction included the infamous Sweeney Todd, Varney the Vampire, the highwaymen Dick Turpin and Claude Duval, the burglars Jack Sheppard and Charles Peace, and the many miscreants whose lives were chronicled in numerous editions of the *Newgate Calendar*. This fiction was not directed at young readers, although there is some evidence that they were part of the audience. One of the publishers of this era, Edward Lloyd, when unsure about the appeal of a new manuscript would 'try it out on the office boy'.[16] It was one of the many small printer publishers operating at this time who brought out the first Robin Hood novel in weekly parts. From the autumn of 1839 to the summer of 1840, Foster and Hextall published a novel by Pierce Egan the Younger in 41 penny weekly parts, entitled *Robin Hood and Little John; or, The Merry Men of Sherwood Forest* (Figure 3.1).

Egan's novel is divided into three books. In Book I, Baron de Beaseant's illegitimate son, Robyn, is deposited with a forester couple called Gilbert and Margaret Head to be brought up as their own son in Sherwood. It emerges that this Robyn Head is the rightful heir to the Earldom of Huntingdon. Robyn (soon spelt Robin) grows up tall and powerful, an excellent archer, a young man with a strong sense of justice, and before long he finds himself combating the evil sheriff, Baron Fitzallan ('a complete epitome of rascality – a walking Newgate Calendar').[17] Subsequently, back in the forest, the male and female outlaws pair off: Robin and Marian, Allan and Christabel, Will and Maude, the three young women being repeatedly saved from the rapacious Normans by their menfolk. In Book II, six years later, Robin is still rescuing Marian from Norman lords determined to rape her ('Bless thee, dear, dear Robin; you have rescued me from shame and misery, to which death would be a blessing!').[18] The three outlaw couples marry; soon three babies are born, although Marian's boy does not survive the harsh winter. Book III returns in part to the legend as recounted in the old ballads, introducing the well-known characters Sir Guy of Gisborne, the Bishop of Hereford, Sir Richard of the Lee and King Richard. More weddings take place in

---

14 Hodgetts, *Edwin, the Boy Outlaw*, p. 10.

15 See Louis James's masterly survey of this literature, *Fiction for the Working Man* (1963, repr. Harmondsworth: Penguin, 1974).

16 E.S. Turner, *Boys Will Be Boys: The Story of Sweeney Todd, Deadwood Dick, Sexton Blake, Billy Bunter, et al.* (1948, repr. London: Michael Joseph, 1975), p. 18.

17 Pierce Egan, *Robin Hood and Little John* (London, 1840), p. 49.

18 Ibid., p. 266.

ROBIN HOOD.   241

Mass! holy abbot, we shall be all the better for his four hundred merks annually.'
"'The lord high justice is staying with me,' said

consideration, in bright golden coin, he was of the abbot's opinion.
"'He will not come at all to-day, I dare wager,' said

the abbot; 'I will ask him if I cannot claim the estates an' he be not here by noon"
"The high justice was sought, and for a handsome

he,' therefore thou mayst well esteem the estates thine.'
"He had scarce uttered the words when I reached the gate. I had clothed myself even in the same

No. 31.

Figure 3.1   Pierce Egan the Younger, *Robin Hood and Little John; or, The Merry Men of Sherwood Forest* (London: Foster and Hextall 1839–40, reprinted by Edward Harrison, *c*.1870). Collection of Kevin Carpenter.

the greenwood: Much and Barbara; Little John and Winifred; Will finds six brides for his six brothers. In a Norman onslaught on their forest stronghold, Marian is hit by an arrow and dies, though not before delivering a two-page valedictory speech. At the age of 55, Robin is overtaken by severe depression and in this state falls an easy prey to the treacherous Prioress of Kirkley Abbey (and Robin, too, has a two-page final speech to the band).

Terrific battles, terrible injuries, violent deaths, attempted rapes, amorous encounters, nocturnal abductions, incarcerations in damp dungeons, wailing Gothic ghosts, lecherous old villains – these are some of the features of Egan's novel. The central confrontations owe much to the popular theatre.[19] When youth and innocence and bravery confront cynicism and wickedness and cowardice, the villain 'roars' in reply:

'Oh, ho! Mighty well! Out upon thee, thou wood-cur! Dost thou beard me, fling thy saucy words in my face? By St. Ignatius! I'll have thee hanged up by thy ears, and whipped with thy own bow, yelping pup! Dare to tell me I liest!'[20]

It is the world of melodrama transferred to the printed page, and the illustrations (by Egan himself) underscore the theatrical source of language, gesture and emotion. Curiously, this novel has been categorised as a children's story by scholars of the Robin Hood legend, but, judging from its style and subject matter, it quite evidently is not.[21] However, by 1870 at the latest it had been *turned into* a boys' book by its readership and by a publisher (Edward Harrison) responding to the interest of its boy readers.

Right from the start, Egan's penny-part novel was hugely successful and 'public demand quickly mounted to hundreds of thousands of copies per week'.[22] Reprints were called for in 1840, 1843, 1844 and 1847 and a revised penny-part edition in 1850, in which the author expressed his surprise at the 'extraordinary success' of his story.[23] For this new edition, Egan tinkered with the text. In Book I, Robin is now 16 years old (he was originally 14); some of the stilted dialogue has been left out, as have references to the theatre; footnotes to Major, Percy and Ritson are added; some of those outrageous 'Norman' names are modified (Caspar Steinkopft drops his final

---

19 Egan compares himself to a 'playright' [*sic*], refers to his characters as 'dramatis personae' and describes one scene depicted in an illustration as 'in theatric phrase, a picture formed' (Ibid., pp. 166, 142 and 93).

20 Ibid., p. 49.

21 Dobson and Taylor, *Rymes of Robyn Hood*, pp. 59–60; J.C. Holt, *Robin Hood* (1982, repr. London: Thames and Hudson, 1989), pp. 185–6; David Blamires, 'Robin Hood', in Ulrich Müller and Werner Wunderlich (eds), *Herrscher, Helden, Heilige* (St Gallen: UVK, 1996), pp. 437–50, p. 449; but not in his *Robin Hood: A Hero For All Times*, p. 43, and not Knight, *Robin Hood: A Complete Study*, pp. 186–9. Egan is listed as a boys' writer in W.O.G. Lofts and D.J. Adley, *The Men Behind Boys' Fiction* (London: Howard Baker, 1970), p. 129; the Johnson edition of his Robin Hood novel appears as item 25 in W.H. Shercliff's catalogue, *Manchester Polytechnic's* [now Manchester Metropolitan University] *Collection of Children's Books 1840–1939* (Manchester: Manchester Polytechnic Library, 1988).

22 Peter Haining, *The Penny Dreadful* (London: Gollancz, 1975), p. 50.

23 Pierce Egan, *Robin Hood and Little John* (London, [1850]), p. viii.

't' and Sir Tristram Uggeleretsche becomes Sir Tristram of Goldborough). This is the version Edward Harrison reissued for boys around 1870.

Not only did Egan's novel become a boys' book, it inspired 'a whole Robin Hood industry'.[24] Towards the end of its first serialisation, the original publisher, Foster and Hextall, brought out a cheap edition of the old ballads (1840).[25] A companion volume by J.H. Stocqueler, *Maid Marian, the Forest Queen*, followed in 31 weekly parts (1849). The first full-length story-version of Robin Hood for children, Joseph Cundall's novel may well have been produced to meet demand for a reworking of the legend in narrative form because older children were reading Egan. In France, a translation of Egan appeared in two volumes as *Le prince des voleurs* (1872) and *Robin Hood le proscrit* (1873), books generally attributed to Alexandre Dumas the Elder that themselves inspired great interest in 'Robin des bois'. It is interesting to note that the French version followed close on the heels of the English edition of Egan specifically issued for the juvenile market.

Egan's novel served as a template for many later versions of the legend. *Little John and Will Scarlett; or, The Outlaws of Sherwood Forest* appears to have been first issued around 1865, in 40 eight-page penny parts. Neither style nor theme suggest that young readers were being targeted. Whatever its title may imply, the novel is basically a rehash of Egan's tale, with Robin Hood as the main character. (In this period, many children's stories also avoid the outlaw's name in their main titles.) Once again, young Robin is unaware that he is the rightful heir to the Huntingdon estates. Once again, the wicked Norman barons lust after pretty Saxon girls. Once again, there is much kissing and courting in the forest, scenes presumably designed for young female readers rather than teenage boys. Again, there are pursuits, battles, last-minute rescues, disguises, japes, feasts. And weddings: Robin marries Marian, Little John weds Rose, Allan ties the knot with Ella, Eveline accepts Will. In all, Friar Tuck performs the ceremony for 'some thirty young and happy couples, so that the race of Sherwood outlaws was not likely to become soon extinct'.[26] Once more, Marian is killed in a Norman attack and Robin dies at Kirklees. In a minor deviation from the legend as recreated by Walter Scott in *Ivanhoe*, it is Little John who splits the arrow, a feat equalled by Robin some time later. A more significant innovation is the more active role of the women characters, Eveline and Marian, proving in times of crisis that they are both crack shots with the bow and arrow. This book, too, was reissued in weekly parts around 1870 by Edward Harrison, who evidently felt there was enough adventure and excitement in it to attract boy readers.

Working-class and lower-middle-class boys had clearly been turning to the thrilling and sometimes lurid penny-part novels put out for adults in the 1850s.[27] But there is no evidence that they were actually being targeted as a paying audience before the mid 1860s, when a group of printers, newsagents and publishers operating from in and around Fleet Street, together created the phenomenon of the boys' weekly

---

24 Haining, *The Penny Dreadful*, p. 51.

25 Along the crease of part 38 of Egan's novel runs an advert for the publication of *Robin Hood Ballads* on 'July 1st' (i.e. 1 July 1840).

26 *Little John and Will Scarlett*, [*c*.1865], p. 155.

27 James, *Fiction for the Working Man*, pp. 87, 186 and 199.

as a viable commercial product. While it had been known since the 1850s that boys were eager to read adventure fiction, eager readership alone did not make popular juvenile fiction – it had to be affordable; it had to be *cheap*.[28] And in the 1860s a number of factors favoured the emergence of a penny press for the young: paper cheaper than ever before, efficient steam-driven rotary presses, a reliable distribution network (newsagents), a high proportion of children in the population (particularly in London) and a relatively high level of pre-Education Act child literacy, wage-earning boys, and a reservoir of unemployed penny-a-liners and illustrators.[29] The first publishing firm to exploit this new situation was the ill-famed Newsagents' Publishing Company, which issued lurid tales of crime in the mid 1860s such as *The Wild Boys of London* (1864–66) and *The Dance of Death* (1865–66). At 30,000 penny parts sold per week, the sales were good, but the harsh criticism of such 'penny dreadfuls' or 'penny packets of poison' led the manager Edwin J. Brett to embark on a magazine of a slightly more respectable nature.[30] The boys' journal he envisaged was to become a major publishing venture, a large-format 16-page boys' weekly miscellany, the backbone of which was to be wild and wonderful fiction, 'wild and wonderful but healthy'.[31] E.J. Brett's *Boys of England* (1866–99) became the first commercially successful boys' weekly magazine, its sales rising quickly to 150,000 copies per week, then rocketing to 250,000 copies in the early 1870s once serials began to appear about a hugely popular adventurer called Jack Harkaway. (The Brett firm would later be renamed Harkaway House.) There were, however, rival publishers; indeed, the competition for boys' pennies was fierce. The Emmett brothers brought out their boys' magazine *Young Englishman* in 1867, then going on to devote much of their energy to penny-part novels about pirates, robbers and highwaymen.[32] Around 1875 their firm (now called Hogarth House) was taken over by Charles Fox, whose publications and reprints attracted much public abuse.[33] Edward Harrison of Salisbury Square has already been mentioned as the publisher reprinting two Robin Hood novels for boy readers. His other publications included the long-running Dick Turpin weekly serial *Black Bess* (1863–65) and a

---

28 In the 1850s, the publishers David Bogue, Grant and Griffith, Nelson, Nisbet and Routledge had already begun to market the talents of boys' writers such as R.M. Ballantyne, Anne Bowman, James Bowman, W.H.G. Kingston and Mayne Reid.

29 John Springhall, '"A Life Story for the People?" Edwin J. Brett and the London "Low-Life" Penny Dreadfuls of the 1860s', *Victorian Studies* 33 (1990), 223–46, and his *Youth, Popular Culture and Moral Panics: Penny Gaffs to Gangster-Rap, 1830–1996* (Basingstoke: Macmillan, 1998).

30 James Greenwood's critical commentaries on the 'gallows literature' put out by N.P.C. and Edward Harrison are to be found in his *Seven Curses of London* (1869) and *The Wilds of London* (1874). His essay 'A Short Way to Newgate' is reprinted in Haining's *Penny Dreadful*, pp. 357–71, under the title 'Penny Packets of Poison'.

31 Editor's Address, *Boys of England* 1 (24/27 November 1866), p. 16. The editor at this time was Charles Stevens.

32 Operating under various names, four brothers were involved: George, Henry Charlton, William Laurence and Robert Emmett.

33 See Francis Hitchman, 'Penny Fiction', *Quarterly Review* 171 (1890), 150–71.

New Newgate Calendar for boys (1863–65), besides more conventional children's magazines.[34]

It was the Emmett brothers who published the first penny-part Robin Hood novel specifically written for boys. Written by George Emmett and entitled *Robin Hood and the Outlaws of Sherwood Forest* (Figure 3.2), it appeared in 52 penny parts from early 1868 to early 1869. It was illustrated by Robert Prowse and Warwick Reynolds, but a number of illustrations from some previous publication were used as stop-gaps (one seemingly showing Robin Hood in a sword duel with a gentleman in Victorian dress).[35] For about a quarter of a century, the text of this book was available in a cheap form to many thousands of office, factory and schoolboys. Later Hogarth House editions were re-set in the same double-column small-print format, the inappropriate illustrations replaced and the title significantly emended to *Robin Hood and the Archers of Merrie Sherwood*. 'Outlaw', 'robber', 'highwayman' – such words in the titles of penny-part novels intended for the young attracted immediate opprobrium.

In his preface, Emmett elaborates on what he sees as the appeal of the legend. The old ballads express 'a love of all that is manly and brave, and a contempt for all that is cowardly and mean [and thus appeal] to the hearts of the freeborn, manly youth of England.' He goes on to say that he has devoted 'immense labour' to his studies of ancient documents, his task 'long and patient' to separate the dross from the metal, finally leading to his discovery that Robin Hood was a Saxon freedom-fighter who betook himself to Sherwood to sustain an incessant and predatory battle against the Norman tyrants and enslavers of the people.[36]

The story opens in the mid thirteenth century. After Simon de Montfort's rebellion is put down at Evesham, Robin retreats to Barnsdale Forest. Mortimer is sent to flush him out, but eventually becomes his friend. Moving to Sherwood, the outlaw embarks on sorties attacking harsh landlords and heartless ecclesiastics, occasionally drubbing Norman knights for impertinence shown towards young village girls. The bulk of Book I represents Robin Hood as a military leader, with much of the narrative devoted to strategy, armour and weapons (Emmett was himself a former cavalry officer). There are many adventures, skirmishes, battles and drinking bouts – many drinking bouts. And there are spirits of another kind. The spectre of the castle helps Robin and Earl Mortimer escape by showing them secret passages. And there is the wood demon that offers Robin power and riches and above all invincibility in archery in return for his soul. Unsurprisingly, the outlaw leader declines. After all, this is the man who – in this version of the legend – regularly wins silver arrows in contests, who can split two arrows in mid flight before hitting the bull's-eye, who as an after-dinner feat sometimes shoots an arrow straight upwards catching it as it falls

---

34 The adverts and editorial comments in Edward Harrison's *New Newgate Calendar* make it quite clear that it was produced for boy readers. Harrison also published the short-lived *Gentleman's Journal and Youth's Miscellany* (1869–72) and the long-running *Young Ladies' Journal* (1864–1920).

35 Cover illustration to part 25 of *Robin Hood and the Outlaws of Sherwood Forest* [1868–89], p. 193.

36 Ibid., p. 2.

and as an encore will shoot apples off Maid Marian's head from a great distance. By now (Book II), hide-and-seek and adventurous escapades have taken over from the military manoeuvring. Robin proves himself to be generous to his enemies outwitted or defeated in battle, apart from the unfortunate Norman messenger who refers to Marian as "'a common woman'" and is cut down without further ado.[37] Adventures with King Henry take up much of Book III. While the king is Robin's enemy, he cannot but be greatly impressed by the outlaw's archery, leadership, generosity and boldness. Finally, the Merry Men are routed by the combined forces of the sheriff's men and the king's Kentish bowmen. Robin is wounded and dies at Kirklees; Marian survives him.

Some of the features of this 1868–69 reworking of the legend – the stylisation of emotion, the ritualised conflict between good and evil, the stagey nature of the language itself ('A malison on thee, thou knave of the blackest dye!') – link Emmett with Egan, and both with conventions of the popular theatre of the early Victorian era. In both stories, for instance, we find 'strong' confrontations between characters embodying Purity and Vice, using dialogue that would have resonated with audiences in the cheap theatres. Here is Emmett's Marian repudiating the licentious king's advances:

> 'Sir!' cried Marian, her eyes flashing with scorn, 'sir! I cannot call you king, or thou would have spared the blush of maiden modesty that thy words have caused to mantle my cheek Away! Leave me untarnished as I am, or return me to the greenwood as you found me, a simple flower, where, under the care and nurture of him thou callest an outlaw, I may grow up free from the vile contaminations of royalty!'[38]

After a further heated exchange, the king, muttering darkly, strides angrily out of the chamber. Such a repudiation scene in one form or another is a regular feature of Robin Hood tales in popular juvenile fiction. It might involve Robin or Marian, but in the later fiction it just as often involves one of the outlaw's boy companions who boldly stand up to the villain: young Cedric taunting Baron Fitzurse; young Guy verbally lashing Sir Humphrey de Brionne; young Edwin berating the Norman lords, to take but a few examples.[39]

Whilst George Emmett's tale was still running, his publishing rival Edwin J. Brett responded. 'Robin Hood and His Merry Men' appeared in Brett's weekly *Boys of England* in the winter of 1868–69. The subtitle 'And the Larks They Played in the Greenwood Shade' and the mock chapbook-style illustrations indicate straight away that this is to be a spoof. Robin, yet again the dispossessed Earl of Huntingdon, here turns to a life of outlawry to escape his creditors, a tailor, a butcher and a publican. His arch-enemy is now one Baron de Beetelbrowze. Some of the original characters are but thinly disguised: the Bishop of Hereford becomes the proud Abbot of St Bumpus's Priory, the old woman in the cottage becomes Old Mother Hubbard. Well-known incidents are recast: Robin's fight with Friar Tuck is now a boxing match (the Queensberry rules were established in 1867). And so on. With its terrible puns, its

---

37　Ibid., p. 176.
38　Ibid., p. 292.
39　From *British Boys* (1897) and *The Boys' Friend* (1904 and 1905).

facetious humour and farce, and the repeated references to contemporary life (the London police, the Band of Hope, patent medicines, the *Daily Telegraph*, etc.), the story clearly owes much to pantomime and to *Punch*, and in particular leans heavily on Francis Burnand's 'original farce' – as he called it – *Robin Hood; or, The Forester's Fate*, which had been drawing large audiences in the mid nineteenth century.[40]

More Robin Hoods followed in Victorian boys' weeklies. Admittedly, such stories form only a fraction of the total number of serials found in the pages of the numerous boys' magazines that flourished between the 1860s and the 1890s, and yet whatever their reading preferences, generation after generation of boy readers would at some point come across the daring exploits of Bold Robin in their preferred weeklies. Up to Jubilee Year, the Merry Men cavorted in novel-length serialised stories in the penny weeklies *Boys of England* (1868–69, 1877 and 1883), *The Young Briton* (1871–72 and 1874), *Our Young Folks' Weekly Budget* (1873–74), *Young Britannia* (1885–86), *Young Men of Great Britain* (1885–86), *Boys and Girls* (1887), *Nuggets* (1896), *The Boys' Comic Journal* (1897) and *British Boys* (1897). While this batch of serials may employ the characters and incidents from the old ballads, they also tap into Egan for elements of melodrama that become standard ingredients in popular juvenile fiction in this century. If the barons sack homes and seize lands, they also carry off women who fiercely challenge their conduct and who at the end of the day have to be rescued by the gallant outlaws. Young women as characters play a stronger role than might be expected, even if their behaviour sometimes has domestic overtones. 'Bold Robin Hood' (1873–74) ends with this comment on Marian's role: 'when [Robin] sorrowed, Marian made him glad; when he brooded over his wrongs, she soothed him lovingly'.[41] She was the angel in the forest cave. But when faced with threats to their liberty and honour, these women are not lost for words to express their disgust at the despicable behaviour of their Norman tormentors, words that act as a cue for Robin and his men, waiting in the wings for their entrance.

Vengeance is another frequent theme in these serials. In 'Allen-a-Dale: The Comrade of Bold Robin Hood' (1885–86), Allen rises to his duty to avenge the death of his father murdered by the ruthless Danish mercenary Tostig at the behest of Sir Clifford de Marmilon. Youngsters being temporarily cheated out of their inheritance is another theme. Royston Gower, in the 1874 serial of that title, is a ruthless old crusader employed by Sir Geoffrey de Marchmont to murder the rightful heir to Nottingham Castle, a plan which, of course, at the end of the day is thwarted. If elements from the old ballads are employed, then it is, on occasion, with a twist. In 'The Prince of Archers' (1883), Little John appears as just that – little (and fat). This story also offers a new explanation of the malicious vengefulness of the Prioress of Kirklees: in her younger days, when she was known by her real name Lady Julia la Grange, her amorous advances were spurned by Robin, and many years later she takes her cruel revenge. Supernatural beings, good and evil, figure in many of these stories. 'Allen-a-Dale' has a forest sprite called Flip. In 'The Prince of Archers' there is a Demon Bowman, who gives Robin a mighty bow with magical properties which

---

40 Gable's *Bibliography of Robin Hood* has acting editions he dates 1850 and 1862, p. 19. On Sir Francis Burnand, see Knight, *Robin Hood: A Complete Study*, pp. 195–6.

41 Quoted from the reprint in *Nuggets* 235 (31 October 1896), p. 13.

the young hero uses to perform stupendous feats of archery. This 'demon' also seems to be an attendant to a mysterious figure clothed in a long black cloak who glides in and out at critical junctures. King Richard returns to England in many disguises; his life is saved by young Robin Hoods on countless occasions.

Towards the end of the nineteenth century, a new publisher introduced a new format into popular juvenile literature. The Aldine Publishing Company brought out the first of its 'libraries' in 1887, the *Boys' First-Rate Pocket Library*, followed by *O'er Land and Sea* (1890), *Invention, Travel & Adventure* (1894) and many others. These booklets were basically abridged reprints of American dime novels relating the adventures of Buffalo Bill, Deadwood Dick and other colourful heroes of the Wild West. As a rule, they were pocket-sized magazines comprising 32 pages of letterpress enclosed in bright chromolithographed covers at the regular price of one penny each, appearing in batches of four or eight numbers per month. In 1901 Aldine embarked on a programme of 'libraries', resuscitating British outlaws and highwaymen popular half a century before. *Robin Hood* (1901–6) was the flagship (see Figure 3.3), the success of which led Aldine to float the companion 'libraries' *Dick Turpin* (1902–9), *Claude Duval* (1902–6), *Rob Roy* ('the Great Scottish Robin Hood', 1903–4) and *Jack Sheppard* (1904–6). The Robin Hood 'library' itself commenced publication on 10 October 1901, soon meeting with 'enormous demand', which necessitated a number of hasty reprints.[42] Aldine kept all back issues in print up to the end of the full run (number 88, brought out on 16 June 1906).[43] In all, eight writers were employed on this project, while Robert Prowse and others illustrators designed the attractive coloured wrappers.[44]

The first number in Aldine's *Robin Hood* is entitled 'Sweet Liberty or Death', this being the war-cry young Robin Fitzooth adopts after swearing to exact revenge for the murder of his father, hanged by the sheriff Baron Oswald de Burgh's men. As the stories progress in this 'library', a succession of Robins have to despatch a series of Norman villains as one sheriff is replaced by another more rapacious than the last (Basil de Vaux, Outram de Saye, Baron Lachelles and many more). As in the earlier fiction, these hissing and snarling villains are put in their place by the bold young heroes in 'strong' scenes. This is Little John replying to De Burgh's threat to have him thrown to the 'loathsome toads and biting reptiles' in his dungeon if he does not lead them to Robin's hideout:

---

42 Front cover, verso, of the fourth edition of no. 1 of Aldine's *Robin Hood*. How successful these 'libraries' actually were is not known. Aldine was in financial trouble by 1906 at the latest, according to John Springhall's '"Disseminating Impure Literature": The Penny Dreadful Publication Business Since 1860', *Economic History Review* 47 (1994), 567–84.

43 All previous numbers were in print according to announcements on the back cover, recto, of undated numbers 33 [April 1903], 76 [23 September 1905] and the back cover, verso, of the final number, 88 [16 June 1906].

44 Robert Prowse, a prolific illustrator of popular juvenile fiction, appears to have been working from *c.*1860 (for Vickers) to *c.*1920 (for Aldine).

Figure 3.3   Cover illustration by F.W. Boyington to 'The Great Fight in Sherwood Forest', no. 11 of Aldine's 'library' *Robin Hood* (London: Aldine Publishing Co., 1902). Originally printed in colour. Collection of Kevin Carpenter.

'There is no more loathsome toad or crawling reptile than yourself, Norman boaster!'
Little John cried. 'I despise your offer, and laugh at your threats! If I am to die – and I
snap my fingers at all that the fiend may put into your mind regarding me – a hundred, nay,
five hundred men will spring to arms to avenge me. You may smile with your lips, but in
your heart you tremble!'[45]

And then there are damsels a-plenty for the Merry Men to rescue (Edith, Editha,
Gwendoline, Hilda, Marian, Martha, Mildred, Winifreda) and a whole gallery of
deformed and supernatural beings to contend with (Meg the Witch, the magicians
Pygoras and Zoastro, the hunchbacked dwarf Quasamodo [*sic*] and many more).
The setting of the stories shifts from place to place in England, Scotland, Wales and
Ireland; Sherwood, Barnsdale, Epping Forest, the Wolds, Wiltshire; Nottingham,
Derby, York, London. Duty even takes the outlaws abroad, to Normandy and the
Holy Land. Robin Hood's tasks, however, remain constant: to save women from
their tormentors, rescue his own men from the enemy, protect King Richard, burn
down Norman castles whenever possible and redistribute wealth to the poor and
needy.

By Edwardian times, it was Alfred Harmsworth (later, Lord Northcliffe) with
his Amalgamated Press who was the principal figure in the production of popular
juvenile fiction. His first boys' weeklies had come out in the mid 1890s at the
startlingly low price of a halfpenny: *Marvel* (1893), *The Union Jack* (1894), *Pluck*
(1894) and *The Boys' Friend* (1895, see Figure 3.4). Harmsworth's avowed intention
was to kill off the penny dreadful, by which term he simply meant any of the penny
magazines put out by his competitors.[46] There is evidently some truth in A.A. Milne's
observation that Harmsworth 'killed the penny dreadful by the simple process of
producing the ha'penny dreadfuller'.[47] He certainly did push his competitors to the
wall: around 1895 Charles Fox sold his Hogarth House stock to the printers Sully
and Ford; in 1900 the newly renamed firm Edwin J. Brett Ltd was close to collapse;
by 1906 Aldine was in debt.[48] Many of Harmsworth's writers were recruited from the
older publishing firms, for instance Escott Lynn and Singleton Pound, who had both
previously worked for Aldine.[49]

To begin with, the Amalgamated Press carefully avoided the literature of roguery
so popular in the preceding half century. Instead, boys were offered a rich fare of
school stories, treasure quests, yarns of espionage, detective stories, tales of darkest
Africa, re-runs of recent military conflicts, up-to-date accounts of life on board
the dreadnoughts and thrilling fantasies about forthcoming invasions. Gradually,
however, the popular heroes – Dick Turpin, Jack Sheppard, Robin Hood and others
– did enter Harmsworth's boys' magazines, but when they did, it was stressed that
these new outlaw tales were not 'blood and thunder trash ... but true stories of real

---

45 *Robin Hood* 1 [19 October 1901], pp. 13–14.
46 See the editorial 'The Penny Dreadful and the Scoundrels Who Write It', *Boys' Friend*
1, 1 (29 January 1895), p. 4.
47 Quoted in Turner, *Boys Will Be Boys*, p. 115.
48 See Springhall, '"Disseminating Impure Literature"'.
49 Escott Lynn went on to write Robin Hood novels for the publishers Blackie and Son
and W. and R. Chambers.

life'.[50] Before *The Boys' Friend* serialised 'Guy of the Greenwood' in 1904, the editor (Hamilton Edwards) emphasised that he felt he simply had to respond to customer pressure as 'hundreds and hundreds of my friends' had been begging for a Robin Hood serial.[51] In 1910 he repeated this dubious claim when Morton Pike was commissioned to write another Robin Hood serial, following requests from 'an enormous number of my boys'.[52] All in all, however, the Amalgamated Press produced few Robin Hood stories for boys up to 1914, apart from what appeared in *The Boys' Friend* in 1903–5 and 1909–10, a single short story in *The Union Jack* in 1904, and just one out of the full run of 764 numbers of the first series of *The Boys' Friend Library* (c.1913).

Robin Hood's fortunes in boys' weeklies declined even further after the Great War. According to the head salesman of a news agency, after 1918, serials about outlaws, pirates and highwaymen were 'out' while adventures in submarines and aeroplanes were definitely 'in'.[53] Apart from the Amalgamated Press's *Robin Hood Library* of 1919–20, there was only the occasional Sherwood story in inter-war boys' weeklies.[54] And yet, in the full field of children's literature, from the turn of the century onwards Robin Hood was consolidating his position. Increasingly, mainstream children's publishers now included Robin Hoods in their lists.[55] Two recent Robin Hood exhibitions had more children's books on display published between 1900 and 1914 than in the entire previous century.[56] The first significant new version of the legend was Henry Gilbert's *Robin Hood and the Men of the Greenwood* (1912), illustrated in colour by Walter Crane. The 'heritage' movement and the Georgian revival of the legend encouraged the publication of Robin Hoods for various purposes: children's novels as 'rewards' and 'prizes'; ballad collections,

---

50 Quoted in Kevin Carpenter, *Penny Dreadfuls and Comics: English Periodicals for Children from Victorian Times to the Present Day* (London: Victoria & Albert Museum, 1983), p. 53.

51 'Your Editor's Den', *Boys' Friend* 3, 152 (new series, 7 May 1904), p. 804.

52 'Your Editor's Den', *Boys' Friend* 9, 457 (new series, 12 March 1910), p. 656.

53 Springhall, '"Disseminating Impure Literature"', p. 580. One of the oddest items of Robin Hoodana is a serial by George Rochester running in the boys' weekly *Chums* in 1932 called 'Captain Robin Hood, Skywayman' about a fighter pilot 'who singlehanded is defending England's peace' (p. 755).

54 The full series of *Robin Hood Library* ran from 15 April 1919 to 10 July 1920. According to Lofts and Adley, *The Men Behind Boys' Fiction*, all 57 numbers were written by one man, Australian-born R. Coutts Armour (p. 39). The series editor was Leonard Pratt. Amongst the inter-war weeklies I know of Robin Hood stories in only *Little Folks* (1917), *The Nugget Weekly* (1920), *Young Folks* (1921), *Magnet* (1924), *Gem* (1924), *The Popular* (1926), *The Modern Boy* (1934) and *Chums* (1934–35).

55 Foremost among them Blackwood and Sons, Cassell and Co., J.M. Dent and Sons, T.C. and E.C. Jack, Thomas Nelson and Sons, Ernest Nister, George Routledge and Sons, John F. Shaw, Raphael Tuck and Sons, Ward Lock and Co. and Wells Gardner and Darton.

56 See Carpenter, *Robin Hood*, pp. 220–2 and Blamires, *Robin Hood: A Hero For All Times*, pp. 45–6 and 53.

play texts and readers for school use.[57] And then in the 1920s, the Merry Men moved into new terrains of popular children's literature – 'bumper books' and comics.[58]

The Robin Hood stories in the Victorian and Edwardian boys' weeklies surveyed in this chapter may not have been well-crafted or thought-provoking or profound. They certainly were grisly at times, repetitive and chauvinistic, regularly stressing thrilling incident and melodramatic posture. The writing was often poor, sometimes atrociously so. However, the assumption that Robin Hood stories written for the young always stick closely to the old ballads and portray the outlaw as a father-figure restoring feudal order does not hold for popular juvenile fiction, where Robin often leads an exciting and sometimes even riotous life. And if, as Dobson and Taylor maintain, children's literature in the pre-Hollywood and pre-TV era became 'the primary vehicle for the diffusion of the Robin Hood legend', then the boys' weeklies of this period certainly contributed their pennyworth to the way millions of British people perceived one of the most enduring heroes of popular culture.[59]

Appendix

This is not a complete bibliography as I have not been able to examine every boys' magazine published in this period.[60] However, despite the lacunae and the guesswork, I believe it is a fair guide to Robin Hood in popular juvenile fiction up to 1914. The list actually begins with Egan's penny-part novel of 1839–40, the novel that prepared the way for so many later re-tellings for boy readers. The entries are arranged in chronological order by first publication in whatever form. Only the main titles of serials and short stories are given; in the case of the Aldine Robin Hood 'library' of 1901–6, the 88 individual story titles have not been listed.

---

57 Some of this ground is covered in Knight, *Robin Hood: A Complete Study*, pp. 205–9 and 210–17.

58 'Bumper books' were cheap books printed on thick lightweight paper enclosed in matt boards. Robin Hoods were published in this format by Aldine, J. Coker and Co., George G. Harrap, John F. Shaw (one of them for Marks and Spencers), Ward Lock and Co. and Wells Gardner and Darton. Robin Hood appeared in a Dreamy Daniel comic strip (drawn by George Davey) in *Lot-o'-Fun* in 1920, in a 20-year run in the comic *Bubbles* from 1922 to 1941 (drawn by Vincent Daniels), in *The Chick's Own* in 1923, in *Merry and Bright* in 1930 and in *Sparkler* in 1937. The comics of this period still contained serialised fiction: *Puck* ran a Robin Hood serial in 1912, as did *The Rainbow* in 1920 and *Sunbeam* in 1931.

59 Dobson and Taylor, *Rymes of Robyn Hood*, p. 61.

60 W.O.G. Lofts and D.J. Adley's *Old Boys' Books: A Complete Catalogue* (London: privately published, 1969), record a staggering total of 295 nineteenth- and early twentieth-century boys' magazines. The British Library holdings of these periodicals (at St Pancras and Colindale) are far from complete.

Egan (the Younger), Pierce, *Robin Hood and Little John; or, The Merry Men of Sherwood Forest*, London: Foster and Hextall, [1839–40], pp. 474. Issued in 41 weekly parts, October or November 1839 to July 1840.[61] Illustrated by the author. One-volume edition for seven shillings in 1840 (the new dedication is dated 25 June 1840). Gable records further editions in 1843 (Hextall and Wall), 1846 and 1847 (both George Peirce);[62] there was another edition by Peirce in 1844.[63] Revised 280-page edition in 35 weekly parts *c.*1850, with illustrations by W.H. Thwaites engraved by John Wall, issued by W.S. Johnson and reissued *c.*1860. The first edition for young readers, a straight reprint of Johnson's version, was brought out by Edward Harrison *c.*1870 and was probably available for a number of years after that. What seems to be the last edition appeared with the shortened title *Robin Hood; or, The Merry Men of Sherwood Forest* as vol. 22 of *Dicks' English Library*, London: John Dicks, [1896], pp. 224.

Little John and Will Scarlett; or, The Outlaws of Sherwood Forest, 'By the Forest Ranger', London: H. Vickers. [*c.*1865],[64] pp. 218 + 99. Issued in 40 weekly parts, later in one vol. Most of the illustrations are by Robert Prowse. The Gable Collection has a straight reprint for young readers by Edward Harrison, *c.*1870, which would doubtless have been available for a number of years thereafter.[65]

[Emmett, George], *Robin Hood and the Outlaws of Sherwood Forest*, London: Temple Publishing Co., pp. 416. Issued in 52 weekly parts beginning March 1868 and concluding – presumably – in March 1869.[66] Illustrations signed 'R.P.' (Robert Prowse) and 'W.R.' (Warwick Reynolds), with 28 illustrations from some earlier publication. Reprinted in one vol. dated 1869. Weekly and monthly reissue in 1871, 1872 (The 'Young Englishman' Edition, issued by Salisbury House) and again in 1873. Three paperback volumes at a shilling each were issued and a cloth-bound book as vol. 1 in the *Hogarth House Volumes* (publisher now Charles Fox) at 3s 6d in 1872. New edition, completely re-set, in 38 weekly parts, bearing the emended title *Robin Hood and the Archers of Merrie Sherwood*, with additional illustrations, probably by Harry Maguire, pp. 456, *c.*1875. Twenty chromolithographed plates were given away with later Hogarth House reprints, of which there seem to have been many, the book still being available in the 1880s, possibly even as late as the early 1890s.

---

61 Approximate dates based on an announcement along the binding crease of part 38.

62 Gable, *Bibliography of Robin Hood*, pp. 34–6.

63 J.J. Rigden Books, catalogue 1, 1984, item 117.

64 Item 369 is dated thus in Elizabeth James and Helen Smith, *Penny Dreadfuls and Boys' Adventures: The Barry Ono Collection of Victorian Popular Literature in the British Library* (London: The British Library, 1998).

65 Gable, *Bibliography of Robin Hood*, p. 41.

66 According to announcements in *Sons of Britannia*, the *Young Englishman* and the *Young Englishman's Journal*, this work was being written in January 1868; the first weekly and monthly parts were issued in March; a pirated edition was on the market in April (unlikely); weekly and monthly parts were reissued in August 1871; three volumes were out by July 1872; a penny-part reissue started in August 1873.

'Robin Hood and His Merry Men'. Illustrated. Serial in *Boys of England*, London: Edwin J. Brett, vol. 5, no. 104 (13 November 1868) to vol. 5, no. 115 (29 January 1869; not seen).[67] Reprinted in the reissue of *Boys of England*, vol. 7, no. 166 (19 June 1877) to vol. 7, no. 177 (4 September 1877).

'The Fighting Friar'. Illustrated by Warwick Reynolds. Serial in *The Young Briton*, London: George Brent, William Emmet Laurence *et al.* [i.e. the Emmett Brothers], no. 114 (8 November 1871) to no. 125 (24 January 1872).

Williams, Will, 'Bold Robin Hood'. Illustrations signed 'W.H.' Serial in *Our Young Folks' Weekly Budget*, London: James Henderson, vol. 3, no 153 (29 November 1873) to vol. 4, no. 164 (14 February 1874). Reprint in book-form in 1874, pp. 52 (not seen).[68] It appeared again as a serial in *Nuggets*. London: Red Lion House, probably commencing in September 1896 (not seen) and concluding in no. 235 (31 October 1896). Book-form 1897 (not seen).[69] Another reissue as 'Bows and Broadswords', no. 72 of *The Nugget Library*, London: James Henderson and Sons, [1907], pp. 48.

[St. John, Percy Bolingbroke], 'Royston Gower'. Illustrations probably from some other source. Serial in *The Young Briton*, London: Charles Fox, vol. 6, no. 244 (2 May 1874) to vol. 7, no. 278 (26 December 1874).

'The Prince of Archers'. Illustrated. Serial in *Boys of England*, London: Edwin J. Brett, vol. 34, no. 851 (9 March 1883) to vol. 34, no. 869 (13 July 1883). Reprint in Brett's *Boys of the Empire*, div. 24, no. 244 (6 June 1905) to div. 26, no. 262 (10 October 1905).

[Clarke, S. Dacre], 'The Young Lord of Huntingdon'. Illustrated. Serial in *Young Britannia*, London: H.J. Brand [i.e. Samuel Dacre Clarke?], commencing vol. 2, no. 27 (11 October 1885); further numbers not seen but probably ending in early 1886.

[Lambe, Robert Justyn], 'Allen-a-Dale'. Illustrated. Serial in *Young Men of Great Britain*, London: Edwin J. Brett, commencing vol. 38, no. 930 (16 November 1885; conclusion – evidently early 1886 – not seen). Reprint in *The Boy's Comic Journal*. London: Edwin J. Brett, commencing vol. 29, no. 743 (5 June 1897) to vol. 30, no. 764 (30 October 1897).

Hope, Edwin S., 'Bold Robin Hood'. Illustrated. Serial in *Boys and Girls*, London: Guy Rayner [i.e. Samuel Dacre Clarke], vol. 1, no. 10 (1 October 1887) to vol. 1, no. 17 (19 November 1887).

Armitage, Alfred [i.e. William Murray Graydon], 'Robin Hood and His Merry Men'. Illustrations signed 'Phil S' and 'Menzies'. Serial in *British Boys*, London: George Newnes and John Marshall, vol. 1, no. 17 (3 April 1897) to vol. 2 (26 June 1897).

---

67 Dates reconstructed by working back from the *Boys of England* reissue of 1877, which has an undeleted note 'Commenced in No. 104' on p. 176.

68 Details from the *National Union Catalog: Pre-1956 Imprints*, vol. 665, p. 426.

69 Advert in *Nuggets* 246 (9 January 1897), p. 15.

Robin Hood, London: Aldine Publishing Co. The first series of this 'library' consisted of a total of 88 penny numbers issued in batches of four every two months from 19 October 1901 to 16 June 1906.[70] Each number has 32 pages with coloured wrappers. The series editor was Walter Light. In alphabetical order, the authors writing a total of around 2 million words in this series of stories were: Charles E. Brand, Alfred Sherrington Burrage, Roderick Dare, G.C. Glover, Escott Lynn (i.e. Christopher George Holman Lawrence), Richard Mant (i.e. George Richard Mant Hearne), Singleton Pound (i.e. Oliver Merland) and H. Philpott Wright (i.e. J. Weedon Birch). The cover illustrations are initialled 'J.A.' (J. Arch), 'C.H.B.', 'F.W.B.' (F.W. Boyington), 'T.K.', 'R.P.' (Robert Prowse), and 'A.W.' (Arthur White?). A reprint of this 'library', begun in 1912 and discontinued in 1914, ran to just 14 numbers). The *Aldine Robin Hood Library* was a complete reprint of the first series, with many altered titles and omitting the authors' names or pseudonyms; two 32-page numbers were issued per month from early 1924 to late 1927, at twopence each.[71] The last reprint had but a brief life, being discontinued after only eight numbers in 1930.

Pike, Morton [i.e. David Harold Parry], 'Robin Hood's Christmas Dinner'. Illustrated by Arthur White. Short story in the Christmas number of *The Boys' Friend*, London: Carmelite House [i.e. Amalgamated Press], vol. 3, no. 132 (19 December 1903).

Pike, Morton [i.e. David Harold Parry], 'Guy of the Greenwood'. Illustrations by Val Reading. Serial in *The Boys' Friend*, London: Carmelite House [i.e. Amalgamated Press], commencing vol. 3, no. 154 (new series) (21 May 1904); conclusion not seen.

Stanton, John [i.e. George C. Wallis], 'The Black Knight'. Illustrated. Short story in *The Union Jack*, London: 'Printed for the Proprietors at Lavington Street, Southwark, E.C.' [i.e. Amalgamated Press], vol. 3, no. 55 (new series) (29 October 1904).

[Graydon, William Murray], 'The Red Earl's Son'. Illustrated by Val Reading. Short story in *The Boys' Friend*, London: Amalgamated Press, vol. 5, no. 224 (new series) (23 September 1905).

[Burrage, Alfred Sherrington], 'Robin Hood and His Merrie Men'. Issued as no. 18 of *The Boys' Own Library*, London: Aldine Publishing Co., [January 1909], pp. 128. A revised reprint of nos 1–4 of Aldine's first *Robin Hood* 'library'.

Pike, Morton [i.e. David Harold Parry], 'The White Monks of Merly'. Illustrated by Harry Lane. Short story in *The Boys' Friend*, London: Amalgamated Press, vol. 8, no. 412 (new series) (1 May 1909).

Pike, Morton [i.e. David Harold Parry], 'The Traitor in the Camp'. Illustrated by Fred Bennett. Short story in *The Boys' Friend*, London: 23, Bouverie Street [i.e. Amalgamated Press], vol. 9, no. 429 (new series) (28 August 1909).

---

70 While the whole series was undated, the dates of this 'library' can be derived from adverts in this and other Aldine magazines.

71 These imprecise dates are based on seasonal adverts on the covers of this 'library'.

Pike, Morton [i.e. David Harold Parry], 'The Outlaw's Christmas'. Illustrated by Harry Lane. Short story in the Christmas number of *The Boys' Friend*, London: 23, Bouverie Street [i.e. Amalgamated Press], vol. 9, no. 445 (new series) (18 December 1909).

Pike, Morton [i.e. David Harold Parry], 'Rough Justice'. Illustrated by Harry Lane. Short story in *The Boys' Friend*, London: 23, Bouverie Street [i.e. Amalgamated Press], vol. 9, no. 455 (new series) (29 February 1910).

Pike, Morton [i.e. David Harold Parry], 'Robin Hood's Ward'. Illustrated by Harry Lane. Serial in *The Boys' Friend*, London: 23, Bouverie Street [i.e. Amalgamated Press], commencing vol. 9, no 457 (new series) (12 March 1910); conclusion not seen.

Walkey, Samuel, 'Hurrah! for Merry Sherwood'. Illustrated by J. Herie. Serial in *Chums*, London: Cassell and Co., vol. 20, no. 1000 (8 November 1911) to vol. 20, no. 1019 (23 March 1912). Issued in book-form by Cassell and Co. in 1920 (undated) with colour plates by C. E. Brock.

Pike, Morton [i.e. David Harold Parry], 'Longbows of England'. Illustrated. Issued as no. 259 of *The Boys' Friend Library*, London: Amalgamated Press, [*c.*1913].[72]

'For Outlaw or King?' Illustrated. Issued as no. 14 of *The Briton's Own Library*, London: Aldine Publishing Co., [*c.*1914].[73]

---

72 Copy seen in the Hess Collection, Walter Library, University of Minnesota at Minneapolis.

73 See previous note.

Chapter 4

From Madame d'Aulnoy to Mother Bunch: Popularity and the Fairy Tale

David Blamires

Among the fine company of French aristocratic writers who devoted themselves to composing fairytales during the period 1690–1720 Madame d'Aulnoy reigned supreme. She was known as 'la reine de la féerie', and her tales enjoyed the widest circulation, not only in French but also in English and German. At least 22 editions in English are known between 1699 and 1799.[1] Another 11 followed in the nineteenth century. Meanwhile, individual tales appeared separately, usually in chapbook format, or were included in general collections of fairy tales. However, enthusiasm began to diminish in the course of the twentieth century, and readers who are familiar with Madame d'Aulnoy today are fewer in number. Her former fame has been largely eclipsed by the tales of her contemporary Charles Perrault and by those of the Brothers Grimm and Hans Christian Andersen.[2]

The history of the transmission of Madame d'Aulnoy's tales, particularly that of 'The White Cat', can be useful as part of an exploration of the concept of popular literature, both in terms of the appeal and endurance of texts, and the connexions

---

1   Melvin D. Palmer, 'Madame d'Aulnoy in England', *Comparative Literature* 27 (1975), 237–53, lists 14 editions, to which may be added *The History of the Tales of the Fairies* (London: E. Midwinter, *c.*1725), *Fairy Tales; Selected from the Best Authors* (London: William Lane, 1788), *The Palace of Enchantment* (London: William Lane, 1788) and *Mother Bunch's Fairy Tales* (six editions between *c.*1773 and 1779 by F. Newbery and E. Newbery). See Judith St John, *The Osborne Collection of Early Children's Books: A Catalogue* (2 vols, Toronto: Toronto Public Library, 1958 and 1975), pp. 39–40, 586–7, 597 and S. Roscoe, *John Newbery and his Successors 1740–1814: A Bibliography* (Wormley, Herts.: Five Owls Press, 1973), p. 49.

2   Several important studies of French women writers of fairy tales have recently appeared, including Lewis C. Seifert, *Fairy Tales, Sexuality, and Gender in France, 1690–1715: Nostalgic Utopias* (Cambridge: Cambridge University Press, 1996); Kathryn A. Hoffmann, 'Matriarchal Desires and Labyrinths of the Marvellous: Fairy Tales by Old Régime Women', in Colette H. Winn and Donna Kuizenga (eds), *Women Writers in Pre-Revolutionary France: Strategies of Emancipation* (New York and London: Garland Publishing, 1997), pp. 281–98; Patricia Hannon, *Fabulous Identities: Women's Fairy Tales in Seventeenth-Century France* (Amsterdam and Atlanta, GA: Rodopi, 1998); Elizabeth Wanning Harries, *Twice Upon a Time: Women Writers and the History of the Fairy Tale* (Princeton, NJ: Princeton University Press, 2003); and Anne E. Duggan, *Salonnieres, Furies, and Fairies: The Politics of Gender and Cultural Change in Absolutist France* (Newark, DE: University of Delaware Press, 2005).

between 'high' literature and popular culture. Not only do we find close translations of her tales being published all through the eighteenth and nineteenth centuries, but fresh translations of individual tales have been made in the last ten years, demonstrating an impressive longevity. In addition, the folktale core of many of their plots meant that the tales did not remain the sole province of the educated upper classes, but were easily tailored to the needs of children and the less well educated. Their adaptation for pantomimes also took them into a broad range of society. The name of the aristocratic French author was replaced in the late eighteenth century by that of the folk figure Mother Bunch, probably in emulation of the Mother Goose who presided over Perrault's tales. The name of Mother Bunch made the tales traditional and disguised their foreign provenance. Madame d'Aulnoy's tales thus achieved popularity in a variety of forms and with widely differing social strata.

Madame d'Aulnoy did not write her fairy tales for children, but rather for adults. They were the product of the literary salons of the age of Louis XIV (1638–1715), stylishly written by a lady who was known for her popular contributions to the literature of memoirs and travels as well as for historical romances and *nouvelles*.[3] D'Aulnoy narrates at a leisurely pace, delighting in hyperbolic descriptions of imagined splendours or horrors, the more bizarre the better. Her stories are complex, self-consciously literary structures, frequently referring to other contemporary writings and culture. They present a fascinating kaleidoscope of the materialistic ideals of the aristocracy, the central importance attached to sentimental relationships, and the moral values expected in ladies and gentlemen. The disasters, intrigues and successes that fill the pages of these tales in some measure reflect the vicissitudes of Madame d'Aulnoy's own life.

Marie-Catherine Le Jumel de Barneville was born about 1650 of a Norman family and was married to François de la Mothe, Baron d'Aulnoy, a man three times her age, when she was 15 or 16 years old. Properly speaking she ought to be referred to as Baroness d'Aulnoy, but for some reason she is always called Countess. She and her husband did not get on well together and separated early. Her mother engineered an accusation of *lèse majesté* against the Baron, but he extricated himself from this, and the two nobles who had brought the accusation against him were arrested and ultimately executed. It is not known what part Madame d'Aulnoy herself had in this gruesome affair, but she was for a time herself under arrest, though never tried. Her mother fled to Spain, where she spent the rest of her life. By the age of 20 Madame d'Aulnoy had three children; later she had three more. She travelled a good deal, to Spain and to England, and wrote about these experiences. In 1690 she was in Paris, living a kind of semi-religious life and conducting a literary salon.[4] It was at this time that she began to write the fairy tales that have kept her reputation alive. She died in 1705.

Her first fairy tale, 'L'Ile de la félicité', was incorporated into her novel *Histoire d'Hypolite, comte de Duglas* (1690), but it has only rarely been reprinted. Between

---

3   See D.J. Adams, 'The "contes de fées" of Madame d'Aulnoy: Reputation and Re-evaluation', *Bulletin of the John Rylands University Library of Manchester* 76 (1994), 5–22.

4   For these details of Madame d'Aulnoy's life see Jacques Barchilon, *Le Conte merveilleux français de 1690 à 1790* (Paris: Champion, 1975), pp. 37–8.

1696 and 1698 she published her first collection, *Contes des fées*, followed in 1698 by *Contes nouveaux ou les fées à la mode*, both of which were frequently reprinted in the eighteenth century. These two volumes contained 24 fairy tales. Although these tales are literary creations, they are to a marked degree based on traditional tales that Madame d'Aulnoy may have known orally. She appears to have had access to the Italian fairy tales of Straparola, which had been translated into French in two volumes (1560 and 1585), and to Giambattista Basile's *Pentamerone* (1634–36), the first European book to consist solely of fairy tales. From Straparola she took the plot of 'La Princesse Belle-Etoile et le Prince Chéri' (IV, 3,[5] 'The Dancing Water, the Singing Apple and the Speaking Bird'), 'Le Dauphin' (III, 1, 'The Magic Tunny Fish') and 'Le Prince Marcassin' (II, 1, 'King Pig'). From the *Pentamerone* came the stimuli for 'Gracieuse et Percinet' (V, 4,[6] 'The Golden Root'), 'La Belle aux cheveux d'or' (III, 7, 'Corvetto'), 'La bonne petite Souris' (III, 5, 'The Cockchafer, the Mouse and the Grasshopper'), 'Belle-Belle ou le Chevalier Fortuné' (III, 8, 'The Booby'). Both 'Le Mouton' and 'Serpentin vert' are examples of the animal bridegroom story (AT 425A),[7] which is best known nowadays through Madame Leprince de Beaumont's 'Beauty and the Beast'. 'Finette Cendron' is d'Aulnoy's reworking of the Cinderella tale. Several other tales have analogues in the Grimms' collection, suggesting that they derived from oral sources. These include 'La Princesse Rosette' ('The White and the Black Bride', KHM 135),[8] 'La Biche au bois' ('Little Brother and Little Sister', KHM 11), 'L'Oranger et l'abeille' ('Darling Roland', KHM 56, and 'The Two King's Children', KHM 113). It was not Madame d'Aulnoy's practice simply to pick up and translate the tales of other writers: she submitted them to the alchemy of her own imagination and often combined plots and motifs from more than one source. 'La Chatte blanche' ('The White Cat') is such a combination. By contrast, 'Le Nain jaune' ('The Yellow Dwarf'), which vies with it in popularity in English translation, is entirely a product of Madame d'Aulnoy's imagination (see Figure 4.1). Seven other tales are likewise invented, though they do contain some typical fairy tale motifs.[9]

Although many of Madame d'Aulnoy's tales achieved wide currency in English, particularly during the eighteenth and nineteenth centuries, 'The White Cat' was the

---

5   References to the tales of Gianfrancesco Straparola are given according to *The Nights of Straparola*, trans. W.G. Waters (London: Lawence and Bullen, 1894), where roman numerals indicate the 'night' and arabic numerals the 'fable'.

6   References to tales in the *Pentamerone* are given according to *The Pentamerone of Giambattista Basile*, trans. and ed. N.M. Penzer (London: John Lane the Bodley Head, 1932), where roman numerals indicate the 'day' and arabic numerals the 'tale'.

7   Tale-type numbers are given according to those in Antti Aarne and Stith Thompson, *The Types of the Folktale: A Classification and Bibliography*, 2nd rev. edn (Helsinki: Suomalainen Tiedeakatemia, 1973).

8   The Grimms' tales are numbered according to the 1857 edition of the *Kinder- und Hausmärchen* (KHM), the standard complete edition.

9   For details of Madame d'Aulnoy's sources see, for example, the Grimms' original notes as reprinted in, Brüder Grimm*, Kinder- und Hausmärchen. Ausgabe letzter Hand mit den Originalanmerkungen der Brüder Grimm*, ed. Heinz Rölleke (3 vols, Stuttgart: Philipp Reclam jun., 1980), vol. 3, pp. 314–18.

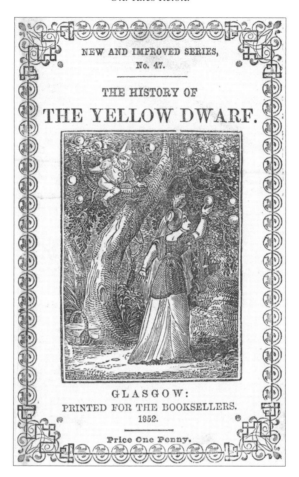

Figure 4.1   Madame d'Aulnoy, *The History of the Yellow Dwarf* (Glasgow: Printed for the booksellers, 1852). Private collection.

one that enjoyed the greatest popularity, a popularity that extended right into the second half of the twentieth century. For this reason it seems appropriate to examine at some length the varied forms in which it was known over a period of 300 years.

'La Chatte blanche' was first published in the *Contes nouveaux ou les fées à la mode*. The story falls into two distinct parts, focusing first on the hero and second on the heroine. The plot runs as follows:

An old king tests his three sons in order to decide who should inherit the kingdom. First, they have to find the prettiest and most intelligent little dog to keep him company. The youngest prince eventually finds his way to a marvellous palace, where he is waited on by bodiless hands. The palace is inhabited only by cats, their queen being a beautiful white cat who provides him with everything he needs. She gives the prince a wooden horse on which to return and an acorn containing a fantastic tiny dog. This pleases the king greatly, but he sets another test: the princes are to bring back some cloth so fine it will go through the eye of a needle. The youngest son returns to the white cat, enjoys himself as before and becomes more devoted to her. This time she gives him a walnut, which contains a hazel nut, inside that a cherry stone, its kernel, a grain of wheat, a millet seed and, finally, 400 ells of the finest cloth imaginable. The king then sets a third test: to bring back the most beautiful maiden to marry. To achieve this the prince is told by the white cat to cut off her head and tail and burn them. He summons up the courage to do this, and the white cat is transformed into a beautiful princess, who then tells her story.

Her mother, while pregnant and out travelling, had discovered a castle and garden belonging to the fairies that contained the most wonderful fruit. She was allowed to have it on condition she gave the fairies her daughter. She promised this, but her husband incarcerated her and only agreed to comply when his kingdom was ravaged by a dragon. The baby princess was handed over and taken to the fairies' castle, where she enjoyed the companionship of a parrot, Perroquet, and a dog, Toutou. One day in her tower there she saw a knight passing by and fell in love with him. The fairies, however, proposed to marry her to the ugly dwarf king, Migonnet. Meanwhile, the princess made a rope ladder to escape, but instead the prince climbed it to see her. On his second visit, they were surprised by the fairies arriving with Migonnet. The fairies' dragon consumed the prince, and the princess was transformed into a white cat. She could only be disenchanted by a prince who perfectly resembled her lover. The youngest prince is, of course, he. The two proceed to the king's court, where the princess, the ruler of six kingdoms, gives a kingdom each to the old king and the two elder brothers, keeping only three for herself and the youngest brother, her husband.

This story is a combination of two tale-types. The first part is a form of AT 402, 'The Mouse (Cat, Frog, etc.) as Bride', while the second part is a version of AT 310, 'The Maiden in the Tower'. A version of AT 402 is to be found in the Grimms' tale 'The Three Feathers' (KHM 63), where the animal bride is a toad. The motif of restoration to human shape being brought about through decapitation is also found in the Grimms' 'The Golden Bird' (KHM 57), in which the ever helpful fox begs the hero to chop off his head and is transformed into a young man as a result. 'The Frog Prince' (KHM 1) contains a related motif, for there the princess unwittingly transforms the frog into a prince by flinging him violently against the wall. However, there does not appear to be any version of tale-type AT 402 extant from the period at which Madame d'Aulnoy was writing. For AT 310, though, she took her inspiration either directly from Basile's 'Petrosinella' (II, 1 in the *Pentamerone*) or indirectly through a literary version by Charlotte-Rose de La Force entitled 'Persinette', published in 1697 in a collection entitled *Les Contes des contes*, thus pointing to its source in the *Pentamerone*, which also goes under the title of *Lo Cunto de li cunti*. The tale-type is best known in modern times from the Grimms' 'Rapunzel' (KHM 12).

Madame d'Aulnoy created a tale of great popularity and staying power in 'The White Cat', but it was designed originally to entertain aristocratic adults rather than children. This is evident above all in many literary and contemporary allusions and in d'Aulnoy's playfulness with linguistic forms. When the prince first arrives at the White Cat's palace, we are told that its transparent porcelain walls display the history of all the fairies from the creation of the world to the present day. Among them are 'Donkey Skin' and 'The Sleeping Beauty' (one verse and one prose tale by Perrault) and 'Finette', 'The Orange Tree', 'Graciosa', 'Green Serpent' and 'The Hobgoblin Prince' (five tales by Madame d'Aulnoy herself). This sort of reference in a work of fiction to printed works of fiction existing in the real world recalls what Cervantes did in *Don Quixote*, where, in the second part of the novel, he has his hero marvelling to see that his previous adventures have actually been published. Madame d'Aulnoy certainly knew *Don Quixote*, since a little later in the tale she has the prince disclaim any resemblance to the Spanish knight errant when he is persuaded to mount a wooden horse when setting out on a hunt.

In her fairy tale d'Aulnoy describes, in a hall inside the palace, pictures of famous cats, among them La Fontaine's Rodillardus and Perrault's Puss-in-Boots. She alludes furthermore to the widespread belief that sorcerers could change themselves into cats and mentions the cat that became a woman, hinting here at the outcome of her own tale. Later, there are further allusions to La Fontaine with the names of Martafax and Lhermite, two famous country rats that are alleged to have conspired with four renegade cats against the White Cat herself. Elements of this kind reflect the sophisticated world within which Madame d'Aulnoy was operating. Her blurring of the boundaries between fact and fiction and her exaggeration of the details of the White Cat's palace suggest a degree of fantastic artifice within the contemporary experience of aristocratic life. Its showiness is totally unreal, full of extremes and, above all, brittle.

The court over which the White Cat presides is a transformation of the royal court of d'Aulnoy's own day, with cats everywhere playing the part of human beings. Perhaps its most extraordinary feature is the cats' orchestra and the prince's reaction to it:

> he saw some cats come and place themselves upon a bench set there for that purpose; one holding a music-book, another with a roll of paper to beat time with, and the rest with small guitars: when, all on a sudden, they every one set up a mewing in different tones, and struck the strings with their talons, which made the strangest music that ever was heard. The prince would have thought himself in hell, if the palace had not been so wonderfully fine, it put him so much in mind of it; then, stopping his ears, he laughed heartily at the several postures and grimaces of these strange musicians.[10]

Madame d'Aulnoy delights in inventing suitable terminology for this feline world and has the White Cat refer to herself as 'ma miaularde majesté' (my meowing majesty), a form of words that this early translation does not attempt to render. Madame d'Aulnoy further indulges her sense of humour in describing the food set upon the table to welcome the prince: it includes a dish of pigeons entirely suitable for human consumption, but alongside are fat mice for the White Cat herself.

A pointer to the resolution of the story is given by a small portrait that the White Cat has at her paw. The prince asks to see it, thinking it will display some haughty cat, and is astonished to see the picture of a young man, so handsome that it seems scarcely credible that nature could have created one like him, and, moreover, bearing a strong resemblance to himself. However, the White Cat's deep, sad silence inhibits him from asking further questions, and it is not until she is transformed back into

---

10 *Fairy Tales and Novels of the Countess d'Anois* (London: Walker and Edwards, 1817) I, pp. 260–1.

human shape that the connexion between the portrait of the handsome young man and the king's youngest son, the hero of the fairy tale, is revealed.

'The White Cat' first appeared in English in a two-volume work entitled *A Collection of Novels and Tales of the Fairies* (1721). This book contains three *nouvelles* framing eight separate tales, all by Madame d'Aulnoy, along with four tales by Madame de Murat. Further editions of this collection appeared in 1728, 1737, 1749 and 1766. It was then republished with the title *Fairy Tales and Novels* by the Countess d'Anois (Walker and Edwards, and congers of sixteen, 1817). 'The Story of the White Cat' in the identical translation was also published in *Fairy Tales; Selected from the Best Authors* (William Lane, 1788; reprinted 1794). All of the other tales in Lane's editions were also by Madame d'Aulnoy except for two by Madame de Murat. The translation printed in all these editions is anonymous. It keeps close to the French original, but occasionally, as noted above, there are small omissions where details prove difficult to accommodate in an English version. What is important about these and other eighteenth-century editions of d'Aulnoy's fairytales (that is to say, editions that do not include 'The White Cat') is the fact that her tales were extremely well known throughout the century and that they were transmitted in a full translation up to 1817.

Towards the end of the eighteenth century, however, we find the first abridgments of Madame d'Aulnoy's ample texts. *Mother Bunch's Fairy Tales* (F. Newbery, *c.*1773) makes clear on its title page that this book is 'published for the amusement of all those little masters and misses who, by duty to their parents, and obedience to their superiors, aim at becoming great lords and ladies'. In other words, the readership for Madame d'Aulnoy is undergoing a change. Her tales are being adapted to make them accessible to younger readers, not simply educated upper- and middle-class adults and their adolescent daughters and sons. There are further editions by Elizabeth Newbery dated 1776, 1784, 1790, 1795 and 1799.[11] The name 'Mother Bunch' as a traditional narrator of fairy tales, like Mother Goose, was applied to Madame d'Aulnoy in ten or a dozen publications up to at least about 1830.[12] Among them are two editions published in London by John Harris in 1802 and 1817 which were almost immediately abridged and pirated by James Lumsden and Son of Glasgow.[13] *Mother Bunch's Fairy Tales* contains, in addition to those by d'Aulnoy, four tales with an Oriental setting by Madame d'Auneuil. Mother Bunch was a figure knowledgeable in English folklore, referred to in the sixteenth century by Thomas Nashe and Thomas Dekker and later made the ostensible source of a collection of

---

11 See S. Roscoe, *John Newbery and his Successors 1740–1814: A Bibliography* (Wormley, Herts.: Five Owls Press, 1973), p. 49.

12 In addition to Roscoe, *John Newbery and his Successors*, see also Marjorie Moon, *John Harris's Books for Youth 1801–1843: A Check-List*, rev. edn (Folkestone: Dawon, 1992), p. 81; S. Roscoe and R. A. Brimmell, *James Lumsden and Son of Glasgow* (Pinner: Private Libraries Association, 1981), pp. 68–9; Gumuchian, *Les Livres de l'enfance* (1930; repr. London: The Holland Press, 1979), no. 4204.

13 Moon, *John Harris's Books for Youth*, pp. 81–2; Roscoe and Brimmell, *James Lumsden and Son*, pp. 68–9.

charms and dreams in a chapbook entitled *Mother Bunch's Closet Newly Broke Open* (P. Brooksby, 1685).[14]

We are, however, concerned with 'The White Cat', and it might not be so easily recognised in the Harris/Lumsden collections because it is divided into two parts, each of which is given a new title. In fact, 'The Story of Prince Lupin' and 'The Story of the Princess Frutilla, as related by herself' together make up what is usually known as 'The White Cat'. The prince bears no name in Madame d'Aulnoy's original text, nor does the White Cat after she has regained human form. The princess is presumably called Frutilla on account of her mother's insatiable longing for the manifold fruits in the fairies' garden. This new format of the tale is not surprising. As has been explained, Madame d'Aulnoy's original tale is long, complicated and full of literary detail. What the abridgement does is to follow the plot of the original, but simplify it. The allusions, asides and lengthy descriptions that were calculated to entertain a sophisticated adult or adolescent readership are carefully eliminated.

'The White Cat' was included in part I of *Tabart's Collection of Popular Stories for the Nursery* (Tabart and Co., 1804, reissued 1809). The collection, which brought together French, Italian and English material, was edited and translated by Mary Jane Godwin, with the stories being told 'in admirably clear and simple language' and the illustrations being 'well drawn and carefully executed'.[15] Like some of the other tales, 'The History of the White Cat' was also issued as a separate booklet (1804; new editions 1806, 1808). The text of the story varies slightly from edition to edition. One of the larger changes is the omission of the episode of the White Cat's would-be husband Migonnet from the 1808 edition. From the publishing point of view, what is interesting here is the issuing of individual stories as separate booklets. With its three copperplates Tabart's 36-page booklet was not cheap at sixpence. Lumsden sold *Mother Bunch's Fairy Tales* (five tales, 72 pages) for the same price.

At a later date individual tales by Madame d'Aulnoy became so popular that they entered the chapbook market. Thomas Richardson of Derby, co-publishing with Robert Sears and Co. of London, published *The History of the White Cat, c.*1835. The text, probably adapted and simplified from one of Tabart's editions, is compressed into 12 pages. A coloured engraving serves as frontispiece, showing (above) the prince on horseback and (below) the lovers embracing. Although much detail has had to be omitted from the story, the text nonetheless retains the verses sung to greet the prince on his first arrival at the White Cat's hall:

---

14 See Humphrey Carpenter and Mari Prichard, *The Oxford Companion to Children's Literature* (Oxford: Oxford University Press, 1984), p. 362; *Mother Bunch's Closet Newly Broke Open*, ed. George Laurence Gomme (London: Villon Society, 1885), pp. i–vii.

15 Marjorie Moon, *Benjamin Tabart's Juvenile Library: A Bibliography of Books for Children Published, Written, Edited and Sold by Mr. Tabart, 1801–1820* (Winchester: St Paul's Bibliographies; Detroit, MI: Omnigraphics, 1990), p. 122. See entries on d'Aulnoy, pp. 28–30 and Mary Jane Godwin, p. 43.

Welcome, prince! no danger fear;
Mirth and love attend you here:
You shall break the magic spell,
That on a beauteous maiden fell.
Welcome, prince! no danger fear;
Mirth and love attend you here.

A similar text was published as *The Surprising Story of the White Cat* by the London publisher Orlando Hodgson, *c.*1835. This had 16 pages and 'a beautiful engraving', hand-coloured, showing the prince standing up at a banquet and looking at the White Cat sitting on the floor. The text seems to be an abridged form of Tabart's 1809 edition, since it includes a reference to the princess's proposed marriage to Migonnet, which is omitted from the 1808 edition.

A slightly later chapbook, *The White Cat* (A. Park, *c.*1840), provides a different text, which is taken from *Fairy Tales and Novels* (1817), but with various excisions and verbal modifications. The chapbook contains seven hand-coloured illustrations. Although it has only 16 pages, the text is printed very closely with approximately 47 lines to the page, so it makes quite an extensive version for a chapbook. Other chapbook publishers also included tales by Madame d'Aulnoy in their repertoire. Francis Orr and Sons, publishing with the imprint 'Glasgow, Printed for the Booksellers' between 1834 and 1851, included a couple of booklets containing tales by d'Aulnoy among their list of 150 items. No. 7 was 'Prince Lupin, Yellow Dwarf, &c.' and no. 30 'The Little White Mouse' according to their catalogue of *c.*1840.[16] These chapbooks comprise 24 pages. As is the case with virtually all of the chapbook versions of d'Aulnoy, no mention is ever made of her name and original authorship.

The chapbook versions of Madame d'Aulnoy's tales, which include others apart from 'The White Cat' and go back as far as the 1760s, indicate a breakthrough into the popular literature available to the poor at this time. Chapbooks typically cost a penny or twopence and were crudely rather than beautifully illustrated – quite a contrast to Tabart's sixpenny tales for children. Huge quantities were printed in London and many provincial towns for pedlars (chapmen) to take around the country. Texts were freely borrowed, adapted and pirated, as were the woodcut illustrations. The subject matter of chapbooks was overwhelmingly traditional and English, so the appearance of Madame d'Aulnoy's tales anonymously in chapbook form is evidence that they were regarded as being of the same kind. In this way they became part of popular culture.

In 1845 the London publisher James Burns issued in three volumes a collection entitled *The Book of Nursery Tales. A Keepsake for the Young.* The pagination makes clear that individual items were also issued separately. The second volume or 'series' (as Burns calls it) includes a version of 'The White Cat' (a 28-page booklet) opening with an anonymous engraving of the prince clasping the princess in his arm and about to strike the rampant dragon. A large decorative initial shows the White Cat

---

16 See Adam McNaughtan, 'A Century of Saltmarket Literature, 1790–1890', in Peter Isaac (ed.), *Six Centuries of the Provincial Book Trade in Britain* (Winchester: St Paul's Bibliographies, 1990), pp. 169–70, 178–80.

with a fan in one hand. As was now usual, the text is an abridgement of Madame d'Aulnoy's original. It includes the first two lines of the verses welcoming him to the White Cat's palace as printed in Tabart, and it omits any reference to Migonnet. Neither the prince nor the White Cat is given a personal name. This booklet was larger and more refined in format and design than the typical chapbook, but it was surpassed a couple of years later by the ambitious bound edition adorned with ten lithographs by J.W. (Edinburgh and London: William Blackwood and Sons, 1847). This unidentified J.W. also illustrated d'Aulnoy's *Fortunio* for Blackwood the same year. Again, the text is an abridgement, and Madame d'Aulnoy's authorship is nowhere indicated. This edition was clearly designed for a discriminating purchaser and not for a popular readership.

From the publication of *Mother Bunch's Fairy Tales* (*c.*1773) onwards Madame d'Aulnoy's tales, whether published in collections or separately, joined the growing corpus of popular tales for children that were regarded as traditional. Like 'Little Red Riding Hood', 'Beauty and the Beast', 'Tom Thumb' and 'Jack and the Beanstalk', they were not credited to any author. Their basic plots were retained, but they were adapted and abridged without comment or excuse. In addition to 'The White Cat', the following representative collections indicate the tales that achieved this sort of currency. *The Child's Own Book* (7th edn, Thomas Tegg, *c.*1850) prints 'The White Cat' along with 'Miranda and the Royal Ram', 'The Fair One with Golden Locks', 'The Invisible Prince' and 'The Yellow Dwarf'. Francis Paul Palmer in *Old Tales for the Young* (George Routledge and Co., 1857) restricts himself to 'Graciosa and Percinet' and 'The Yellow Dwarf' in addition to 'The White Cat'. *Grimm's Goblins* (George Vickers, 1860/61), a volume made up from a series of tales issued as eight-page penny parts, contains 'The Blue Bird', 'The Fair One with Golden Locks', 'Fortunio', 'The Invisible Prince', 'The White Cat' and 'The Yellow Dwarf'. In *Household Tales and Fairy Stories* (George Routledge and Sons, 1877) we find the last two plus 'Graciosa and Percinet', 'The Fair with Golden Hair' and 'Princess Rosette', while *Aunt Louisa's Book of Fairy Stories and Wonder Tales* (Frederick Warne and Co., *c.*1904) prints severely reduced versions of 'The Yellow Dwarf', 'The White Cat', 'The Invisible Prince', 'The Beneficent Frog' and 'The Enchanted Hind'. It is obvious from this brief survey that as Madame d'Aulnoy was absorbed into the corpus of traditional children's tales, the two most frequently reprinted are 'The White Cat' and 'The Yellow Dwarf'. 'The White Cat' was the only one of her tales to be included in *Once Upon a Time*, by R. Marriott Watson and others (Ernest Nister, *c.*1910).

The nineteenth-century popularity of 'The White Cat' was not confined to print: the story was utilised as the basis of theatrical entertainment as early as 1811, when the new comic pantomime *The White Cat: or, Harlequin in the Fairy Wood* was presented at the Lyceum Theatre in London. Pictures published by W. West at his Theatrical Print Warehouse depict a strangely draped female figure with the head of a cat and underneath the caption 'ARBORELLA (Genius of Fairy Wood partially Transformed by an evil Genius, to the White Cat)'.[17] As was usual in such early

---

17 Reproduced in Raymond Mander and Joe Mitchenson, *Pantomime: A Study in Pictures* (London: Peter Davies, 1973), nos 52–5. See also David Powell, *William West and*

pantomimes, the emphasis was on the entertainment provided by the harlequinade rather than by the preceding scenes about the White Cat.

During the 1840s and 1850s James Robinson Planché (1796–1880), one of the great names in Victorian theatre, wrote a considerable number of Christmas entertainments that he called extravaganzas.[18] The term was used to distinguish 'the whimsical treatment of a poetical subject from the broad caricature of a tragedy or serious opera, which was correctly described as a burlesque'.[19] Many were based on fairytales by Madame d'Aulnoy, and an early one was *The White Cat*, performed at Covent Garden under the management of Madame Vestris in the 1841–42 season. The next dozen or so years saw a similar kind of Christmas pantomime each year based on a tale by d'Aulnoy. The Haymarket Theatre staged *The Fair One with the Golden Locks* (1843), *Graciosa and Percinet* (1844), *The Bee and the Orange Tree* (1845) and *The Invisible Prince* (1846). Then came productions at the Lyceum: *The Golden Branch* (1847), *The King of the Peacocks* (1848), *King Charming: or, the Blue-Bird of Paradise* (1850), *Once Upon a Time There Were Two Kings*, which was based on 'La Princesse Carpillon' (1853). The series was rounded off with *The Yellow Dwarf* (1854) at the Olympic Theatre.[20] Another pantomime called *Harlequin and the White Cat* was performed at Drury Lane in 1877. A different pantomime called *The White Cat*, written and invented by J. Hickory Wood and Arthur Collins, entertained the public in 1904.[21] After this the theme seems to have disappeared as a pantomime subject.

Clearly, in the middle of the nineteenth century many individual tales of Madame d'Aulnoy's were well known in outline, although knowledge of her authorship and of the peculiar quality of her original writing was entirely lacking. From having been designed for a refined adult readership her tales, adapted and simplified, had become the province of children. In 1855, however, the situation was completely changed as Planché, enthused by the success of his Christmas extravaganzas, published a new translation entitled *Fairy Tales by the Countess d'Aulnoy* (G. Routledge and Co., 1855). The volume was illustrated by John Gilbert (1817–97) and carried on the title page the severe message 'This Translation is Copyright'. Planché did not translate all of d'Aulnoy's fairy tales: he excluded 'Le Prince Marcassin' and 'Le Dauphin', explaining that 'though not wanting in merit, as far as fancy and humour are concerned, [they] could not, without considerable alterations in their details, have been rendered unobjectionable to the English reader'.[22] These two tales are examples of the animal bridegroom story and were plainly too sexually explicit for the translator's taste.

---

the Regency Toy Theatre (London: Sir John Soane's Museum, 2004), p. 58.

18 T.F.P. Croker and S. Tucker (ed.), *The Extravaganzas of J.R. Planché* (5 vols, London: S. French, 1879).

19 J.R. Planché, *Recollections and Reflections* (2 vols, London: Tinsley Brothers, 1872), vol. II, pp. 43–4.

20 Ibid., pp. 43, 67, 132, 135, 147–8, 153–4.

21 Mander and Mitchenson, *Pantomime*, illustration no. 104, p. 48 and endpapers.

22 *Fairy Tales by the Countess d'Aulnoy*, trans. J.R. Planché (London: G. Routledge and Co., 1855), Preface, pp. xi–xii.

'The White Cat' is, of course, an animal bride story, but as it does not contain any hint of sexual congress between animal and human it remains entirely within the bounds of Victorian propriety. Planché's careful translation made Madame d'Aulnoy's story available once more in its original character, complete with literary allusions and verses; he also appended notes. The translation was reissued in a new format in 1888 and reprinted in 1893 and 1894. Twelve colour plates were created on the basis of John Gilbert's black and white illustrations, to which were added a further 60 by Gordon Browne (1858–1932). The colour plate for 'The White Cat' depicts the princess with her parrot Perroquet and dog Toutou in the room in the tower where she is imprisoned. On the table behind her stands the fairy Violente in grim remonstrating mood. This story in particular offers a multitude of possibilities for illustration, but curiously enough Browne, in his five black and white drawings, avoids depicting the world of cats except in one that shows the veiled White Cat next to the portrait that exactly resembles the prince so intently looking at it. This is quite the opposite of J.W.'s lithographs for the Blackwood edition, which revel in depicting all manner of cats.

While editions of Planché's translation occupied centre stage from 1855 to 1894, the story of 'The White Cat', naturally much abridged, was issued several times in toy book format with illustrations in full colour. It was published by Routledge in 1868 as no. 46 in 'Aunt Mavor's Toy Books', in 1870 as no. 47 in 'Routledge's Shilling Toy Books' and as no. 27 in an advertisement of 1872. An edition illustrated by Kate Greenaway appeared as no. 19 in 'Nursery Toy Books', published by the Edinburgh firm of Gall and Inglis.[23] These colour-printed toy books were the product of technical developments in colour-printing now being transferred to the ever-growing market for attractive books for children. They were, however, more fragile than case-bound books and have not survived as well. The popularity of 'The White Cat' among children's tales and rhymes is further attested by an allusion to it in 'The Golden A.B.C.' printed in *The Golden Playbook*, illustrated by Alfred J. Johnson (Frederick Warne and Co., 1886). Alphabet books are not noted for the brilliance of their lines, and these do no more than sum up the climax of the story:

W is White Cat, whom a Fairy spell
Bound in that shape for a long time to dwell;
When the Prince, at her wish, cut off her head,
A lovely young Princess he saw instead.

Planché's translation was the standard version of Madame d'Aulnoy for the second half of the nineteenth century, but it acquired competition in the last decade from a new translation by Miss Annie Macdonell and Miss Lee with an introduction by Anne Thackeray Ritchie and illustrations by Clinton Peters (Lawrence and Bullen, 1892). Ritchie's introduction is blissfully ignorant of Planché and declares robustly (but erroneously) that d'Aulnoy's stories are 'here once more, after a century or

---

23 For the Routledge toy books see Tomoko Masaki, *A History of Victorian Popular Picture Books* (2 vols, Tokyo: Kazamashoto, 2006). Göte Klingberg, *Denna lilla gris går til torget* (Stockholm: Rabén and Sjögren, 1987), pp. 137, 143–4, 162–4.

so, presented in a new form to the present generation of children'. She dwells at length on Madame d'Aulnoy's biography and her acquaintance with Spain, but has next to nothing to say about the fairy tales. Ritchie's reputation, however, counted more with the publishers on the title page than did the names of the translators, who extended Planché's coverage by adding 'Prince Marcassin' and 'The Dolphin'. The monochrome illustrations are taken from watercolours and reflect a more modern style than those by Gilbert.

There have been no further translations of the full corpus of Madame d'Aulnoy's fairy tales, but two selections were made in the course of the twentieth century. The first was *The White Cat and Other Old French Fairy Tales*, by Mme La Comtesse d'Aulnoy, arranged by Rachel Field and drawn by E. MacKinstry (New York: The Macmillan Company, 1928; reissued 1967). In addition to 'The White Cat' it included 'Graciosa and Percinet', 'The Pot of Carnations' ('Fortunée'), 'Prince Sprite' and 'The Good Little Mouse'. The text used was Planché's, arranged and abridged by Rachel Field. In the introduction Planché is wrongly described as a Frenchman, and his translation is wrongly attributed to the 1860s. The book is attractively illustrated, mainly in black and white, but with six pages in full colour. For the most part they have the character of decorations rather than more complex pictures.

The second collection came just after the Second World War. It too is not a new translation but a retelling of nine tales. *The Hind in the Forest (and Other Tales by the Comtesse d'Aulnoy)*, retold by Hilda Mary McGill (Roger Ingram, 1950, reprinted 1951) includes 'The White Cat' as its second item. Without changing the basic plot this is quite the most engagingly independent version of Madame d'Aulnoy's fairy tale. For example, Hilda McGill tells her readers that the youngest prince in his search for a dog to please his father 'soon learned that the prettiest dogs were quite stupid, while the clever ones, who could do the best tricks, were for the most part lop-eared, cross-eyed, or of no known breed.'[24] In d'Aulnoy's original the White Cat assures the doubtful prince that his food is prepared quite separately from that destined for the cats. Not so in McGill's retelling. The prince cannot bring himself to eat a fricassée of mice, nor a pie of small birds served with beak and claw. The White Cat is perplexed and comments: '"Doubtless the human tongue is less accustomed to delicacy than the cat's."'[25] She regards the prince's refusal of the food as a discourtesy. Later on her feline character is underlined when she admits that 'she slept by day for preference'. She is surprised at the nature of the quest that the king has set his sons and says 'doubtfully, "if there is such a thing in the world as a clever dog, and pretty too, I will find it for you, and none better. If the King your father is taken by the cleverness of a dog he must be sillier than I thought."'[26]

Similar sardonic touches enliven the rest of the narrative and make the story delightfully readable for a twentieth-century audience. At the end of the story the king not only remains on his throne, but actually also remarries 'and added to the cares of a kingdom the responsibilities of a wife and growing family, so that he had

---

24 *The Hind in the Forest (and Other Tales by the Comtesse d'Aulnoy)*, retold by Hilda Mary McGill (London: Roger Ingram, 1950, repr. 1951), pp. 51–2.

25 Ibid., p. 54

26 Ibid., p. 58.

no time to worry lest anyone wanted to rule in his place'.[27] Many of the other versions of the story dispense with the moral with which Madame d'Aulnoy concludes her tale in the original, so it is a pleasure to encounter Hilda McGill's witty invention:

The cat a lady? You'll agree
That ladies may be cats, and often are.
But who is this most admirable She
Who works her feline magic from afar?

A Princess in disguise? Just so
Does my Serena look, a petalled paw
Half white, half rosy, to her cheek of snow
In mock submission to some ancient Law.

The cat a lady? Nothing less
Than an enchanted, exquisite Princess,
Whose altered form reveals another grace
A cat-like beauty in her human face.

Or cat or lady, take your choice,
For both bring th'occasion to rejoice,
He whom a cat or woman loves may hold
Himself as lucky as the Prince of old.[28]

Other retellings of 'The White Cat' mainly content themselves with abbreviating the story and excising Madame d'Aulnoy's allusive passages, so McGill's humorous comments and additions are quite refreshing.

The inclusion of individual tales by Madame d'Aulnoy in anthologies of fairy tales began in the nineteenth century, but with reprints many continued into the twentieth. 'The White Cat' figured along with six more of her tales in *The Fairy Book* by Dinah Maria Mulock/Craik (Macmillan and Co., 1863), which was reprinted until at least 1923 (with an edition in the 'Facsimile Classics' series in 1979). Andrew Lang (1844–1912) included 'The White Cat' in *The Blue Fairy Book* (Longmans, Green and Co., 1889; much reprinted), the first of his 'colour' fairy tale collections. 'The White Cat' and 'The Yellow Dwarf' had formed part of his own childhood reading.[29] Similarly, both stories plus two more by d'Aulnoy appeared in *A Book of Fairy Tales* retold by Sabine Baring Gould (Methuen and Company, 1894; reprinted 1895). Eleven of her tales, including 'The White Cat', were incorporated into Mrs Valentine's *The Old Old Fairy Tales* (Frederick Warne and Co., 1890), while a retelling of 'The White Cat' crept into E. Nesbit's *The Old Nursery Stories* (Henry Froude and Hodder and Stoughton, 1908) as the only representative of her talent. Nesbit's collection was reprinted as late as 1975, with illustrations by Faith Jaques.

---

27 Ibid., p. 78.
28 Ibid., p. 79.
29 Roger Lancelyn Green, *Andrew Lang: A Critical Biography* (Leicester: Edmund Ward, 1946), p. 8.

D'Aulnoy is not well represented in anthologies of fairy tales from the mid twentieth century, which tend either to concentrate on Perrault, the Grimms, Andersen and traditional English tales or to expand their interest to fairy tales and folktales from around the world. Either way d'Aulnoy disappears. The only collection in which I have found 'The White Cat' is M. C. Carey's *Fairy Tales of Long Ago* (J.M. Dent and Sons; New York: E.P. Dutton and Co., 1952), which contains, in addition, 'The Fair One with the Golden Hair'. Other tales occasionally crop up elsewhere, for example, in annuals, but Madame d'Aulnoy's position as a leading fairy tale author was, by this time, on the wane.

The 1967 reissue of Rachel Field's edition of *The White Cat and Other Old French Fairy Tales* possibly prompted two separate editions of 'The White Cat'. With each one, the focus was illustration. The first, *The White Cat by Madame la Comtesse d'Aulnoy 1682* (Dean and Son, 1972) was illustrated by Janet and Anne Grahame Johnstone in typically entertaining manner. The lively, neatly observed figures are set off, mainly in profile, against clear backgrounds. The cats, in their skilful combination of human and animal features, owe much to Louis Wain and nothing at all to Beatrix Potter. The overall effect is of a reassuring theatricality executed in a style the Johnstone twins take for granted. Where '1682' comes from in connexion with Madame d'Aulnoy is a mystery, as 'La Chatte blanche' was not published until 1698. This Dean and Son publication is a studiously traditional production, designed to attract, but not surprise.

By contrast, *The White Cat*, retold and illustrated by Errol Le Cain (Faber and Faber, 1973) is more individual in every way. The illustrations are subtle in colouring, varied in mood and elegantly composed. They capture the oddity of Madame d'Aulnoy's story with a mixture of sophisticated décor, mystery and cartoon-like humour. Le Cain does not take d'Aulnoy's story as an unalterable datum: he adapts and rewrites it to suit his own purpose. So while the Dean and Son version has the king require his sons to find 'the prettiest, tiniest dog they can', Le Cain changes this to 'the cleverest dog in the world'. Moreover, in the crowded scene he paints where the king towers imperiously at the left, there is a jester at the king's feet and a small white cat in the bottom right-hand corner. The Dean and Son version, like the traditional text, ignores the adventures of the older two princes. By contrast, Le Cain provides his readers with a complex picture divided with two diagonals into four, in which the king, at the top, observes his eldest son bowing to a group of court ladies, his middle son going off to sea and his youngest setting off for the enchanted forest. On succeeding pages we have an old-fashioned city street scene with lots of dogs, a ship at sea crammed with dogs and, finally, the youngest prince approaching a cat-shaped house in an eerie forest where animals, reptiles, birds, snails and other creatures, but never a dog, are to be found. The White Cat gives the prince a golden egg (not an acorn), out of which a tiny dog springs: 'He danced, he juggled, he brought tiny rabbits out of his tiny hat, and finally he bowed to the king.' All of this is illustrated with delicate wit. The search for a fabric that can pass through the eye of a needle is omitted, but further pictures delineate the three princes' female conquests. The White Cat appears as the youngest son's bride, but he is not required to cut off her head and tail. Instead, when he says, 'I know she is a cat, Father, but I want her to be my wife,' she flings back her fur and reveals herself as a woman, being immediately accepted as a queen. The White Cat's own story is entirely eliminated. The delight of the book rests in Le Cain's meticulously composed illustrations. He has simplified Madame d'Aulnoy's story ruthlessly, altering aspects of it and adding details of his own. The pictures expand Le Cain's own text and are full of surprises. The result is an inventive re-creation that coheres beautifully.

Around the same time John Lawrence produced a lively version of 'La Princesse Rosette' with the title *The King of the Peacocks* (Hamish Hamilton, 1970). Lawrence's inspiration was a chapbook version of the tale with this title, but neither he nor his publisher knew that it was an abridgement of a tale by Madame d'Aulnoy. In the same year there appeared *The Bluebird*, adapted by Jan Vladislav and illustrated by Mirko Hanak (Hamlyn, 1970). Like many other children's books of this period, it originated with Artia of Prague and is a fine example of their skilfully illustrated and designed productions. More recently, 'The White Cat' resurfaced in a luxurious American version entitled *The White Cat: An Old French Fairy Tale*, by Robert D. San Souci (New York: Orchard Press, 1990; reprinted 2000).

At this juncture we need to ask ourselves why 'The White Cat' has proved to be the most appealing of Madame d'Aulnoy's fairy tales in English over such an extensive period. The only tale that rivals it in popularity is 'The Yellow Dwarf', which contains some rather more threatening features and actually concludes with the death of the King of the Gold Mines, the husband desired by the story's heroine, at the hands of the odious Yellow Dwarf. 'The White Cat', by contrast, is a reassuring story, which follows the traditional fairy tale pattern and ends with a happy marriage. In its focus on cats and dogs it seems calculated to appeal to its audience's love of pets. The White Cat is attractive, gentle, generous and powerful, with a knowledge and understanding that surpasses that of human beings. Her whiteness symbolises her purity. It is hardly surprising that the prince declares after his second year spent with her: "'Lovely White Cat … I own I am so penetrated with your beauty, that if you will give your consent, I will prefer passing my days with you before all the grandeur I may promise myself elsewhere.'"[30] The prince's feelings towards the White Cat are analogous to those of Beauty towards the Beast in Madame Leprince de Beaumont's classic version of the animal bridegroom story, but they are more tender since there is nothing to fear in this charming cat. The prince's only trauma is having to kill the animal he loves in order to win his bride.

The White Cat's own story is an appendix to the tale, and some later versions of Madame d'Aulnoy's fairy tale reduce its importance, truncate or entirely omit it. It explains how the White Cat came to be enchanted, but it is not really essential for an understanding of the king's testing of his three sons. However, it is a typical example of Madame d'Aulnoy's tales of young women threatened by the prospect of marriage to an odious partner. In this case it is the dwarf king Migonnet, and one can't help suspecting that he is a literary embodiment of d'Aulnoy's own hated husband. This second part of 'The White Cat' displays more of the author's sado-masochistic imagination and penchant for the grotesque, but kept within bounds. What appears in the first part shows her imagination in full flight, but engendering feelings of wonder rather than of fear. She keeps closely to the traditional structure

---

30 *Fairy Tales and Novels*, I, pp. 268–9.

of fairytale, controlling the desire to subvert that she often expresses in other tales. The displays of pain and suffering that are prominent in other tales, together with projections of almost uncontrollable hate and anger on to would-be powerful male figures (though the fairies are bad enough), play the smallest role in this story. The result is that 'The White Cat' is a happy story. That lies at the root of its popularity.

Over a period of about 300 years the readership for Madame d'Aulnoy's fairy tales in English has changed considerably, and their textual presentation has varied accordingly. The original public consisted of aristocratic and middle-class adults and their educated children, with a preponderance of female readers. For much of the eighteenth century, they were well provided for, but by around 1770 the audience began to expand and change. Selections and adaptations were made for a younger, though still well-to-do readership, and individual tales entered the chapbook market in severely abridged, crude and cheap formats aimed at a broader, unsophisticated range of readers that included children as well as adults. 'The King of the Peacocks and the Princess Rosetta', along with 'Leander; or, the Blue Bird and the Princess Florina', formed the major part of *Fairy Stories*, a 24-page chapbook 'Printed and Sold in Aldermary Church-Yard, Bow Lane, London', which is listed in a catalogue dated 1764. From this period to the last quarter of the nineteenth century there are widely varying forms of Madame d'Aulnoy's tales available for different levels of readers. Her own name may not be printed on the title pages, but several of her stories circulated very widely.

J.R. Planché's translation of 1855 marks a return to the original form of her fairy tales and to a more or less complete corpus. It dominated the market for the rest of the nineteenth century and made an unabridged text available to the growing readership of children's books, brought about by the rapid increase of the population as well as higher standards of literacy. The translation by Misses Macdonell and Lee kept up this acquaintance with the more demanding original work. All the same, abridgements of individual tales in old and new forms continued to be published.

The twentieth century has seen a decline in the number of d'Aulnoy's tales included in selections and in general collections of fairy tales. Where they are known it is in abridged versions. This is almost certainly due to the belief that fairy tales are mainly the province of small children. One consequence of this belief is the increasing importance of illustrations over text. This can be seen much earlier in the splendid toy books illustrated in striking colour by Walter Crane for George Routledge and Sons. In 1875 he produced *The Yellow Dwarf*, *The Hind in the Wood* and *Princess Belle Etoile*, though Routledge's earlier versions of *The White Cat* had pictures by an anonymous illustrator. Twenty years later illustrations to 'The White Cat' were printed in *Favourite Fairy-Tales* in 'Books for the Bairns', no. 7 (September 1896), where every page has a black and white drawing to accompany the text. This is also the case with the Macmillan Company edition of 1928, which has stylish, well-designed illustrations by E. MacKinstry. By the mid century illustration has come to dominate, as in *The Fair One with the Golden Hair*, illustrated by Tom Kerr in the 'Perry Colour Books' edition of the early 1940s. The four books published in the early 1970s, illustrated by John Lawrence, Mirko Hanak, Janet and Anne Grahame Johnstone and Errol Le Cain, can together be taken as the high point of this trend.

Since that period attitudes towards fairy tales have changed direction again. Interest has turned to the history of fairy tales and the origins of many in the social and literary culture of France in the reign of Louis XIV. Iona and Peter Opie's *The Classic Fairy Tales* (Oxford University Press, 1974), in which they printed the earliest English texts of 24 well-known fairy tales, included most of Perrault's, five of the Grimms' and four of Andersen's, but of Madame d'Aulnoy they chose only 'The Yellow Dwarf'. Each of the tales was preceded by a concise bibliographical essay and accompanied by reproductions of illustrations to a variety of editions. Since then scholars have approached the subject of fairy tales from Marxist and feminist perspectives as well as using historical, sociological, psychological and literary methodologies. One of the most stimulating studies is Marina Warner's *From the Beast to the Blonde* (Chatto and Windus, 1994), which focuses particularly on the female storyteller and has much to say about the historical and literary context of the French fairy tale in the age of Louis XIV. It is thus not surprising that she edited a collection of six French literary fairy tales with the title *Wonder Tales* (Chatto and Windus, 1994), which included translations of Madame d'Aulnoy's 'The White Cat' and 'The Great Green Worm' ('Serpentin vert'). 'The White Cat' was elegantly translated by the American poet John Ashbery, 'The Great Green Worm' by the novelist A.S. Byatt. Jack Zipes, whose work has deeply influenced the cultural interpretation of fairy tales over the past three decades, had also translated this latter tale as 'Green Serpent' in his massive collection *Spells of Enchantment: The Wondrous Fairy Tales of Western Culture*.[31] It seems a fitting if, one might hope, a temporary conclusion to the fortunes of 'The White Cat' in English that we have here a return to beginnings and that Madame d'Aulnoy has at last regained the adult literary readership with which she started. Indeed, her combination of fantasy with critical irony and a deft, allusive style seem almost calculated to appeal to her postmodern readers.

---

31 Jack Zipes, *Spells of Enchantment: The Wondrous Fairy Tales of Western Culture* (New York: Viking, 1991).

Chapter 5

From Chapbooks to Pantomime

George Speaight with Brian Alderson[1]

This chapter is about the absorption into children's culture of a variety of traditional tales, myths, legends, *commedia dell'arte* characters, chivalric narratives and fairy stories, all important manifestations of popular culture in pre-industrial Britain. They reappeared in theatrical pantomimes, first staged in the eighteenth century, and still performed in twenty-first century Britain. And they reappeared in new kinds of children's literature which sprang up in the late eighteenth and nineteenth centuries, such as the 'harlequinade' and the children's chapbook. Some critics might call this 'remediation': the successive reconfiguration of particular texts in new formats and new media.[2] Others might see it as 'materialisation': the way in which orally transmitted narratives were given physical form as either performances or books. Or perhaps the process under discussion here is really 'commodification': the harnessing of tales freely circulating in popular culture to make money, either for theatrical impresarios or for the publishers of books and pamphlets. What is certain is that relatively little work has been undertaken either on the pantomime or on the children's books that developed alongside it.[3] But what lies at the heart of this chapter is the connection between popular culture and children's culture, and the ways in which a popular theatre, aimed at children, acted as a bridge between them.

By the early nineteenth century, at least in middle-class circles in England, the theatre was widely and enthusiastically followed. There were, though, no plays being written and produced especially for children. This is not to say that children

---

1   Parts of this chapter, in particular the sections dealing with harlequinades, were added or rewritten by Brian Alderson.

2   See J.D. Bolter and R. Grusin, *Remediation: Understanding New Media* (Cambridge, MA: MIT Press, 2000).

3   On the harlequinade, see Jacqueline Reid-Walsh, 'Pantomime, Harlequinades and Children in Late Eighteenth-Century Britain: Playing in the Text', *British Journal for Eighteenth-Century Studies*, special issue 'The Cultures of Childhood', ed. M.O. Grenby, 29 (2006), 413–25, and a brief discussion in Brian Alderson and Felix de Marez Oyens, *Be Merry and Wise: Origins of Children's Book Publishing in England, 1650–1850* (London: The British Library, and New Castle, DE: Oak Knoll Press, 2006), pp. 118ff. Pantomimes have recently begun to receive more attention, notably in John O'Brien's *Harlequin Britain: Pantomime and Entertainment, 1690–1760* (Baltimore, MD: Johns Hopkins University Press, 2004), which concentrates on the early eighteenth century, but examines the fascination of young London apprentices with the pantomime, as well as its socially subversive content. Other useful studies include David Mayer's *Harlequin in his Element: The English Pantomime, 1806–1836* (Cambridge, MA, Harvard University Press, 1969) and Allardyce Nicoll's *The World of Harlequin: A Critical Study of the Commedia Dell'Arte* (Cambridge: Cambridge University Press, 1963).

did not go to the theatre. Walter Scott saw a production of *As You Like It* at the age of four. Charles Lamb saw *Artaxerxes* at the age of six. Charles Dickens saw *Richard III* at the age of eight.[4] But there were also some productions which might have fitted children's tastes better than Shakespeare and Plutarch. In 1717, the manager of Drury Lane Theatre had the idea of presenting *The Loves of Venus and Adonis* as a mimed after-piece described as 'a new dramatic entertainment after the manner of the ancient pantomimes'. The idea caught on, largely under the influence of John Rich, who mimed the role of Harlequin with great effect from 1717 to 1760. These new pieces had titles like *The Necromancer, or Harlequin Doctor Faustus*, and *Harlequin Sorcerer, with the Loves of Pluto and Proserpine*, and *Perseus and Andromeda, or the Spaniards Outwitted*. It will be clear from these titles that the art had developed a great deal from the days of Ancient Greeks, on which they were, in theory, based. But as they were mimed without words and supported by beautiful scenery, pretty music and exciting stage effects, they could be enjoyed by children, even though they had not originally been composed with children in mind.

As the eighteenth century drew to a close, there were two developments in this kind of pantomime entertainment in England. First, simple dialogue was introduced, though this did not immediately play a predominant role in the pieces. Second, the idea of linking each play to a particular Greek legend was abandoned. But what was to be put in its place? At this point the characteristic feature of pantomime appeared. For what could be more suitable for plots than the great mass of folk tales, nursery rhymes, original mysteries, and traditional legends of every kind that had for centuries been told round the fire by grandmothers to wide-eyed grandchildren, and which were already part of popular culture, in print in chapbooks designed for children of the poor and barely literate? And so we find, before the end of the eighteenth century, an enormous number of variations on the Harlequin theme: from texts based on folk traditions, such as *Harlequin's Museum, or Mother Shipton Triumphant*, to texts founded on literary motifs, such as *Harlequin and Quixote, or the Magic Arm*, to texts based on topographical marvels, such as *The Wonders of Derbyshire, or Harlequin in the Peak*, or *The Witch of the Lakes, or Harlequin in the Hebrides*. The Harlequin character, lifted from the *commedia dell'arte*, was now dominating the English pantomime.[5]

But the English pantomime did not yet exist in any shape that later generations would have recognised. It did not come into being until after 1806, when Thomas Dibdin's *Harlequin and Mother Goose* was produced at Covent Garden Theatre with Joey Grimaldi in the role of Clown, or Pantaloon's partner. It was under Grimaldi's influence that the character of Clown was greatly developed and the pantomime evolved into two parts: the Opening, in which the bare bones of the story upon which the play was supposed to be based were presented; and the Harlequinade, in

---

4   George Speaight, *The History of the English Toy Theatre* (London: Studio Vista, 1969), pp. 90–1. For Lamb's account, see 'My First Play' (1821), Charles and Mary Lamb, *The Works of Charles and Mary Lamb*, ed. E.V. Lucas (7 vols, London: Methuen, 1903–5), vol. 2, pp. 97–100.

5   These titles are taken from the hand-list of plays in Allardyce Nicoll's *A History of Late Eighteenth Century Drama, 1750–1800* (Cambridge: Cambridge University Press, 1927).

which the chief characters of the Opening (sometimes played by the same actors and sometimes by fresh ones) were transformed by the Fairy Queen into Harlequin, Columbine, Pantaloon and Clown. There then ensued the chase, in which Pantaloon and his servant, Clown, usually chased after Columbine, Pantaloon's daughter, who had run away with Harlequin. Harlequin was provided with a 'bat', a kind of magic wand that could be used to change bits of scenery into something else, often with punning associations, as when a chimney pot was transformed into a chimney sweep or a bottle of blacking into a black woman. The chase took place before a rapid succession of scenes depicting familiar London backgrounds, but eventually concluding with the Fairy Queen blessing the union of Harlequin and Columbine.

The appeal of these theatrical interludes resulted in the first substantial attempt to exploit stage productions in print. The method adopted was that of the 'turn-up', more usually called the 'harlequinade' (see Figure 5.1). These little books were an adaptation of the nursery game of metamorphosis and can best be described as flap picture books. They were made from two sheets of paper, approximately 30 by 18 centimetres in size (12 by 7 inches) which were joined along the long edges, top and bottom. The upper leaf however had been cut once, horizontally, along its centre, and three times vertically, at equal intervals, so that four flaps at the top and four flaps at the bottom could be raised or lowered. Each sheet had initially been engraved with text and pictorial scenes, often hand-coloured, in such a way that the reader made his or her way through the narrative by raising and lowering the flaps of what could amount to 16 changing scenes. When the printing and colouring were complete, the double sheets were folded concertina-wise along the three vertical divisions and the whole was stitched into paper covers.[6] The rarity of surviving examples of these harlequinades cannot be taken as a reflection of their contemporary popularity, for their 'moveable' nature meant that they were delicate, and liable to be easily destroyed in the hands of an impatient child.

The first English publisher to produce a series of turn-ups for sale was Robert Sayer, a map and printseller of 53 Fleet Street, who launched his first effort round about 1766 with *Adam and Eve*, a work for which a much earlier published model already existed. In 1770, however, Sayer thought of a new source of subject matter for a turn-up book: pantomime. The transformations effected by Harlequin's bat were perfectly adapted for representation in the changing pictures. Thus, the fourth number in his turn-up series was a version of *Harlequin's Invasion*, the 'Christmas Gambol, after the manner of Italian Comedy' that Garrick had introduced at Drury Lane in 1759 (see Figure 5.1). It had remained a favourite piece with audiences, and ten performances had been staged by 1769.[7]

---

6   A facsimile of the turn-up *Mother Shipton*, issued in 1800 from plates originally engraved in 1771, was published by Toronto Public Library for the Friends of the Osborne and Lillian H. Smith Collections in 1980. Full-page digital images of another example, *Parnell's Hermit*, text by Thomas Parnell (London: Tabart and Co., 1810), are available online on the Hockliffe Project website: <http://www.cts.dmu.ac.uk/hockliffe/> (accessed 20 December 2007).

7   Copies are located in Britain at Cambridge University Library and the Museum of Childhood in Edinburgh. The original 'Gambol', of which – unusually – a manuscript text has been found, was not a pantomime in the full sense. It has been compared with Sayer's pictorial reduction in an article in George Speaight, 'Harlequin Turn-Ups', *Theatre Notebook* 45 (1991),

Figure 5.1   *Harlequin's Invasion: A New Pantomine [sic]* (London: Robert Sayer, 1770). Private collection.

Sayer went on to produce at least nine turn-ups based upon pantomimes or theatrical interludes. His example was quickly followed by competitors, who continued to produce these turn-ups for some 30 years. One of the last was the energetic Benjamin Tabart, who published half-a-dozen traceable to theatrical performances in 1809–10. Although such booklets can do no more than illustrate a handful of scenes from their sources, for the historian they provide otherwise irretrievable records of the appearance of stage scenery and costume, as well as

---

70–84, which shows how the publisher broadly followed the plot of the play but necessarily with much compression.

changes in fashion. Thus, the yokel who is Sayer's Clown in 1771 develops into a uniformed gentleman's servant as shown in I. Strutt's *Harlequin's Museum, or Mother Shipton Triumphant* in 1800.

In all this, what had happened to the traditional folk tales upon which the pantomime was supposed to be based? They were still there, although not always easily recognisable. A catalogue of chapbooks in print at the end of the eighteenth century lists 124 titles that were issued from the Aldermary and Bow churchyards, then centres of cheap publishing.[8] In this list there are 22 titles that seem to be related to stories we might still recognise as 'traditional': 'The Blind Beggar of Bethnal Green', 'Sir Bevis of Southampton', 'The History of the Seven Champions', 'Chevy Chase', 'The Children in the Wood', 'The Life of Robinson Crusoe', 'Dr. John Faustus', 'Moll Flanders', 'The Life and Death of St. George', 'The Travels of Captain Lemuel Gulliver', 'A True Tale of Robin Hood', 'The History of Jack Horner', 'Jack and the Giants', 'The Wandering Jew', 'Puss in Boots', 'Reynard the Fox', 'The Life and Death of Fair Rosamond', 'The History of Mother Shipton', 'The Life and Death of Jane Shore', 'The Sleeping Beauty in the Wood', 'The Famous History of Tom Thumb' and 'The History of Richard Whittington'. During the nineteenth century, pantomimes adapting such stories were enormously popular. They used traditional folk and fairy tales as a background upon which to paint an entertainment of magic, broad humour, music and dancing, references to public events and masses of changing scenery, concluding with the earthy comedy of the Harlequinade. In the process the original stories on which they were supposed to be built were almost completely lost. But without some kind of familiar story upon which to build, they could never have started.

Further signs of the influence of pantomime on the publishers of children's books begin to emerge during the first decades of the nineteenth century when the turn-up, in its declining years, was joined by a variety of entertaining picture books and nursery stories for children. In one instance at least a direct reference is present in a title: *The Ogre and Little Thumb; or The Seven League Boots. A Tale of Mother Goose. Now Performing as a Pantomime Ballet at the Theatre Royal, Covent Garden*, printed for John Harris in 1807. In fact, Harris's advertisements, along with those of Tabart too, often drew attention to the connection between their publications and that season's theatrical performances in London. As M.O. Grenby has noted, Tabart boasted that his *Cinderella; or The Little Glass Slipper* (1804) featured 'representations of three of the principal scenes in performance at Drury Lane Theatre'. Noticing the connection, Sarah Trimmer, in her censorious 1805 article on fairy tales in the *Guardian of Education*, deplored the fact that Tabart was bringing to child readers 'representations ... of play-house scenes'.[9] The cross-over from stage to page was evident in other ways too. Stage characters such as King Oberon, Queen Mab and Master Puck figure on the title page of the *Popular Fairy Tales*, edited by Benjamin Tabart for Richard Phillips (1818 – though many of the

---

8   These titles are taken from the appendix to John Ashton's *Chap-Books of the Eighteenth Century* (London: Chatto and Windus, 1882).

9   M.O. Grenby, 'Tame Fairies Make Good Teachers: The Popularity of Early British Fairy Tales', *Lion and the Unicorn* 30 (2006), 1–24.

tales anthologised here had already appeared in the early years of the century in Tabart's *Popular Stories* series). Harris similarly made reference to the theatre when he bound up his collection of fairy tales by Charles Perrault and Madame D'Aulnoy as *The Court of Oberon* (1823). The conversion of the prose tales into verse, as in Tabart's *Little Red Riding Hood* (1807) or Harris's *History of Mother Twaddle* (an early version of 'Jack and the Beanstalk', 1807), suggest connections to recitations and glees. The exploiting of comical magic tricks, as in Richard Scrafton Sharpe's *The Conjurer* (R. Dutton, 1808), also suggests a link to theatrical farce.

This period was also notable for the emergence of the do-it-yourself drama that established the tradition of toy theatre. The beginnings of this phenomenon lay in the trade in printed theatrical characters to be sold as adjuncts to performances (as were the turn-ups) but it did not take long for lively entrepreneurs to add the appendages of cut-out proscenium, scenery and play-books of the text, so that the characters could be provided with their proper settings. Probably the first publisher to produce a complete kit was William West of Exeter Street, London, and among his earliest complete sets was *Harlequin Jack and Jill*, based on the pantomime produced at the Lyceum in 1812.[10] The images in these toy theatre sheets provide some kind of visual record of the pantomimes that children would have enjoyed at the start of the nineteenth century, and it is not altogether fanciful to see a theatrical quality in many of the Regency picture books that exploited the folk tale medium. Just as many individual illustrations of fairy tale events, in, say, Tabart's *Popular Fairy Tales*, were, in effect, 'stills' from a pantomime performance, so stories set largely indoors, like *Old Mother Hubbard*, published by Harris in 1805, and her neighbour *Old Dame Trot*, by W. and T. Darton in *c.*1806, present a sequence of scenes almost as if the book itself were a stage.

Pantomime's penetration of the world of children's books, their composition and publication, could not help growing as the century progressed. On the one hand, the facilities for elaborate publishing projects developed. On the other, the nation was in thrall to all manner of theatrical performances alongside, and sometimes related to, pantomime: melodrama, grand guignol, burlesque, and music hall. In considering the children's books related to these entertainments, a significant division can be discerned: the separation of material into works that continue the tradition of cheerful or rumbustious anonymity, and those resulting in the enthusiasm of identifiable authors and illustrators. Among the first group the most prominent are the toy books – the cheap picture books – in which the popular themes found in many of the Regency 'chapbooks' are adapted for Victorian families. The format gradually alters from modest duodecimos to larger quartos and folios; hand-colouring gives way to colour printing, often of eye-boggling gaudiness; and typographical or line-printed covers develop into excursions in showmanship, whether pictorial or with ornate,

---

10 This subject has been dealt with at length in George Speaight, *The History of English Toy Theatre* (London: London Book Co., 1946). George Speaight, *The Juvenile Drama ... Comprising Holdings of Five Libraries or Museums in England and Three in America* (London: Society for Theatre Research, 1999), a union catalogue, lists some 58 titles of pantomimes that found their way into the juvenile drama.

decorative lettering, so that they might as easily be advertisements for theatrical publications as book bindings.

Many London publishers attempted to establish series of these offerings with what they hoped might be encouraging series titles: 'Aunt Mavor's Toy Books' (Routledge), 'Aunt Friendly's Series' (Warne), 'Fairy Fairstar's Cabinet of Gems' (Park), 'Uncle Buncle's Pictorial Books' (Dean), and so on. Pantomime elements were seldom far away. Thus, the 16-page *Sleeping Beauty* in 'Marks's Comic Nursery Tales' series (price sixpence) is told in doggerel quatrains:

> In the City of Norland, a fam'd place you must know,
> Liv'd a King and Queen, a long time ago;
> They quarrel'd all day, and at night could not rest,
> Because with an Heir they had not been blest.

Each page of verse is faced by a caricature picture, such as the Bad Fairy reading 'The Court Gazette', in a frame of printer's flowers, as though within a stage-setting.

Without doubt, the long-lived firm of Dean were the most prolific purveyors of comic toy-book series, to which they joined a varied array of moveable books which could be seen as the legitimate successors to the eighteenth-century turn-ups. Their 'Surprise Picture Books' were advertised as having 'wonderful Turn-up Corners, which transform One Picture into Fourteen or more at will'. These included, at number five in the series, *Clown and Pantaloon; Pantomimic Fun and Tricks*, priced at one shilling and sixpence in 'stout boarded covers'. Even more significant was the shilling series of 'Pantomime Toy Books': five titles with 'five set scenes and nine trick changes'. The centre spread of these books consisted of an ornate proscenium arch, with orchestra pit below, and within the arch was a series of differently sized flaps attached to the central hinge, producing a sequence of different scenes as the 'play' progressed. This play, in fact, has no script. All that the publisher provides is a re-telling of the story in couplets, followed by a prose version, so that the child reader would have to remember the events of the drama while turning the scenic flaps. Nevertheless, gestures are made towards tradition. The conclusion of *Aladdin*, for instance, reads:

> By magic the runaway building [was] brought down,
> And the wicked Magician was changed into CLOWN!
> Aladdin in HARLEQUIN's spangles that shine
> Like his jewels, leads on the Princess COLUMBINE!
> The King's PANTALOON! and the lamp a lime-light,
> And its Geni the most India-rubberish sprite!

The final scene shows them in their *commedia* costumes.

The hack artists and dogerellists responsible for these *jeux* are unknown to history. In the case of major toy-book series published by prominent firms like Nelson, Routledge, and Warne, authors and illustrators are sometimes named or can sometimes be identified through their appended monograms. Such a one was A.H. Forrester, who wrote and illustrated toy-book versions of fairy tales (not always free of moral injunctions) as 'Alfred Crowquill' and, occasionally, 'Baron Krakemsides'. According to the *Dictionary of National Biography* he was also involved in 'designs, devices and effects' for London pantomimes, and he may be seen as a representative of the *Punch* humorists, many of whom had a liking for burlesque. Among them was Charles H. Bennett, whose children's books are infused with a delight in farce and who was the illustrator of a picture-book version of another traditional entertainment deriving from *commedia*, *The Wonderful Drama of Punch and Judy* (London: H. Ingram and Co., 1854).

The author of the script for this little work, writing as 'Papernose Woodensconce', was Bennett's friend Robert Brough, who brought to his task both a love and knowledge of popular theatre and who here gives us perhaps the most authentic glimpse of *Punch* as performed by Victorian showmen. Nor was this the only evidence of Brough's playful reworking of comic performances. In his *Cracker Bon-Bon for Christmas Parties* (1852), for example, he includes three 'Christmas Pieces. Not all suited to the stage, but the very thing for the Front Drawing-room', which came complete with many caricature vignettes (probably by H.G. Hine, who supplied a handsome, hand-coloured comic frontispiece to the book). And Brough also produced 'a Dragon Story for Christmas' in *Ulf the Minstrel; or the Princess Diamonducks and the Hazel Fairy* (1859), which introduces into the genre of the invented fairy tale that satiric view of court life that was one of the staples of pantomime.[11]

Authorial ventures of this kind naturally differ in tone and substance from the free-wheeling inventions of the harlequinade and its successors, but their inspiration remained a continuing presence at the time when Victorian children's literature was emerging in all its imaginative diversity. The crucial example here is William Makepeace Thackeray's *The Rose and the Ring* of 1855, subtitled 'a fire-side pantomime for great and small children', and a work which surely stands godfather to fictions like *Ulf the Minstrel*. On the admission of Thackeray himself in his 'Prelude', the idea for *The Rose and the Ring* came from traditional Twelfth-Night festivities as much as from pantomime itself (the naming of characters is especially close to the naming of players at Twelfth-Night parties), but there can be no doubt of Thackeray's delight in the pantomime tradition, for he composed just such a thing in *Harlequin and Humpty Dumpty*, 'by E. Fitzball, author of "Za-Ze-Zi-Zo-Zu"', first performed at the Theatre Royal, Drury Lane, on 26 December 1850.

Rare though it is, this pantomime text signals the arrival of the 'official' publication of the substance of a Christmas pantomime, and hence firmer evidence than we have yet had as to what actually happened on stage (although there must have been plenty of opportunity for the players to add 'business' related to contemporary events, or to the known interests of the audience). Here then is an example of the structure of the mid century style – *Whittington and his Cat, or Harlequin Lord Mayor of London*, as performed at Sadlers Wells in London in 1853:

---

11 Peter Newbolt gives a welcome account of the Brough family and their place in the Bohemian milieu of mid Victorian London in his *William Tinsley (1831–1902), 'Speculative Publisher'* (Aldershot: Ashgate, 2001), especially pp. 21–8.

Scene 1. The Miss-managed abode of Miss-Fortune.

Miss-Fortune laments to her court that 'My throne to dust is tumbling / Our friend John Bull has given over grumbling.' To which her courtiers respond, 'But there's old Ireland, still, where once you reigned', to which Miss-Fortune replies, 'Ah, even Ireland is improved and drained.'

Scene 2. The Temple of Fortune, where Dame Fortune reigns.

Miss-Fortune asks, 'Then what do you propose to do this time?' To which Dame Fortune answers, 'To illustrate it in a pantomime.' Miss-Fortune asks, 'But for the subject?' Dame Fortune replies, 'I'll take care of that / We'll have our old friend Whittington and Cat.'

Scene 3. Outside of Fitzwarren's House, before which Dick Whittington collapses from exhaustion.

Scene 4. The Kitchen in Fitzwarren's House.

Dick is beaten and scolded by the Cook, but makes friends with Alice, the kitchen maid, and the Cat.

Scene 5. Fitzwarren's Counting House.

All the servants must invest something in a ship that is making a voyage. Fitzwarren asks Dick, 'And Whittington have you no goods to send?' Dick replies, 'I've nothing but this Cat, my only friend', which Fitzwarren advises him to send on the ship.

Scene 6. Highgate Hill, on which Dick falls asleep.

Dame Fortune leans over him, 'Sleep on Dick Whittington, and dreaming see / The wealth your Cat will soon bring back to thee.'

Scene 7. Interior of the Palace of Flibbidee Flobbodee.

Dinner is served, but rats swarm on to the table. Dick's Cat drives them off and eats them up. The King rewards him generously. 'Puss come to my arms – much is thy due for that: / Ten thousand killed! Long live the Cat!'

Scene 8. Highgate Hill.

Dick is discovered asleep. Dame Fortune leans over him. Bells ring and chorus sings, 'Turn again, Whittington, thrice Lord Mayor of London,' Dick wakes: 'I'm off at once! those bells shan't plead in vain. / For London ho! Richard's himself again.'

Scene 9. Exterior of Fitzwarren's House. A procession enters carrying the fortune Whittington's cat has earned for him. Fitzwarren, however, has other ideas:

> What all for Whittington? No sight but that,
> Besides it warn't your doing, 'twas the cat
> And now I think of it, that Cat must be
> My own Uncle Tom come back to me,
> So all those treasures are not yours but mine.

Scene 10. The Temple of Fortune. Dame Fortune speaks:

> Hold treacherous merchant, cease your petty spites,
> While Fortune gives to every one their rights.
> Dick Whittington to lead the chase begin
> And appear as magic Harlequin.

Whittington exits and re-appears as Harlequin.

> Fair Alice still shall share your fortune too,
> So now as Columbine appear to view.

Alice exits and re-appears as Columbine. Fitzwarren is changed into Pantaloon, the Cook to Clown, and the Cat to Sprite.

> Now then for fun – the path before you lies.
> Shoot as you run at folly as it flies.

Scene 11. Richard Whittington's Almshouses at Highgate.
Scene 12. A Fishmonger and Linendraper's shop.
Scene 13. Hardware and Confectioner's shop.
Scene 14. A Greengrocer's shop and Servant's Register Office.
Scene 15. An Emigration Office and Oil Shop.
Scene 16. End of the Cat's Tale.

Scene 17. The Temple of Fortune. Line-up of the characters. Chorus:
> The Christmas dish once more complete,
> Poor Puss for pardon sues;
> And trust that she each night may meet
> Kind friends to well amuse.

The Curtain to descend slowly.

One can see from this that by the mid nineteenth century, the pantomime had moved significantly nearer to what is today generally thought of as pantomime. However, the text and 'business' indicated in this synopsis still suggest a theatricality that was distantly in touch with the interludes of the eighteenth century. Few better examples of this cultural continuity could be found than John Hart's pantomime *Goody Two-Shoes*, written by J. Hickory Wood (a joke name, perhaps) and performed at the Theatre Royal, Bradford 'on Tuesday December 24th, 1907 at 7-15 and every evening until further notice'. Here, interestingly enough, the original story came not from folklore but from the famous didactic tale written for children in 1765. The heroine's name, however, had passed into a sort of folklore by the nineteenth century, and John Newbery, its original publisher and perhaps its author, would have had great difficulty in recognising his progeny. By 1907 Goody Two-Shoes was no longer the orphaned daughter of Farmer Meanwell but had become the child of the Baron Bounder. A text was published to go with the performance, complete with photographs of performers and production staff, and advertisements for anything from 'The Colonial Overstrung Piano' to Raven's Corsets ('2000 always in stock'). The 'book' has similar shortcomings to its eighteenth-century harlequinade counterparts. The plot is foolish, being merely a slack line on which to hang effects created by the actors. (The story, such as it is, is nearer to 'Cinderella' than John Newbery, with the heroine's two shoes – made by fairies to bring good luck – being stolen by a demon, who substitutes a pair that have the opposite result.) There are many references to the locality, to current Bradford events, often accompanied by puns ('my friend, Alderman Hartley says it won't be long, but I think it's *hartly* likely'; 'Where are the village maidens, from Horton Bank Top, strewing roses? Instead of roses the corporation have been strewing the path with their short weight coke'; etc., etc.); and there are numerous cues for the inclusion of current popular songs with notes on the copyright holders ('DUET – Jack and Baron. "Dinkey, Do! 22." Exclusive performing rights for Bradford secured from the publishers.') One must hope that Miss Lulu Valli, Mr Jack Pleasants, the Valdo Bros, *et al.*, were able to make something of this stuff.

And so the pantomime has continued to this day. In the process there have been many changes. It has become widely linked to Christmas (at least for commercial pantomime productions), whereas up to the 1840s it was popular at Easter and Whitsun as well; Principal Boys are now usually played by girls, and Dames by men; music hall and television stars took over the best parts from straight actors; the Harlequinades declined, and have now disappeared altogether; the rhyming couplets in which the stories used to be conveyed have now usually shrunk to a few lines in the opening scene; cricketers and pop stars and other 'celebrities' now turn up in totally irrelevant parts; the proportion of children in the audience has increased. Often parents now complain about what their children are being shown, but the pantomime is not, and has never been, an entertainment solely addressed to children. It is for all the family: a familiar nursery rhyme for the younger children, some smutty jokes for the parents and old-fashioned songs for the grandparents, the whole cobbled together with some circus tricks. There is nothing else like it, and it is not easily understood by those who have not been born and raised with it.

Despite the changes, pantomime continues to provide a genuine 'people's theatre', free from the narrow commercialism of West End management, presenting a loosely structured and partly extempore theatre, open to exploit any kind of contemporary satire and parody, deeply grounded in native traditions, reflecting the legends of childhood, full of fun and colour and jolly songs that the audience can join in. And all this sprang from traditional stories. The connections between pantomime and popular literature are now more stretched than they were in the late eighteenth and early nineteenth centuries. But it is clear that it was only the absorption of popular stories into children's commodity culture – their books, their games, their theatre – that has enabled the popular culture of early modern Britain to survive today at all.

PART II
Forgotten Favourites

Introduction

Julia Briggs

The history of children's literature is strewn with forgotten favourites; they moulder in attics because we cannot bear to throw them away. Who today has heard of *Marigold in Godmother's House* (1934) by Joyce Lankester Brisley (remembered, if at all, for the adventures of 'Milly-Molly-Mandy'), yet for me it opened magic casements.[1] It is difficult to overestimate the imaginative hold of our earliest reading, and impossible to reduplicate its impact, though parents so often try. Copies of the best-loved early children's books are now notoriously rare, because they were so often 'read to death'. A typical example might be William Godwin's *Bible Stories*, written under the pseudonym William Scolfield, and published in 1802. Of this, as William St Clair has observed, 'no copy has been found in any library in Britain nor any copy of the original edition'. Single copies of a later edition have survived, but only the first volume (there were two), one in the United States and one in Britain. And this is despite the fact that 'The book was evidently a commercial success', it 'was still being advertised in London in 1828', and it was in print until 1831.[2] Another popular and rather better-known children's book (by title, at least), suffered a similar fate: John Newbery's *History of Little Goody Two-Shoes*, of which the first edition of 1765 exists in a single copy in the British Library.[3] Presumably, the rarity of these two books results from the pleasure they gave their earliest readers. Today, some surviving Puffin books are far rarer (and thus more highly valued) than their hardback equivalents.

Goody Two-Shoes reflects mid eighteenth-century attitudes in a number of ways. As well as recommending rational and sceptical views of old superstitions, it illustrates self-help through literacy, and thus contributes to Newbery's wider project, to persuade children of the value and pleasure of reading. It is highly didactic in the most literal sense, for not only does the narrative show how the abandoned orphan Margery Meanwell (also known as Goody Two-Shoes) learned to read, and then put her reading to use in teaching others, but the book itself can be used as a 'teach-yourself-to-read' manual, providing an alphabet, then lists of letters to be identified, followed by short words and phrases, and building up to complete sentences: 'Now, pray little Reader, take this Bodkin, and see if you can point out the Letters from these mixed Alphabets, and tell how they should be placed as well as little Boy

---

1   It also did so, apparently, for Primrose Lockwood: see her 'Centenary Celebration' of Brisley in the *Children's Books History Society Newsletter,* 56 (1966), 15–16.

2   William St Clair, 'William Godwin as Children's Bookseller', in Gillian Avery and Julia Briggs (eds), *Children and Their Books: A Celebration of the Work of Iona and Peter Opie* (Oxford: Clarendon Press, 1989), pp. 165–79 (p. 168).

3   See F.J. Harvey Darton, *Children's Books in England: Five Centuries of Social Life*, 3rd edn, rev. Brian Alderson (Cambridge: Cambridge University Press, 1982), pp. 131–2.

Billy.'[4] At the same time, its plot is a variant on the theme of 'Cinderella', or even of Richardson's *Pamela* (1740), where the heroine rises in society through her own virtues, skills and efforts, winning respect and financial independence – and not merely through marriage. *Goody Two-Shoes* was often reprinted (though later editions omitted the opening critique of social injustice) and further adventures were invented for Margery's brother Tommy. Like several of the children's authors discussed in this section, it retained its popularity for a number of generations, but did not quite achieve a permanent niche among the classics (though it enjoyed a curious afterlife in pantomime – in the early 1950s it was still being staged with Arthur Askey in drag and the Dagenham Girl Pipers). And though Margery's story is forgotten today, tales of magic makeovers and self-transformations are more popular than ever on television.

This process of slow decline also applies to other forgotten favourites, so that, while individual writers may go out of fashion, the particular formula or genre they opened up is often reworked by a later generation of writers. As Dennis Butts explains in Chapter 6, Barbara Hofland was particularly enjoyed for her stories of family life, a genre that increased in popularity during the nineteenth century. Examples include *Little Women* (1868) and *What Katie Did* (1872) in the United States, and *The Daisy Chain* (1856), and the family stories of Mrs Ewing, Mrs Molesworth and E. Nesbit in Britain. Family stories achieved their greatest popularity when families were large and (middle-class) family life was idealised, and regarded as a crucial source of moral education. As Butts shows, Hofland's work was regularly reprinted until the end of the nineteenth century, though it is largely forgotten today.

One of Hofland's successes was *The Young Crusoe* (1828), part of the prolific and continuous history of adaptations of Defoe's *Robinson Crusoe* (1719), which, like Swift's *Gulliver's Travels* (1726), had been abridged and adapted for children almost as soon as it was published.[5] These and old folktales such as 'Jack the Giant Killer', provide the roots of boys' adventure stories, a well-established genre when G.A. Henty, a former soldier and journalist, took it up and made it his own. Henty despatched his boy heroes to exciting locations, at exciting moments in history, in a steady stream of books for boys, written to encourage them to advance and defend the power of Victoria's empire – a purpose he shared with public schools like Thomas Arnold's Rugby (the subject of *Tom Brown's Schooldays*) or the United Services College at Westward Ho! (Rudyard Kipling's old school, featured in *Stalky & Co.*). As Butts demonstrates in Chapter 8, Henty wrote to a formula in which the young hero's manly virtues always won the day, and British superiority over foreigners was maintained, justifying the colonial enterprise and promoting its continuance. Recently, Henty's work has begun to be reprinted in digital form in

---

4   *The Renowned History of Little Goody Two-Shoes*, a facsimile of the 1766 edition, introduced by Charles Welsh (London: Griffith and Farran, 1881), p. 31. See Patricia Crain, 'Spectral Literacy: The Case of *Goody Two-Shoes*', in Andrea Immel and Michael Whitmore (eds), Childhood and Children's Books in Early Modern Europe, 1550–1800 (New York and Abingdon: Routledge, 2006), 213–42.

5   See Darton, *Children's Books in England*, pp. 106–7.

the United States, in part for its endorsement of precisely those values that make it suspect for many modern readers.

Where Henty's work focuses on courage and self-discipline, Angela Brazil rejoices in high spirits and 'giggling in the shrubbery' (the title of Arthur Marshall's 1985 book on stories for girls). Like the boy's adventure story, the school story has a long history, going back to Sarah Fielding's *The Governess or, Little Female Academy* (1749), and forward to Harry Potter's adventures at Hogwarts Academy. School stories play out the difficult process of socialisation, reflecting the desire to make friends and be valued within a community, at a stage when, for some readers, social interaction may be problematic or even painful. As Judy Simons shows, Brazil gave the form a new currency by celebrating the disruptive energy of her 'madcaps', and the pleasure of belonging to a coterie.

Hofland, Henty and Brazil have their modern equivalents, but the type of novel that Hesba Stretton was writing has lost currency, for it was a product of a particular moment of social history: Victorian London was a city of unwanted children, who played or struggled to find work, roaming ragged and barefoot through the streets. Several high-minded writers, among them Charles Dickens, felt it their duty to publicise the appalling circumstances in which such children lived. Evangelical writing aimed to acquaint its middle-class readers with the plight of London's outcast children, its waifs and 'street arabs'. Maria Charlesworth's much derided *Ministering Children* (1854) represents children as more responsive to mute suffering than adults, and within her novel, they form an underground society in which each does what she can to relieve the suffering of others. Though this may sound dull and pious, it evidently appealed to the idealism of its earliest readers, imaginatively empowering them by representing them as morally superior to adults.

Hesba Stretton gained popularity through her sharply observed stories of destitute children, and the power of their innocence in a corrupt adult world. She made it her business to find out about the lives of the very poor, and vividly imagined what it felt like to be cold, hungry and friendless. As Elaine Lomax shows, she used fiction to extend her readers' social sympathies. So, while Hofland idealised the family life that was a part of most middle-class readers' experience, and Henty and Brazil took their readers to imaginary worlds (the heroism of empire, the high jinks of school), Stretton used her fiction to expose the bleak lives of children at the bottom of society. When we have made allowances for the distribution of her books through Sunday school and other such groups (a popularity imposed, one might say), it remains a measure of her courage and imaginative power that she created so wide a readership for her tales.

Chapter 6

Finding and Sustaining a Popular Appeal: The Case of Barbara Hofland

Dennis Butts

Barbara Hofland (1770–1844) is a classic example of a woman writing in the early years of the nineteenth century – what Ellen Moers has called the 'Epic Age of Women's Literature' – who turned to a career as a professional writer partly for intellectual satisfaction, but mostly in pursuit of economic security.[1] At its best, her work provides genuine insights into family life, work and moral character, and those skills give her a real, if limited, individuality among the numerous writers for children at the beginning of the nineteenth century. This chapter argues that her biography reveals a remarkable series of attempts to re-invent herself as a popular writer as her career developed and her sales fluctuated. Mrs Hofland is the consummate example of an early children's writer, first finding and then struggling to sustain her popular appeal through a variety of forms and genres.

The vicissitudes of Mrs Hofland's long, hard and ultimately heroic life were largely responsible for this. She was born Barbara Wreaks in Sheffield in 1770, the daughter of an ironmonger who died when she was three, leaving his widow to bring up Barbara and a younger brother. To judge from the use of quotations in her books, she seems to have acquired some kind of education, for she was well-acquainted with the Bible, Shakespeare and many of the English poets, and had some knowledge of geography and history.

A lively and talented young woman, Hofland began by writing decorous eighteenth-century verse, which first appeared in the pages of the new Sheffield newspaper the *Iris* in 1794. But these were turbulent times, and it is a tribute to Hofland's liberal sympathies and courage that when James Montgomery, the editor of the *Iris*, was imprisoned in 1795 for publishing an allegedly seditious libel, she published a sonnet in praise of his defence lawyer.

In 1796 Hofland married a prosperous businessman, Thomas Hoole. A baby daughter was born and a period of great happiness ensued. But tragedy was never far away. The baby died in 1798 and Hoole himself died in 1799, leaving his widow to bring up a son aged only four months. To make matters worse, Hoole's business collapsed shortly after his death, and money left to his son was also lost when Hoole's trustees became insolvent.

But Hofland was nothing if not resilient. Throughout her marriage she had continued to write poetry, and encouraged by James Montgomery she now collected together her best verses and published them in a volume to be sold by subscription at six shillings a copy. With the help of advertising in the *Iris*, Barbara Hoole's *Poems*,

---

1   See Ellen Moers, *Literary Women* (London: The Women's Press, 1980), pp. 13–41.

published in 1805, sold over 2,000 copies. Such remarkable sales figures were perhaps more of a tribute to the young widow's personal history than to the quality of her poetry. Today, her verses sound disappointingly conventional and pedestrian.

With money raised from the sales of her book, Mrs Hoole was able to send her son Frederick to a Moravian school and also to open her own girls' boarding school in Harrogate. Encouraged by the success of the *Poems*, she continued writing and produced her first children's tale, *The History of an Officer's Widow*. John Harris, London's leading publisher of children's books, paid her £6 for it, bringing it out in 1809, the year that the Harrogate school opened.

Other children's books soon followed. So too did a handsome suitor in the person of Thomas Christopher Hofland, a talented but impecunious landscape artist, who met Mrs Hoole when poverty forced him to teach art. Though her friends had doubts about the match, there was no doubt about Thomas Hofland's ability. He had exhibited at the Royal Academy since 1798. Barbara Hoole fell deeply in love with this attractive and engaging artist, and they were married in 1810.

At first all went well. Hofland showed his paintings at various exhibitions and his wife's writing developed. But the school proved a disappointment, not only because of its many difficult pupils but because of their parents' reluctance to pay the fees. Even more worrying was the state of Mr Hofland's health. He was ill in January, and again in March 1811. He and his wife decided to make a fresh start elsewhere. In November 1811 they sold up in Harrogate and before the year was out had settled in London.

Again, all went well initially. Hofland exhibited regularly at the Royal Academy and his picture 'A Storm at Scarborough' won a 100-guinea prize awarded by the Royal Institution. Mrs Hofland's career also prospered. Her moral tale for children, *The Daughter-in-Law* (1812), so impressed Queen Charlotte that she gave Mrs Hofland permission to dedicate her next book, *A Visit to London* (1814), to her. *The Son of a Genius*, first published in 1812 and Hofland's most successful book overall, quickly became extremely popular, reaching a tenth edition by 1826. She made friends with various celebrities, including the architect John Soane and fellow writers Maria Edgeworth and Mary Mitford.

In *The Son of a Genius* Mrs Hofland told the story of a talented but imprudent artist who wasted his gifts and almost ruined the lives of his wife and children through his erratic and unstable temperament. Reading it, it is difficult not to suspect that Mrs Hofland was beginning to draw on some of the experiences of her own second marriage. Hofland had been brought up as a gentleman of leisure and, despite the fact that he now had to earn a living, that was how he still regarded himself. He was, for example, frequently away from home, not only on painting expeditions but also on fishing jaunts. And, though he had artistic successes, these were erratic, perhaps because of his poor health. Saddest of all, however, was that Hofland's career failed to develop. His tragedy is not unlike that of his friend Benjamin Haydon, whose resentment at his lack of recognition led to a series of disputes with the major artistic arbiters of the day, his ostracism from their circles, and eventually his suicide. Hofland never became quite so desperate, but he was certainly extremely difficult to live with, and, at his worst moments, abused his wife.

Furthermore, in 1816 Hofland fathered an illegitimate son, Thomas Richard Hofland, whom his wife took in, nursed, and treated as her own for the rest of her life. Whether it was to avoid embarrassment or for business reasons, the Hoflands moved to Twickenham that year. Together they began work on an important commission for the Marquis of Blandford, heir to the Duke of Marlborough. The Marquis had bought the mansion of Whiteknights near Reading, and, having spent large sums on its garden and library, engaged the Hoflands to produce a book which would describe his showplace, with illustrations by Hofland to accompany a text written by Barbara. For nearly three years husband and wife worked together on the project, making sketches and employing engravers and printers. But by the time the handsome volume was completed in 1819, although the Marquis had become Duke of Marlborough, he was virtually bankrupt, and the Hoflands never received a penny for their labours.

Thomas Hofland's career continued on its unpredictable way. In 1821 an exhibition of his paintings failed, and his outbursts of temper became more noticeable to outsiders. But Mrs Hofland supported him cheerfully and her publications continued to flow: *Theodore, or the Crusaders* (1821), *The Daughter of a Genius* (1823), *William and his Uncle Ben* (1826). She had also published a first novel for adults, *Says She to Her Neighbours, What?* (1812) and further novels appeared in 1813 and 1814. Few of her novels reached a second edition. It is significant that when the periodical *La Belle Assemblée* published her portrait as a well-known authoress in 1823, it associated her with *The Son of a Genius* and her other children's books, rather than with her adult novels.

Throughout the 1820s Mrs Hofland continued to publish copiously: children's stories, textbooks, essays for the *Annuals*, anything that would bring in money. By the 1830s she often found authorship physically painful because of a shoulder injury, but she still kept on writing. All this time she had been cheered and sustained by the love of her son Frederick who, after taking a degree at Cambridge, became a curate in Holborn, London. In 1833, though, he fell ill and died.

In 1840 Hofland fulfilled a lifetime's ambition when he visited Italy on a painting expedition, but his health continued to deteriorate after his return and he died in January 1843. Despite her loss Mrs Hofland went on working. In the summer of 1843 she took a holiday in France, a trip which gave her the idea for her final children's book, *Emily's Reward; or, The Holiday Trip to Paris*. She finished it in the summer of 1844, but then an attack of erysipelas was aggravated by a fall – she was now in her seventy-fourth year – and she did not have the strength to resist a second attack when it came. She died on 4 November 1844.

Mrs Hofland's literary career (as Barbara Wreaks) had begun before her first marriage, when she had a handful of poems published in the pages of Montgomery's weekly newspaper the *Iris*, so clearly the creative impulse was present in her before widowhood and financial difficulties forced her to turn to the economic rewards of authorship. The death of her first husband and his business losses suggested writing as a way of earning money, and the success of her first book, the *Poems* of 1805, must have seemed immensely encouraging. The book was published by subscription, and skilfully advertised in the *Iris* as 'this solitary tribute' of 'A Widow's Mite.'[2] Some readers may have bought it for compassionate rather than literary reasons, but, even so, the sales were still extraordinarily high, the 43-page list of subscribers showing that 1,620 customers bought no fewer than 2,040 copies at six shillings each. Although the *Gentleman's Magazine* may be guilty of hyperbole when it described its success as 'an event (for a first publication) unequalled, we should imagine, in the annals of literary history', these figures compare extremely favourably with other poetry published by subscription in the eighteenth century.[3]

Searching for other ways of achieving literary success, Mrs Hoole noticed how popular William Roscoe's light-hearted poem for children, *The Butterfly's Ball*, had been upon its appearance in 1807. This charming rhymed fantasy enjoyed such an enormous success that it produced a flood of imitations and sequels, for instance, *The Peacock 'At Home'* (1807) and the *Lion's Parliament* (1808). Here was a literary formula, a rhymed, poetic fantasy about animals, birds or insects, treated anthropomorphically and with humour, which Mrs Hoole enthusiastically followed when she wrote *La Fête de la Rose: or, The Dramatic Flowers. A Holiday Present for Young People* in 1808.

Following the format of *The Butterfly's Ball*, she makes the Rose decide to give a party for all the other flowers:

Since Birds, Beasts and Insects, together combine
To give invitations, to dance or to dine;
Pray why may not I, who am Queen of the Flowers,
Just invite a few friends to enliven my hours?[4]

The Lily joins in with enthusiasm and suggests building a theatre on the lawn for after-dinner entertainment, and the other flowers combine to perform a Tragedy followed by a pantomime, in the early nineteenth-century tradition. It is all rendered with an engagingly light-hearted touch, but there is no doubt that Mrs Hofland knew exactly what she was doing when she sent detailed instructions to the ever-willing Montgomery. 'The more it can be made to look like the Butterfly's Ball Lions Fete &c. &c. the more likely it must be to sell,' she told him in December 1808.[5] When the little pamphlet came out in 1809 it did reasonably well, being sold by Longman's of London and reaching a third edition by 1810.

The possibility of achieving commercial appeal by the successful exploitation of a popular formula was a lesson quickly grasped by Mrs Hoole, though her often successful application of it also included an element of chance. In late eighteenth-

2   *Iris* (23 February 1804); repeated 1 March and 8 March.

3   *Gentleman's Magazine* (January 1845), 23, 100. William Cowper's *Homer*, for example, had a subscription list of just 300, and Matthew Prior's *Poems* attracted 1,445 subscribers, according to J.W. Saunders, *The Profession of English Letters* (London: Routledge and Kegan Paul, 1964) p. 134.

4   *La Fête de la Rose: or, The Dramatic Flowers. A Holiday Present for Young People* (1809), Sheffield, Montgomery, p. [3].

5   Barbara Hoole to James Montgomery, 5 December 1808, Sheffield City Library, SLPS36, 141 (1).

and early nineteenth-century England many women were writing children's books – Lucy Cameron (1781–1858), Maria Edgeworth (1767–1849), Maria Hack (1777–1844), Mary Martha Sherwood (1775–1851) and Sarah Trimmer (1741–1810) were among the most notable. Other writers, such as Hannah More (1745–1833), while not addressing themselves exclusively to children, were indirectly contributing to children's reading through publications such as her 'Cheap Repository Tracts' of 1795–98. The literature produced by these writers was predominantly moral, didactic and realistic fiction. At a time of great change, characterised by the French Revolution abroad and the Industrial Revolution at home, they aimed to provide books and stories more serious and edifying than those associated with John Newbery and his successors, earlier in the eighteenth century. Instead of verses about games and play, they offered serious stories about children in realistic situations. Typically, a child encounters a dilemma of some kind and has to cope with a crisis, usually with the help of a sympathetic but not necessarily soft-hearted parent or friend, who emphasises the moral or religious implications of the event for the child and the reader. The joys and troubles of ordinary family life are present in many of these stories, from little Rosamund learning the folly of impulsive desire in Maria Edgeworth's famous 'The Purple Jar' (1796) to Hannah More's fable of a poor but contented Christian family in 'The Shepherd of Salisbury Plain' of 1795.

Barbara Hoole is likely to have been influenced by this school of writing when beginning her first children's story. She certainly paid generous tribute to Maria Edgeworth in 1815, when writing to her father, Richard Lovell Edgeworth, to say that 'In so far as I am a Tale teller, Sir, I am rendered such by the ardent admiration and the deep sense of their utility, with which the unparalleled excellence of Miss Edgeworth's tales have inspired me.'[6]

The idea of the family story was not new, then, but Mrs Hoole was able to stamp it with considerable individuality in her first fiction, *The History of an Officer's Widow, and her Young Family* (1809). Perhaps this was because she drew on her own experiences. The story it tells is simple and episodic, but the anxious words of her preface suggest that she was conscious that of trying to write something rather different:

> In addressing the following history of a worthy family to young readers, it may be thought, by some, that I have presented pictures of too gloomy a nature, and scenes of too affecting a kind, for their season of life; but I am persuaded that children themselves will not accuse me of lessening their pleasure, by withdrawing them for a few hours from noisy sports and frivolous occupations, to trace with me the various joys and sorrows of boys like themselves.[7]

The story portrays the Belfield family, concentrating on the period after their father, an army captain, is wounded and dies, leaving his widow, a clergyman's daughter, to bring up their five children. The family moves to a small cottage in Lincolnshire, and the eldest son Charles, though he had wanted to become a clergyman, is found a

---

6   Mrs Hofland to R.L. Edgeworth, 29 May 1815, Oxford, Colvin Collection.

7   Mrs Hofland, *History of an Officer's Widow and her Young Family*, 'New Edition' (London: John Harris, 1834), pp. [v–vi].

commission in the army. His younger brother Henry, who would actually have liked to join the army, has to become a linen-draper in Hull, while his sisters learn to do muslin work at home. Despite their disappointments, the family pull together and survive. Charles performs gallantly in the army, while Henry has his adventures at home too, rescuing an old lady from a house fire, and later foiling an attempted robbery. The story is rounded off with various marriages in a conventionally happy ending.

The moral of this story is plain and clearly enunciated to her children by Mrs Belfield in the book's final pages. Children should follow their professional inclinations if they can, but, if that is not possible, 'in every situation of life, a man may find occasions to display those virtues he does possess, and acquire those in which he is deficient'.[8] What is particularly interesting in the story is its acute sense of monetary values. While the children behave well for moral and religious reasons, good and brave behaviour tends to bring swift and unexpected material rewards. When Henry rescues a young girl from drowning, he is not only immediately recompensed with a half-crown by a passing gentleman, but is later offered an apprenticeship by the same philanthropist. When he saves an old lady from a house fire, she gives him £220 in gratitude, and when Charles looks after a dying soldier, the soldier's father gives Charles £1,000.

It is clear that Hofland sees, or wishes to see, some kind of relationship between what she regards as the upholding of Christian virtues and their reward, not simply as spiritual blessings but on this earth as well. What she had stumbled across in the tale of an *Officer's Widow* is a narrative formula which she was to make her own, the tale of people, often a family or group of young folk, struggling in adverse circumstances to sustain some kind of integrity and Christian virtue, and at the same time displaying all kinds of industry and business acumen to support themselves and their families. It is part of her belief that this combination of qualities is related in some way, and though tested out in many trying circumstances, is nearly always rewarded. She seems to articulate some of the main features of the system of belief known as the 'Protestant work ethic,' but without any of the signs of hypocrisy, or that theological justification of *laissez-faire*, found later in the Victorian period, though the changing climate of Victorian opinion (reflected, for example, in the response to Samuel Smiles' *Self-Help* of 1859) may partly explain Mrs Hofland's enduring popularity in the second half of the nineteenth century.[9] The successful publication of *The History of an Officer's Widow* in 1809 was followed by frequent reprintings, with a second edition of 1812, a third in 1814, and new editions by John Harris in 1818, 1820, 1823, *c.*1830 and 1834. It was also often reprinted in America.

Alan Richardson has shown how often in this period from the last years of the eighteenth century through the opening decades of the nineteenth, many women writers, perhaps barred from or not wishing to participate in political or commercial life, began producing realistic fiction advocating care and reform in the domestic

---

8   Ibid., p. 170.
9   See R.H. Tawney, *Religion and the Rise of Capitalism* (London: Penguin, 1964); W.E. Houghton, *The Victorian Frame of Mind 1830–1870* (New Haven, CT: Yale University Press, 1957).

sphere.[10] It is not surprising, then, that Mrs Hoole, or Mrs Hofland, as she became in 1810, exploited this successful formula again and again. The background of her stories is nearly always a family, but sometimes she focuses upon the careers of the sons, as in stories of industrious apprentices, and sometimes she focuses upon the career of an unhappy young girl, a sort of nineteenth-century Cinderella. In either case we can see that Hofland's incorporation of familiar folklore motifs within her own more realistic formula helped to strengthen her popularity.

In the next few years she produced a series of similar tales: *The History of a Clergyman's Widow and her Young Family* first appeared in 1812 and reached a seventh edition by 1825. *The Son of a Genius; a Tale for Youth*, published by John Harris, also in 1812, reached a fourteenth edition by 1841. *The Merchant's Widow and her Family*, published by A.K. Newman in 1814, reached its sixth edition by 1826. *The Blind Farmer and his Children*, published by John Harris in 1816, reached a seventh edition in 1831, and *Elizabeth and Her Three Beggar Boys* was published by Newman in 1833 and often reprinted. The structure of these moral and didactic tales is formulaic and predictable, for Mrs Hofland knew it to be popular. A middle-class family is living in relative prosperity until a domestic or financial crisis occurs. The father, a shadowy figure although the ultimate authority in family matters, dies or loses his power, leaving the mother to become the guiding force in the family. In fact, she is often revealed to be intellectually as well as morally his superior. The children are usually depicted as stereotypes, the boys, though employed as industrious apprentices, are either manly or scholarly; the girls tend to be either prudent or very foolish in some way. But when the crisis occurs, whether it is a family death or a bankruptcy, the family learns to rally round. In *The History of a Merchant's Widow*, the children of the recently-widowed and impoverished Mrs Daventree begin to develop the virtues of tenderness and self-reliance as they settle into their strange new home:

'But who will be our cook, mamma?' said Sophia.

'And who will wait on us when William is gone?' cried Louisa.

'Who is to wash me and hear me my prayers, now I have no good Jackson?' asked little Edward.

'How silly you all are,' interrupted Charles, 'to tease poor mamma in this way! Don't you know we are going to be like poor people, and to wait on ourselves? For my part, I like it of all things, and know I can do it better than anybody, because papa always told me to do it, and said it was the way to make a man of myself; and that if I meant to be a sailor, I must learn to do everything; and I remember one day, when Admiral Bennington was at our house, he told me he could mend his own stockings; and so I shall mend my stockings, and my shoes, and all: and I shall – '

'Well, well, you needn't talk so fast, Charles,' said Sophia; 'I suppose we can *all* do something as well as you: I am sure I will do anything mamma tells me.'

---

10 Alan Richardson, *Literature, Education and Romanticism: Reading as Social Practice 1780–1832* (Cambridge: Cambridge University Press, 1994), pp. 170–89.

'I will tell you,' said Henry, 'what we must *all* do; we must all wait on mamma and
the little ones, quietly as it were, without pretending to do anything; because,
if we make a noise about it, that will put her in mind of poor papa's death,
and all the comforts she has lost; and as everybody had better be orderly, and
manage *one* thing well, than go bustling about a *many*, Edward, my little man, *I*
shall take charge of you, and though I shall perhaps not dress you very handily
at first, yet I can teach you your lessons and hear your prayers, you know.'

'And I will do the same for Elizabeth,' said Sophia joyfully.

'Well then, Anne shall be my child,' cried Louisa.

'So,' quoth Charles,' you have got each of you your portion of work before me;
well I am glad of it, for I am neither much of a nurse or a scholar; but I will
work in the garden, and run errands, and read voyages to mamma on winter
nights; and in another year, I hope the admiral will send for me to go on
shipboard, and then all the world will see how I can work.'

'And how you can talk,' said Henry with a smile.[11]

This picture of unselfish and co-operative family love, countered with the good-
natured irony of the eldest son, is effectively handled and encapsulates the formula
of Mrs Hofland's most successful tales. She shows ordinary human beings pulling
themselves together and demonstrating their strengths after some great domestic
grief or crisis. We see it when Mrs Belfield's family rallies round after their father's
death in *The History of an Officer's Widow*, when Ludovico goes off in *The Son of
a Genius* to sell his drawings in Leeds Market, and when the Norton family, evicted
from their farm, with the father going blind from cataracts, stop at Birmingham
when their coach has an accident. There Mrs Norton gets work helping the tailor next
door, Frank gets a job in a button factory, Betsy a job in a factory making trays, and
blind Mr Norton sets to cultivating his landlord's neglected garden. 'In this way, by
unremitting industry, though with very small profits, the distressed family made shift
to support themselves,' says Mrs Hofland.[12] This call for labour and endurance was
the staple of her most successful books. Stephen Behrendt goes further and suggests
that in the three books about widowhood, *The Officer's Widow*, *The Clergyman's
Widow* and *The Merchant's Widow*,

> Hofland's novels ... outline an alternative feminist model of women's (and families')
> response to sudden reversal that painted for generations of 'younger' readers, in particular,
> a group portrait of principled personal development that was grounded in the evangelical
> principles of industry, humility, self-awareness, and the ennobling generosity of self-
> sacrifice that makes the fully individuated persona.[13]

---

11 Mrs Hofland, *The History of a Merchant's Widow and her Young Family* ([1814],
'New Edition', London: A.K. Newman, n.d.), pp. 32–4.

12 Mrs Hofland, *The Blind Farmer and his Children* ([1816], 'New Edition', London:
A.K. Newman, n.d.), pp. 39–40.

13 Stephen C. Behrendt, 'Women without Men: Barbara Hofland and the Economics of
Widowhood', *Eighteenth-Century Fiction* 17 (2005), 481–508 (p. 508).

Certainly something similar is present in some of Mrs Hofland's later 'teenage' stories, such as *Decision* of 1824.

These early stories sold well, but they did not earn Hofland much money. The firm of John Harris in particular seems to have treated her very badly, offering her only the most modest sums as outright payment for some of her most successful books. Indeed in 1815 she told R.L. Edgeworth that 'My Officer's widow now in its fourth edition was sold to Mr. Harris for only 6£ nor did he give me a single copy so that asking ten for "Son of a Genius," was a bold thing.'[14] The author and editor Samuel Carter Hall added a footnote to the history of Mrs Hofland's most famous tale:

> She received for the book £10. It was so rapidly and frequently reprinted that the publisher made by it as many hundreds. I remember Mrs. Hofland telling me this – on the very day it occurred. She called upon Harris concerning a new edition, time (twenty-eight years) having exhausted his claim to the copyright, which consequently reverted to her. The worthy publisher refused to acknowledge any such right, protesting against it on the ground that such a thing had never happened to him before! The discussion ended in his giving the author another £10.[15]

With earnings like this it is not surprising that Hofland looked round for other literary genres to supplement her husband's erratic income. She tried adult novels from time to time, but these, though often published by the Minerva Press, only seem to have earned her about £30 each, and, consisting of three or four volumes, took much longer to write. Furthermore, only *A FATHER As He Should Be* (1815) reached a second English edition in her lifetime.

Having worked in a school for young ladies in Doncaster before running her own boarding school in Harrogate, Hofland had some experience as a school teacher. Supplementary textbooks at the beginning of the nineteenth century tended to be what F.J. Harvey Darton has called 'catechisms', of which Richard Mangnall's *Historical and Miscellaneous Questions* of 1800 is perhaps best-known.[16] There was obviously a market for writing here, and Mrs. Hofland produced several of these dialogue instruction-amusement books. A good example is *The Panorama of Europe: or, A New Game of Geography* (1813) in which Mr and Mrs Davenport try to educate their nine children by a mixture of entertainment and instruction. The children are encouraged to put on exhibitions about different countries, but the game soon degenerates into long lectures about each country, chiefly given by Mr Davenport. The book must have been fairly popular, however, for it reached a sixth edition by 1828. Another geographical text, *Africa Described in its Ancient and Present State* (1828), intended perhaps to exploit the anti-slavery interest of the time, was only reprinted once, while a late attempt to blend amusement with instruction, *Emily's Reward; or, The Holiday Trip to Paris* (1844) failed to earn a single reprint.

---

14 Mrs Hofland to R.L. Edgeworth, 29 June 1815, Oxford, Colvin Collection.

15 S.C. Hall, *Retrospect of a Long Life from 1815 to 1883*, (2 vols, London: Richard Bentley, 1883), vol. 2, 77–8.

16 F.J. Harvey Darton, *Children's Books in England: Five Centuries of Social Life*, 3rd edn rev. Brian Alderson (Cambridge: Cambridge University Press, 1982), pp. 47–9.

Another genre of children's books related to the geographical textbooks that Hofland sought to develop is what might be called the 'travelogue', in which the young hero undertakes a journey to foreign parts and describes his experiences either through letters or in conversation with a sympathetic companion. Hofland first described northern Europe. *The Young Northern Traveller*, subtitled *Being a Series of Letters from Frederick to Charles during a Tour through the North of Europe*, was first published in 1813, and later editions appeared in 1829 and *c.*1835. More exotic is *Alfred Campbell, The Young Pilgrim; Containing Travels in Egypt and the Holy Land* of 1825. It narrates the journey of 14-year-old Alfred and his father through the Middle East. *The Young Pilgrim, or Alfred Campbell's Return to the East*, published the following year, describes further travels in Asia Minor and Arabia, and suggests that the format enjoyed some popularity, being reprinted four times by 1841. *The Young Cadet; or Henry Delamere's Voyage to India* (1828) sought to build on the success of Alfred Campbell's travels by describing the adventures of its 15-year-old hero, who obtains a cadetship in the East India Company and takes part in the Burmese War.

These books did moderately well, as did two historical tales, *Theodore, or The Crusaders, A Tale for Youth* (1821), which reached a seventh edition by 1838, and *Adelaide; or, The Intrepid Daughter*, a melodramatic tale of 1823. Involving the St Bartholomew's Eve Massacre, *Adelaide* looks like a crude attempt to cash in on the popularity of Sir Walter Scott's works, and it did rather less well.

Another source of Hofland's income came from her frequent contributions to the *Annuals* and *Keepsakes*, which began to appear, often with beautiful illustrations, from 1823 onwards. Andrew Boyle has identified no fewer than 36 contributions from her, including items for Ackermann's *Forget-Me-Not*, S.C. Hall's *The Amulet* and Mrs S.C. Hall's *Juvenile Forget-Me-Not*.[17] Many of these poems, sketches or stories were intended for adults, but some were written especially for children, and short moral tales like 'The Passionate Little Girl, or, More than One in Fault' (*New Year's Gift*) and 'William and his Story Books' (*Juvenile Forget-me-Not*) appeared in *Annuals* before being printed together in the collection *Rich Boys and Poor Boys*, published by A.K. Newman in 1833. These simple tales remind one of Hofland's debt to Maria Edgeworth, particularly 'The Passionate Girl; or, More than One in Fault' in which 11-year-old Sophy, after over-reacting angrily to a domestic accident, learns to improve her self-control – but through the encouragement of her family rather than parental punishment.

The major attempt Hofland made to revive her literary career, after the first flush of success had abated in the 1820s, resulted in a series of stories for young girls – 'teenage novels' we might term them today – published initially by the firm of Longman. Beginning in 1823 with *Integrity*, Longman published *Patience* and *Decision* in 1824, *Moderation* in 1825, *Reflection* in 1826 and *Self-Denial* in 1827. The series was then taken over by the firm of A.K. Newman, who published *Fortitude* in 1835, *Humility* in 1837 and *Energy* in 1838.

---

17 Andrew Boyle, *An Index to the Annuals*, vol.1: The Authors (Worcester: Andrew Boyle, 1967), pp. 129–30.

Lynne Vallone has shown how conduct manuals giving girls and women advice about their behaviour had been published since the seventeenth century, and she demonstrates how in the early nineteenth century books appeared – often a mixture of the tract and the realistic novel – which also attempted to give young female readers advice on marriage and domestic happiness.[18] Mrs Hofland's series are related to this genre. The novels, which reflect Mrs Hofland's moderately liberal Anglican values, are not linked in any way but are all realistic tales about young middle-class girls. The titles of the books suggest the moral themes which the stories aim to articulate. *Moderation*, for example, is about three sisters – Sophia, who becomes a religious fanatic, Harriet, who is worldly and extravagant and Emma, who remains steadfast in her reasonable moderation (with shades of Jane Austen's *Sense and Sensibility*). Hofland's *Reflection*, on the other hand, is about 17-year-old Clara, who, though orphaned and ill-regarded by her relatives, learns Christian endurance and wins the hands of a curate (with a hint of *Mansfield Park*?).

Foster and Simons have pointed out that during the nineteenth century there was far less rigid division between adult and youthful readership than is accepted today (if we exclude recent works by Philip Pullman and J.K. Rowling), and that as a result many books for young readers 'can be viewed as "hybrids," appealing to both young and adult readers and consequently inviting complex readings'.[19] Mrs Hofland's *Decision* can be seen as one such example. The theme of the novel is the need for moral firmness and self-control, expressed through Mrs Hofland's familiar plot of a family's economic distress and its gradual recovery. Mr Falconer, an Irish gentleman of wealth and property, lives extravagantly, and, when his business collapses, his daughter Maria learns that he has squandered his wife's fortune as well as his own. Although she is sorry for her father's plight, she is indignant at his mismanagement. She decides that their remaining money and property must be used to repay their outstanding debts, and then, with £6 borrowed from a friend, 19-year-old Maria declares her astonishing intention of becoming an iron merchant! She packs her plainest clothes and moves to a manufacturing town where she rents a warehouse and begins selling steel to the poorer artisans in smaller quantities than the great iron masters find profitable.

Despite the roughness of the work and the genteel protests of her parents and friends, Maria prospers because she is meeting a real need. The business expands, and when she is lent £200, she enters the German market and also visits Holland and Flanders. Maria continues in business after it would have been possible for her to sell the concern and return to her former way of life. Although she is disappointed in one love affair, she turns down two proposals of marriage. The reader, familiar with Hofland's other tales, confidently expects her to marry the amiable German she meets through business, and then, when she declines him, to accept the hand of her first love when he returns to her, now a widower. She rejects both offers, however, preferring instead to go on living with her aged mother. The truth is that Maria,

---

18 Lynne Vallone, *Disciplines of Virtue: Girls' Culture in the Eighteenth and   Nineteenth Centuries* (New Haven, CT: Yale University Press, 1995), pp. 69–78.

19 Shirley Foster and Judy Simons, *What Katy Read: Feminist Re-Readings of 'Classic' Stories for Girls* (Basingstoke: Macmillan, 1995), pp. 8–11.

an early example of the career woman, is married to her job, to use the well-worn phrase. Although Mrs Hofland would have denied it, *Decision* might be interpreted as a subversive book. This story of a teenager taking on such unusual work reminds us of Judith Rowbotham's observation – 'the creation of a body of fiction concentrating specifically on an adolescent middle-class market actually aided the expansion of women's role in society'.[20]

Writing of such liveliness is not common, however, and Mrs Hofland's series of books for young women readers gradually ran out of steam. Whereas, *Integrity*, for example, was first published in an edition of 1,000 copies by Longman in 1823, with reprints of 750 in 1824 and another 1,000 in 1826, *Self-Denial* was only published in a first edition of 750 copies in 1827 with a reprint of 250 copies in 1830. Finally, Longman sold off unsold copies of Mrs Hofland's books to A.K. Newman in the 1830s, and it is significant that a later title *Humility*, published by Newman in 1837, was reprinted only in the 'Hofland Library' in the 1850s.

With such dwindling sales, Hofland did not earn much money from her work for Longman. She was paid a lump sum for the copyright of the first edition, which was always £25. Subsequent editions, however, were published on a shared profits basis, Longman dividing the profits equally with the author after the costs of publication had been covered. Thus, on subsequent editions of *Patience*, first published in 1824, and reprinted in 1825, 1827 and 1833 – a reasonably popular book, in other words – Hofland's earnings were as follows:

1826   £15-07-09
1827   £ 9-08-05
1828   £ 3-10-11
1829   £ 1-08-05
1830   £ 5-07-07
1831   £ 4-05-01
1832   £ 3-05-12
1833   £ 3-04-11
1834   £60-07-10 (on transfer of all books to A.K. Newman.)[21]

One irony of Hofland's energetic search for a literary form that would bring her financial success was that she did actually find one in her modest attempts at adventure stories. But she was born too soon to be able to capitalise on their success or see the astonishing development of the genre. *The Stolen Boy: An Indian Tale*, the story of a Spanish boy's capture by and escape from Comanche Indians, first appeared in the *Juvenile Souvenir* for 1828, and, after appearing in book form in 1829, was frequently reprinted, perhaps because of its American setting. The success of *The Young Crusoe, or The Shipwrecked Boy* was even more remarkable, for this simply-told Robinsonnade, first published in 1828, though only reprinted twice in Mrs Hofland's lifetime, was reprinted no fewer than nine times after her death, the

---

20 Judith Rowbotham, *Good Girls Make Good Wives: Guidance for Girls in Victorian Fiction* (Oxford: Blackwell, 1989), p. 9.

21 The Longman Archives, University of Reading Library, accession no. 1393.

last known English edition being published in Manchester in 1894. It was not until the great achievements of Captain Marryat's *Masterman Ready* (1841) and *The Children of the New Forest* (1847) that the children's adventure story really took off, with the successes of R.M. Ballantyne, W.H.G. Kingston and G.A. Henty following shortly thereafter. Otherwise, Hofland's gift for writing surprisingly brisk narratives might have brought her greater rewards than her realistic moral tales did.

Despite her modest financial earnings, there can be no doubt that Hofland was a popular author, read widely overseas as well as in Britain in the nineteenth century. Her work was widely advertised. Her books were often noted in such periodicals as the *Critical* and *Monthly Reviews*, and were often listed among the book lists to be found at the back of other publications, notably those produced by A.K. Newman. Though there is no evidence of deliberate puffing, at least one of Hofland's adult books, *The Captives in India* (1834), received a favourable review in the *New Monthly Magazine*, which was edited by Hofland's old friend S.C. Hall. Her *Integrity* of 1823 was praised in the *Literary Gazette*, which was partly owned by Hofland's publisher Longman. She was, in other words, well-known in literary circles.

T.W. Ramsay in *The Life and Literary Remains of Barbara Hofland* (1849) calculated that 'upwards of three hundred thousand copies' of her works had been sold by the time that he was writing in 1849.[22] He was including all her works, those for adults and children, but even so, his figures should be treated with respect. If we average out the size of each recorded edition of her 45 juvenile works as a 1,000 copies, except for those for which we have exact figures, this means that British sales up to her death in 1844 total 163,250. These calculations ignore the probability that many editions may have exceeded 1,000 copies. Ramsay said of *The Clergyman's Widow*, for example, that 'altogether, as many as seventeen thousand copies have been sold by the London publishers'.[23]

Hofland's work was also widely published overseas, particularly in America, where no fewer than 31 different titles were published as well as compilations such as *Mrs. Hofland's Domestic Tales* (New York, 1850). *The Son of a Genius* was again enormously popular with editions recorded in New York in 1814, 1818, 1832, 1839, 1844, 1854 and 1858; in Boston in 1826, 1863, 1865 and 1868; and in Ohio in 1852, 1853 and 1854. Hofland also edited the *American Juvenile Keepsake* from 1834 to 1836, and, altogether, if we adopt the 1,000 copies per edition formula, she achieved sales of over 127,000 in the nineteenth century. Hofland herself claimed that *The Son of a Genius* had been translated 'into every European language; and in France, Germany and Holland gone through numerous editions'.[24] *The Stolen Boy* of 1830 also seems to have enjoyed enormous popularity overseas, being translated into French, German and Spanish. The catalogue of the Bibliothèque Nationale records nine different French editions from Paris, Rouen and Lille.

We have, furthermore, to remember what Ramsay could not have known – the enduring popularity of Hofland's works after her death. The firm of Arthur Hall,

---

22 T.W. Ramsay, *The Life and Literary Remains of Barbara Hofland* (London, W.J. Cleaver, 1849), p. viii.

23 Ibid., p. 21.

24 Mrs Hofland, *The Son of a Genius* (Paris: Baudry, 1829), pp. vi–vii.

Virtue and Co., taking over from A.K. Newman, found it profitable to produce what was called 'The Hofland Library' in the 1850s, publishing no fewer than 30 of Mrs Hofland's tales 'for the instruction and amusement of youth', handsomely bound in embossed scarlet cloth with gilt edges, sold at either two shillings and sixpence, or one shilling and sixpence each (see Figure 6.1). Griffith and Farran, successors to John Harris, included four of Hofland's books – *The Son of a Genius*, *The Daughter of a Genius*, *Ellen* and *Theodore, or The Crusaders* as volumes IX, X, XI and XII of 'The Favourite Library', which they published between 1871 and 1883. In addition between 1866 and 1881, Nelson and Sons published at least 11 of her titles, including *The Blind Farmer*, *Alicia and her Aunt* and *The Young Crusoe*.[25]

Popularity is a relative and ambiguous virtue, however. Despite Hofland's impressive sales figures, especially in the first half of the nineteenth century before national education developed, we must keep a sense of proportion by reminding ourselves that *Alice's Adventures in Wonderland* alone sold 150,000 copies between 1865 and 1898.[26] We have also to bear in mind what Dr Johnson told Mrs Thrale –'Remember always that the parents buy the books, and that the children never read them.'[27]

Not much evidence survives, in fact, as to what children did think of Mrs Hofland's books. Contemporary adult notices, such as those in the *Monthly Review* or the *Gentleman's Magazine*, tend to emphasise their healthy morality, and it is only occasionally that a critic comments on a book aesthetically, as when Elizabeth Eastlake praised *The Son of a Genius* in 1844 as 'A very beautiful tale, and the very best of this lady's numerous books.'[28] Mrs Molesworth, born in 1839, reminisced in 1898 about the favourite books of her childhood; she remembered 'one or two of Mrs. Hofland's with pleasure', and Marjorie Moon recalled reading *Adelaide; or, The Intrepid Daughter* as a child in the early years of the twentieth century.[29] But, though William Caldwell Roscoe said in 1855 that Mrs Hofland 'continues popular', his description of her 'deliberate sesquipedelian manner' anticipates the gradual loss of popularity which followed.[30] This was to be confirmed when *The Young Crusoe* was reprinted for the last time in 1894 with a 'Preface' by Alfonzo Gardiner. 'The only one of Mrs. Hofland's books that are read in the present day', he wrote, 'are *The Son of a Genius*, *The Captives in India*, and the tale which is here presented.'[31]

Yet Hofland's popularity and influence arguably extended far beyond the confines of the modest tales she wrote in the first half of the nineteenth century. It is not difficult to see how the story of the patient and virtuous heroine, tested

25 For much of this publishing information, see Dennis Butts, *Mistress of Our Tears: A Literary and Bibliographical Study of Barbara Hofland* (Aldershot: Scolar Press, 1992).

26 Morton N. Cohen, *Lewis Carroll: A Biography* (London: Macmillan, 1995), p. 134.

27 Quoted in Samuel Johnson, *Dr. Johnson. Some Observations upon Life and Letters*, chosen by John Hayward (London: Zodiac Books, 1948), p. 26.

28 Elizabeth Eastlake, 'Children's Books', *Quarterly Review* 74 (June 1844), 1–26.

29 Mrs Molesworth, 'Story-reading and Story-writing', *Chambers Journal* 75 (1898), 772–5; Marjorie Moon, private communication to the author.

30 Quoted in Lance Salway, *A Peculiar Gift: Nineteenth Century Writings on Books for Children* (London: Kestrel, 1976), p. 38.

31 *The Young Crusoe*, ed. Alfonzo Gardiner (Manchester: John Heywood, 1894), p. 10.

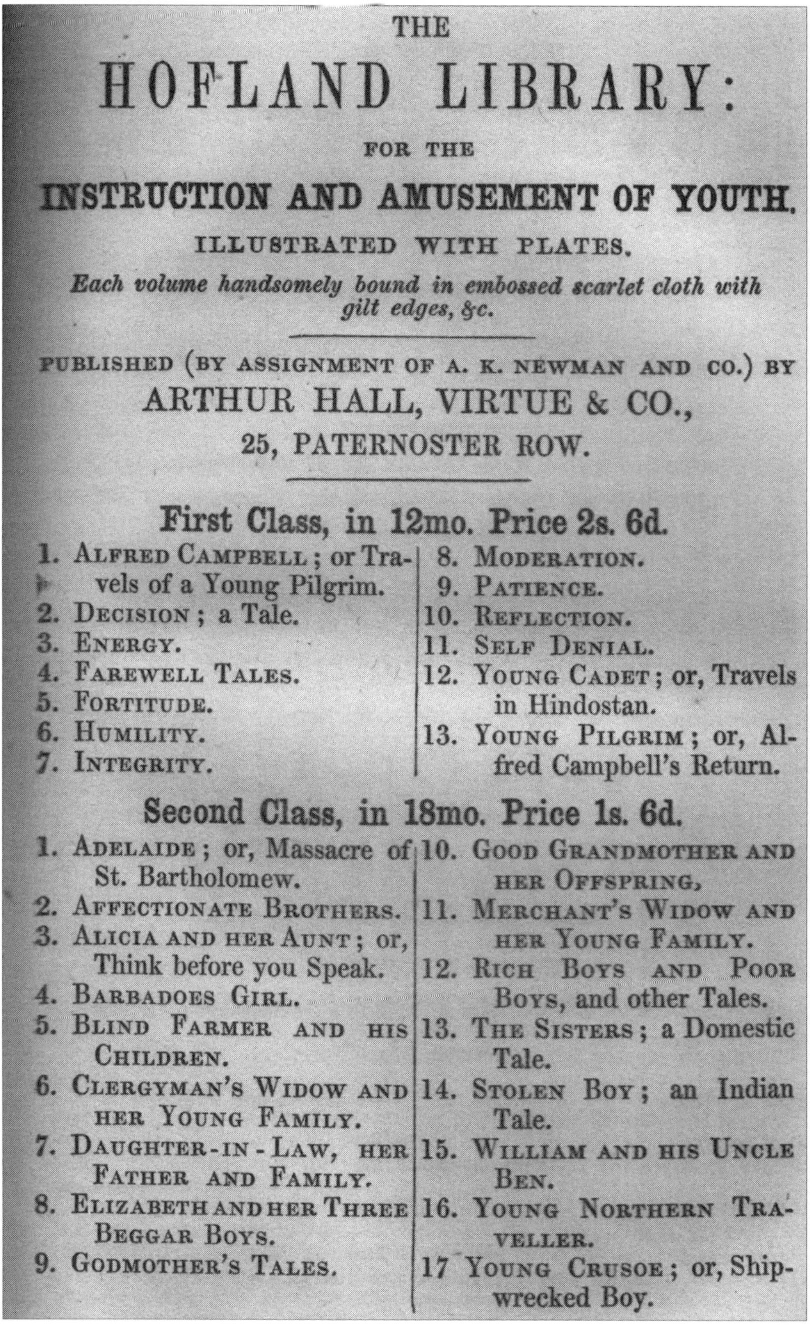

THE

HOFLAND LIBRARY:

FOR THE

INSTRUCTION AND AMUSEMENT OF YOUTH.

ILLUSTRATED WITH PLATES.

Each volume handsomely bound in embossed scarlet cloth with gilt edges, &c.

PUBLISHED (BY ASSIGNMENT OF A. K. NEWMAN AND CO.) BY

ARTHUR HALL, VIRTUE & CO.,

25, PATERNOSTER ROW.

First Class, in 12mo. Price 2s. 6d.

1. ALFRED CAMPBELL; or Travels of a Young Pilgrim.
2. DECISION; a Tale.
3. ENERGY.
4. FAREWELL TALES.
5. FORTITUDE.
6. HUMILITY.
7. INTEGRITY.
8. MODERATION.
9. PATIENCE.
10. REFLECTION.
11. SELF DENIAL.
12. YOUNG CADET; or, Travels in Hindostan.
13. YOUNG PILGRIM; or, Alfred Campbell's Return.

Second Class, in 18mo. Price 1s. 6d.

1. ADELAIDE; or, Massacre of St. Bartholomew.
2. AFFECTIONATE BROTHERS.
3. ALICIA AND HER AUNT; or, Think before you Speak.
4. BARBADOES GIRL.
5. BLIND FARMER AND HIS CHILDREN.
6. CLERGYMAN'S WIDOW AND HER YOUNG FAMILY.
7. DAUGHTER-IN-LAW, HER FATHER AND FAMILY.
8. ELIZABETH AND HER THREE BEGGAR BOYS.
9. GODMOTHER'S TALES.
10. GOOD GRANDMOTHER AND HER OFFSPRING.
11. MERCHANT'S WIDOW AND HER YOUNG FAMILY.
12. RICH BOYS AND POOR BOYS, and other Tales.
13. THE SISTERS; a Domestic Tale.
14. STOLEN BOY; an Indian Tale.
15. WILLIAM AND HIS UNCLE BEN.
16. YOUNG NORTHERN TRAVELLER.
17. YOUNG CRUSOE; or, Shipwrecked Boy.

Figure 6.1   'The Hofland Library', advertisement by Arthur Hall, Virtue & Co., in Thomas Ramsay, *The Life and Literary Remains of Barbara Hofland* (London: W.J. Cleaver, 1849). Collection of Dennis Butts.

and tried by difficult circumstances, one of the most popular situations in her moral tales, was taken up and developed in such novels as Jane Austen's *Mansfield Park* (1814) and Charlotte Brontë's *Jane Eyre* (1847). Hofland's *Ellen the Teacher* (1814) in particular, has many parallels with *Jane Eyre*, for Ellen is warned not to be so passionate by her mother, the same fault of which Mrs Reed accuses Jane. Similarly, when she is sent away to an unpleasant school, Ellen is accused of lying and locked in a closet, just as Jane would be locked in the red room. Like Jane, Ellen falls ill but manages to get away and find a better home elsewhere, where she nurses a sick child in the way Jane comforts the dying Helen Burns (there is even a minor character in *Ellen* called Betsey Burns). When she meets the grandmother who wronged her, Ellen forgives her on her deathbed in the way Jane forgives the dying Mrs. Reed, and if Ellen does not finish up falling in love as memorably as Jane does, there is at least the hint of a happy marriage. Because of the popularity of Hofland's tales at the Keighley Mechanics' Institute Library, where the Brontës borrowed their books, and which contained no fewer than 30 of Mrs Hofland's titles in 1841, it seems at least possible that the Brontës, especially Charlotte, could have been influenced by Hofland.[32]

Another of the recurring situations in Hofland's tales is one in which poor boys, often disadvantaged in some way and frequently orphans, by their virtue and industry achieve prosperity and happiness. Ludovico's adventures in Leeds Market might have ended up in Fagin's Den, one feels, and the early nineteenth-century popularity of such books as *The Son of a Genius* or *Elizabeth, and her Three Beggar Boys* (1833) may well have played some part in the making of *Oliver Twist* (1837–38) and *David Copperfield* (1849–50), as well as later popular successes such as the American rags-to-riches tales of Horatio Alger (from 1867).

One of Hofland's greatest themes is the strength and happiness of family life, especially in such books as *The Merchant's Widow* and *The Blind Farmer and his Children*. As we have seen, she was not afraid to show tensions within families: between husbands and wives, as in *The Son of a Genius*, or between children and parents, as in *Decision*. But her most powerful and recurring motif is the demonstration of family love and co-operation in the face of some crisis or disaster, often the loss of a parent, and her influence may be suspected on such books as Charlotte M. Yonge's *The Daisy Chain* (1856), Louisa M. Alcott's *Little Women* (1868) and E. Nesbit's *The Railway Children* (1906), where similar situations and attitudes appear.

Hofland was not a great children's writer, but she had a genuine if slender talent; she was particularly adept at the depiction of domestic tragedy and moral triumph within a realistic setting. Having achieved a literary and popular success with such early works as *The History of an Officer's Widow* (1809) and *The Son of a Genius* (1812), she often repeated the narrative pattern of those tales, but also energetically set about finding and exploiting other popular formulae, with textbooks, travelogues, historical fiction, tales of adventure and stories for young girls. Perhaps because of the unhappy circumstances of her own life, Hofland produced too many books quickly and carelessly. With such modest royalties, she seems to have come to

---

32 Clifford Whone, 'Where the Brontës Borrowed Books', *Brontë Society Transactions* 11 (1950).

depend upon the lump-sum payments initially made for her books, and so wrote more books to earn more lump-sums. R.L. Edgeworth probably put his finger on the problem when he wrote to her in 1815:

> For the paltry and inadequate remuneration you have hitherto received for your writings you are induced to endeavour, by *quantity*, to make up for what ought to be paid for the quality of a production … If my daughter has obtained any literary reputation, it has not been won, by sudden fits of exertion, but by patient changes & corrections which have cancelled more than three fourths of what she has written.[33]

It was, however, one among many misfortunes of her life that Hofland was never able to give her books the care and revision they needed. But who can doubt that there was something poignantly heroic about her continuing to do so until well into her infirm seventies?

---

33 R.L. Edgeworth to Mrs Hofland, 28 December 1815, Oxford, Colvin Collection.

Chapter 7

Telling the Other Side:
Hesba Stretton's 'Outcast' Stories

Elaine Lomax

If the modern reader is familiar with the work of Hesba Stretton (Sarah Smith 1832–1911), it is likely to be in the general context of her reputation as a writer of Evangelical 'street Arab' stories.[1] Her name is permanently linked with the highly successful – and deceptively simple – 'waif' narrative, *Jessica's First Prayer* (see Figure 7.1), published in book form by the Religious Tract Society (RTS) in 1867 and followed by other famous titles such as *Little Meg's Children* (1868) and *Alone in London* (1869). Bibliographies and histories of children's literature, whilst acknowledging her influence in this field, have concentrated on limited aspects of her work. Commentators have emphasised the contemporary popularity of her narratives, but have, for the most part, only briefly discussed – or dismissed – them as belonging to a body of didactic, simplistic and, to modern taste, overly religious and sentimental writing. Although the more detailed accounts by M. Nancy Cutt and J.S. Bratton, written over 20 years ago, indicated the complexity and socio-historical significance of Stretton's writing, few writers have engaged with the issues raised.[2] The range of Stretton's work – which includes numerous full-length novels (some for the secular market), as well as stories and articles of journalism for periodicals such as Dickens's *Household Words* and *All The Year Round* – has remained largely unexplored, its complex nature and wide-ranging implications underestimated or overlooked.

There is now a need to move beyond an understanding of Stretton founded only on the reputation of one or two celebrated works and limited both by the

---

1   The name 'Hesba Stretton' was adopted by Smith not long after she commenced her writing career, the first name formed from the initials of her siblings and the surname taken from the Shropshire village where she lived.

2   Lance Salway in 'Pathetic Simplicity: An Introduction to Hesba Stretton and Her Books for Children', *Signal* 1 (1970), 20–8, suggests the reforming influence of Stretton's narratives. M. Nancy Cutt's longer account in *Ministering Angels* (Wormley, Herts.: Five Owls Press, 1979), examines aspects of Stretton's life and work in relation to its historical context, and J.S. Bratton in *The Impact of Victorian Children's Fiction* (London: Croom Helm, 1981), places Stretton's writing within the context of Victorian children's publishing. More recently, Sally Mitchell in *The New Girl: Girls' Culture in England 1880–1915* (New York and Chichester: Columbia University Press, 1995), discussing the possible effects of narratives of this kind on the inner lives of girls, identifies the potential for both emotional release and empowerment in Stretton's fiction. Suzanne Rickard in '"Living by the Pen": Hesba Stretton's Moral Earnings', *Women's History Review* 5 (1996), 219–38, relates Stretton's work to the wider publishing environment, noting how her dealings with publishers crossed the usual boundaries.

Figure 7.1   Frontispiece for 'Hesba Stretton', *Jessica's First Prayer* (London: Religious Tract Society, no date but 1867). Private collection.

awareness that her popularity has receded and a perception of outdatedness. It is time to revisit the range of Stretton's work, to uncover the political, social, moral and emotional intricacy of her writing and to reopen the debate concerning its appeal and significance. Much can be gained by exploring these comparatively marginalised narratives alongside more widely discussed classic works (for both adults and children), and in the light of contemporary textual forms such as journalism, art and melodrama.[3] Although Stretton is principally categorised as a children's writer, many stories occupy an uncertain territory on the boundaries of juvenile and adult literature, in terms of theme and potential audience. The issues addressed are much broader than is generally recognised, encompassing many of the prominent interests, anxieties and debates of the period; more importantly, her narratives shed light on

---

3   Stretton's themes and motifs overlap in clearly identifiable ways with those of writers such as Charles Dickens, Mrs Gaskell, Charlotte Brontë, George Eliot, Victor Hugo and others; they echo and interact with culturally significant concerns which surface across all media forms.

crucial aspects of the nineteenth-century imagination. Focusing on the poor or displaced child, and directing attention towards other marginalised, disenfranchised or persecuted figures or sections of society, Stretton's writing highlights interrelated questions of gender, class and race. Her stories reveal a discourse of 'otherness' at the heart of Victorian society, exposing the simultaneous fear and allure of that which is perceived as different, unknown or undesirable. The significance of her work lies not only in the searchlight it directs onto contemporary structures, attitudes and ambivalence, but also, perhaps surprisingly, in the continued resonance of many of its themes.

Stretton was born in the Shropshire town of Wellington in 1832. As the child of a publisher and bookseller, she grew up surrounded by books of all kinds, and, like her protagonist, Hester Morley, was exposed to adult discussions on 'every possible religious and political question'.[4] Stretton's mother, acknowledged to be an important influence on her religious understanding and her compassion for humanity, died when her daughter was not yet ten years old. The significance of their relationship, and of its subsequent loss, is highlighted in the author's intensive literary focus on the maternal and the mother–child bond. The childhood games enjoyed by Stretton and her siblings (a brother and three sisters) reflect an openness to the realms of the imagination – an awareness which emerges in conflicting strands in Stretton's writing, feeding elements of sensation, and embodying the simultaneous appeal and terror of the supernatural or the forbidden.[5] Her enjoyment of the open Shropshire countryside, and her fear of containment, are translated in her books into diverse motifs of freedom and enclosure – both literal and metaphorical. At the same time, a resentment of the monotony or stagnation of day-to-day life underlies her appreciation – in tension with her disapproval – of the 'change and stir', the 'chances and changes', which the city inferno or an adventurous nomadic existence offer her characters.[6]

Although we should not assume an uncomplicated relationship between life and texts, Stretton's journals and related material reveal numerous personal preoccupations, tensions and contradictions which, mirroring wider contemporary interests and uncertainties, operate as themes or undercurrents in her work. Writing during an era of social, cultural and political change, in which recurrent economic crises were accompanied by fears of social unrest, Stretton exposes the effects of poverty and deprivation on individual lives and communities, reflecting an awareness formed, in part, through personal observation of the conditions in urban Manchester and London. In a society where scientific ideas were unsettling religious

---

4　'A Talk with Hesba Stretton', *Sunday Hours* 1, 7 (1896), 164; see also *Hester Morley's Promise*, p. 22. For full bibliographical details of Stretton's works cited here see the list at the end of this chapter.

5　See *Michel Lorio's Cross*, p. 25, and many other texts, for the expression of similar tensions. The sense of 'fearful pleasure' aroused, during Stretton's childhood, by firelit talk of ghosts, winding-sheets in candles, howling dogs and strange tappings at windows ('A Talk with Hesba Stretton', p. 165), clearly finds expression in the gothic settings and incidents which figure in a number of Stretton's narratives.

6　See, for instance, 'Log Book': Period to 4 December 1860; *Carola*, p. 11; *The Lord's Pursebearers*, p. 129.

beliefs, and altering ideas about the nature of childhood and the rights of women were increasingly accompanied by programmes of reform and legislation, Stretton's narratives both reflect and challenge dominant ideas.

Serious-minded, but with a sense of fun and irony, and displaying attitudes which were sometimes openly rebellious and radical, Stretton was a far more complex and less conventional figure than might be suggested by the legend that developed around her. Possessing a strong, but open-minded Evangelical faith, she was deeply distrustful of religious hypocrisy and narrow dogmatism; her narratives contain trenchant social criticism and exhibit scorn for the ineffectiveness of the establishment. At the same time, alongside her condemnation of inequality and her mockery of pretentiousness, we can find reflected in her writing commonly held assumptions and anxieties concerning social status; we can identify ways of perceiving or discussing the outcast which are characteristic of an ambivalent contemporary mindset.

Hesba Stretton's spirited attitudes towards men, whom she generally regarded as alien and unfathomable, surface in expressions of hatred, suspicion or lack of understanding between characters in her stories. An overall endorsement of woman's role as homemaker competes with Stretton's own sense of independence, her disapproval of domestic slavery and a scepticism about the marital state which translates into a textual indictment of marriage as both an economic solution and a yoke. Marking an end to freedom and happiness, matrimony represents a form of entrapment which sees the lively young woman as a butterfly flying 'heedlessly into a damp and chilly cave', able only to 'fold its wings'.[7] Stretton's journals reveal a playful interest, shared with her unmarried sisters, in potential suitors. Nonetheless, despite her mockery of old maids, and a suggestion in her narratives of single women letting chances pass by (for example, *Bede's Charity*, p. 6), spinsterhood actually allowed her greater freedom to participate in practical social investigation, and to conduct business and publishing affairs on her own terms. Together with a not inconsiderable income from writing, it enabled Stretton to avoid the state of dependence bemoaned by many of her female protagonists; in common with Felicita of *Cobwebs and Cables*, she could assert, 'I am a woman, and I will act for myself' (p. 128). Consistently appreciating the company of children, and displaying a deep concern for their welfare, Stretton undertook – by practical as well as literary means – to address childhood poverty, neglect and abuse. She was a leading campaigner and founder member of the London Society for the Prevention of Cruelty to Children, which was established in 1884.[8] Confessing herself, in correspondence, 'thoroughly a Radical',[9] she collaborated, towards the end of her career, with revolutionary Russian émigrés in the writing of narratives such as *The Highway of Sorrow* (1894), followed in 1897 by *In the Hollow of His Hand*. In these novels, which centre on the treatment

---

7   *Hester Morley's Promise*, p. 41; see also *The Highway of Sorrow*, in which girlhood is seen as 'the only happy time we women have in life' (p. 176). Such sentiments are echoed in numerous other works. Mature marriage between like-minded individuals, however, generally meets with less criticism.

8   Later the National Society for the Prevention of Cruelty to Children.

9   Letter to [Mr] Pattison, 16 April [1886?].

of the persecuted Christian Stundist minority in Russia, Stretton integrates religious and socialist ideas, and condemns the abuse of power by Church and State.[10]

In reassessing the impact of Hesba Stretton's work, it is important to relate it to the circumstances of its publication, and to consider the diverse, sometimes conflicting, agendas which underlie its production. In this respect, the role of Evangelical publishers such as the non-denominational Religious Tract Society, which produced and/or reissued many Stretton texts, is significant. Rapidly expanding in the 1860s, these publishers marketed fiction and non-fiction, educational and scientific texts as well as religious material, targeting all ages, but, importantly, playing a crucial role in the expansion of juvenile literature. From the 1850s, periodicals such as the *Leisure Hour* and the *Sunday at Home* (the latter including material for a younger audience) formed part of a drive to entertain, inform and provide an improving alternative to mass literature deemed 'pernicious' and 'sensational or worse'.[11] They provided a testing ground from which many texts – including those of Hesba Stretton – graduated to book form.

Tract Society minutes afford an insight into intended audiences: the publishers aimed to reach a range of classes, through differentiated reading matter or material offering cross-class appeal.[12] Editions suitable for prize/reward purposes were directed at the Sunday, Ragged, National or, later, Board School pupils, more expensive texts or editions at middle-class readers. Minutes often refer, overtly or ambiguously, to social category. Books might be deemed suitable for 'all classes', sometimes with the additional comment 'especially for the young' (as in the case of Stretton's *Max Kromer*, 1871).[13] Whilst certain texts were designed for 'young educated girls',[14] others were 'adapted to every class ... but especially to the lower'.[15] Stories were

---

10 In her letter to [Mr] Pattison (University of London Archives, AL225), Hesba Stretton declares her republican sympathies. An early log book entry (22 July 1861), reveals the stirring of such sentiments. During the 1890s, Stretton collaborated with the Russian exile Stepniak and attended the London lectures of the revolutionist Kropotkin. There was support among British intellectuals for the cause of the exiles, and considerable public interest in the oppression of the Russian peasantry, whose sufferings were recounted, often in sensational form, at public meetings.

11 Such descriptions abound. See, for example, Samuel Green's *The Story of the Religious Tract Society for One Hundred Years* (London: Religious Tract Society, 1899), pp. 127 and 126.

12 This information, and general examples which illustrate the attitudes, agendas and criteria of publishers, are drawn from the Religious Tract Society Archives, held at the University of London School for Oriental and African Studies, 'Executive Committee Minutes and Minutes of the Joint, Copyright and Finance Sub-Committees', RTS H8501 and H8502.

13 See RTS H8501, Fiche 284, 24 January 1871.

14 H8501, Fiche 232, 26 July 1864.

15 The entry continues 'such as that to which the principal persons of the story belong' (H8501, Fiche 251, 4 December 1866). The experiences on which such texts focus, are, of course, filtered through the lens of the middle-class writer/spectator; the voice of the poor is mediated, even though, as in Stretton's fiction, it may be suggested by personal observation. Those suffering the extremes of deprivation were also, in general, the least likely to read these narratives, as Anna Davin observes with reference to late nineteenth-century 'waif' stories in *Growing Up Poor: Home, School and Street in London 1870–1914* (London: Rivers Oram,

directed at those of 'humble condition' (whose conduct in Stretton's *The Fishers of Derby Haven*, 1866, met with Committee approval[16]), at 'working boys' and those with 'little advantage of education'.[17] Many were produced specifically with the servant class in mind.[18] Even where books were ostensibly aimed at a young audience, publishers were also targeting parents and adults of the lower classes, whose inferior understanding (as it was thought) and need for instruction were in some respects equated with those of children. Adults might absorb ideas through reading to children, but increasing literacy among younger family members meant that children often read to their elders. Furthermore, a narrative designed to prove salutary or uplifting for the poor, could also appeal to middle-class readers, extending awareness of material conditions beyond their own sphere, eliciting sympathy and charity, and encouraging mutually beneficial good works in terms of the spiritual state of the giver and both the body and the soul of the recipient.

Publishers increasingly walked a tightrope between the religious and the secular, between economic and moral imperatives. As early as 1859, Stretton herself, in 'The Postmaster's Daughter', had voiced an awareness – gained through family experience – that 'very few persons care to buy [religious books], except to give away'.[19] The Tract Society, whilst undertaking to supply important information on 'moral and religious truth in this intellectual and reading age',[20] and discouraging the inclusion of 'sensational incident[s]',[21] was anxious to 'enliven' texts[22] and to exploit, as far as they dared, the growing market for sensation fiction. No doubt the 'adventures' and 'dangers' related with 'vividness and interest' identified in *The Fishers of Derby Haven*[23] suited this requirement, as, from a more subtle perspective, did her portrayals of the underside of society. With the widening of child audiences, the publishers were alert to the financial potential of a rapidly expanding market, noting in 1865, that, along with devotional books, children's books were 'among the most saleable issues of the Society'[24] and regularly highlighting a shortage of original material.

2001), p. 69. Cutt, in her *Ministering Angels*, writes of the occupant of a Great Ormond Street Hospital 'Aunt Judy's Magazine [Charity] Cot', who was impressed by *Little Meg* (p. 144).

16 H8501, Fiche 246, 27 March, 1866.

17 H8501, Fiche 258, 22 October 1867 and Fiche 251, 1 January 1867.

18 Servants, many of whom, like Stretton's Cassy, were little more than children, were deemed particularly susceptible to the temptations around them. Like Cassy, they were often subject to exploitation by their employers. Doris Langley Moore, in *E. Nesbit: A Biography* (1933; London: Ernest Benn, 1967), quotes from a letter from E. Nesbit to Ada Breakell, written during the 1880s, in which Nesbit speaks of reading *Jessica's First Prayer* to her maid (p. 107). Nesbit was later to draw on Stretton's portrayal of urban poverty in her own writing, for example in *The New Treasure Seekers* (1904) and *Harding's Luck* (1909).

19 'The Postmaster's Daughter', *All The Year Round* (5 November 1859), 38.

20 37th AGM, December 1866, RTS Minute Book, Additional Papers.

21 H8501, Fiche 311, 24 February 1874.

22 H8501, Fiche 254, 26 February 1867.

23 H8501, Fiche 246, 27 March 1866.

24 H8502, Fiche 28, Copyright Sub-Committee, 27 September 1865.

Developments in children's literature were also entwined with women's struggles to forge a place in the literary market. Commonly focusing on the concerns of home and family, writing for children constituted an acceptable female literary activity. A respectable means of generating an income, it offered a degree of independence, and relief from conventional domesticity. In addition, it afforded an outlet for various forms of subversion and social comment, as critics have demonstrated.[25] For the forthright Hesba Stretton, an aspiring writer of adult novels – many of which were to contain more than a modicum of sensation – publishing for a younger market provided an alternative vehicle for social and political projects, through which cultural expectations and limitations could be exposed, and personal dissatisfactions articulated. It also afforded a springboard for establishing a wider reputation within the literary establishment.

During the early 1860s Stretton had begun to achieve some success with magazine stories and articles, and had embarked on two full-length novels for the secular adult market.[26] However, before publishing these works, she had already gravitated into the area of what she described in her diary as the 'child's story'.[27] Her Evangelical background and family connection with Sam Manning, Book Editor for the Religious Tract Society, rendered the Society's book department a

---

25 J. Briggs cites Stretton as a possible exception to the prevailing tendency amongst Evangelical writers, the majority of whom were women, to accept existing social structures: 'Women Writers and Writing for Children: From Sarah Fielding to E. Nesbit', in G. Avery and J. Briggs (eds), *Children and Their Books: A Celebration of the Work of Iona and Peter Opie* (Oxford: Clarendon Press, 1989), pp. 238–9. Mitzi Myers also explores the uses of the child figure for the women writer and argues the importance of taking child-centred texts seriously from a political point of view; see, for example, her 'Canonical "Orphans" and Critical *Ennui*: Rereading Edgeworth's Cross-Writing', in M. Myers and U.C. Knoepflmacher (eds), *Children's Literature* 25 (1997), 116–36.

26 *The Clives of Burcot* and *Paul's Courtship* both appeared in 1867, the former published by Tinsley, the latter by Wood. *The Clives of Burcot* attracted a number of favourable reviews, with several critics remarking upon the complexity of the issues. The critic for the *Observer* (6 January 1867), deemed the interest of the book 'unquestionable', and considered its status as a 'general favourite with the public' to be assured. Reviewers for the *Morning Star* (14 January 1867) and the *Standard* (30 August 1867) both commented on the strength of characterisation. The former made comparisons – not unfavourable to Stretton – with Charlotte Brontë's *Jane Eyre*, and placed Hesba Stretton 'in the foremost rank of living authoresses'; the latter declared Stretton's book 'one of the soundest and healthiest novels of the season', containing 'finished pictures, of which George Eliot would have no need to be ashamed'. Although *Paul's Courtship* attracted less favourable reviews, a number of Stretton's long novels were well received, with *The Doctor's Dilemma* (1872) and *Hester Morley's Promise* (1873), both published by H.S. King, presented as novels of the week by the *Athenaeum* (15 February 1873 and 6 September 1873, respectively). Full-length texts such as these – unequivocally for the adult market – can be seen as important both in their own right and as part of a discussion of Stretton's work as a whole. Encapsulating central ideas surrounding, for example, the figure of the child or the social outcast, and articulating the complexities and ambiguities of the human condition, these longer novels confirm, elaborate and explicate the currents, patterns and sentiments identifiable in her more familiar texts and her writing more generally.

27 'Log Book': Period to 16 November 1863.

natural destination for such fiction. Their 'Readers', who applauded the originality of her narratives, were swift to recognise writing 'far above the usual average of such works'[28] and the first four titles were quickly published in book form.[29] Just as Stretton's successful early writing had emerged in periodicals, however, so her most famous story was also to appear in that medium, this time as a serial in the *Sunday at Home*, during 1866. 'Numerous and urgent requests' were made for *Jessica's First Prayer* to be issued as a separate text;[30] later, a similar response led to the publication of *Alone in London*, which had been 'attracting much attention' as a serial and was 'highly recommended'.[31]

By February 1867, when *Pilgrim Street* was recommended for publication, publishers were confidently using the phrase 'popular author' to describe her.[32] Whilst mindful of the potential of her books to 'do good' – *Little Meg's Children* was 'thought even to exceed *Jessica's First Prayer* in pathos and power'[33] – they were increasingly aware of her commercial importance to the Society. The Committee was alert to the fact that by 1869 her books accounted for over one-third of new books, and in excess of one-fifth of their book circulation; her high sales made it particularly desirable that she should provide another book for Christmas.[34]

Texts such as *Jessica's First Prayer*, *Little Meg's Children* and *Alone in London* enjoyed an unusually wide and sustained popularity. Within approximately two years of publication, the sixty-thousandth copy of *Jessica's First Prayer* (1867), to take one example, had been produced. The hundred-thousandth had made its appearance by about 1871, and by the mid 1880s sales were approaching four hundred thousand.[35] Total sales at the time of Stretton's death were estimated to be in the region of two million.[36] Originally to be sold at sixpence or one shilling,[37] it was issued in numerous editions and large numbers of cheaper formats were produced. In 1886 an announcement in the Society's archives of a new series of 'Cheap Reprints' refers

---

28 H8501, Fiche 231, 21 June 1864.

29 *Fern's Hollow* (1864), *Enoch Roden's Training* (1865), *The Children of Cloverley* (1865), *The Fishers of Derby Haven* (1866).

30 H8501, Fiche 251, 4 December 1866.

31 H8501, Fiche 273, 17 August 1869. The question of serial publication (in which format many of her stories continued to make their first appearance, both with the RTS and with other publishers), is of particular interest, not only in terms of the narrative momentum encouraged by the form, but also for the sustained connection which it guaranteed between author and reader. This relationship with an audience over the duration of the career of a popular and prolific author is significant both in terms of prolonged familiarity, identification and anticipation, and in relation to the gradual dissemination of ideas and values, political and social.

32 H8501, Fiche 254, 26 February 1867.

33 H8501, Fiche 264, 21 April 1868.

34 H8502, Joint Sub-Committee, Fiche 34, 15 July 1869.

35 J. White, 'Further Notes on Children's Best Sellers', *Children's Books History Society Newsletter* 29 (1984), 3–4.

36 Anon., 'Hesba Stretton – Born 1832, I. Memoir', *Sunday at Home*, 1911, 121–4, p. 122. According to this Memoir, in addition to the numbers acknowledged, numerous unauthorised editions were produced (ibid.).

37 H8501, Fiche 251, 4 December 1866.

to the publication over the preceding four years of well-known tales like *Jessica's First Prayer* and Mrs Walton's *A Peep Behind the Scenes* (1877), at prices from a penny to threepence. Although figures for Stretton's stories are not specified, overall sales of two and a half million copies of such books for the four-year period cited give an idea of the volume of editions produced.[38] Advertisements in RTS texts show that by 1911, in addition to *Jessica*, *Little Meg* and *Alone in London*, stories such as *Jessica's Mother*, *Lost Gip*, *Cassy* and *No Place Like Home* were all appearing in the 'Bouverie' Series of Penny Popular Stories.[39] Throughout the latter part of the nineteenth century and beyond, Stretton's books, including the earliest titles, continued to be published in a variety of sizes and editions, with many appearing in the Shilling 'Gift' series as well as more elaborate and costly formats. As Stretton herself records, by 1870 the story of Jessica had been made into lantern-slides ('Log Book': 3 June, 1870). It later appeared as a 'Service of Song'.[40] In 1909 a silent film was produced, and another film version released in 1921.[41]

The publishers expected *Little Meg's Children* to 'prove a most successful work, to sell at 1s. 6d.'[42] They were not mistaken: by November 1868 sales had already reached 10,000, and in February 1869 Stretton received a cheque for £131.[43] By summer 1869, another 14,000 had been sold, and its continuing popularity ensured considerable sums in royalties.[44] An indication of early sales of other Stretton stories can be gleaned from textual advertisements, which show, for example, that numbers of *The King's Servants* (first published in 1873 by H.S. King) had by 1877 reached 36,000, with *Cassy* (1874) at 30,000 and *The Storm of Life* (1876) – commended by critics for its beauty and pathos – at 11,000. By the following year, according to

---

38 H8501, Fiche 444, March/April 1886.

39 See lists in RTS texts such as *Harry's Magic Glasses* by C.A. Mercer (n.d. but *c.*1911 (label), author's private collection.

40 'Hesba Stretton – Born 1832', p. 123.

41 Stretton's diary records her attendance during 1870 at a Magic Lantern show that included 'the Jessica slides, some of which were very good' ('Log Book', 3 June 1870). The British Film Institute indicates that the 1909 film, by Walturdaw, like many silent films, may have been lost or destroyed (letter to the author of this chapter from the BFI, 18 April 2001). The later 35 mm version, by Seal Film Company (1921), is included in the National Film and Television Archive (Title Ref. 435684).

42 H8501, Fiche 264, 21 April 1868.

43 Stretton records these milestones in her diary during 1868–9. She also records her dealings with publishers over the publication of *Little Meg*, during which she risked playing various publishers off against each other in order to obtain the best offer per 1,000 copies, in addition to the outright sum normally accepted. She reluctantly agreed a figure of £6.5s. per 1,000 from the Religious Tract Society. ('Log Book': April/May 1868). There is no mention in her diary of a time restriction, although RTS minutes suggest an arrangement for ten years, with copyright reverting to them after this period (H8502, Fiche 33, 21 May 1868). Research into their archives reveals numerous occasions when Stretton attempted to push back boundaries and negotiate special terms, although she was sometimes forced to accept a compromise.

44 According to the 1911 memoir in the *Sunday at Home*, the combined circulation of *Little Meg* and *Alone in London* reached 750,000 ('Hesba Stretton – Born 1832', p. 123).

the 'sixty-first thousandth' *Lost Gip* (1878, first published 1873), reprints numbered 43,000, 38,000 and 21,000 copies respectively.[45]

Labels and inscriptions show that Stretton's texts were being awarded as prizes in Sunday and mainstream schools from the 1860s through to the early decades of the twentieth century, and their dissemination was not confined to Britain. A number of the titles which Stretton published with H.S. King and other establishments were produced in America by Dodd, Mead and the American Tract Society and various other publishing houses continued to issue her work in that country. The Religious Tract Society also produced and distributed literature in Europe, the colonies and places of missionary activity worldwide. Minutes record early requests for French translations of *Alone in London* and *Little Meg*.[46] By the time of Stretton's death, according to sources such as the RTS Quarterly *Seed Time and Harvest* (December 1911), *Jessica* had been translated into at least 15 languages, and its impact noted in places such as Beirut, Liberia, Asiatic Turkey, Budapest and Russia.[47]

Whilst information concerning publishing agendas and aspects of distribution may point to particular assumptions about readership, identifying the books' ongoing dissemination and their actual readers is more difficult. The Tract Society made grants to public libraries, and the accounts of Henry S. King, with whom Stretton started publishing in the 1870s, indicate that copies were routinely distributed to libraries at the time of publication. However, evidence about reactions and reading patterns is limited, and often confined to the middle classes.[48] Library information on particular authors is scarce, and contemporary reader surveys such as those conducted by Edward Salmon during the 1880s inevitably give an incomplete picture. Salmon's findings reveal Hesba Stretton as a popular author for girls, and *Little Meg's Children* as a favourite book.[49] No doubt boys also read Stretton, but may have been prevented by peer pressure from citing her books because of the perceived emotional, and by implication, feminine, appeal. Yet her engagement with the emotions, and the alternative masculine models offered by Stretton's role reversals, which present and value the young or adult male as caring and nurturing,

---

45 The 1877 figures are taken from advertisements contained in an 1877 edition of *David Lloyd's Last Will* (published by Henry S. King). Stretton continued to receive royalties from H.S. King for particular texts until after the end of the nineteenth century (King/Kegan Paul Archives, University College London).

46 H8502, Fiche 35, 16 June 1870 and Fiche 36, 20 April 1871.

47 Stretton records an encounter with a missionary and a 'black man from Liberia', who were both familiar with her books ('Log Book': 19 June 1871). Tsar Alexander II ordered that *Jessica's First Prayer* should be placed in all Russian schools, although this order was later revoked ('Hesba Stretton – Born 1832', p. 123).

48 Mitchell, *The New Girl*, cites an East End free library, used by poor and working-class women during the 1890s, which records the popularity of writers such as Stretton and Mrs Henry Wood (p. 142).

49 Edward Salmon, 'What Girls Read', *Nineteenth Century* 20 (1886), 515–29 (p. 528). See also Salmon's *Juvenile Literature As It Is* (London: Henry J. Drane, 1888). Salmon prepared his summary from responses to a series of questions put to boys and girls (aged 11–19) in various schools.

might have constituted a vital aspect of boys' reading experience.[50] Within the pages of these narratives, the reader can encounter or identify with young Sandy (*Lost Gip*), who completely accepts the maternal role in assuming responsibility for the new-born Gip, or Don in *A Thorny Path*, who describes his adopted 'sister' Dot as 'my little gel' (p. 112). Don becomes the self-sacrificing mother, going hungry in order to feed the child.

As Salmon recognised, survey results are inevitably distorted by the fact that the books offered to children as presents or prizes were chosen and purchased predominantly for, rather than by them. Sales figures, therefore, are not a direct measure of popularity. Likewise, certain commendations reflect perceived effectiveness in relation to particular Evangelical aims. Information gleaned from biographies and autobiographies suggests that while some readers were impressed by the power of Stretton's portrayals, others expressed distaste for their moral imperatives and the unrealistic piety of particular protagonists.[51] Yet the comments retrieved represent only a fraction of her readership; many are drawn from twentieth-century sources, and relate predominately to *Jessica* and *Little Meg*. What can we say of the response of the vast number of readers whose views have remained unrecorded, or of other aspects of her fiction which may have made an impact? What can be surmised about the reaction to texts such as *Cassy*, *Lost Gip*, *Carola* and others – perhaps less popular than those very famous titles, but still published in large numbers? Not necessarily chosen by readers, Stretton's books nevertheless found their way into countless homes, augmenting perhaps meagre collections, to be read, arguably, within and across families and generations, forming part of a common reading experience, and engaging with individual interests, desires and needs.

---

50 Although Stretton does not feature in Salmon's lists of boys' favourites, award labels confirm that boys were among the recipients of her texts. During the last decades of the nineteenth century, efforts to promote 'manliness' and to steer boys away from 'feminine' behaviour in preparation for their dominant role were self-consciously taken up by Board Schools – see E. Ross, *Love and Toil: Motherhood in Outcast London 1870–1918* (New York and Oxford: Oxford University Press, 1993), p. 153. In such a climate, Stretton's narratives perhaps answered to needs that were not addressed in wider literature for boys.

51 In a letter to the *Record* in November 1867, Lord Shaftesbury declared *Jessica's First Prayer* unrivalled for its 'simplicity, pathos, and depth of Christian feeling', and noted the author's 'minute, and accurate, knowledge of that class, its wants, and its capabilities'. He identified it as the work of a woman, as 'no man on earth could have completed a page of it'. The Reverend C.H. Spurgeon found *Little Meg's Children* 'equal to Jessica's First Prayer in simple pathos', adding 'What encomium can be higher? We confess to having gone upstairs for a dry handkerchief after reading this tale. The writer has the key of our heart' (quoted in the anonymous (but signed 'C.H.I.') 'Hesba Stretton', *Seed Time and Harvest* (December 1911), 12). Praise for its 'pathetic simplicity' was later echoed by E. Nesbit, according to Langley Moore, *E. Nesbit*, p. 107. The journalist Hulda Friederichs found no trace of 'mawkishness' or 'weak sentimentality' in Stretton's books in 'Hesba Stretton at Home', *The Young Woman* (22, July 1894), 327–33 (p. 332), but Lilian Faithful disliked its moral didacticism, according to Kate Flint, *The Woman Reader 1837–1914* (Oxford: Clarendon Press 1993), p. 221, while Leonora Eyles was impressed by its 'heart-rending portrayals' (quoted in Flint, *The Woman Reader*, p. 222). Herbert Read was struck by the 'grim pathos', but retained positive memories of the influence of *Little Meg's Children* (quoted in Cutt, *Ministering Angels*, p. 143).

If readers (like Stretton's characters) were likely to be drawn from different social classes, agendas of both publishers and author also indicate the fluidity of boundaries between child and adult literature – boundaries which were, in any case, more permeable in the nineteenth century than they are today. The identification of Stretton's books as specifically for a particular age range, whether in terms of targeted or potential readers, is problematic. Clearly, a number of stories chronicle the experiences of child/juvenile protagonists, offering a child's perspective and inviting identification or empathy. Children often figure in the longer novels, but are less likely to be the central character. Although Stretton apparently regarded the early RTS texts as children's stories, Society 'Readers' identified *The Children of Cloverley* as likely to 'interest adults as well as the young'.[52] Underlining this ambiguity, the author of a memoir of Stretton reported comments that *Jessica* was 'a child's book truly ... but its effect upon sailors was marvellous'.[53]

Her narratives are less easily recognisable as children's stories than those of contemporaries such as Mrs Walton. Hesba Stretton rarely employs a maternal narrator–child tone, or directly addresses an identifiable child reader, as, for example, does Mrs Castle Smith, who refers to 'my little readers'.[54] Stretton views child and adult (within the story and as reader) not as categories, but as individuals whose experiences, needs and rights are significant – in short, as equally valid subjects and audiences. If adults are addressed over the shoulder of a potential child reader, this is seldom at the expense of the child, and often serves to emphasise the vulnerability of the young and to expose the failings of those in authority. Stretton explores the concerns of both child and adult, highlighting bonds and differences.

Hesba Stretton's writing consistently demands at least a reasonable level of literacy and comprehension; the reader is expected to engage with mature and serious concerns. In terms of narrative simplicity, certain texts – albeit carrying deeper resonance – might appeal to a younger or less sophisticated reader, whilst the stylistic and thematic complexity of others suggests a mature audience. Many stories, including *Bede's Charity*, *The King's Servants*, *Carola* and others, occupy a place in what might be regarded as a continuum within which adult and children's

---

52 H8501, Fiche 243, 3 October 1865.

53 'Hesba Stretton – Born 1832', p. 123. According to this memoir, rough young sailors, apparently choking and red-eyed, were among the 'strong men' reduced to tears by this tale (ibid.). Textual lists of other works/editions tended to place Stretton's work under a general category rather than as children's stories. The *Day of Rest Annual* (n.d., Strahan and Company), which includes Stretton's *The Lord's Pursebearers*, does not list this under the Children's Section in the Contents Table. Advertisements in the *Sunday at Home* for forthcoming inclusions do not place *Under the Old Roof* under titles/material for children, and textual advertisements for *Carola* appear with those relating to full-length adult novels. On the other hand, the 'Favourite Gift Series' (in about 1911) lists a number of Stretton titles, including texts as diverse as *Jessica's First Prayer* and *Under the Old Roof*, as 'approved stories for Boys and Girls'.

54 *Froggy's Little Brother*, p. 4. In appealing for charity, Mrs Castle Smith includes parents in her direct address (p. 198). Mrs Walton's novels include *Christie's Old Organ* (1874) and *A Peep Behind the Scenes* (1877).

literature intersect and overlap. For some, perhaps, they served as stepping-stones on the path to full-length novels.

In order to broaden our understanding of the complex appeal of Stretton's themes, we must bring this awareness of a potentially varied readership (in terms of both age and class) to a closer examination of her stories, exploring their relationship to the individual psyche and the wider cultural imagination. The experience of reading and making meaning is a process of interaction and negotiation, which involves the words on the page, but a great deal more than that. All the elements that writer and reader bring to the text – the influences of the world around them, their experiences, knowledge and value-judgements – come into play, at conscious and unconscious levels.[55] These elements intermingle, combine and sometimes clash, producing tensions and contradictions. If we consider a particular text as one among many 'cultural texts' – which include, as well as works by the same author, wider literary, non-literary, artistic and visual images – we can see that words and illustrations, ideas, patterns and motifs, overlap and call attention to each other in various ways, generating diffuse echoes, associations and meanings. Writers and texts may, at one level, invite the reader to adopt one position over another. However, narratives may – intentionally or unintentionally – offer alternative positions, and readers, because they read in diverse ways and bring with them individual priorities and needs, are liable to make different connections, engage with particular aspects, and take different things from the books they read. They can question and read against the grain, overlooking or resisting some elements, finding relevance and taking pleasure in others.

If publishers instantly recognised Stretton's ability to tell a good story, textual advertisements underline this enduring strength, with reviewers stressing that 'from first to last the interest of the story [*Carola*] never flags'. Also highlighted is the 'peculiar force' given to her writing by 'a breadth in Miss Stretton's views of life'.[56] Clearly, the greater the range of interests and viewpoints a narrative offers, the greater the opportunity for alternative readings, which may or may not be the most obvious. The many issues and perspectives which Stretton explores, the ideas and counter-currents within her work, ensure a range of possibilities – complementary and competing. Embodying tensions, and tapping into wider preoccupations and anxieties, her themes invite different forms of identification, offering something for everyone. The freedom of choice denied the reader of prize texts is, arguably, afforded in other ways within the narratives.

---

55 For a useful discussion of the possibility of diverse readings and responses, see, for example, Lissa Paul, *Reading Otherways* (Stroud: Thimble Press, 1998). Readings depend, as Paul suggests, on who is looking, on the conditions under which they are looking and the angle from which readers approach the text. For an overview of approaches which focus on the relationship between 'texts' in the broadest sense, see Christine Wilkie, 'Relating Texts: Intertextuality', in Peter Hunt (ed.), *Understanding Children's Literature* (London and New York: Routledge, 1999), 130–6. See also Peter Hollindale's 'Ideology and the Children's Book', *Signal* 55 (1988), 3–22, and John Stephens's *Language and Ideology in Children's Fiction* (Harlow: Longman, 1992).

56 Reviews quoted in an advertisement contained in an RTS edition of *The King's Servants* (author's private collection).

Clearly, these stories contain didactic currents: designed, at least in part, as tools for evangelism and moral improvement, they incorporate the principles which publishers routinely required to be 'interwoven in the narrative';[57] they form part of a programme of socialisation motivated by political as well as religious concerns. Themes served, in the eyes of publishers, to 'inculcate a spirit of contentment' with one's lot,[58] to 'enforce submission' to God's authority (*The Children of Cloverley*),[59] or to guard against temptation (*Pilgrim Street*).[60] Hesba Stretton's stories generally complied with requirements, striking the right note with publishers and critics, although additions to the religious teaching were sometimes required, and her satirical portraits of Church figures occasionally provoked irritation.[61] However, if her narratives met with the approval of those concerned with evangelical effectiveness, they undoubtedly also appealed for reasons beyond those imperatives; there is so much to interest, attract and provide food for thought. Stretton exploits theme and character to convey personal, religious and social messages, but these are wide-ranging, radical as well as conservative, and her stories are as likely to provoke questioning as to encourage submission. She demonstrates that faith empowers, and religion can be harnessed for liberating as well as restrictive or regulatory purposes.

Espousing a fundamental belief in a loving and personal God, Stretton exposes and satirises the coldness, bigotry and inadequacy of aspects of organised religion and the ways in which society has distorted and exploited religious ideas for its own ends. Her sympathies permit doubt and uncertainty, suggesting a moral complexity which undercuts moralising, redirects blame and shows how social and family structures which are supposed to reflect biblical models are, in fact, found wanting. In *Pilgrim Street* and other texts, God's paternal role is contrasted with earthly models in ways which chime with Stretton's evident anger at the patriarchal abuse of power and authority – both within the family and in public institutions, whether this involves male domination and abuse of women across classes, or the oppression of minorities by the 'Autocrat of All the Russias' in *The Highway of Sorrow* (p. 391). Stretton constantly draws attention to the way in which Jesus treated outcasts, women and children – as though (in the innocent but, for the attentive reader, sardonically charged words of Cassy) 'they were almost as good as men' (*Cassy*, p. 138). It is, in fact, the renewed religious conviction of Mr Shafto (in *Lost Gip*) which promotes a reshaping of gender relations within the household, establishing a degree of sexual equality which sees him hastening to clean his own boots for the first time in years (p. 85).

If the potential audience is hybrid, there is also a blending of many different elements and influences within the texts, in which realism, romance and fairy tale, fact and fiction intermingle. Although Stretton's socially-grounded fiction might, at first sight, be considered the very opposite of fantasy – a genre often frowned upon by moral and religious writers, its concerns clearly overlap with the themes explored

---

57 H8501, Fiche 254, 26 February 1867.
58 H8501, Fiche 299, 20 August 1872.
59 H8501, Fiche 243, 3 October 1865.
60 H8501, Fiche 254, 26 February 1867.
61 See, for example, 'Log Book': 11 December 1868.

by Charles Kingsley and George MacDonald in their classic fantasies.[62] At the same time, interwoven into Stretton's narratives – perhaps tapping into archetypal fears – are familiar fairy tale patterns and allusions, ranging from the wild wood or forest with its grasping, menacing shapes and shadows, and its associations with sexual abuse (evoked, for example, in *Cassy*, p. 14), to motifs of Bluebeard, the wicked stepmother, the bountiful godmother/benefactress or the sinister fur-wrapped Snow Queen of Hans Christian Andersen, across a number of texts. Attention is drawn to the fact that, in their shared highlighting of opposing moral forces and supernatural intervention, the concerns of religion and fairy tale are not so far removed from one another, relating the same kinds of stories about lives and relationships, and requiring a not dissimilar act of belief. At another level, although faith may ostensibly be promoted as superior, the unbelieving Jessica's first impression of the Church as fairyland – and perhaps, by association with her past acting role in stage fantasy, as theatre – might prompt a reader, in a climate of wavering belief, to question not only the external manifestations of religion, but its status as truth.

Stretton's themes engage with the significant preoccupation of her age – evidenced in art, literature and social enquiry/legislation – with the child. Such interest reflects a personal and cultural nostalgia; the child figure, embodying all that is natural, uncontaminated and innocent, serves as a repository for adult yearnings; it represents that which is lost, the child in the self, an individual and collective past, as well as a locus of future possibility. At the same time, the poor child is seen both as a threat to society, and, increasingly, as victim of material circumstances, in need of protection and redirection. Along with novelists like Dickens, and social commentators such as Henry Mayhew and Benjamin Waugh, Hesba Stretton paints a picture of 'thousands and thousands of poor children … everywhere' (*The Lord's Pursebearers*, p. 87). Referring to the role played by Elizabeth Barrett Browning's 'The Cry of the Children' (1844) in awakening consciences, Stretton speaks of 'eyes growing keener to discern any evil threatening childhood'.[63] Underlining collective responsibility, Stretton angrily exposes society's reluctance to intervene in the exploitation of children, because it is not 'a matter affecting property', but only ' the lives of little friendless children' (*The Lord's Pursebearers*, p. 247). Samuel Green, writing in 1899, suggested the importance of Stretton's texts in arousing interest in the condition of the poor and outcast child; 100 years later, the historian Raphael

---

62 See, for example, Kingsley's *The Water-Babies* (1863) and MacDonald's *At the Back of the North Wind* (1871). Contemporary disapproval of fairy tales can be found, for example, in Charlotte Yonge's comments that 'too much of impossible unreality' is likely to lead to a 'morbid craving for excitement', in *Womankind* (London: Mozley and Smith, 1876), pp. 64–5. Modern studies of children's literature, in contrast, tend to favour works of fantasy and imagination over texts of realism.

63 'Women's Work for Children' in A. Burdett-Coutts (ed.), *Woman's Mission* (London: Sampson Low, Marston, 1893), p. 5. For contemporary accounts of children swarming in the streets, see, among others, Charles Dickens, *Oliver Twist* (1838); Henry Mayhew, *London Labour and the London Poor* (1861–62); Benjamin Waugh, *The Gaol Cradle: Who Rocks It?* (1873, repr., ed. M.J. Wiener, New York and London: Garland, 1984).

Samuel pointed out their significance in promoting the 'social compunction' which fed into progressive reforms.[64]

These stories underline the extent to which financial circumstances and social class determine not only childhood experiences, but the ways in which people define what it means to be a child. It becomes abundantly clear that boundaries between adult and child – in relation to independence, responsibility, maturity and awareness – are not set in stone. Contrasting the 'rosy and merry face[d]' (middle-class ideal) child, safe in its rural Eden of 'unbroken childish happiness', with 'thin and meagre-face[d]' waifs such as Jessica, or the 'living skeleton[s]' of children exploited as begging attractions in *The Lord's Pursebearers*, Stretton confronts the reader with alternative versions of childhood, offering experiences of what critic Peter Hollindale has termed 'differential childness'.[65] Her fiction draws upon, explodes and reshapes idealised myths of childhood; while her portrayals incorporate romanticised or sentimentalised versions of the poor child, they also register stark materialities and carry dark undercurrents.

There is, within these narratives, an overlapping of the material and the psychological. The lost, orphaned or quasi-orphaned child who figures prominently in Stretton's texts – in middle-class as well as poor settings – reflects the physical realities of loss, from the perspective of child, siblings and parents. The displaced child – like the excluded adult in her narratives – stands in for the individual's experience of vulnerability, powerlessness, insecurity or rejection, and has a resonance across classes. The image also taps into wider uncertainties, embodying experiences of alienation, rootlessness and loss of identity in an increasingly industrialised and commercialised society – feelings reinforced by Stretton's evocation of 'a depressing sense of forlornness in the midst of crowds' which characterises the City, where strangers may be 'lost forever'.[66]

The unconfined child of the streets – free to stay away from its home 'as long as [it] will' – excites fascination, pity and revulsion.[67] Perceived as an anarchic figure, its difference also embodies the fear of the other in the self. The wild-faced waif with its thick, dark mass of tangled hair, along with the black-eyed 'reg'lar little gipsy' (*Lost Gip*, p. 4), the forest-dweller Cassy, or the half-savage mountain child (*Half Brothers*), suggests a Heathcliff, a Maggie Tulliver, or even a Caliban, and

---

64 Green, *Story of The Religious Tract Society*, p. 79. Raphael Samuel *et al.* (eds), *Island Stories: Unravelling Britain*, vol. 2: Theatres of Memory, ed. Alison Light with Sally Alexander and Gareth Stedman Jones (London and New York: Verso, 1998), pp. 306–7.

65 *The Lord's Pursebearers*, p. 248; *Jessica's First Prayer*, p. 12; *The Lord's Pursebearers*, p. 177. Peter Hollindale, in 'Odysseys: The Childness of Journeying Children', *Signal* 94 (2001), 29–44 (p. 41), uses this phrase in relation to the encounters which 'journeying' characters – and readers, as voyagers – experience, and their responses to different environments and life patterns.

66 *The Soul of Honour*, p. 79; *Bede's Charity*, p. 105.

67 This idea of 'wildness' outside the home – expressed here in *Bede's Charity* (p.108), and echoed by many contemporary commentators – reflects the importance given to the socialising influence of home and mother. 'Wildness' can be seen as desirable in terms of the 'natural', as privileged by the Romantics and by educators such as Jean-Jacques Rousseau; at the same time, it may be associated with chaos and resistance to socialisation.

resonates with society's attraction to, yet fear of, the untamed, the foreign or exotic. The street Arab, Tony, with his bare, mud-*black* feet, stands in for, but is never far from, the real ethnic other or colonial subject, who, like the child or the degraded lower-class adult, needs to be civilised and schooled (*Alone in London*, pp. 68–9, italics added). The language of these narratives, even more than that of texts such as Kingsley's *The Water-Babies*, highlights the overlapping of moral, social and racial black and whiteness, dirt and cleanliness, revealing how meanings and attitudes can be transferred and exploited.

The street child's premature independence is alluring – potentially attractive to the middle-class child reader constrained by the limitations of its protected domestic environment. Yet for the waif of Stretton's novels, it is a freedom born of a fundamental dislocation – a not belonging, a having '[no]wheres' to go (*Lost Gip*, p. 13). Like Jo in Dickens's *Bleak House*, or Nanny, the girl crossing-sweeper in MacDonald's *At the Back of the North Wind*, Stretton's Sandy (*Lost Gip*) and his nomadic counterparts are constantly being moved on by authority without any possibility of destination, denied the right to occupy any existential space.[68] Identities are elusive: Don, of *A Thorny Path*, has no 'proper' name, having 'lost it afore I can remember'. The sibling relationship, or surrogate sibling connection, may represent the only possible source of an affirmative sense of self: 'I'm all she's got, and she's all I've got' (pp. 17 and 113).

In portraits such as that of Jessica, Stretton reaches out to the reader's fundamental needs. Linking physical hardship with emotional starvation, she captures and conveys with an immediacy that betrays intimate observation, the child's experience of sensory deprivation. We become intensely aware of Jessica's gaze, reduced and sharpened to 'a pair of very bright dark eyes', and 'as hungry as that of a mouse ... driven by famine into a trap' (*Jessica's First Prayer*, pp. 11–12). Carefully chosen detail directs attention to 'two bare little feet curling up from the damp pavement', and underlines the yearning for respite as Jessica lifts 'first one and then the other' and lays them 'one over another to gain a momentary feeling of warmth' (p. 12). The situation exposes the vulnerability of the waif, who becomes the object of society's – and, potentially, the reader's – objectifying gaze. However, the focus on body parts invites participation, at a primal level, in Jessica's lack: her eyes gleam 'hungrily', and she 'smack[s] her thin lips, as if in fancy she was tasting the warm and fragrant coffee' (p. 12).

This cameo encapsulates the experience of basic physical needs denied; it is simultaneously charged with a sense of fear and a longing for human warmth and contact, which prefigures and heightens the explanation of Jessica's exclusion by her mother and persecution by the police (p. 13). Stretton utilises the physical blue-blackness of Jessica's limbs (p. 15) to set up a doubled-edged image in which signs of coldness and abuse merge, generating a sense of emotional, as well as material, chill and bruising. Later, when the child reaches out to touch the velvet mantle worn by one of the congregation (p. 36), the unaccustomed tactile experience speaks not

---

68 Charles Dickens, *Bleak House* (1853, repr., ed. N. Bradbury, Harmondsworth: Penguin, 1996), p. 308; George MacDonald, *At the Back of the North Wind* (1871, repr. New York, Airmont, 1966), p. 41.

only of curiosity about a social world beyond Jessica's knowledge, but equally, of multiple deprivation and a yearning for primary comfort and interaction.

Families in Stretton's stories are shown to be fragmented or dysfunctional, with adults flawed or absent. Fathers may be unknown, mourned or, in many cases, feared as tyrants, as they are in a number of her longer novels. Motherlessness, and the yearning for a mother's touch, kiss or even the rustle of her dress – echoed in countless contemporary texts, from Maria Charlesworth's *Ministering Children* to Christina Rossetti's *Speaking Likenesses* – is an insistent, and powerfully resonant motif.[69] At the same time, mothers – as in Dickens's novels – are sometimes unworthy of the name, showing neglect and even cruelty. The abuse suffered by Jessica and Cassy at the hands of adults – parents and step-parents alike – like the beatings experienced or witnessed by the protagonists of Silas Hocking's *Her Benny*, and viewed as a part of life by Kingsley's Tom, or Dickens's Oliver and Nancy – are class-specific, drawing attention to the effects of poverty, oppression and brutalisation.[70] Yet, the poor street child is at once different, and, perhaps, disturbingly the same, his or her experiences functioning as displaced arenas for unvoiceable experiences which transcend class.

Protagonists like the slum girl Meg, with her 'anxious air' and slow step 'less like that of a child than of a woman', responsible for the physical, financial and emotional care of siblings, are, like Henry Mayhew's 'Watercress Girl', neither child nor woman.[71] If childhood is equated with sexual innocence (and sexuality is a subject ostensibly avoided by children's literature), the implications of potential or imminent sexuality are, in Stretton's texts, never far from the surface. Kitty, in *Little Meg's Children*, has already succumbed to the life of prostitution from which Meg – whose influence in fact redeems the older girl – is at risk. Descriptions of the barefoot Jessica, her torn dress 'slipping down over [her] shivering shoulders' (p. 12), or the 'overgrown' Joan of *The Lord's Pursebearers*, with her too-short frock, barely-covered legs, 'promise of beauty' and potential for earning 'a mint o' money' (p. 37), also place these protagonists in a commonly understood context. Along with figures such as Barnardo's 'City Waif' and, more obliquely, Lewis Caroll's photograph of Alice Liddell as a Beggar Girl, they can be seen as innocent, yet on the edge of knowing, available and corruptible, their future clearly signposted.[72]

---

69 Maria Charlesworth, *Ministering Children* (1854, repr. London: Seeley and Company, 1895), p. 2; Christina Rossetti, *Speaking Likenesses* (1874), repr. in N. Auerbach and U.C. Knoepflmacher (eds), *Forbidden Journeys: Fairy Tales and Fantasies by Victorian Women Writers* (Chicago: Chicago University Press, 1992), p. 326.

70 Silas Hocking, *Her Benny* (1890, repr., Manchester, 'Memories', n.d.), p. 19.

71 *Little Meg's Children*, pp. 13–14; Henry Mayhew, *London Labour and the London Poor*, selected and ed. Victor Neuburg (Harmondsworth: Penguin, 1985), pp. 64–8. Mayhew's young interviewee – approximately eight years old – maintains that she 'ain't a child, and I shan't be a woman till I'm twenty' (p. 68).

72 T.J. Barnardo, 'A City Waif: How I Fished for and Caught Her', 1885, collected in *Tracts on Dr. Barnardo's Homes* (London: Shaw and Company, 1886); Charles Dodgson (Lewis Carroll), 'Alice Liddell as The Beggar Maid' (*c.*1859), reproduced in Anne Higonnet, *Pictures of Innocence: The History and Crisis of Ideal Childhood* (London: Thames and Hudson, 1998), p. 124 (plate 59).

The outcast child, it might be suggested, stands in for the middle-class child whose sexuality is denied, but feared.

Stretton's narratives investigate questions of individual morality, but also expose society's class-related responses to deviancy, underlining the consequences of scapegoating and labelling. They highlight the ineffectiveness of a prison system which corrupts and fails to rehabilitate the juvenile offender – issues addressed in similar terms by contemporary progressives such as Benjamin Waugh, and which remain the subject of heated debate even today.[73] Assumed to be 'born and bred liars and thieves', deemed 'slippery as eels', the poor protagonists of Stretton's stories are constantly hounded and held under the torchlight of authority, permitted no voice in their own defence (*Pilgrim Street*, p. 16; *Lost Gip*, p. 50).

In *Bede's Charity*, young Cor voices the plain truth that 'Folks oughtn't to die of thinness' (p. 62). Stretton highlights the fact that waifs like Don (*A Thorny Path*) die as a result of the inadequacies of the system; the final chapter of this story contains a diatribe against an affluent society which allows the vulnerable to be 'stinted in the absolute necessaries of life' (pp. 157–8). At the same time, Stretton's fictional children demonstrate their perceptiveness, self-possession and resilience – their ability to become entrepreneurs and mature, effective managers when adults and those in authority fail them. Given the chance, many succeed in transcending their circumstances. As Romantic agents of transformation, they may exert a moral and spiritual influence on their elders – sometimes by their mere presence; they also act as social commentators and mediators, with the power to change attitudes and behaviour. It is Jessica who exposes the double standards of the church official, Daniel; she not only turns the parent–child socialising relationship upside-down, admonishing her mother for her impropriety, but also crosses the boundary of traditional male spiritual authority.[74] Sandy (*Lost Gip*) – initially deemed scarcely fit to eat and sleep alongside his working-class surrogate family (p. 61) – directly confronts the father (p. 78), exposing the latter's hypocrisy and underlining the creation of 'otherness' within as well as between classes. More subtly, it is Cassy (pp. 64 and 75) who points to the cultural acceptance of men's oppression of women, and Jessica whose matter-of-fact interpretation of the phrase 'reckoning day' suggests, not only an untroubled conscience, but the irrelevance of other-worldliness to those preoccupied with immediate material needs.[75] Through the eyes of the young protagonist of *Max Kromer* (1871), machismo, patriotic fervour and war are exposed as anything but glorious, their effects on ordinary citizens, women and children being clearly devastating. Although awareness and agency might be said to be confined to the

---

73 See Waugh, *The Gaol Cradle*.

74 *Jessica's Mother*, pp. 59–60. *Jessica's Mother* first appeared in periodical form in 1867. A proposal for its issue as a separate volume was put forward, but declined by RTS 'Readers', in 1870 (H8502, Fiche 35, Copyright Sub-Committee Minutes, 19 May and 16 June), and it is thought that it did not appear separately in hardback until early in the twentieth century.

75 Unaware of the spiritual interpretation of this phrase, Jessica talks about liking 'reckoning days' during her career as a stage fairy (*Jessica's First Prayer*, p. 62). Whilst, from certain perspectives, the incident may function to point up her religious ignorance, various – more subversive – readings are also possible.

pages of the texts, fictional empowerment may serve not only to make readers *feel* powerful, but also to impart the confidence to speak and act.

If, as the narrator of *Hester Morley's Promise* suggests, hearts may feed upon fancies 'half romantic and half religious' (p. 97), Stretton herself does not shy from interweaving Evangelical and romantic themes. Perhaps in ironic self-mockery, she adopts as subject matter (in *Cassy*, for example) the perceived corrupting influence of romantic novels, demonstrating, nonetheless, their power to generate action, however ill-judged, on the part of women yearning to escape the limitations of their lives.[76] Engaging with the contemporary appetite for melodrama and sensation fiction, Stretton, in stories and longer novels, blends elements of passion with themes of scandal, attempted murder and an 'actual adultery'.[77] In fact, those texts generally regarded as juvenile fiction trouble the borders of acceptability in numerous respects. Tapping into a fascination with the dark side of life, the content and language of Stretton's narratives overlap with the pressing social issues being addressed by reformers, journalists and urban explorers, who, in their melodramatic reports and narratives, transferred the notion of the unknown Dark Continent to descriptions of the murky and uncivilised underworld or hell of the City.[78] Taking as their themes the very elements they ostensibly aim to counteract, many Stretton stories focus on the urban inferno, with its low lodging-houses and gin-palaces, portraying in colourful and suggestive, if sometimes ambiguous, language, the degradation and vice to be found in the labyrinthine slum neighbourhoods in which Jessica, Little Meg and others struggle to survive. In a review of Stretton's *The King's Servants* – a text dealing with the rescue of painted-faced 'fallen girls' – the *Athenaeum* critic, recognising that Stretton's name would 'attract readers to anything she may write', condemned the inclusion of such mind-darkening subject matter, which rendered it 'not a book we should put into the hands of young people'.[79]

These stories open a window onto the world of prostitution, infanticide, crime and juvenile delinquency. Reviewers of *Carola*, which, in a blend of religion, romantic fiction and urban melodrama, taps into widespread anxieties about the adolescent girl, found the writing 'real and graphic'.[80] Striking a balance between intimation and exposition, narratives such as this, with their echoes and innuendoes, highlight the dangers which lurk in such a depraved environment. Nonetheless,

---

76 Mrs Gaskell refers in her novel *Ruth* (1853, repr., ed. A. Easson, Harmondsworth: Penguin 1997), p. 157, to 'castle-building' – encouraged by the reading of Minerva Press romantic novels – as an outlet which permitted escape from 'the pressure of [a] prosaic life'.

77 Review of *Hester Morley's Promise*, *Athenaeum* (6 September 1873).

78 See, for example, the accounts written in the 1880s by George Sims and Andrew Mearns (extracted in P. Keating (ed.), *Into Unknown England 1866–1913: Selections from the Social Explorers* (London: Fontana/Collins, 1976)). An urban philanthropist character in Stretton's *Half Brothers* enjoys the strange sights of unexplored London as much as the strange scenes in foreign lands (p. 58). See also Judith Walkowitz's discussion, in *City of Dreadful Delight: Narratives of Sexual Danger in Late-Victorian London* (London: Virago, 1992), of W.T. Stead's melodramatic report on child prostitution, 'The Maiden Tribute of Modern Babylon', which appeared in the *Pall Mall Gazette* in 1885.

79 *Athenaeum* (13 December 1873).

80 Advertisement in the RTS copy of *The King's Servants* (author's collection).

glimpses of this forbidden world, combined with Stretton's sympathetic portrayal of the wayward young girl – who, like the author and many of her protagonists, resists being shackled by rules or kept under authority – might conceivably act as an invitation as well as a warning.[81] True, Carola's wild energies are eventually tamed, and she marries her prince. In the process, however, she proves herself capable, like Jane Eyre, of surviving independently, and is shown to be morally superior to the members of her suitor's family whose middle-class prejudices against her tainted background are exposed and overturned.

Narratives often reflect the viewpoint of the child or young adult, but this is by no means always the case. Stretton alternately draws the reader into the thought processes of different characters, changing perspectives, experimenting with different narrators and highlighting moral complexity, with criticism implied or withdrawn. The position of the deserted child in *A Thorny Path* is juxtaposed with that of the mother who searches for her family, perhaps tapping not only into the dread of being abandoned, but also into adult fears of being the abandoner.[82] In *The Storm of Life* and *Bede's Charity*, although the child figure is important, the woman protagonist takes centre stage. The attitudes and experiences of the maturing heroine of *Carola* are set alongside those of her elderly Jewish guardian, the vicissitudes of their relationship explored. Although Matthias is, predictably, destined for eventual conversion to Christianity, Stretton promotes the superiority of many Jewish values. At a time when Jews were often regarded with suspicion, and their rising population in London's East End was provoking concern, she undermines negative stereotypes and shows how prejudices and misperceptions create other religions and races as alien. The importance of the family is underlined in her writing, but family, home and parenting may take many different forms, with traditional patterns interrogated. Not only can the young of both sexes become providers and nurturers, and men act as carers and protectors, but different generations – equally marginalised – may provide effective mutual support.

Hesba Stretton writes that the sacred idea of the Mother and Child 'almost dominates the Christian religion'.[83] Such iconography is, of course, widely reflected in art and literature, and the intensity of the relationship powerfully experienced in life. Stretton's themes highlight this fundamental bond, expressing the all-consuming desire for oneness, the unbearable nature of separation. Love for the child may be exploited as a lever, as in *The Storm of Life* or *In the Hollow of His Hand*, in which

---

81 Margaret R. Higonnet, 'A Pride of Pleasures', in E. Lennox Keyser and J. Pfeiffer (eds), *Children's Literature*, 28 (2000), p. 31 endorses critic Perry Nodelman's view in 'Pleasure and Genre: Speculations on the Characteristics of Children's Fiction' in the same volume, p. 4, that the 'activities of the wise' are less appealing than those of the unwise; she argues that seemingly didactic texts often have the opposite effect, directing attention onto activities normally inhibited. Despite Stretton's exposure of merciless exploitation, the world of the circus, presented in *An Acrobat's Girlhood* [1889], as a spectacle of movement, glitter and cheering crowds, can appear exhilaratingly free from conventional restraints – tantalisingly exotic, anarchic and 'other'.

82 See Lissa Paul, *Reading Otherways*, for more on the power of such stories to engender a fear of abandoning as well as abandonment (p. 32).

83 'Women's Work for Children', p. 4.

children are prime weapons in the authorities' armoury, pawns in a game of religious
and political manipulation: 'Give me the children ... and the mothers will follow' (*In
the Hollow of His Hand*, p. 49). If the ties between mother and child are paramount,
so is the shared subordination of these figures. Often, as in the record of village
inhabitants in *In the Hollow of His Hand* (p. 152), they literally do not count. Images
of the excluded mother and her child abound in Stretton's stories, as they do in
contemporary literary and artistic images. The concerns of women and children are
entwined: 'where women have their rights, childhood is happy'.[84]

The moral and spiritual influence of mothers – the power of a mother's
name, or even memory – is emphasised, its restraining and humanising potential
highlighted. It is only Cassy's mother 'as kept her father tolerably decent' (*Cassy*,
p. 25). These narratives reveal that, if mothers are often venerated, they are also
fallible. Motherhood may, for some, be 'the perfection of a woman's happiness'
(*The Clives of Burcot*, p. 188); for others it entails untold burdens, the mismatch
between expectations and reality only too evident. Stretton recognises that mothers
are among the first casualties of poverty, their physical and economic constraints,
and the need to act as breadwinner, competing with, and sometimes overwhelming,
maternal instincts. Hagar (*A Thorny Path*) has 'toiled and slaved', 'gone hungry and
famished herself', sacrificing her own portions, before, in despair, she throws off
her burden and abandons her family (pp. 9–10). Slum mothers like those of Jessica
or Sandy – figures viewed, on the one hand, as unnatural or even akin to vermin
– are, nonetheless, driven by environmental factors to drink, child neglect and the
brink of infanticide. The working guardian of Fantine (*Left Alone*, p. 23) must leave
the child alone, and locked in, because she is denied community support.[85] Cassy's
employer is easily enticed by romantic notions of adventure to flee the hardships
of marriage and responsibility when poverty and abuse loom large (*Cassy*, pp. 93–
4). Mixed with the condemnation of irresponsibility and moral weakness, there is
an exploration of causal factors, with active sympathy, or at least understanding
– reminiscent of the empathy displayed by Mrs Gaskell – of many a misguided or
transgressive protagonist.

Stretton speaks on behalf of poor women, but simultaneously reaches out to
women's collective experience, voicing shared grievances and expressing proto-
feminist sentiments. Women protagonists of the respectable working classes
shoulder most of the burden of household management – the worrying 'for the
morrow' (*Enoch Roden's Training*, p. 13); they forgo proper nourishment, while
husbands enjoy a 'comfortable and tasty breakfast' (*Lost Gip*, p. 84) and stretch
themselves out across the hearth, dominating physical space (*Lost Gip*, p. 59 and
A Thorny Path, p. 45). More darkly, the violence signalled by a woman's bruises

---

84 Ibid., p. 4.

85 Stretton writes of the importance of crèches set up for the children of poverty-
stricken women who are the breadwinners of the family ('Women's Work for Children',
p. 7). *Lost Gip*, highlighting the burden which motherhood may represent for the poor (pp. 2–
3), touches on the issue of infanticide (p. 20). The crime of infanticide, and the factors which
served to undermine maternal instincts, were extensively debated during the latter half of the
nineteenth century.

(*Alone in London*, p 18) may strike a chord beyond the environment in which it is fictionalised. The idea of women – regardless of class – as slaves, as the property of men, surfaces throughout Stretton's writing, from the long novels to the ostensibly child-directed texts, from slum settings to the drawing rooms of the affluent, or the distance of foreign lands. Indignation at men's – and society's – manipulation of women permeates her fiction from the early identification, in *The Clives of Burcot*, of woman as man's plaything – an article of luxury to be admired and either bent 'into some degree of conformity' or 'drive[n] … into desperate revolt' (p. 378). It culminates in the uncompromising declaration of women's superiority in *The Soul of Honour*, one of her last texts, which recognises the need for emancipation and questions the idea of marriage as the 'aim and end of every woman's life' (p. 84). Stretton is also concerned with the inequalities of women's position under the law – with their legal right to property, and to the fruits of their toil. Echoing the sentiments of feminist campaigners such as Annie Besant, she fictionalises, in *Under the Old Roof* (1882), the concerns addressed by the Married Women's Property Acts, and underlines, once again, women's lack of identity apart from their husbands: 'by the law a married woman is nobody' (p. 49).[86]

In Stretton's stories, men are often castigated, labelled as 'foolish' or 'domineering', as akin to 'savage wild beasts' or 'despots'. At the same time, male characters compare women to watches which need regulating, their ways – like their fashions – unaccountably alien and unsettling.[87] There is, however, room for negotiation; despite their differences, both sexes have 'human hearts' (*A Thorny Path*, p. 59) and potentially share a common consciousness. Stretton's narratives display an understanding of human failings and the need to examine and bridge the gulf between individuals, communities, religions and nationalities. They mirror, and at the same time seek to change, society's perceptions of the other, in all its guises and manifestations.

The Victorian fascination with the outcast city and its inhabitants – as objects of curiosity, contempt or pity – is reflected in various artistic media, including the popular theatre and the illustrations of artists such as Gustave Doré.[88] If 'how the poor live' is, to some, merely an 'interesting problem' (*Half Brothers*, p. 58) or something they are 'too refined and sensitive to look upon' (*David Lloyd's Last Will*,

---

86 Similar expressions of women's grievances, and discussions of their rights are to be found in many other Stretton texts. For a contemporary discussion of women's rights in relation to property, see Annie Besant, 'Marriage: As It Was, As It Is and As It Should Be' (1882), reprinted in S. Jeffreys (ed.), *The Sexuality Debates*, Women's Source Library (London: Routledge and Kegan Paul, 1987). On The Married Women's Property Acts, see Lee Holcombe, 'Victorian Wives and Property: Reform of the Married Women's Property Law, 1857–1882', in Martha Vicinus (ed.), *A Widening Sphere: Changing Roles of Victorian Women* (London: Methuen, 1980), pp. 3–27.

87 See, for example, *Carola*, p. 109, *A Thorny Path*, pp. 44 and 48, *Bede's Charity*, pp. 67 and 55.

88 See, for example, Dion Boucicault's play *The Streets of London*, a performance of which Stretton attended during 1866. Many of Stretton's descriptions evoke the arrangement and atmosphere of the famous engravings of London by Doré (1832–83), depicting its scenes and inhabitants.

1:54), it is of immense concern to Stretton, who scorns such views.[89] She highlights the widening gulf between rich and poor, with different sides of London, as in *Bede's Charity* (p. 141), as far removed from one another as separate countries. Like Mrs Gaskell, Stretton satirises those for whom unendurable privation means giving up luxuries – being reduced to 'poverty and cotton gloves'.[90] At the same time, her themes reflect a contemporary awareness of the importance of economic security – of how easily the better off may, through various kinds of misfortune, join the ranks of the outcast. They also highlight the Victorian tendency both to separate and to confuse ideas of poverty, class and manners. However, whilst Stretton does reproduce certain stereotypes of the coarse or vicious underclass, and often sets her central protagonists slightly apart, in terms of nature, breeding or integrity, from the real, so-called dregs of society, she exposes the inequality and oppression which lead to the poor being 'pinned down to suffering and crime' (*In Prison and Out*, p. 195). The criminal voices his resentment against the rich, for whom the poor are 'born to be trodden on, like their slaves', and who use religion to 'keep [them] down' (*The Storm of Life*, pp. 110 and 107.) The strong may exploit or humiliate the weak, and wealthy employers abuse their position to grind down workers (*Fern's Hollow*, p. 29), but the utopian vision, put forward in the early novel *Enoch Roden's Training* – a story which leans towards exposing, rather than condoning, ideas of knowing one's place – proposes a coming together of rich and poor, and a society in which the needs of all are taken into account (p. 127).

This chapter can only hint at the complexities which surface when we permit ourselves to look with other eyes at these narratives. We discover, I would argue, that Hesba Stretton's writing is surprisingly readable, perceptive and unsentimental, and that her novels hold attention and interest. The more we delve into this body of work and relate it both to the Victorian imagination, and to our own, the more we find of significance and relevance. Stretton clearly took advantage of popular forms and themes to promote pressing social, moral and spiritual agendas, to articulate the shared needs of the dispossessed or disenfranchised, and to expose – wittingly and unwittingly – society's fears, prejudices and shortcomings. As a strongly opinionated, intelligent and ambitious writer, she skilfully negotiated the mores of the Evangelical and juvenile publishing environment to create a platform for the morally complex popular fiction she was determined to publish, and for the expression of a powerful, if sometimes contradictory, female voice. It is rewarding to recover these cast-aside narratives, to reclaim the network of voices embedded within them, and to uncover the 'other' stories they tell.

---

89 See also remarks by Friedrich Engels concerning the barring of the working classes from the main streets of Manchester, in order to protect the 'tender susceptibilities of the eyes and nerves of the middle classes' in his *The Condition of the Working Class in England* (1845, repr., trans. W.O. Henderson and W.H. Chaloner (Stanford, CA: Stanford University Press, 1968), p. 56.

90 See, for example, *David Lloyd's Last Will* (2:164) and similar sentiments expressed at 1:33. See also Mrs Gaskell's *Mary Barton*, in which the masters are accused of 'cut[ting] short' in 'things for show', while the poor have to 'stint' in 'things for life' (1848, repr., ed. E. Wright, Oxford: Oxford University Press, 1987), p. 453.

Works by Hesba Stretton cited in this chapter (listed chronologically)

Dates and publishers refer to first publication as a volume, followed by the edition cited in this chapter.

Fern's Hollow (1864/n.d.), London: Religious Tract Society.

Enoch Roden's Training (1865/label 1902), London: Religious Tract Society.

The Children of Cloverley (1865/label 1876), London: Religious Tract Society.

The Fishers of Derby Haven (1866/label 1884), London: Religious Tract Society.

The Clives of Burcot (1867), London: Tinsley/(n.d.) London: Miles and Miles. (This text was reissued early in the twentieth century as *The Price of a Secret; or, The Clives of Burcot*. London: R.E. King.)

Paul's Courtship (1867), London: Wood.

Jessica's First Prayer (1867/n.d.), London: Religious Tract Society.

Pilgrim Street (1867/inscr.1890), London: Religious Tract Society.

Little Meg's Children (1868/label 1889), London: Religious Tract Society.

Alone in London (1869/inscr.1872), London: Religious Tract Society.

David Lloyd's Last Will (1869), 2 vols, Manchester: Tubbs and Brook; London: Sampson Low, Son and Marston.

Max Kromer (1871/n.d.), London: Religious Tract Society.

Bede's Charity (1872/*c.*1890), London: Religious Tract Society.

The Doctor's Dilemma (1872), London: Henry S. King.

Hester Morley's Promise (1873), London: Henry S. King/(1898), London: Hodder and Stoughton.

The King's Servants (1873), London: Henry S. King/(label 1911), London: Religious Tract Society.

Lost Gip (1873), London: Henry S. King/(1878), London: C. Kegan Paul.

Cassy (1874), London: Henry S. King/(*c.*1888), London: Religious Tract Society.

Michel Lorio's Cross (1876), London: Henry S. King/(inscr. 1888), London: Religious Tract Society.

Left Alone (1876), London: Henry S. King/(n.d.), London: Religious Tract Society.

The Storm of Life (1876), London: Henry S. King/(label 1910), London: Religious Tract Society.

A Thorny Path (1879/*c.*1882), London: Religious Tract Society.

In Prison and Out (1880), London: Isbister.

No Place Like Home (1881/inscr.1904), London: Religious Tract Society.

Cobwebs and Cables (1881/n.d.), London: Religious Tract Society.

Under the Old Roof (1882/n.d.), London: Religious Tract Society.

The Lord's Pursebearers (1883), London: Nisbet/(n.d.), published in an edition of *Day of Rest*, Strahan and Company.

Carola (1884/label 1898), London: Religious Tract Society.

An Acrobat's Girlhood [1889], London: Society for Promoting Christian Knowledge.

Half Brothers (1892/n.d.), London: Religious Tract Society.

The Highway of Sorrow (1894/1897), London; Paris; Melbourne: Cassell.

In the Hollow of His Hand (1897/inscr.1912), London: Religious Tract Society.

The Soul of Honour (1898). London: Isbister/(label 1905), London: Religious Tract
Society.

Jessica's Mother (*c.*1904, hardback edition/label 1912), London: Religious Tract
Society. (This text, which first appeared in the *Sunday at Home* in 1867, was
included in the RTS 'Penny Tales for the People' series before 1900, and was
issued by the Bible Institute Colportage Association, Chicago, as Part II of the
complete 'Jessica' Story [1897]. It is thought, however, that a separate-volume
hardback edition did not appear until early in the twentieth century.) See also
Brian Alderson and Pat Garrett, *The Religious Tract Society as a Publisher of
Children's Books* (exhibition catalogue), Hoddesdon: The Children's Books
History Society, 1999, pp. 22–3.

'The Postmaster's Daughter', *All The Year Round* (5 November 1859), 37–44.

Log Books: 1858–71 and 1875 (Shropshire Archives, Ref. 6001/5556). These consist
of a series of small notebooks containing a record of early submissions of magazine
articles and payments received, together with Stretton's journal for 1860–71 and
part of 1875. Entries chart day-to-day personal, domestic and business activities,
and afford an insight into Stretton's attitudes and relationships. They also provide
useful information regarding publishing matters for certain periods.

'Women's Work for Children' (1893), in A. Burdett-Coutts (ed.) *Woman's Mission*.
London: Sampson Low, Marston.

Chapter 8

Exploiting a Formula: The Adventure Stories of G.A. Henty (1832–1902)

Dennis Butts

Literary popularity is an unpredictable phenomenon. It can come overnight, as Rider Haggard found with *King Solomon's Mines* or it can come gradually as with J.R.R. Tolkien's *The Hobbit*. Only occasionally do the right author, the right publisher and the right moment of the *Zeitgeist* coincide, as happened when the firm of Blackie and Son began to publish the boys' adventure stories of G.A. Henty in the third quarter of the nineteenth century. This chapter argues that Henty's popularity came about because Henty so faithfully reflected the spirit of an imperialist age, because he used popular narrative devices, and because he was skilfully promoted by a vigorous and enterprising publisher.[1]

The great Education Acts of 1870 (England and Wales) and 1872 (Scotland) made elementary education compulsory for all children, and created an urgent need for school books. The firm of Blackie and Son (originally based in Scotland, but also operating in London from about 1860) was eager to meet the new demand and began educational publishing from 1879. Many Victorian schools and Sunday schools also began to give stories as prizes to their pupils about this time, and, to quote Peter Newbolt, 'From educational publishing to "rewards" was a natural line of progression which it only took three years for Blackie and Son to follow.'[2] So

---

1 Henty's work has been until recently largely neglected by modern scholars. At least one monograph has now been published, Leonard R.N. Ashley's *George Alfred Henty and the Victorian Mind* (San Francisco, CA; London: International Scholars, 1999), but it is in the wider field of literature and imperialism that analyses of Henty's writing, or more often, its ideological contexts, are increasingly to be found. See, for instance, Kelly Boyd, *Manliness and the Boys' Paper Story in Britain: A Cultural History, 1855–1940* (Basingstoke: Palgrave Macmillan, 2003); Patrick Brantlinger, *Rule of Darkness: British Literature and Imperialism 1830–1914* (Ithaca and London: Cornell University Press, 1988); Joseph Bristow, *Empire Boys: Adventures in a Man's World* (London: Harper Collins, 1991); Dennis Butts, 'Shaping Boyhood: British Empire Builders and Adventurers', in Peter Hunt (ed.), *An International Companion Encyclopedia of Children's Literature* (2 vols, London and New York: Routledge, 2004), vol. 1, pp. 340–51; Martin Green, *Dreams of Adventure, Deeds of Empire* (London: Routledge and Kegan Paul, 1980); M. Daphne Kutzer, *Empire's Children: Empire and Imperialism in Classic British Children's Books* (New York: Garland, 2000); and Jeffrey Richards (ed.), *Imperialism and Juvenile Literature* (Manchester: Manchester University Press, 1989). Other relevant studies of these themes are noted later in this chapter.

2 Peter Newbolt, *G.A. Henty 1832–1902: A Bibliographical Study of his British Editions with Short Accounts of his Publishers, Illustrators and Designers, and Notes on Production Methods Used for His Books* (Aldershot: Scolar Press, 1996), p. 587.

Blackie began publishing 'Reward Books' as well as educational books. One of their leading writers, Thomas Archer, introduced Henty, a friend and fellow club member, to the firm, and in 1882 Blackie's first catalogue of publications for the young included two of Henty's books for boys, *Facing Death* (1882) and *Under Drake's Flag* (1883).

George Alfred Henty was already an experienced journalist and writer. When the Crimean War broke out, he left Cambridge and joined the Hospital Commissariat of the army, reaching Balaclava in the spring of 1855 with his brother Fred. Working to organise provisions amid the chaos of the Crimean campaign, Henty visited the battlefield of Inkerman and also witnessed the siege of Sevastopol. During this time some of his letters home describing the war were seen by the editor of the *Morning Advertiser*, who invited him to contribute regularly to the paper. So began Henty's career as a writer. Frederick died at Scutari during an outbreak of cholera and a short time later, Henty himself was invalided home after a severe illness.

On his recovery Henty was sent abroad again to help organise the hospitals of the Italian Legion. He also served in Belfast and Portsmouth before leaving the army. For the next few years he tried mining engineering in Wales and Sardinia before, in 1865, he became special correspondent of the *Standard* newspaper, covering the Austro-Italian war in 1866. Then in 1867–68 Henty accompanied Lord Napier's expedition against King Theodore of Abyssinia.

During these years Henty's career as a writer was also taking off. In 1867 he brought out an adult novel, *A Search for a Secret,* and in 1868 had several articles published in such magazines as the *Cornhill* and Dickens's *All the Year Round.* His despatches from Abyssinia also appeared as *The March to Magdala.* Most important of all, during 1868 Henty seems to have written his first book for children, *Out on the Pampas,* the tale of a family settling in Argentina. Though the book was not published by Griffith and Farran until November 1870, there is little doubt that it is Henty's first book for juveniles, originally intended for his own children, Charles, Hubert, Maud and Ethel, whose names are shared by the main characters.[3]

The book was no immediate bestseller, and soon Henty was busy reporting on the Franco-Prussian War. He was actually in Paris during the time of the Commune and was deeply affected by the whole conflict, using some of his experiences to write his second children's book, *The Young Franc-Tireurs* (1872), There was a gap of eight years before Henty wrote for children again, for he next revisited Russia, and then, in 1873, sailed with Sir Garnet Wolseley on the Ashanti Campaign, which again produced a book of despatches, *The March to Coomassie* (1874). Revolution in Spain sent Henty off to report the struggles of the monarchy there, and a year later he reported on the tour of India made by the Prince of Wales. Shortly after, in 1876, the Turco-Serbian War broke out, and once more Henty's duties as a war correspondent claimed him. By the time an armistice was announced Henty was thoroughly worn out. Though he struggled on, his health broke down and he never worked as an active war correspondent again; instead, he settled down to his last career as a full-time professional storyteller.

---

3   Peter Newbolt, 'G.A. Henty: The Earlier Books for Boys, 1871–1885', *Antiquarian Book Monthly Review* 4 (1977), 438–47.

Henty was writing in the heyday of British imperialism. In 1815 the British Empire had hardly existed. Although the West Indies supplied Britain with sugar, Australia was regarded as little more than a convict station, and on the African continent Cape Colony was the only part inhabited by white people and they were mainly Dutch. Canada was largely unexplored and New Zealand was inhabited only by its indigenous population. India was the one major possession overseas Britain cared about, although three-quarters of what was to become the Raj was ruled by native princes and the rest by the East India Company. However, new forces were at work, and during Henty's lifetime Britain vastly extended its overseas territories, forming the New Zealand Colonisation Company, consolidating its control of India, and acquiring the whole of Burma and large areas of Africa, including Uganda, Nigeria and Zanzibar. The area over which Queen Victoria ruled in 1897, usually painted red in British maps of the world, was four times greater than at her accession in 1837.

Improvements in communications by railways, steamships and the electric telegraph, together with the availability of cheaper newspapers, made the British public more aware of overseas affairs. Newspaper reports from Special Correspondents, such as W.H. Russell of the *Times* and Henty himself, helped to sharpen the public consciousness of such events as the Charge of the Light Brigade, the Indian mutiny, the Zulu Wars and the Relief of Mafeking during the second Boer War.

The explorations of Captain Cook and Mungo Park in the late eighteenth and early nineteenth centuries, the dramatic encounter of Livingstone with Stanley in Africa in 1871 and the travels of such men as Sir Richard Burton, all intensified the interest in adventures in exotic places. When the domestic economic situation seemed to offer only the grim alternatives of either unemployment or dreary factory work, many began to look overseas. As well as searching for opportunities of trading with British colonies, hundreds of thousands of Britons emigrated to America, Australia, Canada and South Africa, often because there was more scope for enterprise and even the possibility of adventure. In the process, links between Britain and its great Empire overseas were gradually extended and strengthened.

Thus Henty's literary career coincided with the high tide of imperialism. Although there was a significant amount of debate on the question of empire, most Britons under the leadership of imperialist politicians such as Benjamin Disraeli, Lord Salisbury and Lord Rosebery, generally supported the maintenance and expansion of British territorial possessions overseas, and endorsed the notion that the British Empire was an unrivalled instrument for peace and justice. In particular, many Victorian children, especially boys, shared in this interest in the Empire. Many expected to work there when they left school, in commerce, the armed forces or as public servants. For their part, many girls, according to conventions of the age, probably expected to become the loyal companions or helpmates of their husbands. The United Services College at Westward Ho! in Devon was actually founded to help prepare boys to serve in such countries as India, and it is no coincidence that Rudyard Kipling (1865–1936), the poet of Imperialism, was a pupil there. In such a climate, it is no surprise that boys and girls clamoured for adventure stories, full of thrilling deeds in faraway places (generally under British control), in which the heroes and (less often) the heroines were young people like themselves.

G.A. Henty participated enthusiastically in the literary tradition which endorsed these views. His works embodied the *zeitgeist*. As Kathryn Castle has said, 'Henty … exemplified the ethos of the new imperialism, and glorified its military successes,' and, to quote Mawuena Logan, his works were popular because they 'reflect the attitudes, anxieties and aspirations of the Victorian people'.[4] Earlier writers, such as Captain F.W. Marryat (1792–1848), R.M. Ballantyne (1825–94), and W.H.G. Kingston (1814–80) had already produced children's books exploiting the appeal of adventure, but none of them matched his intense imperialism. He was, said his colleague Edmund Downey,

> the most Imperialist of all the Imperialists I ever encountered. I remember well the day when the news of [the British defeat of] Majuba Hill reached London. Henty appeared at Catherine Street a little later than his usual hour. 'Have you heard this awful news?' he asked me as he arrived in the office. And then the big man burst into tears. 'The disgrace can never be wiped out," he blubbered. "Never! Never!'[5]

What kind of stories did Henty write for his youthful late Victorian readers? We know from various accounts that he gave of his literary methods that when Henty began work on a novel, he usually borrowed ten books from the London Library and read up the appropriate historical background. He then worked in his study with two or three books around him and plenty of atlases. Apparently he did not plan his stories in advance but began work at half-past nine in the morning lying on his sofa and smoking, while dictating to his secretary. At one time Henty even used his secretary to provide synopses of the historical battles for his books, and this might help to explain what can now seem their frequently dull character. He usually worked in the mornings till one o'clock, and then in the evenings from half-past seven until ten. In this way Henty reckoned to produce 6,500 words in a fair day's work, and, though he often devoted six months of the year to his great hobby of sailing, he could produce three books a year. The shortest time in which he wrote a book was the twenty-four days it took him to produce *With Buller in Natal,* a story of 140,000 words.[6]

Not surprisingly, writing at such speed led to a heavy reliance on a formulaic approach, with the same elements recurring in volume after volume, whether the stories involved the distant past or comparatively recent events. To begin with, the moral purpose of Henty's writing never changed. When, in 1883, he lamented the closing of the weekly magazine, the *Union Jack,* which he had edited, he reminded his readers of the lessons he had tried to teach on every page, that 'lads should be

---

4   Kathryn Castle, *Britannia's Children: Reading Colonialism through Children's Books and Magazines* (Manchester: Manchester University Press, 1996), p. 55; Mowuena Kossi Logan, *Narrating Africa: George Henty and the Fiction of Empire* (New York: Garland, 1999), p. 80.

5   Quoted by Guy Arnold, *G.A. Henty: Imperialist Boys' Writer* (London: Hamish Hamilton, 1980), pp. 26–7.

6   Henty's own accounts of his writing methods are quoted by Newbolt, *G.A. Henty 1832–1902*, pp. 556–7.

true, honourable, manly and brave under all circumstances'.[7] Although Henty was never as Evangelical as earlier children's writers, he was almost as didactic as far as teaching moral behaviour was concerned.

Another element was that Henty wanted to teach history. In an article in the *Boy's Own Paper*, published after his death, according to Guy Arnold, Henty had said:

> The idea of writing historical books first occurred to me in consequence of the success which attended the production of *The Young Franc-Tireurs* which I wrote on the conclusion of the Franco-German War. I next wrote *The Young Buglers* a story of the Peninsular War, and the result determined me to stick to historical stories, and if I lived long enough, to treat all the wars of England. My object has always been to write good history. Of course, to make it go down with boys it has to be mixed with a very large amount of personal adventures, but I have never permitted myself to deviate in the very slightest degree from historical facts, except when the boy hero is, so to speak, on the loose. That is the reason of the popularity of my books among parents.[8]

Henty's stories are saturated with his belief in the British Empire, and these explicit values often provide the basis of the *Prefaces* addressed to 'My Dear Lads' with which he liked to begin his tales. Although Henty is not uncritical of aspects of British policy or of personal misbehaviour, his pride in the acquisition and administration of the British Empire as a wonderful story clearly shines through. At the opening of the *Preface* to *With Clive in India: or, The Beginnings of Empire*, for example, we read:

> In the following pages I have endeavoured to give a vivid picture of the wonderful events of the ten years which at their commencement saw Madras in the hands of the French – Calcutta at the mercy of the Nabob of Bengal – and English influence apparently at the point of extinction in India – and which ended in the final triumph of the English both in Bengal and Madras. There were yet great battles to be fought, great efforts to be made, before the vast Empire of India fell altogether into British hands; but these were but the sequel of the events I have described.[9]

The heroes of the books are usually potentially 'manly' boys of fourteen or so, of no great intellectual or social distinction, perhaps the son of a clergyman or a doctor, but endowed with a good deal of pluck. Charlie Marryat, the hero of *With Clive in India* (1884), is typical:

> He was slight in build, but his schoolfellows knew that Charlie Marryat's muscles were as firm and hard as those of any boy in the school. In all sports requiring activity and endurance rather than weight and strength he was always conspicuous. Not one in the school could compete with him in long-distance running, and when he was one of the hares there was but little chance for the hounds. He was a capital swimmer and one of the best boxers in the school. He had a reputation for being a leader in every mischievous prank,

---

7 Robert L. Dartt, *G.A. Henty: A Bibliography* (New Jersey: Dar-Web Inc., 1971), p. 155.

8 Quoted by Arnold, *G.A. Henty: Imperialist Boys' Writer*, pp. 92–3.

9 Henty, *With Clive in India: or, the Beginnings of Empire* (1884, London: Blackie and Son, n.d.), p. 5.

but he was honourable and manly, would scorn to shelter himself under the semblance of a lie, and was a prime favourite with his masters as well as his schoolfellows.'[10]

These boy-heroes are not perfect, Henty says, and indeed quite often get into trouble for fighting a bully or neglecting school rules, but they are intrinsically loyal and true, especially to their mothers. They may forget an important cricket match, but they never forget their friends, and their self-confidence may degenerate into 'cheek' but never into cowardice.

The other characters in Henty's stories are less important but often just as predictable. The books are generally dominated by male values and there is a good deal of gender stereotyping. Women usually appear as patient mothers, girls as gentle sisters, and the pretty girl next door often survives to marry the hero at the end of the story. But Henty's attitudes are not crudely sexist. Brave heroines do play a prominent part in such books as *The Plague Ship* of 1889 and *A Soldier's Daughter* of 1906, to give just two examples. Although much writing for children did begin to split along gender lines during the Victorian period, Henty's stories were regularly enjoyed by girl readers.[11]

The hero's parents, however, are shadowy figures, usually dismissed from the tale very quickly. Headmasters are sternly just but with a friendly twinkle in their eyes to show their sympathy for the hero's minor offences. Villains are often foreigners characterised by two main features, physical cruelty and treachery. The king of the Ashantees in *By Sheer Pluck* (1884) is a bloodthirsty tyrant, responsible for many human sacrifices, and James Pearson, the overseer of the slave plantation in *With Lee in Virginia* (1890), beats his slaves cruelly; but both men get their just deserts. Loyal and faithful servants, on the other hand, are generously rewarded, and foreign servants, such as Hossein, the Indian cook in *With Clive in India*, often accompany the hero on his return to England.

The story usually opens with some crucial incident in the hero's early boyhood which disturbs the expected tenor of his career. Ralph Conway's father's death is announced in the first chapter of *One of the 28th: A Tale of Waterloo* (1890), for example, leaving him with a widowed mother to protect, while Cuthbert Hartington's father dies and his estate is bankrupted at the beginning of *Two Sieges* (1916). Consequently, the hero is forced to make his own way from early on, and by the end of the novel has usually managed this, often by great feats of courage and enterprise, – acquiring prize money, business profits or rapid military promotion, and sometimes all three.

The hero's exploits usually involve battles and war, of course, though it is wrong to think of Henty simply as a military writer. He could and did write about social disturbances, such as the Luddite Riots in *Through the Fray* (1886), and even the tales of war include much else: struggles against natural disasters, mysteries about missing wills and so on. There are even attempts at humour and romance. However,

---

10 Henty, *With Clive in India*, p. 11.

11 See, for example, Deborah Cogan Thacker and Jean Webb, *Introducing Children's Literature: From Romanticism to Postmodernism* (London: Routledge, 2002), pp. 53–4, and Dennis Butts, *Tales of Heroines and Heroes: Rare Short Stories by G.A. Henty* (Winchester: The Henty Society, 2003).

Henty's formula usually led him to place his hero in a historical situation of some moment, and then to interweave his adventures with those of known public events along lines suggested by the novels of Sir Walter Scott. Thus young Charlie Marryat, leaving England for India at the age of 16, not only meets the legendary military genius Captain Clive but also survives the 'Black Hole of Calcutta'. Similarly, Ned Hearn sails with Francis Drake to the Spanish Main in *Under Drake's Flag* and Beric, the hero of Henty's Roman-era novel *Beric the Briton* (1893), is actually appointed as the Emperor Nero's librarian!

After a crisis near the beginning of the book, then, probably connected with the loss of a fortune or the death of his father, the hero, who has already shown some taste of his mettle by defeating the school bully or catching a thief, sets off on a series of adventures in each of which he triumphs, before a great culminating crisis, which again is successfully surmounted and followed by a prosperous homecoming. Ralph Conway, the hero of *One of the 28th*, meets his new protector Herbert Penfold in Chapter 2, only to learn that he is dead a chapter later. In the meantime, though, Ralph, has successfully avoided being captured by a French privateer, so that the difficulties he encounters when he obtains a commission in His Majesty's 28th Regiment of Foot do not prove too daunting. After some skirmishes with smugglers in Ireland, the regiment is posted to Belgium on the news of Napoleon's escape from Elba. Ralph survives the battle of Waterloo to inherit half his guardian's estate and to marry the local vicar's daughter. Often, about halfway through the narrative, the hero is captured and thrown into prison. Thus the eponymous hero of *Jack Archer* (1883) is incarcerated by the Russians during the Crimean War and Vincent, in *With Lee in Virginia* (1890), is jailed by Union soldiers. Inevitably the hero quickly manages to escape, perhaps helped by his faithful servant, and then eludes his pursuers. Frequently, at another point in the book, a minor character will tell the story of his adventurous life, partly as a contrast with the hero's activities, and partly, too, as a way of delaying the hero's own crisis. He may even learn that he is not who he thought he was but discover his true identity and inherit unexpected wealth, as happens at the conclusion of *With Kitchener in the Soudan* (1903). There is often, though not always, a happy wedding to accompany the hero's homecoming.

Henty did vary the pattern of these formulaic elements, sometimes modifying the treatment of an episode, but the structure of his narrative tends to be highly consistent. His story-patterns reproduce the same kind of structures – dealing with the hero, quest, adventures and homecoming – as are found in many traditional tales from epics such as the *Odyssey* to more modern folk tales such as *Dick Whittington*. Henty's popularity in terms of sales, therefore, may be related in part to his use of popular formulae. Such narrative structures offer readers many advantages. Young people, struggling with long and difficult books, having already read one of Henty's stories, soon recognise that they are on familiar ground. The reader is thus reassured psychologically, but also aesthetically, as he or she learns to appreciate the skilful way with which the writer varies his formula.

By Sheer Pluck: A Tale of the Ashanti War (1884) is a good example of the way Henty reproduces the familiar formula, and yet freshens it with inventive modifications. Frank Hargate, the 15-year-old hero, is the only son of his widowed mother, and is well-defined as a games-playing schoolboy whose hobby is natural history. In the opening section of the book, Frank shows his courage and resource when he saves three schoolfellows from drowning. He later wins the admiration of a local farmer by protecting his daughter from an attack by a mad dog; and when Frank saves his school friends again, this time from a rising tide, the whole school gives him a gold medal as a reward for his courage. The complications which follow arise from the death of Frank's mother, who leaves him virtually penniless and with a younger sister to support. Using his last resources to place her in a good boarding school, Frank follows the pattern of all young heroes and leaves home to seek his fortune. He finds it hard to obtain work, and in Chapter 5, Henty paints a picture of poverty in London that is unusual for him. But Frank's skill at preserving dead animals, acquired through his interest in natural history, enables him to secure a job with a kindly shopkeeper. His unusual skill here may be compared to the magic gifts that heroes often possess in folk stories.

The second phase of Frank's quest begins when an old school friend's father introduces him to Mr Goodenough, a celebrated traveller and naturalist, who is looking for an assistant to accompany him on a two-year expedition to Africa to gather specimens of natural history. Frank and his patron leave Liverpool for the West Coast of Africa, where he undergoes a number of minor tests. He is lost in the forest, encounters a hostile tribe and then helps the friendly Christian natives of Abeokuta to drive off the cruel king of Dahoney. By now Henty is well into his stride, using the experiences of his own journey to the Ashantees with Wolseley's expedition of 1873 to depict the atmosphere of the fever-ridden land and to describe the cruelties of the bloodthirsty king of the Ashantees. The king now becomes the story's real villain, for, though he initially greets Frank and Mr Goodenough in a friendly manner, he soon makes them virtual prisoners, and, after Mr. Goodenough has died of fever, the king makes Frank accompany his army, led by General Ammon Quatia, against the British. However Frank quickly wins the general's gratitude by saving him from an assassination attempt by his own men, and is allowed to escape and join the advancing British army. Frank now accompanies the British commander, General Sir Garnet Wolseley, as he and his men march into Ashantee territory. The British win a great battle at Amoaful, and, crossing the river Dah, enter the Ashantee capital of Coomassie. Wolseley decides to burn the town down as a punishment for the Ashantee cruelties, and the British then withdraw their forces. Frank returns to England two and a half years after he left. With a heavy gold necklace Ammon Quatia gave him and an inheritance from Mr Goodenough, he is now prosperous. The story ends with Frank no longer a poor orphaned naturalist but becoming a successful physician with a house in Harley Street, looked after by his sister Lucy.

Here we can see how Henty uses the adventure story structure of the hero, the quest, the crisis and the triumphant homecoming, in ways which are familiar and yet with interesting variations. The hero and the loss of his parents are conventional enough, but the hero's special gift, his knowledge of natural history, and the report of his deprivation on the streets of London, are new features. The account of his journey from the West Coast of Africa inland is again fresh and unfamiliar, but the triumphant military exploits return to familiar territory. Even the ending reveals a gentle surprise to the reader expecting wedding bells, for Frank makes a home with his sister, not with some childhood sweetheart.

Henty's stories usually work most smoothly as narratives when he is most confident with his ideology, and *By Sheer Pluck* is, in Mawuena Logan's words, 'a prime example of a colonialist point of view.'[12] But his formula does not always work so well. It sometimes creaks a little or shows signs of tension, when, for instance, his narratives reflect ideological tensions either within Henty himself or within British society more generally. Henty's treatment of the American War of Independence in *True to the Old Flag: A Tale of the American War of Independence* (1883) is an example. Henty was a British imperialist, and his attitude towards the War of Independence is totally coloured by this doctrine. He thought that Britain was right and that the American colonists were wrong. Although he admits that the British did some foolish things, he was incapable of seeing that many Americans, brought up on the same ideals of *Magna Carta* as he had been, felt that they were being deprived of rights which they were entitled to *as British citizens*. Though an imperialist, Henty resembled a Palmerstonian Whig, who wanted freedom for all abroad, but not at home – for places such as Greece and Italy, which were ruled by outsiders, but not for British colonists. Henty would have approved of Patrick Henry's great cry 'Give me liberty or give me death' in almost any circumstances except the actual ones. Thus his account of the War of Independence is both partial and grudging: the British fought bravely in a just cause, but were incompetently led and overwhelmed by numbers. Henty found it difficult to believe that the Americans fought well because, like such Britons as Burke, Chatham and Tom Paine, they believed in the justice of their cause and were led by a man of genius in George Washington.

The story opens with the young British/American hero Harold Wilson growing up in Boston with his loyalist family. When war breaks out Harold journeys north to Canada to warn of an impending American attack. The warning is ignored and Washington triumphs at Trenton Ferry. There then follows a long and curious interlude in which Harold hears of the British defeat at Saratoga, but, realising that there will be no further fighting until the following spring, decides to return to Canada where he rescues a young girl from the Iroquois. Fighting his way through blizzards and across frozen lakes, Harold outwits the Indians and returns to Detroit. He now rejoins the British army in the south and helps in the defence of Savannah, and then spends the rest of the war scouting for the army until Cornwallis's surrender at York Town. Harold then decides to leave republican America, and settles down on a farm in loyalist Canada.

Even from this brief summary, it is obvious that something is not right with the story. Henty has chosen to tell a tale about the American War of Independence, but failed to treat the war with any kind of justice. References to George Washington are extremely scarce in the book, and there is no mention at all of the heroic episode of Valley Forge. Defeats and victories are sometimes led up to with considerable preparation, but the ensuing battles tend to be dealt with very briefly – only a single paragraph in the case of Trenton Ferry, for example. Oddest of all is the way Harold is simply detached from the major events of the war, while he goes off north enjoying adventures among the Iroquois in episodes reminiscent of Fenimore Cooper's

---

12 Mawuena Logan, 'History and the Ashantis', *Children's Literature Association Quarterly* 16 (1991), p. 82.

Leatherstocking tales. In a book of 21 chapters, no fewer than 10 are concerned with fighting the Iroquois, and even in the 11 chapters dealing with the War of Independence Harold is often only marginally involved, as a scout or an observer.

Thus, whereas in most of his historical novels Henty normally managed to integrate the personal adventures of his fictitious hero with the historical events of his story by depicting his hero working close to a great public figure, such as Clive in India, here Henty portrays Harold's adventures as almost independent of the great historical events with which he claims to deal. Harold misses the battles of Lexington and Concord, attends Bunker's Hill only as a spectator and then misses the battles of Philadelphia, Saratoga, Camden and York Town almost completely. There is thus a sharp dislocation in the book between Harold's personal adventures, which are mainly accounts of successes and triumphs over the Indians, and the major historical events of the war, which are mainly accounts of British defeats and failures against the American colonists. It is almost as if Henty's honesty and objectivity compelled him to record these episodes of imperial disaster in America, while his emotional sympathy and patriotism forced him to seek consolation in historically irrelevant chapters recounting Harold's personal successes in Canada.

Despite occasional imbalances of this kind, Henty generally remained true to his narrative formula, and exploited it successfully for over three decades. And the familiarity of the formula helped to ensure Henty's popularity with his young readers, for the stories all carry the psychologically reassuring message that even ordinary boys and girls can survive, and indeed triumph, under the most adverse circumstances.

In addition to their reassuring conventionality, the other crucial factor in the promotion of Henty's books was John Alexander Blackie, Henty's main publisher. The firm of Blackie was large and diversified, controlling the various processes of printing, binding and publishing. Alexander Blackie persuaded many writers to work for him, including G. Manville Fenn and Ascot R. Hope, as well as Henty, devising a system of mass-production whereby their books could be produced with some uniformity in print, page-size and even length. This standardisation meant that the binding-cases for all these books could be planned in advance, which made for greater economy.

Although Blackie planned to publish books at a wide range of prices, many of the novels were published at just two prices, five shillings or six shillings each. Those at five shillings had 352 pages and those costing a shilling more contained 384 pages. And it is an extraordinary fact that of the sixty-nine full-length books Henty wrote for Blackie, thirty-six came to exactly 384 pages, and twenty-three reached exactly 352 pages. Six of his other ten books made totals of between 380 and 392 pages. Henty was an experienced journalist, of course, used to writing to order, so that knowing an agreed length was expected probably helped him to write his stories to a regular formula. For their part, Blackie must have realised that Henty would be likely to prove an efficient and reliable author, particularly after they had published *Facing Death* (1882) and *Under Drake's Flag* (1883). Thus in 1887 they offered him a contract to produce three books a year of 90,000–120,000 words for £100 each. The contract was renewed in 1891, with the stipulated length slightly raised to 100,000–140,000 words, and payment increased to £150 plus royalties after sales had reached 5,000 copies. Though they did not apparently meet very often, it is clear from their correspondence that Henty got on well with Alexander Blackie, and their commercial partnership was a happy one.[13]

Blackie's mass-production methods enabled the company to lavish a good deal on the quality and design of their books and sell them in attractively-coloured cloth with gold blocking and full-page illustrations which many collectors still appreciate today. But they were particularly skilful in promoting and advertising Henty's books. First, they sent out many review copies, and by the late nineteenth century many newspapers and magazines were publishing accounts of juvenile fiction. Reviews and notices of Henty's works can be found in publications as diverse as the *Academy*, *Saturday Review*, *Observer*, *Spectator*, *School Guardian*, *Times*, *Harper's Monthly Magazine* and *Standard* (Henty's old newspaper). Their policy seems to have reaped dividends. The *Sunday Magazine for 1896*, for instance, in a feature on 'A Boy's Bookshelf' by the Rev. R.E. Welsh, emphatically affirmed 'When in doubt, buy Henty.'[14]

Blackie then further exploited any favourable reviews or comments by including them among the advertisements which appeared in many of their own publications. Thus, as well as mentioning other works by G.A. Henty on a book's title page under the heading 'Author of ...', most of Blackie's publications included copious advertisements for their other titles in a mini-catalogue sometimes of as much as 48 pages, at the back of a particular work. Henty's *With Wolfe in Canada* (1887), for example, points out on its title page that Henty is also the author of *With Clive in India*, *The Lion of the North*, *In Freedom's Cause*, *The Dragon and the Raven*, *By Sheer Pluck* and *Facing Death*. But a Catalogue of 'Blackie and Sons' Books for Young People' at the close lists no fewer than 16 different books by Henty, giving brief accounts of each with its price, and extracts from favourable reviews. Thus we find a short synopsis of the plot of *Through the Fray* (1886), followed by appreciative remarks from the *Standard* and the following extract from the *Journal of Education:* 'The interest of the story never flags. Were we to propose a competition for the best list of novel writers for boys we have little doubt that Mr. Henty's name would stand first.'[15] The repetition of such praise from book to book must have helped to build up Henty's name and reputation.

There is no doubt that Blackie brilliantly exploited the educational market. They had been developing educational publishing since 1879, and because of Henty's declared aim of teaching history, they could appeal to parents and teachers who might have dismissed less serious works. Not only did Henty's books receive glowing tributes from the educational press, Blackie even published them as part of their quasi-didactic schemes. They persuaded Henty to write a history of Queen Victoria's reign, published in 1887 as *The Sovereign Reader*, and intended 'For

13 Peter Newbolt, 'G.A. Henty: Some Notes on the Blackie First Editions', *Antiquarian Monthly Review* 4 (1977), 83–92; and *G.A. Henty: 1832–1902*, pp. 586–90.

14 Rev. R.E. Welsh, 'A Boy's Bookshelf', *Sunday Magazine for 1896* (London: Isbister, 1896), p. 35.

15 G.A. Henty, *With Wolfe in Canada: or the Winning of a Continent* (London: Blackie, 1887), 'Advertisement', p. 7.

Upper Classes in Schools.' Ten years later, they published extracts from his earlier books as a 'School Reader', under the title *Tales from the Works of G.A. Henty*. In a similar attempt to exploit this market, *A Chapter of Adventures*, written originally in 1891, was reprinted as one of 'Blackie's Continuous Readers' in 1899. Blackie also published small advertising leaflets publicising the works of Henty and other writers, which seem to have been inserted into their books in the same way that some booksellers place bookmarks in their works today (see Figure 8.1). A slip from Blackie advertising 'New Books for 1900–1901,' for example, lists three titles by Henty, and includes a dramatic black-and-white illustration from *With Buller in Natal*.

Thus Blackie's mass-production methods enabled them to establish a recognisable publishing style for their attractive books, giving them what might be called a brand, and through assiduous advertising they established a powerful place for Henty and his stories for boys in the development of children's books by the end of the nineteenth century. Unlike many popular authors, Henty never created a single enduring hero such as Jim Hawkins or Biggles or 'Just William', but the familiar structures of his historical tales, and their recognisable format, brought him enormous popularity.

That popularity did not come immediately, nor did it depend upon the remarkable success of individual titles. We know, for example, that Henty's most popular book *With Buller in Natal*, achieved first year sales of 17,342 copies, while his most successful Blackie publication up to 1917 (when Blackie's records cease) was *With Clive in India,* which had sold 38,238 copies.[16] As well as publishing most of his works with Blackie, Henty also published with the Tinsley Brothers, Griffith and Farran, Sampson Low, Chatto and Windus, SPCK and Chapman and Hall. There were numerous reprints too. Extremely popular in America, Henty's books were published in an authorised edition by the New York firm of Scribner's Sons, as well as by numerous publishers of unauthorised or 'pirated' copies.[17] He was also published in such parts of the British Empire as Australia, Canada and South Africa, and was translated for sale in various European languages, though publishing details have never been properly established. Thus Henty's cumulative sales were simply enormous. He himself wrote over 100 full-length books, as well as contributing to many anthologies, newspapers and periodicals, so his name was constantly in the public eye, and his work continued to be reprinted long after his death. There was a particularly attractive 'New and Popular Edition' of his works selling at three shillings and sixpence in 1917, for example, and paperback editions were still being published even after World War II. Henty's tale of the French Revolution, *In the Reign of Terror*, first published by Blackie in 1888, was reprinted in 'A Specially Abridged Edition' for boys and girls aged 8–12 years by the Atlantic Book Publishing Co. in London in 1967, and then in comic-book format by Classics Illustrated of New York in 1968. And further reprints are still being published in America today. Preston Speed of Pennsylvania, for example, republished Henty's *For the Temple: A Tale of the Fall of Jerusalem*, which had first appeared in 1888, as recently as 1995, and

---

16 For Blackie's sales of Henty's books, see Newbolt, *G.A. Henty, 1832–1902*, pp. 659–63.

17 See Harland H. Eastman, *The Scribner-Welford Editions of G.A. Henty*, Literary Supplement No. 9 (Reading: The Henty Society, 1996).

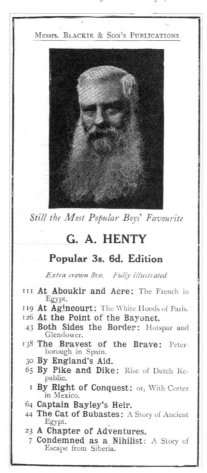

Figure 8.1　　Advertisement in the form of a bookmark by Blackie & Son for works of G.A. Henty, no date. Collection of Dennis Butts.

Robinson Books of Oregon have now reprinted all of Henty's books, primarily, they say, for their use with home-schooled students.[18]

Although it is not possible to quantify precisely how many copies of Henty's books have been published or sold because of the absence of accurate publishers' records, some estimates have been hazarded. W.G. Blackie, a member of the firm which sold Henty's books for nearly 100 years, recalled that he was 'brought up to believe that Henty was Boys' Author No. 1 of his time', adding that 'The figure of 150,000 [copies] a year in the days of his popularity I do not think can be under

---

18 Current prices are listed at <http://www.robinsonbooks.org> (accessed 24 April 2007). Robinson Books have made 99 of Henty's books available on CD-ROM. Thirty-seven historical novels by Henty were also available on CD at <http://www.samizdat/henty.html> (accessed 4 November 2005).

the mark.' His estimate was that Blackie and Son printed and sold some 3.5 million copies of Henty's books, and that with Scribner's, and Donohue's, 'plus an unknown quantity for other pirated editions', total sales of 25 million might not be impossible.[19] Certainly the frequency with which his books turn up in second-hand bookshops in Britain and America continues to testify to the enduring phenomenon of Henty's popularity.

A select list of G.A. Henty's novels (listed chronologically)

A Search for a Secret. A Novel (1867), 3 vols, London: Tinsley Brothers.

The March to Magdala (1868), London: Tinsley Brothers.

Out on the Pampas; or, The Young Settlers. A Tale for Boys (1871), London: Griffith and Farran.

The Young Franc-Tireurs and their Adventures in the Franco-Prussian War (1872), London: Griffith and Farran.

The March to Coomassie (1874), London: Tinsley Brothers.

The Young Buglers. A Tale of the Peninsular War (1880), London: Griffith and Farran.

Facing Death: or, the Hero of the Vaughan Pit. A Tale of the Coal Mines (1882), London: Blackie and Son.

Under Drake's Flag: A Tale of the Spanish Main (1883), London: Blackie and Son.

Jack Archer. A Tale of the Crimea (1883), London: Sampson Low, Marston, Searle, & Rivington.

With Clive in India: or the Beginnings of an Empire (1884), London: Blackie and Son.

By Sheer Pluck: a Tale of the Ashanti War (1884), London: Blackie and Son.

In Freedom's Cause: A Story of Wallace and Bruce (1885), London: Blackie and Son.

True to the Old Flag: A Tale of the American War of Independence (1885), London: Blackie and Son.

The Dragon and the Raven: or, the Days of King Alfred (1886), London: Blackie and Son.

The Lion of the North: A Tale of the Times of Gustavus Adolphus and the Wars of Religion (1886), London: Blackie and Son.

Through the Fray: A Tale of the Luddite Riots (1886), London: Blackie and Son.

The Sovereign Reader: Scenes from the Life and Reign of Queen Victoria [1887], London: Blackie and Son.

With Wolfe in Canada: or, the Winning of a Continent (1887), London: Blackie and Son.

In the Reign of Terror: The Adventures of a Westminster Boy (1888), London: Blackie and Son.

For the Temple: A Tale of the Fall of Jerusalem (1888), London: Blackie and Son.

The Plague Ship [1889], London: SPCK.

---

19   Quoted in Dartt, *G.A. Henty: A Bibliography*, p. v.

One of the 28th. A Tale of Waterloo (1890), London: Blackie and Son.

With Lee in Virginia; A Story of the American Civil War (1890), London: Blackie and Son.

A Chapter of Adventures: or, Through the Bombardment of Alexandria (1891), London: Blackie and Son; reprinted as one of *Blackie's Continuous Readers* in 1899.

Tales from the Works of G.A. Henty (1893), London: Blackie and Son.

Beric the Briton: A Story of the Roman Invasion (1893), London: Blackie and Son.

With Butler in Natal or, a Born Leader (1901), London: Blackie and Son.

With Kitchener in the Soudan. A Story of Atbara and Omdurman (1903), London: Blackie and Son.

A Soldier's Daughter and Other Stories (1906), London: Blackie and Son.

Two Sieges or Cuthbert Hartington's Adventures [1916], London: S.W. Partridge.

Chapter 9

Angela Brazil and the Making of the Girls' School Story

Judy Simons

In a radio programme broadcast in the 1980s on the influence of books read in childhood, Lord Goodman, a celebrated lawyer and pillar of the British establishment, proudly announced that whatever he had become, he owed to Angela Brazil.[1] It is a startling admission, but one which would have found resonance with thousands of like-minded readers who had grown up in the early years of the century – although few of them are likely to have achieved such public eminence as Arnold Goodman. The name Angela Brazil is even now synonymous with a complete and discrete genre of children's literature: the girls' school story. Even those who have never picked up a Brazil novel in their lives will recognise the archetypal characters: the plucky prefect, the madcap heroine, the spirited head girl. All these inhabit the closed, arcane and sometimes thrilling world of the fictional girls' boarding school. It is a world that Brazil to a large extent created. It is also a world that has entered the popular imagination, has given rise to countless imitators and parodists and has put under its spell succeeding generations of girls and women (to say nothing of prominent lawyers). The charm of the fictive English public school continues to fascinate readers of all ages and backgrounds, as the runaway success of J.K. Rowling's Harry Potter books, set in Hogwarts Academy, confirms. To understand the enigma of its enduring appeal, and to appreciate the unique contribution made by Angela Brazil to a form which was to dominate girls' reading habits for nearly three-quarters of a century, we need to go back to some of its earliest audiences.

In the years from the First World War until well into the 1960s, girls between the ages of ten and sixteen on both sides of the Atlantic succumbed wholeheartedly to the allure of the boarding school myth, overcoming barriers both of age and social class in the process. Brazil's immediate successors, either directly or by implication, continually refer to the impact of her work on impressionable young minds. In Elinor Brent-Dyer's *The Princess of the Chalet School* (1927) the motherless little Princess Elisaveta of Belsornia sums up the attraction of school life as represented by Brazil's fiction. Living in a royal household with only a governess for company, Elisaveta longs more than anything to attend a boarding school, where there would be 'lots of nice girls who were all anxious to be friendly and work and play with her, as she had read of girls doing in the school stories which her father had given her'.[2] Significantly

---

1   Quoted in Isobel Quigley, *The Heirs of Tom Brown: The English School Story* (London: Chatto and Windus, 1982), p. 217.

2   Elinor Brent-Dyer, *The Princess of the Chalet School* (London: Harper Collins, 1992), p. 8.

it is not the experience of isolation *per se* that stirs the Princess Elisaveta's longings, but the imaginative power of fiction and the visions it arouses: the little girl in the story does not know that she is lonely until books tell her that she is. In this respect she is a perfect representative for the ten-year-old reader of her day.

For if Elisaveta's imagination is fired by her reading, the same was true of Brazil enthusiasts from all social strata. Angela Brazil received fan mail from admirers as grand and as distant as the Sharfunisa Begum of Hyderabad, who wrote glowingly to her favourite author in 1928 that 'I was one of the lucky girls who got one of your nicest books as a prize ... and I cannot tell you with what breathless interest I read it from cover to cover.' Brazil also heard from those of a very different rank who poured out their hearts to her: 'It has always been the dearest wish of my heart since I was a little girl to go to a boarding school', confided another devotee. 'Unfortunately we are poor and I just had to go to a board-school ... I don't know why I am telling you all this rigmarole, perhaps it is because I want a friend.'[3] Brazil's writing touched a nerve that allowed girls everywhere to identify with her youthful heroines and their situation, and that furthermore invited readers to think of their author as a sympathetic ear, responsive to their personal problems. The vast majority of Brazil's readers had no direct experience of English boarding schools, but the school story paradigm satisfied fantasies of girlhood friendship, community and equality in which all could share. It also reflected a corresponding shift in the educational and literary cultures of the age, especially as these related to young and adolescent girls and women.

Angela Brazil's own lifetime saw radical changes in British social and cultural mores. Born in Preston, Lancashire in 1869, at the very zenith of Victorianism, she lived through the reigns of five monarchs and survived two world wars. She began writing for children at the age of 30, although her first school story, *The Fortunes of Philippa*, did not appear until 1906. Based on the experiences of Brazil's own mother, *The Fortunes of Philippa* heralded the start of the extraordinarily successful narrative formula that was to capture the imaginations of girl readers in an unprecedented way. Brazil's work dramatically charts the transformation in ideologies of girlhood that occurred in the early years of the twentieth century. In part this can be linked to the more general cultural shift which resulted from the heated nineteenth-century debates on the 'Woman Question'. These culminated in the movement for women's suffrage with its attendant controversy, and the consequent changes in women's roles and opportunities that occurred after the First World War. Social reforms that were taking place round about the turn of the century would profoundly affect women's legal standing and, in turn, extend educational opportunities and career prospects for girls.

Much of the underlying anxiety relating to the changing social role of girls and women is recorded in Angela Brazil's schoolgirl fiction, which provides a remarkably accurate register of the times. Her girlish societies are insular communities in which the debates of the day are re-enacted: debates about female education, about careers, about militarism, about class, nation and power and, most importantly perhaps, about adolescence. Brazil's work also denotes the real arrival of the tomboy in British

---

3   Gillian Freeman, *The Schoolgirl Ethic: The Life and Work of Angela Brazil* (London: Allen Lane, 1976), pp. 110 and 109.

fiction – *A Terrible Tomboy* (1904) was the title of one of her early successes – and the centrality of the tomboy figure, wild, active and reluctant to accept the restrictive codes of conventional femininity, could well have been responsible for the success of her contemporary American sales. From the mid nineteenth century onwards, tomboys were familiar figures in North American fiction for girls. *Little Women*'s Jo March (1868), Katy Carr, the eponymous heroine of *What Katy Did* (1872), and Anne Shirley of Green Gables (1908) were all transatlantic favourites by the time Angela Brazil made the wild, impulsive and sometimes transgressive heroine central to the school story.[4] The English forerunners of Brazil's madcap heroines, Ethel May in Charlotte M. Yonge's *The Daisy Chain* (1856) or Annie Forrest in L.T. Meade's *A World of Girls* (1886), were neither as bold nor as untameable as their North American counterparts, nor were they prepared to flout authority with the confidence and the carelessness of Brazil's modern schoolgirls.

Outwardly Brazil herself showed no sign of the tomboy or the unconventional spirit that her novels celebrated. From 1911 she lived quietly with her unmarried brother and sister in a highly respectable household in Coventry. She was a well-known local figure, the stalwart of a number of civic societies, with an abiding interest in local history and antiquities, and committed to supporting charitable causes. She also developed a reputation as a formidable hostess with a penchant for throwing children's parties, and for entertaining adult guests at soirées with juvenile food and entertainment, jellies and party games, diversions that her guests understandably approached with trepidation. Throughout her career, and despite the fact that she had no children of her own, Angela Brazil remained close to the sources and the experience of youthful, especially girlish, pleasure – her children's parties were notable for the predominance of female guests. Her description of herself as 'an absolute schoolgirl' would appear to be an accurate one, for, as her biographer, Gillian Freeman, has pointed out, Brazil's most cherished memories remained those of her own schooldays, and her most intense relationships were those which she had nurtured since childhood or which had developed with young girls later in life.[5] Angela Brazil also read widely. She was an inveterate collector of early children's fiction – her personal collection is now held in Coventry City Library. Like so many writers for children, she was fascinated by her predecessors, and their fictional models informed her own writing.

In her discussion of women's magazines at the turn of the century, Margaret Beetham has suggested that the very form of periodical literature empowers its readers in specific ways that encourage the possibility of diverse readings.[6] The same is true of the school story which by 1914 had overtaken the family stories of selfless heroines typical of the Victorian age or the more action-packed narratives of

---

4   See Shirley Foster and Judy Simons, *What Katy Read: Feminist Re-Readings of 'Classic' Stories for Girls* (London: Macmillan, 1995), for a more extended discussion of the tomboy figure, and Judy Simons, 'Girls Will Be Boys', *International Review of Children's Literature and Librarianship* 13 (1996), 123–34.

5   Freeman, *Schoolgirl Ethic*, p. 18.

6   Margaret Beetham, A *Magazine of Her Own? Domesticity and Desire in the Woman's Magazine, 1800–1914* (London: Routledge, 1996), p. 11.

adventure or of Girl-Guiding, which constituted popular reading for girls in the period immediately preceding the First World War. In contrast to many of her successors, Angela Brazil never wrote a series based around a single fictional school, such as the Abbey School created by Elsie Oxenham or Brent-Dyer's Chalet School. Rather, her school stories were discrete entities, each with its own school and cast of characters, and with its individual inventive scenario – although as her career developed these began to look increasingly formulaic. In her heyday, from 1909 to 1925, in order to keep pace with market demand she was producing on average two full-length novels of boarding school life per year, plus half a dozen magazine stories. Blackie and Son, who from 1906 became Brazil's main publisher, sold an astonishing 3 million copies of her books. By the 1920s the school story was firmly established as the most popular of literary genres for girls.

Yet why did the girls' school story so capture the imagination? And why at this particular moment in history? Who were its readers, and how were their tastes determined? The answers to these questions rely heavily on the power of the myth which Brazil's novels realised so graphically. For although they seem to be firmly rooted in specific class and period conventions, girls' school stories exert a readerly fascination that transcends both. After all, Angela Brazil continued to write and publish school stories for over 40 years. Moreover, by the time of her death in 1947, the genre had become sufficiently embedded in girls' reading experience to flourish without her. Her most famous successors, Elinor Brent-Dyer and Enid Blyton, outlived her, as did the popularity of their respective series about the Chalet School and the schools at Malory Towers and St Clare's. Brent-Dyer's original novel, *The School at the Chalet*, first appeared in 1925. Seventy years later, the series, which ran to an amazing 58 books in total, was still selling 150,000 copies a year without ever having gone out of print.[7] In 1994, reviewing Rosemary Auchmuty's study of four of the best known writers of school stories to follow in Angela Brazil's wake (Brent-Dyer, Blyton, Dorita Fairlie Bruce and Elsie Oxenham), the critic Jonathan Sale could not account for the fact that his own two daughters, who both attended an inner London primary school, were also enthusiastic 'old girls of both Malory Towers and the Chalet School'.[8] What could these books with their archaic midnight japes, heroic hockey deeds and gutsy head prefects offer late twentieth- or early twenty-first century girls, whose own school experiences were so radically different from those of their literary counterparts? Perhaps, as with Brent-Dyer's Princess Elisaveta and with fans of J.K. Rowling's Hogwarts pupils, it is that very difference which is the key to their appeal.

Yet the genre which found such immediate empathy among girl readers was by no means accepted with approval by adults. Headmistresses banned Angela Brazil's writings from their schools, fearful of their apparently subversive influence on impressionable minds. 'I was one of the Assembly summoned to hear the High Mistress forbidding us to read any of Angela Brazil's books – if any found, instant burning,' testified one old public school pupil, reminiscing 60 years later. 'I have since wondered if she had any right to do such a thing, but it was 1920 and times have

---

7   *Guardian*, 7 April 1994, p. 8.

8   Jonathan Sale, 'Top of her Form', *Sunday Times*, 6 September 1992.

changed considerably since then.'[9] Brazil's work, with its cast of lively heroines who openly flouted authority, was evidently suspected of having seditious tendencies. And why should we be surprised? The stories made a feature of naughtiness, venerated the cult of personality, described with relish the antics of the hoyden who was contemptuous of order and control, and definitively established a world where youth reigned supreme and adults were unquestionably relegated to the shadows.

All this undermined existing models of perfect girlhood that were still being touted around by hopeful publishers. At the turn of the century the typical schoolgirl heroine was still the self-sacrificial prototype which had formed the Victorian ideal. Elinor Davenport Adams' *A Queen Among Girls*, published by Blackie and Son in 1900, depicts its central character, Augusta Pembroke, in terms that have little in common with the untidy, energetic adolescents who flout authority and run wild in Angela Brazil's schools. The publishers' blurb for Davenport Adams's work emphasises the exemplary dimension of Augusta's role as 'the head of her school, the favourite of her teachers and fellow pupils who are attracted by her fearless and independent nature and her queenly bearing'. The narrative is a standard one of heroic ordeal, starring the 'queenly' Augusta, who 'dreams of a distinguished professional career; but the course of her life is suddenly changed by pity for her timid little brother, Adrian, the victim of his guardian-uncle's harshness.'[10] This paragon, having taken over her brother's gender role, is out of a very different stable from Brazil's Raymonde Armitage, the eponymous *Madcap of the School* (see Figure 9.1), who

> would certainly not have won a medal for exemplary behaviour, had any such prize been offered at her school. There was no harm in her but her irrepressible spirits were continually at effervescing point, and in fizzing over were liable to burst into outbreaks of a nature highly scandalizing to the authorities.[11]

In the same year as *A Queen Among Girls* appeared, Blackie and Son, who were to become Brazil's publishers, also announced other titles in terms that reveal unambiguously their didactic and reforming bias. The title of *A Girl's Loyalty* is self-explanatory. *The Two Dorothys: A Tale for Girls* retells the classic tale of the triumph of youth over proud old age when 'the shy, dreamy, unselfish Dorothy Heriot comes to live with her great-aunt, the other Dorothy'. *The Lady* hailed it as a book which 'will not only interest and please all girls, but will also stimulate and encourage to better and higher things, youthful hopes and ambitions'. A third title in the series, *A Girl of Today* was endorsed with a recommendation from the *Educational Times* as the sort of book that is 'exactly what is needed to give a school-girl an interest in the development of character'.[12] The pleasure principle was not yet the point; instead,

---

9   Quoted in Arthur Marshall, *Giggling in the Shrubbery* (1985, repr. London: Fontana, 1986), p. 146.

10   Elinor Davenport Adams, *A Queen Among Girls* (London: Blackie and Son, 1900).

11   Angela Brazil, *The Madcap of the School* (London: Blackie and Son, 1917), p. 12.

12   Frances Armstrong, *A Girl's Loyalty*; Mrs Herbert Martin, *The Two Dorothys: A Tale for Girls*; Elinor Davenport Adams, *A Girl of To-Day* (All three published London; Glasgow; Dublin: Blackie & Son Ltd, 1900).

Figure 9.1   Outside front cover and spine of Angela Brazil, *The Madcap of the School* (London: Blackie and Son, no date but 1917). Collection of Judy Simons.

character-building and moral improvement reigned, as in the days of Charlotte Yonge's *Monthly Packet*, founded in 1851.

J.S. Bratton has observed that,

> In practical terms, new narrative and character models, which would maintain the old values but offer a more modern standard of activity for girls, were not easy to set up. A century of writing for girls had established the norm of the domestic tale, in which the trials of the heroine were involved with the learning of discipline, the internalisation of the feminine values of self-abnegation, obedience and submission.[13]

By radically departing from these conventional models, Angela Brazil's work broke through such barriers. Her school stories, with their intensive focus on a world that is exclusively female, where women are in command and where girls can be invested

---

13 J.S. Bratton, 'Girls' Fiction 1900–1930' in Jeffrey Richards (ed.), *Imperialism and Juvenile Literature* (Manchester and New York: Manchester University Press, 1989), p. 197.

with authority, were simultaneously innovative and reassuring. And in defiance of its bourgeois limits – for Brazil's boarding school girls are almost unfailingly middle class and proud of it – the narrative constructs a democratised society run on principles of equality where the nine-year-old child has as much right to be heard as the senior prefect or headmistress. Indeed, ever since Brazil cast the mould, young readers of all classes and generations have been able to locate their own potential for development within the school story. When little Patty Hirst packs her belongings in preparation for her new life at the Priory in *The Nicest Girl in the School* (1909), her mother tries to bolster her spirits: 'It's no use crying, Patty; young birds must leave the nest some time, and learn to fly for themselves.' And as Patty makes the transition from home life to school, she gains comfort from the thought of her possessions stacked neatly above her and nearby, and the identity they confer. 'It seemed so important to be sitting there with a new brown leather bag in the rack over her head, and a new box in the luggage van marked with her own initials, and to feel she was bound for such a particularly interesting destination.'[14]

With between 20 and 50 pupils on average, Brazil's fictional schools are small enough to give the sense of an extended family, yet sufficiently substantial to create what is described in *The Leader of the Lower School* (1913) as 'a state in miniature', with 'its own particular institutions and its own system of self-government'.[15] The advent of prefects, so resisted at first by the more rebellious youngsters – 'Who wants prefects?' groaned Elizabeth Homes, 'The school's done very well without them for all these years, and I can't see why they should be fastened on us now!'[16] – grants responsibility to girls, as does the College Council, an exemplar of government by consensus, which features in *A Popular Schoolgirl* (1920). Via the autonomous societies that they depict, Brazil's stories suggest the possibility of escape from restrictive home life and a culture of compliance. They establish instead a definitive and distinctive world of girl power.

It is also a world where girls themselves are the stars. In describing the fictional girls' school, Brazil invented the modern schoolgirl, a prototype figure who functioned as an inspirational model for generations of youthful readers. Unlike the tomboy heroines who preceded them, such as Jo March, Brazil's schoolgirls are not unorthodox creatures in conflict with the dominant mores governing female propriety. They are normal girls in a transitional period of their lives, active, healthy and lively. High spirited, fun loving and adventurous, they exhibit characteristics with which all readers could identify. At 14 or 15 years old, the typical Brazil heroine has left childhood behind, but is not yet mature enough to take the full responsibilities of adulthood. As Miss Lincoln, the headmistress of the Priory School admits, girls of that age are at their most interesting but also their most problematic stage of development. They were

---

14 Angela Brazil, *The Nicest Girl in the School* (London: Blackie and Son, 1909), pp. 14 and 27.

15 Angela Brazil, *The Leader of the Lower School* (London: Blackie and Son, 1913), p. 44.

16 Angela Brazil, 'The Third Form Strike', *British Girls' Annual* (London: Cassell and Co., 1918), p. 9.

too old to be treated as children, and had already begun to set up standards of their own; indeed they thought they knew most things a little better than their elders. They were impatient of discipline, yet their ideas were still crude and unformed, and they had not the judgement nor self-restraint which might be counted upon in the higher forms.[17]

Thus, Gwen Gascoyne, the *Youngest Girl in the Fifth* (1913),

was at a particularly difficult and hobbledehoy stage of her development. She was tall for her age, and rather awkward in her manners, apt at present to be slapdash and independent, and decidedly lacking in 'that repose which stamps the caste of Vere de Vere'. Gwen could never keep still for five seconds, her restless hands were always fidgeting or her feet shuffling, or she was twisting in her chair, or shaking back a loose untidy lock that had escaped from her ribbon.[18]

Inevitably such restlessness finds its outlet in naughtiness and adventure. In this way Brazil's novels recognise what was just beginning to be acknowledged in educational and medical theory as a discrete stage in the psychological and social process of development: the state of adolescence. Not only do they recognise it, they foreground it and recreate it in all its confusion, messiness and fascination. It is this age group and its evolutionary character that essentially determines the nature of the action with which the stories engage, action which frequently involves escapades that get the girls into trouble, but which also celebrates their essential energy. Girls are stranded when the tide comes in over the rocks, they engage in heroic rescue operations, they search for suspected spies, or more mundanely put on disguises, play tricks on one another and on their teachers and climb out of their dormitory windows at night. The world of Brazil's schools becomes discrete; characterised by its own special behavioural codes and its own private language – the school slang was one of the genre's most excoriated features; its most passionate relationships were those of friendship between the girls themselves.

For in the fantasy world of the fictional school, the most compelling fantasy of all is that of immediate and unrestricted friendship. It is this which captivates Brent-Dyer's Princess Elisaveta, just as it captivated the girl readers who flocked in their thousands to buy Brazil's books. As noted earlier, most Brazil readers never went to boarding school; consequently they were entranced by the visions of community and companionship her writing evoked. This was largely because, in stark contrast with the reality, the fictional school was a place where loneliness did not exist and where unconditional loyalty was the norm. As Sally Mitchell has pointed out in her study of girls' culture in England at the turn of the century, 'Freedom to choose friends was a heady experience for girls previously taught at home or at private schools selected for their social tone.'[19] Intimate friendships provided emotional release and essential support in an environment where all forms of girlish self-expression were licensed.

---

17 Brazil, *The Nicest Girl in the School*, p. 193.

18 Angela Brazil, *The Youngest Girl in the Fifth* (London: Blackie and Son, 1913), p. 19.

19 Sally Mitchell, *The New Girl: Girls' Culture in England, 1880–1915* (New York: Columbia University Press, 1995), p. 81.

Thus, in *A Harum-Scarum Schoolgirl* (1919), troubled Diana Hewlitt turns to her best friend, Loveday, for physical as well as emotional solace:

> But up in the ivy room, when she went to bed, the mask fell off. The Diana that cuddled in Loveday's arms was a very different Diana from the don't-care young person of downstairs. Loveday – who understood her now – consoled and kissed where a term ago she would have scolded. There are some dispositions that can only be managed by kisses.[20]

The passionate relationships which flourish between Brazil's adolescent girls clearly overflow into the sentimental and romantic, yet without the overt eroticism that would make them threatening. Strong attachments are accompanied by admiration of girls' beauty (see Figure 9.2) and by physical closeness, but the intimacy suggests the pleasures of mothering and being mothered as much as those of sexual encounters. Girls climb into bed together, cuddle and kiss unashamedly and develop ardent friendships that can be interpreted in different ways by different readers. Their names – either ungendered like Loveday or masculinised abbreviated versions of their given names – Ray, Phil, Tony – intensify the romantic dimension of these relationships. In her autobiography Angela Brazil wrote about one of her own juvenile friendships in terms of passionate longing. 'How immensely, frantically, intensely I had loved her – loved her even then! ... My friendships were so white-hot, I see now it must have been difficult for a girl of a different temperament to keep pace with me'.[21] Inevitably the physical intimacy of the girls and the heady sensationalism of their exploits has encouraged aficionados, detractors and parodists of the school story to insert the sexuality that Brazil left out. In 2002, for example, 'Trouble at Willow Gables' and 'Michaelmas Term at St Bride's', two lesbian schoolgirl tales by the late Philip Larkin, were posthumously published, both clearly inspired by the stories of Angela Brazil and her cult status.[22]

Angela Brazil had hit upon a winning narrative formula, one which provided the template for her successors, and which was sufficiently attention grabbing to attract hordes of imitators as well as critics. By 1920 her fictional versions of boarding school life had entered the literary imagination to such an extent that they had already become something of a cliché. Dorita Fairlie Bruce's *Dimsie Goes to School* (1920), the first of nine Dimsie books and of thirty school stories by Bruce, shows how Dimsie's own expectations of boarding school life were clearly determined by books. Waking up on her first morning at the Jane Willard Foundation for Girls, after a surprisingly undisturbed night's sleep, Dimsie innocently enquires of a bemused room-mate why she has not yet fallen victim to the schoolgirl pranks which she had expected.

> 'P'raps, then,' she said hesitatingly, 'in real schools like Jane's, you don't put hair-brushes into new girls' beds?'

---

20 Angela Brazil, *A Harum-Scarum Schoolgirl* (London: Blackie and Son, 1919), pp. 175–6.

21 Angela Brazil, *My Own Schooldays* (London: Blackie and Son, 1925), p. 116.

22 Philip Larkin, *Trouble at Willow Gables and Other Fictions*, ed. James Booth (London: Faber, 2002).

Figure 9.2   Illustration by Balliol Salmon for Angela Brazil, *The Madcap of the School* (London: Blackie and Son, no date but 1917), opposite page 180. Collection of Judy Simons.

'What for?' inquired Rosamund, who was not fond of reading; 'it sounds a silly sort of thing to do.'

'Nor jugs of water on the top of the door?' pursued Dimsie, determined to go thoroughly into the matter while she was about it. 'To drop on one's head, you know, when one comes in.'[23]

Dimsie has evidently been overdosing on Angela Brazil, who by 1921 (when *Dimsie Goes to School* appeared) had written over 20 full-length novels and 50 magazine stories about boarding schools. Like Brent-Dyer's Princess Elisaveta, Dimsie has unquestioningly absorbed the boarding school ethos as promoted by Brazil's writing – note that the more down-to-earth Rosamund is 'not fond of reading' – and the degree of referentiality in post-1920 boarding school stories for girls indicates both their young readers' acceptance of the fictional culture and the extraordinary success of the genre in which it was perpetuated. Indeed so familiar had the features of the girls' school story become in the immediate post-war period, that authors such as Bruce and Brent-Dyer could modify what had already become a standard narrative

23 Dorita Fairlie Bruce, *Dimsie Goes To School* (Oxford: Oxford University Press, 1921), p. 19.

format in order to suggest that their pictures of school life were more authentic than those of their pioneering predecessor.

Brazil's schoolgirl tales exerted a mythic appeal that reached across continents and generations. To understand the ingredients of this appeal for a contemporary audience it is also important to appreciate something of the fictional heritage of the school story and the explosion in the publishing market for girl readers that occurred in the early years of the twentieth century. This shift in girls' reading practices needs to be seen in the context of the increased spread of literacy brought about by the education acts of 1902 and 1907 and their effects upon girls' education. Brazil's own nostalgia for schooldays as an opportunity for carefree joys and self-expression was not in fact located in her own experience. Rather it expresses her yearning for an imagined paradise, the sort of school which she believed to have come into existence after her own schooldays had ended in 1887. 'When I go to see modern girls' schools, and know what jolly times they have with games and clubs and acting, I feel I missed a very great deal,' she wrote in 1925.[24] Her stories may have taken their inspiration from a naïve fantasy of 'jolly times', but they hit the marketplace at a particularly opportune moment.

In 1900 there were 20,000 girls at recognised girls' grammar schools in England. By 1920 this figure had grown to 185,000.[25] Brazil's novels and those of her successors must be seen in the context of that changing educational climate and the corresponding transition in attitudes towards intellectual and career opportunities for girls. By the 1920s the girls' boarding school had come to be an acceptable and respected institution, even an establishment of choice for middle-class parents with aspirations for their daughters' future. Alongside the academic syllabus, its curriculum typically included sports of all kinds, hockey, lacrosse, fencing, archery and cricket. The physical freedom conferred by these sports was matched by a corresponding release of opportunities in the intellectual and professional world beyond. The school story thus reflected external changes that were transfigured by Angela Brazil's imagination into a rapturous celebration of girlish pleasure. And as the form developed, it came to represent a self-contained world of youthful liberation and female licence, a temporary haven from reality but with sufficient resemblance to it to be plausible and supremely desirable.

It has been suggested that the girls' school story developed in response to the rise in popularity of boarding school stories for boys, and that it appealed to girls who wanted to enjoy a reading experience which matched that of their brothers. This assumption denies the well-documented history of girls' reading and the development of gender-specific children's literature from the eighteenth century onwards. Although until recently more critical attention has been paid to the growth of boys' boarding school fiction, and some of the most famous nineteenth- and twentieth-century classic texts for children are of this genus – Thomas Hughes's *Tom Brown's Schooldays*; Frank Richards's *Greyfriars* tales – girls' stories of school life have their

---

24 Brazil, *My Own Schooldays*, quoted in Gillian Freeman, *The Schoolgirl Ethic: The Life and Work of Angela Brazil* (London: Allen Lane 1976), p. 25.

25 Mary Cadogan and Patricia Craig, *You're a Brick, Angela: A New Look at Girls' Fiction 1839–1975* (London: Victor Gollancz, 1976), p. 178.

own provenance and culture. They were, of course, also read, if somewhat guiltily, by boys. Lord Goodman is by no means an isolated example of the male Brazil fan. The distinguished academic Fred Inglis has also owned to a youthful penchant for reading Brazil's novels secretly under the bedclothes or concealed beneath innocuous brown paper wrappings labelled, 'Billiards for Boys'.[26] Likewise, Arthur Marshall, journalist, broadcaster and one-time schoolmaster, remained fascinated by the culture of the girls' boarding school and the almost surreal time warp it represented. The very title of his book, *Giggling in the Shrubbery*, and its opening quotation from Brazil's *The School by the Sea* (1914) – 'GIRLS! Girls everywhere! Girls in the passage, girls in the hall, racing upstairs and scurrying downstairs, diving into dormitories and running into classrooms, overflowing onto the landing and hustling along the corridor – everywhere, girls!' – suggest the voyeuristic allure of Angela Brazil's all-female society.[27]

If the novels of Angela Brazil and her successors borrowed elements from their male counterparts, so did the schools themselves. As Gillian Avery has observed, Cheltenham Ladies College, Badminton, Roedean and Wycombe Abbey, some of the first major public schools for girls, made explicit their aspirations to intellectual attainment by introducing a standardised curriculum that reflected those of the famous boys' schools, such as Rugby, Eton and Harrow. But whilst the syllabuses of the girls' schools included the traditional subjects of classics, grammar and mathematics that formed the staple diet of the boys' public school curriculum, they also widened and modernised their scope so as to incorporate modern languages and the creative arts, such as painting and music, which would extend and cultivate the mind.[28] Initially girls' public schools might well have adopted the boys' public schools as models, with their accent on classical languages, physical sport and character building, but they subsequently used this as a convenient framework on which to graft a discrete and feminised culture, often with new emphases on the individual. Whereas boys' school stories tend to promote a masculine ethos and advocate the values of toughness and independence, girls' stories place the accent on love, warmth and the security of friends, features as attractive to boy readers as to girls.

These changes in the curriculum, which allowed for a more liberal approach to girls' education, were correspondingly reflected in the fiction. Patty Hirst, for example, the protagonist of Angela Brazil's most popular novel, *The Nicest Girl in the School*, and by no means a natural scholar, finds her métier in the art studio. The book features lessons that indicate the breadth of the academic curriculum and also give an impression of its intellectual rigour. They include a history lecture on the reign of James I, a French translation class, a grammar exercise on the origins of the English language, a translation from Caesar and a study of Shakespeare and Molière. At the same time the novel draws attention to the qualities of imagination and observation that distinguish the non-scholarly pupil, whose talents might well

---

26 Fred Inglis, *The Promise of Happiness: Value and Meaning in Children's Fiction* (Cambridge: Cambridge University Press, 1981), p. 65.

27 Marshall, *Giggling in the Shrubbery*, p. 7.

28 Gillian Avery, *The Best Type of Girl: A History of Girls' Independent Schools* (London: Andre Deutsch, 1991,), p. 3.

be neglected in a more formal, classical programme of study. In common with more traditional turn-of-the-century novels, such as *A Queen Among Girls*, Brazil's early fiction stresses the character-building element of schoolgirl life. Tellingly, Patty receives a copy of Ruskin's *Of Queen's Gardens* as a school prize. This would have been an unthinkable accolade in Brazil's later work, such as *The Madcap of the School*, where the girls collectively deride the nineteenth-century image of the angel in the house.

> 'This isn't a school for saints!' grumbled Valentine one day. 'If we followed all Gibbie's pet precepts we should have halos round our heads.'
>
> 'And be sprouting wings!' added Raymonde. 'A very uncomfortable process too. I expect it would hurt like cutting teeth, and it would spoil the fit of one's blouses. I don't want to be an angel! I'm quite content with this world at present.'[29]

It is interesting to trace the shift in attitudes from the pre- to post-war fictional market, as represented in these two examples of Brazil's work written less than ten years apart. The Victorian heritage retains a strong influence in girls' fiction written before 1914, and Brazil's early school stories reflect this accordingly. The changes that the war effected in opportunities for women, changes which have been extensively analysed by social and cultural historians, had a corresponding impact on the expectations of young readers. The girls' school story as pioneered by Brazil underscores the essential modernity of the twentieth-century world that her heroines enjoy. At the height of her career, both pre- and post-war Brazil books are packed with references to contemporary events and to the progressive society which the girls inhabit. Raymonde Armitage, for instance, 'not a girl to stop and consider risks',[30] has an adventure involving a German prisoner of war. In *A Popular Schoolgirl*, the girls bemoan the signing of the Armistice. 'It's too bad', grouses one disappointed young woman, 'that just when I'm old enough all the jolly things are closed to women ... Life's going to be very slow now. There's nothing sporty to do at all!'[31] Readers will be heartened to know that later in the story a career as an aviator is held out as a tantalising possibility. Despite the fictional nature of her work, Brazil came to be regarded as something of an expert on 'the modern schoolgirl', invited to give lectures and broadcasts on the subject. Her novels make explicit reference to differences between current educational practice for girls as advanced in the modern school and the restrictive precepts of previous generations.

Even Brazil's early stories insist on the advanced nature of her fictional schools in comparison with the sort of establishment she herself had attended and had heard about from her mother. Nina Forster for example, the heroine of one of her first novels, *The Third Class at Miss Kaye's* (1908), startles her schoolmates by reeling off the horrors of her grandmother's schooldays when girls

> had to learn their lessons off by heart, and stand with their hands behind their backs and say them just like parrots ... They had to use backboards every day, and chest expanders

---

29 Brazil, *The Madcap of the School*, p. 59.
30 Ibid., p. 148.
31 Angela Brazil, *A Popular Schoolgirl* (London: Blackie and Son, 1920), p. 18.

... They hardly ever went on picnics or excursions; they only used to go for stupid walks along the roads, two and two, with a mistress at each end. The music mistress had a silver pencil with a heavy knob at the end, and if a girl played a wrong note she used to bring it down with a thump upon her hand.[32]

How unlike the lives of Brazil's schoolgirls, with their emphasis on physical activity, their school uniform that allowed unhampered movement, their enjoyment of 'dangerous' team games such as hockey, and their indulgence in free (if not always decorous) speech. 'Top-hole'; 'How ripping'; 'Twiggez-vous?'; 'Jubilate': the linguistic community which Brazil's fictional slang established – and which shocked parents and teachers – perhaps more than anything defined the difference between the reticence expected of yesterday's young women and her up-to-date youngsters.

The origins of the modern school story for girls lie in the late nineteenth century, although stories of boarding school life go back to the eighteenth century – Sarah Fielding's *The Governess* (1749) being the first known example. *The Governess or, Little Female Academy*, despite its digressive narrative and its overt moral messages, does contain certain embryonic features of the school story as Brazil and others were to develop it. In Fielding's novel, Mrs Teachum's school, like its twentieth-century counterparts, is a self-contained all-female community whose pupils rarely venture into the outside world. The school is small, consisting of nine girls and their schoolmistress, and the most important lessons it teaches are those of social responsibility and mature leadership, the same themes that were to figure so centrally in Brazil's books and those of her contemporaries. Although Fielding's work is driven by its didactic thrust, the story also represents the world of the school as one of emotional crises, profound friendships, jealousies and anxieties, a world where relationships between the girls assume a heightened intensity in the closed society that nurtures them. Consider, for example, the episode where Miss Sukey Jennet is so distraught over her relationship with a schoolmate

> that she could not utter one Word more; but sat herself down, reclining her Head upon her Hand, in the most melancholy Posture that could be: Nor could she close her Eyes all Night; but lay tossing and raving with the Thought how she should act, and what she should say to Miss Jenny the next Day.[33]

Sukey's despair over how to restore her reputation in the eyes of her friends anticipates that of Raymonde Armitage, Angela Brazil's tomboy protagonist, a century and a half later. After a moment of carelessness, Raymonde agonised,

> the whole of her gay, careless world seemed to have crumbled to ashes. She wondered what her chums were thinking of her. Did they, like Veronica, mistrust her conduct? A sense of utter desolation swept over her, and, pushing aside the tea things, she leaned her arms on the table, with her hot face pressed against them.[34]

---

32 Angela Brazil, *The Third Class at Miss Kaye's* (London: Blackie and Son, 1908), p. 222.

33 Sarah Fielding, *The Governess or, Little Female Academy* (1749, repr. with an introduction by Jill E. Grey (London: Oxford University Press, 1968), p. 115.

34 Brazil, *The Madcap of the School*, p. 280.

The inspirational quality of Fielding's novel and in particular her original conception of the girls' school as an appropriate narrative vehicle for young readers, can be seen both in the number of her contemporary imitators and in the way in which variations on *The Governess* model persisted well into the nineteenth century.[35] What is especially striking about the extracts quoted here, and indeed, what is characteristic of the genre as it subsequently developed, is the seriousness with which schoolgirl emotions are treated. The power of childhood feeling is neither brushed aside nor seen as relative to other more weighty or adult considerations. Brazil's novels above all take the emotional crises which characterise the unstable world of adolescent experience as the pivot of their psychological action. In the twentieth-century school story for girls, as distinct from that written for boy readers, much of the excitement has its source in the subtle interplay of personal relationships, the loves, hates, jealousies and misunderstandings that create an emotionally charged world.

Although Fielding's *The Governess* had its imitators in both the eighteenth and nineteenth centuries, the girls' school story genre only began to assume its current form in the 1870s. With titles such as *Maggie's Mistake: A Schoolgirl's Story* (1874), *The New Girl, or: The Rivals* (1879), and *That Aggravating Schoolgirl* (1885), these books give tantalising indications of the central themes of community, exclusion, unfamiliarity, jealousy and the assertion of identity which were to typify the form.[36] Most crucially perhaps they introduce that new creature, the modern schoolgirl, a distinctive creation quite unlike her antecedents in that she relishes her freedom from the bounds of home, identifies with a community of peers rather than with her family, and during the process of the story, discovers herself as an independent and educated being.

Perhaps the best known of such early heroines is Annie Forrest in L.T. Meade's *A World of Girls* (1886), often credited with being the first modern girls' school story, although, as the examples quoted above illustrate, Meade did not invent the genre. *A World of Girls* contains many of the salient features that came to be associated with the rise of schoolgirl fiction, and Meade herself, probably the most widely read of Brazil's immediate predecessors, was voted the most popular author of 1898 in a poll organised by *Girls' Realm*. It was no mean achievement to head a list that also included her now more famous contemporaries, Charlotte M. Yonge and Frances Hodgson Burnett.[37]

As its title suggests, *A World of Girls* depicts an enclosed female community, which is self-regulating and which attempts to construct an environment independent of the world of male authority. Lavender House is the sort of small school that became the prototype of those featured in Brazil's early works, although by the 1920s her settings had evolved into much more substantial and well-organised establishments. In the world of Lavender House, girls from the ages of five to sixteen live in a collective,

---

35 For the history of publishing details of the text and its imitators, see Jill E. Grey's 'Introduction' to Fielding, *The Governess*.

36 Anon, *Maggie's Mistake: A Schoolgirl's Story* (London: Edis Searle, 1874); M.E. Gellie, *The New Girl, or: The Rivals* (London: Griffith Farran Browne, 1879); Grace Stebbing, *That Aggravating Schoolgirl* (London: Nisbet, 1885).

37 Quoted in Cadogan and Craig, *You're a Brick, Angela*, p. 51.

its divisions into classes and dormitories creating smaller communities each with its own ethos and boundaries. The narrative focus of the book, as in Brazil's texts, falls upon personal allegiances and tensions, the development of friendships, exclusive alliances between groups or pairs of girls, jealousies and experiences of alienation or exclusion. The girls, like their twentieth-century equivalents, enjoy midnight feasts and prize-giving ceremonies, and prepare end-of-term entertainments. But Lavender House is both an educational establishment and a training ground preparing the girls for the womanhood that awaits them. In this it differs from the majority of Brazil's novels, which, although they might pay lip service to the idea of a life beyond the school grounds, essentially celebrate girlhood itself as a state to be enjoyed, rather than a necessary preparation for the life to come.

Angela Brazil did not invent the school story but she became its consummate exponent. In establishing a paradigmatic narrative model, she shaped the development of a genre that influenced writers from Brent-Dyer in the 1920s to the contributors to the bestselling comic, *Bunty*, in the 1960s, and that continues to inspire J.K. Rowling in the twenty-first century. This genre has come to acquire mythic status for generations of readers, irrespective of whether boarding school life bears any relation to their own. Through establishing revised parameters for a world which licenses youthful female freedom, Brazil brings to a logical conclusion the undercurrents of rebellious independence to be found in girls' fiction from Louisa M. Alcott to E. Nesbit, and locates them in a context in which they can be isolated and allowed to flourish. Whilst giving her characters freedom to explore alternatives to normally prescriptive gender codes, Brazil also makes a point of addressing their gendered identity. Her characters are not watered-down versions of their male counterparts in the schoolboy fiction of the same period – they do not compete with Harry Wharton, Bob Cherry and their chums. They are substantial creations, spirited, resourceful and independent, and they validate feminine independence and authority for girl readers everywhere.

Some modern critics of children's literature have derided school stories and Brazil's novels in particular as 'inescapably silly, childish and insubstantial … limiting and wrong and absurd'.[38] In their study of girls' literature from the Victorian to the modern period, Mary Cadogan and Patricia Craig condemn Brazil largely on the grounds that her work had given rise to the travesties of schoolgirl experience in cartoons and parodies, so brilliantly realised in Ronald Searle's images of the monstrous St Trinian's. For Cadogan and Craig, 'the schoolgirl as a joke owes its inception … to Angela Brazil'.[39] Similarly, in a full-length study of school stories that tellingly ascribes only one brief chapter out of seventeen to writing produced for girls, Isobel Quigly suggests that Angela Brazil 'killed the girls' school story stone-dead before anyone else could get at it'.[40] Yet Brazil's self-evident popularity confounds her critics. She was without a doubt the greatest exponent of a genre

---

38 Isabel Quigly, *The Heirs of Tom Brown: The English School Story* (London: Chatto & Windus, 1982), p. 218.

39 Cadogan and Craig, *You're a Brick, Angela*, p. 179.

40 Quigly, *Heirs of Tom Brown*, p. 218.

that signals a new direction in girls' fiction, a genre that reflected the new century's distinctive break with the conventions of model girlhood that many authors still held dear. Her influence remains deeply, if perhaps often unconsciously, felt today.

PART III
Popular Instruction,
Popularity Imposed

Introduction

M. O. Grenby

When we consider popular books, we tend to think straightaway of fiction and poetry, for these are the texts, we imagine, which people most enjoy. In this section, though, three essays deal with a different kind of popular literature: those books designed with a purpose – to instruct, improve, edify and reward. Many such books have achieved popularity in terms of their sales and longevity. For example, alphabet books have never, since the very beginning of children's literature, ceased to be produced and consumed in great numbers. Similarly, as Aileen Fyfe points out in her essay on popular science books, a text such as John Aikin and Anna Laetitia Barbauld's rather didactic *Evenings at Home* could remain in print from the 1790s until the First World War. Nor is there any reason to doubt its editors' claims that *The Children's Encylopedia*, which Gillian Avery investigates, sold an astonishing 5.3 million volumes in Britain and the Empire, and 3.5 million sets in the USA. Evidently, then, as well as delighting the publishers who sold them, such books were liked or admired by those who bought them, even if the majority of purchasers may well have been adults. The question is whether they were also popular, in the sense of being enjoyed, by their actual users, mostly children.

This question is brought into sharp focus by Kimberley Reynold's chapter on reward books. These titles were purchased in their thousands for distribution as prizes or institutional presents. The texts generally reflected the values of the organisations which distributed them – Sunday schools, missionary societies, temperance leagues, youth groups and so on – and, to modern eyes, even if many were works of fiction, they often seem too moral, didactic or earnest. Was their popularity imposed, then? Did they sell so well merely because they were fit for their purpose, and nothing more? And if reward books were so successful only because they were acceptably improving, should it be thought that all educational books sold so well and endured so long only because they too fulfilled the demands of parents and teachers who pressed them on reluctant children? Avery argues, for instance, that the *Children's Newspaper* (1919–65) may have been long-lived but it was not much loved, being principally designed to appeal not to child readers but to aspirational parents, who wished their offspring to absorb the upper-class, public school values with which Arthur Mee filled it.

Moreover, the essays here suggest that the popularity of many of these instructive texts was at least partly manufactured, imposed from without, rather than arising naturally out of any qualities of the text. For Reynolds, the producers of reward books quickly learned to mould their products to the requirements of the organisations which gave them away. Not only did this affect the text, with, say, temperance or Evangelical themes coming to dominate, but it shaped the books' appearance too. The aim was to make the gift appear valuable and the donor appear generous while keeping the cost to a minimum, ideally below that of ordinary books. One technique was to produce books with gold lettering or page-edges, leather binding or built-in presentation plates, but with thin paper and highly compressed print. Often the same publishing company would publish the same text in a variety of different formats to suit the budgets of the various reward-giving institutions. Likewise, Fyfe makes the point that certain titles could remain in print because their publishers continually rebranded them. By the mid nineteenth century, *Evenings at Home*, first published in the 1790s, hardly represented cutting-edge science, nor did it provide a recognisable picture of modern children's lives, so it was reinvented as a classic of the nursery which, like *Robinson Crusoe* or *Tales from Shakespeare*, all children ought to have read. Marketing strategies probably lay behind much of the success of the *Children's Encyclopedia* and the *Children's Newspaper* too (although this is not to say that they were not greatly enjoyed by their readers as well). In the early twentieth century, there was probably no-one who knew the consumers of print quite as well as Lord Northcliffe, their publisher, and his determination to pioneer this unexploited market lay behind their initial success in 1908–10. Thereafter, it was doubtless the constant re-publication of the *Encyclopedia* in slightly differing editions which kept it in print until the 1950s.

Innovating distribution strategies were also central to the success of this kind of instructional material. The *Children's Encyclopedia*, like the *Encyclopaedia Britannica*, was sold from door to door, or could be subscribed to so it accumulated in stages. Many of the children's science texts discussed by Fyfe were distributed by the Religious Tract Society. Operating with an agenda different from that of any commercial publisher – an Evangelical determination to provide good books for all, rather than to make a profit – as well as with huge economies of scale, the Society overrode the normal operation of the market. We might see this as a manipulation of popularity. Considering the seemingly unpalatable nature of many of these popular science books, reward books and encyclopedias (to modern readers), it is difficult to curb the suspicion that the popularity of all these books was artificially constructed and externally imposed.

Yet it is evident that some instructional texts achieved success on their own merits. Reward books, Reynolds concedes, may have been commercially successful at least partly because children actually liked them. The narratives, however pious and didactic, could also be involving – as Elaine Lomax pointed out earlier in this volume in her essay on Hesba Stretton, one of the mainstays of the reward book industry. And even if the intention of these texts was generally to condemn dissipated behaviour, and to promote a life of moral probity, the reader, Reynolds suggests, could still subversively enjoy the depiction of vice before the narrative finally stamped it out. Children's pleasure in these books could also derive from extra-textual factors: the fact that such books were trophies, earned by good behaviour or diligent attendance, must have added to their appeal. And in the nineteenth century, especially for children from the poorer sections of society, the personal ownership of any possession would surely have been an attraction. That these books were often ostentatiously luxurious doubtless deepened the pleasure their owners derived from them.

It seems probable, then, that while the vast sales of all these edifying books were partly externally imposed by publishers, parents and gift-giving organisations, they were also genuinely welcomed by their young end-users. Reward books, for example, were designed primarily to coax children into good behaviour, and that bribe would hardly have worked if children had not actually desired the books they were being tempted with. But to quibble about whether or not the sales of these titles was matched by the pleasure of their readers is, ultimately, to miss the point. Reward books, reference books and science books were all enduring bestsellers in a way that reminds us that popularity has never been limited to books intended only to entertain. Each of these forms of children's literature and many others not discussed here – alphabets and primers, mathematics and geography books or conduct and hobby manuals – constituted important sectors of the market in children's books, from the eighteenth century through to the present, and have been crucially responsible both for funding publishers' continuing operations and for immersing children in print culture.

Chapter 10

Rewarding Reads?
Giving, Receiving and Resisting
Evangelical Reward and Prize Books

Kimberley Reynolds

The tradition of giving young people books as rewards or prizes to mark an achievement, and to reinforce a lesson or set of values in the process, is long and enduring.[1] Isaac Watts, for instance, suggested that children who learned ten or so of the verses from his *Divine Songs* (1715) be given a copy of the book for themselves, and to the present day, the prizes given during annual end-of-year prize-giving events at schools largely consist of books.

Initially, at least, the giving of reward books tended to be done on an informal and individual basis: a parent, tutor or other adult might choose to reward a child for any number of reasons at any time of the year, perhaps inscribing on the flyleaf the date and reason for the event. With the rise of commercial publishing and the increased availability of attractive books at attractive prices, institutions quickly realised that the practice of giving books as rewards and prizes could be beneficial in a number of ways, and by the end of the eighteenth century, many private schools and a number of Sunday schools in Britain and many of its dominions and former colonies had initiated formal occasions when books were presented to children to celebrate specific achievements. These varied considerably in nature, from good attendance, collecting for a society, good conduct, 'knowledge of the golden text', scripture, drawing, composition and first position in class, to 'the best essay on total abstinence'.[2]

It soon became customary when giving a book as a reward or prize to include an ex-libris or ornamental bookplate, which frequently recorded not only the date and reason for the prize, but also included details of the awarding institution. Any collection of reward fiction will contain a wide range of such examples, generally including prizes awarded by denominational groups such as the Wesleyan Methodist Juvenile Foreign Missionary Society, the Salvation Army and the Band of Hope, alongside those awarded by school boards, groups such as the National Temperance League, and a variety of other secular youth organisations. Two good early examples of ex-libris designed to denote that a book has been given as a reward or prize are the Bridport Sunday School plate, and that devised for the Duke's School in Alnwick,

---

1   For the purposes of this chapter, giving books as presents is regarded as a different kind of activity.

2   All the examples cited here are taken from books in the Bratton Collection at Roehampton University. The Collection is composed of reward books.

Northumberland (see Figures.10.1 and 10.2). While both of these specially designed ex-libris leave room to record the recipient's achievement, they are primarily concerned with directing attention to the donor. In the case of the Sunday school, this may have been intended primarily to develop a sense of belonging and allegiance to the school, and through it to the Church, but it is difficult not to interpret plates such as the Duke's School's as a form of advertisement which works by mingling a sense of the importance of the institution with the successes of its scholars. In his history of premium or prize ex-libris, Brian North Lee makes the related point that the giving of handsome prizes to students was a good public relations exercise aimed at parents who had paid substantial fees for their children's education, and who were likely to be gratified by a prize which suggested that their investment had been worthwhile.[3]

Whatever the reason for the prize, and whether given to 'the young, folk in service, members of societies or organisations, or whoever, the volumes in which we find these ex-libris were intended to be improving, or at least wholesome and safe in terms of the mores of the time.'[4] As the practice of giving books as rewards and prizes became widespread and institutionalised, the need for a substantial body of appropriate books which could be given as rewards and prizes stimulated publishers to look to their lists. They began to identify and advertise the books they published which were particularly suited for this purpose, and, perhaps more importantly, to

Figure 10.1   Prize label for Bridport Sunday School. From Brian North Lee, *Premium or Prize Ex Libris* (London: The Bookplate Society, 2001), p. 68. Reproduced by kind permission of the Bookplate Society (see <www.bookplatesociety.org>), an international society of collectors, bibliophiles, artists and others dedicated to promoting bookplate study.

3   B.N. Lee, *Premium or Prize Ex-Libris* (London: The Bookplate Society, 2001), p. 39.
4   Lee, *Premium or Prize Ex-Libris*, p. 2.

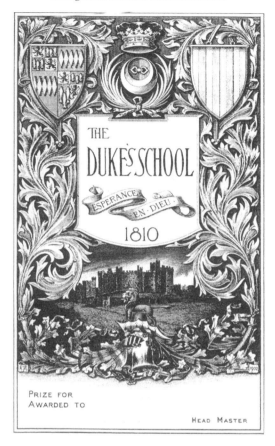

Figure 10.2   Prize label for The Duke's School, Alnwick, engraved by R.A. Mills.
From Brian North Lee, *Premium or Prize Ex Libris* (London: The
Bookplate Society, 2001), p. 55. Reproduced by kind permission
of the Bookplate Society (see <www.bookplatesociety.org>), an
international society of collectors, bibliophiles, artists and others
dedicated to promoting bookplate study.

seek out and commission books specifically intended for this market. It transpired
that the market was more substantial than might have been expected, since the kind
of wholesome, informative and improving books deemed suitable for rewards and
prizes were also appropriate for the increasing numbers of Sunday school libraries.

Reward books, then, became a recognisable publishing activity in the early
nineteenth century. The 1810 catalogue of the Religious Tract Society (RTS) began
what was to become the standard practice of advertising certain titles as suitable
for giving as 'reward books to the children of Sunday-schools'. Within five years a
separate juvenile list specialising in such prizes was established, under the direction

of William Freeman Lloyd.[5] The Society for Promoting Christian Knowledge (SPCK) was a little later on the scene, but brought out a 'supplemental catalogue' of books combining amusement and instruction, evidently intended to appeal to the young, in 1817. In 1832, it went on to establish a Committee of General Literature and Education, which was responsible for producing the kind of wholesome fiction used as rewards.[6] The 10 December 1864 Christmas number of the *Bookseller* included 'A Complete List of Illustrated and Other Books suitable for Presents, School Prizes or Rewards,' and by 1870, under the impetus generated by legislation to provide universal education, producing reward fiction had become a major area of publishing activity. As this chapter will show, however, what kind of books, and which precise books were given, could in many ways be less important to both the institutions which presented rewards and prizes and the young people who received them than the actual acts of giving and receiving.

Deceived by Appearances: A Tale of Book Giving

Despite the scale and financial success of the reward book business, estimating the popularity of reward books with their readers is more problematic than it is for some of the other examples considered in this study. One significant problem is the distortion of what can now be identified as reward fiction, caused by time. Many of the reward books found in collections today have survived precisely because they were *not* popular – physical evidence such as pristine pages, stiff spines, lack of annotation, stains, bookmarks or other inserted material suggests that these books were read infrequently, if at all. Books that were read and relished by their recipients tended to disintegrate with use. The popular end of reward fiction is often represented by the most dilapidated books in a collection, read repeatedly by their owners and, from serial inscriptions, obviously passed on within families and friendship circles.

If the books given as rewards had been chosen by their recipients, as is usually the case today, it would be easier to ascertain which examples were more popular with their readers. However, the method of selection was commonly predicated on judging books largely by their covers. In most cases, the choosing of reward books was not an exact science in which care was taken to match the book with the recipient. Rather, initial selection tended to be based on a number of criteria that had little to do with the text *per se*. No doubt because reward books were almost invariably given to the less well off by schools or charitable organisations with limited budgets, considerations such as compatibility with the aims of the organisation, price and appearance, rather than literary merit, tended to dominate. Those responsible for choosing the prizes, who might be members of a school board, or Sunday school teachers, their resident cleric, superintendents or members of the Parish Council,

---

    5   G. Avery, *Childhood's Pattern: A Study of the Heroes and Heroines of Children's Fiction 1770–1950* (London: Hodder and Stoughton, 1975), p. 67.

    6   W.O.B. Allen, and E. McClure, *200 Years: The History of the Society for Promoting Christian Knowledge 1698–1898* (London: SPCK, 1898), pp. 192–5.

began by agreeing the selection criteria.[7] Then, requests for a selection of suitable reward books would be sent to one of the regular suppliers.[8] Rather like a schools library service today, which will send a pre-selected box of books that teachers are likely to find useful for supporting standard National Curriculum topics, so suppliers of reward books would send mixed boxes of their wares, unashamedly advertising them in terms of value for money and suitability, rather than literary merit. Thus books might be described as 'Eighteen Penny Present Books for boys and girls in attractive bindings and illustrations' or 'Threepence Each: series of reward books with handsome covers printed in gold and colours. *The handsomest books published at the price.*'[9]

The differences in price related entirely to the quality of the production of the book: often identical titles or other works by the best-known authors on a publisher's list would be offered in different editions in the same catalogue or advertisement. More expensive editions were distinguished by such things as costly bindings and endpapers, use of gold lettering, high-quality paper, and coloured illustrations. Because rewards and prizes were often presented in public, were meant to signify accomplishment and needed to reflect well on both giver and receiver, considerable attention was given to appearance, whatever the price. In the closing decades of the nineteenth century, publishers became expert at exploiting every technological development that made it possible to produce books more attractively and cheaply. Covers received particular attention as printers devised effective ways of creating ornately printed designs on relatively inexpensive toughened paper or paper-board covers. Whatever the literary merits of such books, their aesthetic and decorative qualities were likely to be appreciated, and a book that was never read could still be displayed to enliven a poor room while also serving as a reminder of achievement.

During the Victorian period, the more expensive books generally featured in catalogues or advertisements which included brief plot summaries or justifications of their suitability for the reward market, and these tell us a great deal about how reward literature was perceived and what qualities it was supposed to embody. Thus George Cauldwell's most expensive gift or prize books (ninepence each) are briefly described for potential selectors in the following manner:

---

7   This practice pertained not just in Britain but also in its colonies and North America. For instance, writing about morally improving nineteenth-century books in the USA, Joanna Gillespie observes, 'Sunday school commissions or superintendents, not the individual consumer, were the buyers of these little books', mostly didactic religious stories produced in pocket-sized editions (J. Gillespie, 'Schooling through Fiction', *Children's Literature* 14 (1986), 61–81 (p. 62)).

8   Then as now, purchasing bodies tended to be pragmatic. If they had received an acceptable selection of books from a supplier whose publications were in sympathy with the mission or ethos of the organisation, it was likely that future orders would be placed with the same supplier.

9   Announcements found at the back of E.J. Moore's *Dorothy Lavender* (London: George Cauldwell, n.d. but inscribed 1891) and M.E. Winchester's *Lost Maggie* (London: John F. Shaw, n.d.) respectively.

All but Lost. By C.L. Balfour. A story of a youth who learnt by bitter experience that 'the way of transgressors is hard.'

Archie's Old Desk. By Sarah Doudney. Gives the career of two youths; their temptations, victories, and failures; teaching the necessity of daily praying, Lead us not into temptation; but deliver us from evil.

The Irish Scholar; or, Popery and Protestant Christianity. By the Rev. T.W. Aveling, D.D. A Protestant story, suitable for young boys and girls.

The firm of John F. Shaw described their eighteen-penny books as volumes that '*will be found most suitable for Sunday-School Rewards and Libraries. The Stories are full of interest, and their tone and tendency unexceptionable.*'

To modern eyes, such descriptions and means of selecting works may seem doomed to make recipients equate 'reward' with 'tedium'. As Mitzi Myers points out, 'If a work is "didactic", critics usually assume, it must be intellectually unproblematic and literarily uninteresting, especially if it is rational, realistic and domestic.'[10] Undoubtedly, many books given as rewards consisted of badly written, trite stories. But we should not automatically assume that just because descriptions emphasised the moral and spiritual suitability of stories and do not immediately appeal to modern taste, these texts failed to please contemporary readers. For one thing, comparing standard reward fiction with what else was readily available to young readers enables us to see why even formulaic tales of errors, enlightenment and salvation might be regarded as entertaining. Especially for children of the poor and those living in very remote and isolated areas, the only approved alternatives to tract and reward fiction would be the Bible, or educational books intent on cramming readers with useful knowledge. And while many examples of reward fiction are not well written, it would be misleading to categorise them all as boring or uneventful. In order for sinners to learn the error of their ways, they have to sin, so reward fiction is as densely populated with drunkards, villains and fallen women as it is with the pious and virtuous. Though ultimately God can be relied upon to effect a change in the wicked, His method is usually a tragic one, requiring the deaths of beloved children or partners, degeneration, disability, false accusations and other tragic and sensational plot devices. Much reward fiction enacts the philosophy of the prominent nineteenth-century American revivalist, Charles Grandison Finney, who pointed out that, '"religion without excitement" was boring, absurd, and finally unavailing'.[11] Another way in which evangelical reward fiction often succeeded in appealing to its original readers was by employing a highly emotional and manipulative style attempting, as the Methodists put it, to make each book 'an arrow directed at the heart'.[12] What may strike modern readers as sentimental and bathetic could evidently speak powerfully to many of its intended readers.

---

10 Mitzi Myers, 'Socialising Rosamund: Educational Ideology and Fictional Form', *Children's Literature Association Quarterly* 14 (1989), 52–8 (p. 53).

11 J. Gillespie, 'An Almost Irresistible Enginery: Five Decades of Nineteenth Century Methodist Sunday School Library Books', *Phaedrus*, 7 (1980), 5–12 (p. 63).

12 *Minutes* 69, in Gillespie, 'An Almost Irresistible Enginery', p. 65.

However, no matter how emotionally charged such books might be, contemporary evidence suggests that books written specifically as rewards, as distinct from those that might have been *chosen* for this purpose, though not written with the reward market in mind, were not held in high literary regard and that the profession of the reward book writer was derided in cultured circles. George Gissing, for instance, condemned the kind of writing appreciated by the new generation of Board School scholars (the intended readers of much reward fiction) for requiring 'a particular kind of vulgarity', which he equated with cynical commercialism.[13] Certainly from the 1870s onwards, there were clear expectations about what a reward book should and should not contain. Justly or not, the writing of reward fiction was regarded as formulaic and facile – especially by 'proper' writers. Gissing was not alone in mocking them. Shortly before the publishing of reward fiction reached its peak, Charles Dickens also made a point of mocking it. In *Our Mutual Friend* (1864–65) he includes an account of a 'Good child's book, *The Adventures of Little Margery*', the story of a girl

> who resided in the village cottage by the mill; severely reproved and morally squashed the miller when she was five and he was fifty; divided her porridge with singing-birds; denied herself a new nankeen bonnet on the ground that the turnips did not wear nankeen bonnets, neither did the sheep who ate them; who plaited straw and delivered the dreariest orations to all comers at all sorts of unseasonable times.[14]

Whatever their literary failings, writers of reward fiction were both eclectic in the means used to capture their audiences and alert to their tastes and interests. While most of what young people read was carefully monitored to ensure that they did not read anything shocking or unsuitable, gruesome and deliciously exotic content could be justified under the right conditions. For instance, accounts of reportedly barbaric life in foreign lands as witnessed and described by respected travellers and missionaries, in particular, provided a variety of opportunities to move beyond the stories of error and redemption generally considered the stuff of reward fiction. This is evident from the following summary of an anonymous account of an attack on Methodist missionaries in the early 1800s included in *The Praying Mother*:

> The writer seemed to relish portraying the fierce chieftain and his 'cookies' (slaves), as they handled one of the missionaries on the thighs, sides and arms, apparently anticipating how he would taste. And the little son of one of the captives … shrieked heartrendingly, 'Will it hurt to be eaten after we have been killed?'[15]

An extension of this practice is found in a book which was both deservedly popular for many decades and frequently given as a reward or prize, R.M. Ballantyne's *The*

13 From George Gissing's *New Grub Street* (1891), quoted in Brian Alderson, 'Tracts, Rewards and Fairies: The Victorian Contribution to Children's Literature', in Asa Briggs (ed.), *A History of Publishing in Celebration of the 250th Anniversary of the House of Longman 1724–1974* (London: Longman, 1974), p. 275.

14 Quoted in Amy Cruse, *The Victorians and Their Books* (London: George Allen and Unwin, 1935), p. 81.

15 Gillespie, 'An Almost Irresistible Enginery', p. 11.

Coral Island (1858), which contains many scenes in which, before their timely conversion by dedicated missionaries, brutal cannibals murder indiscriminately in the anticipation of enjoying the delicacy of roasted 'long pig'.

Sensational stories and emotional rhetoric alone do not account for the success of reward fiction with some readers. Tastes have changed to such an extent that it is hard for modern readers to appreciate that the very qualities that make a book seem over-written, tedious, or too difficult today might be precisely what made it meaningful a century ago, especially to children of the poor. The extent to which tastes and audiences generally have changed since the zenith of reward fiction can readily be seen in relation to a book often given as a reward, Bunyan's *Pilgrim's Progress* (1678). For at least the last half of the twentieth century, this text has been regarded as too demanding and unappealing for child readers. Indeed, many undergraduates need detailed annotation and considerable encouragement to help them understand and enjoy Bunyan's allegory. Yet there is a substantial amount of evidence to demonstrate that *Pilgrim's Progress* was not only popular with publishers and donors, but also with child readers themselves.[16] Our objection to texts that preach and teach too overtly, then, was not necessarily shared by members of the Victorian reading public, who were more likely to reject texts for espousing faulty doctrine, displaying the wrong kind of sentimentality, or over-simplifying theological debates. This is the accusation made by an anonymous critic in the *Quarterly Review*, writing generally about the merits and demerits of the available range of books for children. While welcoming in principle the kind of religiously motivated fiction typified by reward books, the critic warns against 'the presumption with which authors undertake to explain the mysteries of Christianity'. An author's 'desire to render himself intelligible is apt to betray him into a style of explanation and illustration, which is not only beneath the dignity of the subject, but wholly inadequate even for the purposes contemplated', the critic continued. What is worse, the piece goes on, is the tendency to rely on child characters who embody remarkable goodness

---

16 *Pilgrim's Progress* came ninth in the *Pall Mall Gazette's* poll of the best books for ten year olds in July 1898, beaten only by *Alice in Wonderland*, the fairy tales of Andersen and the Grimms, *Robinson Crusoe*, *Little Lord Fauntleroy*, Charles Kingsley's *The Water-Babies* and *The Heroes*, and *The Jungle Book* (Gillian Avery, *Nineteenth-Century Children: Heroes and Heroines in English Children's Stories 1780–1900* (London: Hodder and Stoughton, 1965), p. 137). F.J. Harvey Darton confirms its great appeal, confessing to having read Bunyan 'rapturously' (*Children's Books in England* (1932, repr., rev. Brian Alderson, Cambridge: Cambridge University Press, 1982), p. 63). In an article on Bunyan's lesser known *Book for Boys and Girls*, Mary Trim includes the following quotation from an 1826 letter written by George Crabbe, which also testifies to the popularity of *Pilgrim's Progress* with young readers in the days when books were almost the only source of stories and entertainment that children could access for themselves on demand: 'Caroline, now six years old, reads incessantly and insatiably. She has been travelling with John Bunyan's Pilgrim, and enjoying a pleasure never perhaps to be repeated. The veil of religious mystery that so beautifully covers the outward and visible adventures is quite enchanting. The dear child was caught reading by her sleeping maid at five o'clock this morning, impatient, t'is our nature, to end her pleasure' (Mary Trim, 'A Rediscovery of John Bunyan's *Book for Boys and Girls*', *International Review of Children's Literature and Librarianship* 8 (1993), 149–67 (p. 150)).

or wickedness. Such 'extraordinary models' hold up 'an impossible standard of youthful piety', which must cause the reader either to give up the thought of religion, or, worse still, 'to use the phrases and imitate the outward deportment of the hero of the book,' and so become 'a dissembler before God and himself'.[17]

A final but important difference in taste and expectation between nineteenth- and twenty-first-century readers centres on the inclusion of lengthy descriptions of sermons, churches, hymns and prayers. From today's comfortable, broadly secular perspective, such material can constitute heavy-handed longueurs, arousing the suspicion that readers learned to skip such passages in search of the story. However, attending church and Sunday school (which, for poor children, was closely linked to the acquisition of books, either through libraries or rewards) represented for many a highlight of the week and a temporary refuge from the grinding poverty and dreariness of their lives. Descriptions of church, Sunday school and the learning they acquired there could evoke moments of pleasure and significance. *Froggy's Little Brother* (1875), an indisputably popular book often given as a reward, vividly captures the mixtures of aesthetic, spiritual and physical comforts and pleasures which church-going was capable of providing:

> After mother's death, Froggy noticed a great change in father. He began to brush himself up on Sunday mornings, and to lead his little boy to the free seats of a neighbouring church, which Froggy used to think the most wonderful and beautiful place the world had ever seen. And well he might; for Froggy's standard of comparison for everything was the poor garret at Shoreditch! The grand sounds of the organ and the voices singing he always associated with his ideas of the Better Land where mother had gone. He remembered she used to speak of the angels, and the golden harps, and the songs of praise in heaven, and he thought that surely this must be something like it.[18]

Though we may accept that the inclusion of lengthy passages relating to religion would not necessarily have alienated early readers, it is still tempting to dismiss such interpolations as evidence of a middle-class agenda to inscribe appreciation of the benefits of attending church in literature for the poor. While clearly such an agenda *is* present, the sentiment need not be entirely discounted. Moreover, such accounts were not unique to fiction for children. Arnold Bennett's *Clayhanger* (1910), a meticulous and minutely detailed evocation of the Staffordshire Potteries where Bennett grew up, includes a comparable account of the place of church and Sunday school in the life of his eponymous character, Darius Clayhanger. From the age of three, Darius 'joyously frequented' a Primitive Methodist Sunday school in the 1830s and, as 'he grew older the Sunday school became more and more enchanting to him'.

> Sunday morning was the morning which he lived for during six days; it was the morning when his hair was brushed and combed, and perfumed with a delightful oil, whose particular fragrance he remembered throughout his life. At Sunday school he was petted and caressed. His success at Sunday school was shining.

---

17 *Quarterly Review* (26 January 1860).

18 'Brenda' [Mrs G. Castle Smith], *Froggy's Little Brother: A Story of the East-End* (London: John F. Shaw), p. 27.

When, at the age of seven Darius is required to leave school and find work, the superintendent of the Sunday school takes him aside and gives him what amounts to a reward book, 'an old, battered Bible'. This volume, Bennett adds, 'was the most valuable thing that Darius had ever possessed. He ran all the way home with it, half suffocated by his success.'[19] Not all recipients were as gratified as Darius Clayhanger by the books they received, as will become clear in the final section of this chapter, which will deal with working-class responses to the books they were given as rewards and prizes. Before then, however, it is necessary to consider what rewards and prizes were given for and how they were intended to function.

They Knew They Were Right: A Story of Reward Fiction and the Uses to Which It Was Put

Books given as rewards or prizes were intended to be taken home to form a bridge between the awarding institution and the child's daily life, perhaps by being read aloud with other family members as part of the tradition of Sunday reading.[20] For those travelling to new lives overseas, such textual links were particularly important; indeed scholars interested in the movements of books over the centuries argue convincingly that they played an important role in the creating and sustaining of empire.[21] Because information about what books were actually given as prizes and their recipients' responses to them is limited and largely anecdotal, it is useful to look briefly at the contents of libraries associated with Sunday schools, where pupils had a better chance of helping choose the books they were given to read. Like reward books, the books contained in Sunday school libraries were carefully vetted for 'suitability', which meant that they studiously avoided bad language while offering models of pure behaviour and elevating morals. Books for libraries seem generally to have been chosen with more care than those given as prizes; discussions of the vetting panel were minuted, and provide evidence that the selection committees consulted reviews in religious periodicals and papers such as the *Methodist Recorder*.[22]

The diaries of Mamie Pickering, begun in 1893 when Mamie was 13 and living in a small town in Manitoba, Canada, describe in detail the system devised to organise children's borrowing of books from the Sunday school library, as well as the carefully monitored exchanges between friends who attended other churches and so might have access to different books. As was characteristic of such libraries, the

---

19 Arnold Bennett, *Clayhanger* (1910, repr. Harmondsworth: Penguin, 1975), pp. 37–8.

20 See Darton, *Children's Books in England*, p. 321.

21 See I.R. Willison, 'Across Boundaries: The History of the Book and National Literatures in English', pp. 130–40, in Bill Bell, Philip Bennett and Jonquil Bevan (eds), *Across Boundaries: The Book in Culture and Commerce* (Winchester: St Paul's Bibliographies; New Castle, DE: Oak Knoll Press, 2000).

22 Dorothy Entwistle, 'Embossed Gilt and Moral Tales: The Purpose and Practice of Giving Reward Books in Nonconformist Sunday Schools in Northwest England, 1870–1918', copy of article prepared for publication, sent without further details, n.d., p. 5. See also another, article by Entwistle, 'Embossed Gilt and Moral Tales: Reward Books in English Sunday Schools', *Journal of Popular Culture* 28 (1994), 81–96.

collection located in Mamie's Sunday school contained only the kind of novels that would have been categorised as reward books, avoiding all other kinds of fiction. The process was overseen by librarians, who either selected for children or supervised their choice of books, somewhat to Mamie's disgruntlement: 'I took back *Eric* and got *The Upward Path.* I have read it too. I'd like to kick that bloomin librarian for giving me it and old Silas [the Deacon] for marching us out so quickly that you don't get a chance to change it.'[23]

In her study of the catalogue of the Stockport Sunday school library for the period 1870–1918, Dorothy Entwistle found a total of 3,000 books recorded, 1,242 of which were specifically intended for children and adolescents. Not all were fiction. She classifies the range of books represented into nine groups: nature, geology, invention, travel and exploration, history, biographies, self-help, religion and fiction. Books from any of these categories were likely to be given as rewards or prizes, but, as a rule, only the fiction tended to be written with such an end in mind and to be subject to a conscious vetting process. Entwistle's analysis of the library's fictional titles shows the collection to have been more eclectic in its selection than that used by Mamie Pickering (the logistical problems of obtaining books in rural Manitoba undoubtedly contributed to the limited size and scope of the collection there), with a large number of authors and titles represented. There were, however, clear preferences for particular authors, founded, she presumes, on the basis that they were 'safe and reliable'.[24]

Many of the authors and titles that dominate these collections were frequently given as prizes, presumably for the reasons adduced by Entwistle, and were made available in many editions at a range of prices. They can thus be said to have achieved popularity with at least the selectors, and since many of them continued to be reprinted well into the twentieth century, it is likely that some were also popular with their readers. Other chapters in this study describe individual texts, authors and genres that have been popular over time. To develop a sense of what young people themselves chose to read when they had the opportunity, it is worth looking at Richard Altick's classic study, *The English Common Reader* (1957). Altick reports that boys sought out novels by Marryat, Henty, Cooper, Verne and Mayne Reid, while girls preferred books by Mrs Henry Wood, Miss Braddon and E.P. Roe. It is notable that while the books and authors chosen by boys were also likely to be given as prizes, the girls' preference was for adult sensation fiction.[25] While, as Bratton points out,

---

23 N.J. and A.E. Williamson, 'Mamie Pickering's Reading, Part One: The Role of Books in the Social Life of a Late Victorian Child', *Children's Literature Association Quarterly* 9 (1984), 3–6 (p. 4).

24 Entwistle, 'Embossed Gilt and Moral Tales: The Purpose and Practice of Giving Reward Books', p. 4.

25 According to Edward Salmon, *Juvenile Literature As It Is* (London: Henry J. Drane, 1888), p. 29, this was because girls were given the kind of insipid writing he associated with reward fiction: 'Girls as a rule don't care for Sunday-school twaddle, they like a good stirring story, with a plot and some incident and adventures … This is also, I am sure, why girls read so many novels of the commoner type – they have, as a rule, nothing else in any way interesting.' It is worth comparing the list of authors Altick identifies with working-class readers (*The English Common Reader: A Social History of the Mass Reading Public 1800–1900* (Chicago: University

there was a tendency for publishers to seek to merge religious novels and sensation fiction by creating a hybrid genre she describes as the 'religious romance', such books would certainly not have met with the approval of a selection committee.[26]

Charlotte M. Yonge, who took it upon herself to guide those responsible for putting reward fiction in the hands of the young on the grounds that 'if good [literature] be not provided, evil will only too easily be found', regarded such books as dangerous and misguided. She suggested that they could have the 'grave and really injurious effect of teaching little girls to expect a lover in anyone who is good-natured to them. Nothing ought to be more rigidly avoided.'[27] The upshot of this situation is that boys had greater access to and greater approval of the fiction they read, while girls were more likely to have to look outside official channels to obtain works by the writers of their choice. More likely to be chosen *for* girls, as evidenced by a list of books compiled for the London School Board 1887–88, were books by writers like A.L.O.E. and Hesba Stretton.[28]

Unlike the religious romance, which combined sexual fantasy and religion, reward books tended to be preoccupied with four main themes, often used in combination. The first requirement was to provide gender role models that conformed to the dominant ideal of the period (notable examples included national heroes such as Lord Nelson); the second was to show character development; the third was to illustrate the dangers of specific vices (usually drinking, smoking and bad company); and the fourth was to emphasise the importance of family life.[29] These themes overrode denominational consideration. Class distinctions, though, remained more firmly in place. Constructions of the working class, in particular, dominate reward fiction, both in terms of characterisation and implied audience, and this undoubtedly accounts for the ambivalent feelings such books could prompt in some of their poorer recipients.

---

of Chicago Press, 1957), p. 237) with the responses young people gave Salmon in reply to a survey sent to schools. From the 2,000 responses he received, Salmon constructed a list of the ten favourite writers for boys and girls. These were, for boys: Charles Dickens, W.H.G. Kingston, Sir Walter Scott, Jules Verne, Frederick Marryat, R.M. Ballantyne, Harrison Ainsworth, William Shakespeare, Thomas Mayne Reid and Lord Lytton; and for girls: Dickens, Scott, Charles Kingsley, Charlotte Yonge, Shakespeare, Mrs Henry Wood, Elizabeth Wetherell, George Eliot, Lord Lytton and Hans Christian Andersen. In his autobiographical work, *My Book of Memory*, Silas Hocking describes how, when distributing copies of Hesba Stretton's *Jessica's First Prayer* at a Sunday school prize-giving, he was inspired to write his own, more accurate accounts of the lives of street children. For a detailed account of Hocking's work, see Chapter 5 of Carole Dunbar's 'The Other Nation – an Examination of the Depiction of the Poor in the Children's Fiction of Mrs Molesworth, Mrs Ewing, Silas Hocking and Frances Hodgson Burnett' (PhD thesis, Dublin City University, 2001).

26   J.S. Bratton, *The Impact of Victorian Children's Fiction* (London: Croom Helm, 1981), p. 156; Altick, *The English Common Reader*, p. 237.

27   C.M. Yonge, *What Books to Lend and What to Give* (London: National Society's Depository, 1888), p. 5, in Bratton, *Impact of Victorian Children's Fiction*, p. 155.

28   Bratton, *Impact of Victorian Children's Fiction*, p. 192.

29   Entwistle, 'Embossed Gilt and Moral Tales: The Purpose and Practice of Giving Reward Books', p. 6.

Even the occasions and venues where rewards were given and the reasons for making such presentations would have been influenced by class.

If we look more closely at the books given and their chances of succeeding with those who received them, other significant class differences emerge. For instance, while upper- and middle-class children were likely to be given books chosen specifically for them and not necessarily from the list of books categorised as rewards or prizes, the children of the poor tended to be given books chosen *en masse* by the kinds of groups and methods described earlier. Minimal attention was paid to the individual child's interests, abilities or circumstances, and this, together with the kinds of messages about children and families like themselves must have affected the way many poor children felt about the books they received – no matter how attractive they were made or how moving their stories might be. Class, then, affected all aspects of reward fiction, from its reception to its narrative concerns and energies.

The contrasting autobiographies of Robert Roberts (1884–1985) and H.C. Barnard (1905–74) illustrate how class-based was the experience of receiving a book as a school prize. Writing about his working-class childhood at the turn of the twentieth century, Roberts recalls being given the class prize when he left school, 'a heavy volume which I had had no hand in choosing entitled *Heroes of the United Services*'.[30] Significantly, he does not mention reading the book, and his tone does not suggest familiarity with its contents. By contrast, the more affluent H.C. Barnard's autobiography, *Were Those the Days? A Victorian Education* (1970), also includes an account of being rewarded with a book, but in his case it was one chosen specifically for him by a teacher who knew him well. While working-class children like Roberts would have been taught in very large groups of up to 60 pupils, making it difficult for teachers to get to know individual children personally, Barnard went first to a Froebel kindergarten and then to a progressive private school where children were taught in small groups. The book he received, and which he describes affectionately, was Juliana Horatia Ewing's *Mary's Meadow* (1886), an attractively illustrated family story (a precursor to those by E. Nesbit) centring on the ownership of a field.[31]

Better to Give than Receive: Stories of Those Who Turned Away from the Messages They Received

As the cases of Robert Roberts and H.C. Barnard show, the circumstances under which young people received books as rewards and prizes varied considerably. That such books were valued by at least some of their recipients is evident from the way so many of them travelled with their owners when they emigrated to make new lives in new worlds. Copies of books received as rewards in England are regularly found

---

30 R. Roberts, *A Ragged Schooling: Growing Up in the Classic Slum* (London: Fontana/Collins, 1976), p. 153.

31 See Percy Muir, *English Children's Books 1600–1900* (London: Batsford, 1969), p. 117.

in North America, Australia and countries that were once part of the empire.[32] Their owners must have cared about them sufficiently to take the trouble to transport and preserve them under difficult circumstances. However, the reasons why such books were valued may be complex, and again cannot be accepted as incontravertible evidence of their popularity. For instance, the care publishers took over covers, which may have attracted those choosing books to give them in the first place, may also have given them an aesthetic value for the recipients. The stories might be dull or even obnoxious to some readers, but the covers were bright, and displayed on a shelf offered a tangible link to home. Similarly, a book received from school or Sunday school might well be the only visible evidence of achievement in a family, and the only prize an individual received in a lifetime.

Research has recently been conducted into the importance of books in the lives of emigrants, drawing attention to the role played by books from home in renegotiating the self in a new country. Bill Bell's contribution to *Across Boundaries* takes as its starting point the objects which Robinson Crusoe lists as he begins to take stock of his situation. For the purposes of 'personal definition and orientation in an unfamiliar landscape', Bell writes, Crusoe's books, ink and paper are just as valuable as the paraphernalia of science which he had also managed to salvage from his ship. 'Cultural memory is in exile contingent on – even reinforced by – the continued practices of reading and writing', Bell asserts.[33] Indeed, his study offers a wide-ranging investigation into groups who actively maintained relationships with home and its institutions through the books they were given and which they subsequently obtained, notwithstanding the fact that many had been deceived by books written as propaganda to encourage them to emigrate in the first place! Whether pioneers in North America, uprooted groups such as those resulting from the Highland clearances and the Irish famine or transported convicts, migrants were often given books – if not as official rewards, then for many of the same reasons: to mark an occasion and to help prepare individuals for their futures. In such cases the books received tended to be either religious or practical – very little fiction was given. Since these were likely to be the only books to which the children of migrants initially had access, it is worth trying to identify what they were, how they were received and how they were regarded by their recipients. I know of no accounts by children which document their responses to books given on the occasion of migrating, but work done to reconstruct the books which travelled with the First Fleet of convicts to Australia in 1788 offers some insights that may usefully act as indicators of reactions closer to home.

The SPCK, which published many reward books, provided the Fleet's Chaplain with 'one hundred Bibles, four hundred New testaments, one hundred prayer books, two hundred catechisms, as well as numerous tracts such as the Rev Stephen White's *A Dissuasive from Stealing* and Josiah Woodward's *A Dissuasive from Profane Swearing and Cursing offered to such unhappy persons as are guilty of those horrid sins and are not past counsel.*' Also included were numbers of 'Dixons Spelling

---

32 See M. Nancy Cutt, *Ministering Angels: A Study of Nineteenth-Century Evangelical Writing for Children* (Wormley, Herts: Five Owls Press, 1979), p. 179.

33 Bill Bell, 'Crusoe's Books: The Scottish Emigrant Reader in the Nineteenth Century', pp. 116–28, in Bell, Bennett and Bevan (eds), *Across Boundaries*, p. 116.

Books' for distribution to children in the colony and to illiterate convicts. Johnson was 'discouraged' by the response to his attempts to distribute books, some of which he reports were torn up and used as waste paper. Equally indicative of the First Fleeters' lack of interest in the books provided for them is a journal entry of 1 May 1792, set down by Lt Ralph Clark: 'Two sharks were caught this morning – in the belly of one of them was found a Prayer Book quite fresh not a leaf of it defaced' – so, clearly unread – and 'on one of the leaves was wrote Frances Carthy'. [34] Carthy was a convict sent out with the First Fleet, and on being given one of the SPCK prayer books (presumably), he demonstrated what he thought of everything it represented by hurling it into the sea in the manner of Thackeray's Becky Sharp, another rebellious recipient of a reward book.

Anger at an awarding institution and rejection of the messages contained in the books offered as prizes is more obviously and understandably associated with the poor – so often both the subjects of and the intended audience for reward fiction – than their wealthier peers. Indeed, it could be argued that reward books have their origins in books distributed to the children of the poor with a view to encouraging them to change their behaviour to something more acceptable to the middle classes. Usually this meant striking a careful balance between urging the acceptance of middle-class values and practices while clearly indicating the importance of 'knowing your place'. The pitfalls of aping social superiors were pointed out time and again in reward fiction. For instance, in *Dorothy Lavender, A Temperance Story* by Emily Jane Moore (the copy consulted for this chapter was given as a reward by the Band of Hope in June 1891), the eponymous heroine's good character is established in part by her reaction to being given a brooch by an Earl who is commissioning some work from her talented but 'weak' wood-carver father: 'No, thank you, my lord,' says Dorothy', explaining for the benefit of readers that 'My mother would not wish me to accept such a costly thing. She says that jewels do not become a poor young girl like me.' The Earl is insistent, so Dorothy and her mother put the jewel away in a drawer until the time comes when their family fortunes improve as a consequence of Mr Lavender's signing the pledge. Once his earnings are saved rather than squandered on drinking with his companions, the Lavender family rapidly rises to a new social level. Mrs Lavender is able to hire some help in the family's new home, freeing Dorothy to resume her education, beginning with a trip to Italy where she and her father will study 'the productions of the old and modern masters in several lines of art'. [35] With their new found wealth and stability, small jewels are no longer out of Dorothy's sphere, and she jubilantly removes the Earl's brooch from its hiding place as a sign of her new status and happiness.

Because they have known their place, worked hard and patiently borne the trials of living with a drunkard father, Dorothy and her family are rewarded. Those who are less wise find inappropriate gifts a trial, even if the original mistake is not theirs. In *Poison in the Packet*, published by the RTS in the 1880s, a country carpenter's

---

34 C. Steele and M. Richards, 'Bound for Botany Bay: What Books did the First Fleeters Read and Where Are They Now?' *Antiquarian Book Monthly Review* 15 (1988), 412–16 (pp. 413 and 414).

35 Moore, *Dorothy Lavender*, pp. 54 and 87.

family is sent a gift of fancy clothing from a friend in the city and it makes their lives a misery. The quarrelling, envy and dissatisfaction that the garments provoke work like 'poison' on the previously happy family.[36]

Such messages are characteristic of reward books, for it was hoped that by giving youngsters something tangible for them to take into their homes to consult when times were difficult, the messages of church, Sunday schools, youth groups, temperance societies and other establishments where the young were given moral, spiritual, social and academic instruction, could be strengthened to help the recipients withstand the temptations associated with privation and the 'degenerate' life-style of the poor.[37] This sense underpins many early reward books, which were given to children who were perceived as being 'Wanderers like the Arabs of old, dwelling in tenements instead of tents', children who formed 'no attachment to any habitation or any locality', with no teacher, local magnate or clergyman standing out 'as the familiar figure of their childhood'.[38] It was for precisely such children that in 1795 Hannah More began publishing what can be regarded as a very early form of reward literature, her series of Cheap Repository Tracts. Although primarily intended to be sold very cheaply to the poor, Hannah More herself gave them as prizes to the children in her Sunday school.[39] Whether they were popular as prizes is debatable; especially when the custom of giving reward books impinged on the practice of rewarding children with gifts such as money, clothing, sweets, teas, buns, oranges, pincushions, nosegays, extra privileges, outings or swimming lessons.[40]

The narrative drive of typical reward fiction is to show the benefits of conforming to the prevailing image of the 'respectable poor', which involved demonstrating precisely the kinds of qualities associated with a governable, committed, undemanding and socially quiescent work force. The need to be thrifty, independent, teetotal and good tempered was stressed, as was the value of home life and education,

---

36 This story is discussed in some detail in Avery's *Childhood's Pattern*, pp. 88–90.

37 In *Growing Up Poor: Home, School and Street in London 1870–1914* (London: Rivers Oram Press, 1996), Anna Davin convincingly argues that middle-class constructions of working-class lifestyles were often misguided, seeing degeneracy and deprivation in what were often merely different patterns for child rearing. She points out that poor families tended to be closer and to have more immediate and indulgent interactions with their children than their middle-class counterparts, as well as including them in the vital work of keeping the family fed and sheltered.

38 Davin, *Growing Up Poor*, p. 31. According to a parliamentary speech by Lord Shaftesbury in 1848, there were 30,000, 'naked, filthy, roaming, lawless and deserted children in and about the metropolis' (p. 162).

39 According to Alderson's 'Tracts, Rewards and Fairies', her intention was 'to furnish the People at large with useful Reading, at so low a price as to be within the reach of the poorest purchaser' (p. 266). Gillian Avery notes that 'Hannah More doled out pennies and gingerbread to the meritorious who performed well on Sundays, with a Bible as first prize at the end of the year, A Prayer Book as second, and her tracts as consolation prizes' (*Childhood's Pattern*, p. 68).

40 Davin, *Growing Up Poor* lists all of these as possible rewards for children in Board Schools (p. 106); Avery notes that Mrs Trimmer, 'distributed caps, handkerchiefs, pincushions, huswifes to girls' and that 'boys were rewarded with books and halfpence … not because they were the more intellectual sex, but because boys' clothing was so much more expensive' (*Childhood's Pattern*, p. 68).

the importance of trusting in God, of accepting dominant ideals of masculinity and femininity, and of assuming responsibility for caring for others.[41]

Even when disseminated through the medium of an exciting story, lessons such as these were inevitably resented by some readers, and just as the First Fleeters rejected the books they were given to 'improve' their characters, so some physical evidence suggests that resentment about what reward literature represented and, perhaps especially, its links to institutions that could be seen as invalidating working-class ways of living and social codes, resulted in its being rejected or symbolically purged of its associations.[42] It is striking, for instance, how many of the bookplates/ certificates detailing the reason for an award are defaced in examples of reward books that have survived. Sometimes this takes the form of cutting or tearing out the offending item, at other times scribbling over all but the name of the recipient. Presumably this reflects a desire to disassociate the prize from the awarding institution or individual giver (although sometimes it may have been an attempt to obliterate former owners when the book was inherited or sold). Accounts of the lives and educational experiences of the working classes during the years following the institution of compulsory education make such evidence of resentment unsurprising and mirror the antipathy of the First Fleeters to the books they were given. Although reward fiction itself might call attention to the hardships and virtues of the poor, working-class children in practice tended to be treated as the brutalised offspring of a primitive and degenerate race. Schools in particular were associated with efforts to eradicate working-class culture and traditions, while reinforcing class divisions and social inequality. This resulted in hostility towards and rejection of much associated with school, including religious knowledge and sentiments. As David Vincent points out, the moral and scriptural lessons taught at school and for which prizes were often given, ignored the personal experience of many pupils:

> In the domestic curriculum [of the working class], moral education was largely a matter of people rather than books, example rather than instruction. It was not Christ but their parents, and especially their mothers, who had most obviously suffered that they might live. The 'exemplary and heroic character' of those who had sacrificed food, comfort and rest for their growing children provided the most powerful lessons.[43]

In their memoirs and anecdotes, working-class children have recalled resenting being coerced into ways of behaving and thinking, and seeking ways of subverting the messages of school, Sunday school (though perhaps to a lesser extent) and everything associated with them. While teachers, inspectors, and those who were responsible for administering the education system were determined to regard

---

41   Entwistle, 'Embossed Gilt and Moral Tales: The Purpose and Practice of Giving Reward Books', p. 11.

42   For a lively account of conscious resistance to the attempts of the education authorities to dismantle working-class culture, see Steve Humphries, *Hooligans or Rebels? An Oral History of Working-class Childhood and Youth 1889–1939* (Oxford: Blackwell, 1981).

43   David Vincent, 'The Domestic and the Official Curriculum in Nineteenth-Century England', pp. 161–79, in M. Hilton, M. Styles and V. Watson (eds), *Opening the Nursery Door: Reading, Writing and Childhood 1600–1900* (London and New York: Routledge, 1997), p. 171.

working-class pupils as deficient, many regarded themselves as representatives of an entirely different, but no less legitimate culture, which provoked them to ridicule the tools used to 'socialise' them. In an interview with social historian Steve Humphries, Ernie Till remembered school children chanting in the playground, 'I one the Bible, I two the Bible, I three the Bible ... I EIGHT' – that is to say, hate – 'the Bible!'[44] Such behaviour never finds its way into reward fiction.

As evidenced by the disparaging attitudes of Gissing and Dickens, even those who were not subjected to such coercion rejected the relentless message and the formulaic attributes associated with reward fiction. Nevertheless, the strong sense that this kind of writing was both suitable and necessary for working-class readers persisted. For instance, even so strong an advocate of stirring stories as Edward Salmon, who defended girls' rights to something better than the 'Sunday-school twaddle' they were offered, was primarily concerned with giving the working classes suitably moral works. Salmon entirely rejected the literature which was truly popular in the sense that readers were prepared to purchase it for themselves – 'penny dreadfuls' and comics. If that kind of production was to be their reading matter, he said, teaching them to read was 'to sharpen their wits to the inception and comprehension of the criminal motives'.[45]

Like many of his contemporaries, Edward Salmon was eager to put the kind of wholesome, improving stories typified by reward books into the hands of the poor. Reward fiction, then, had the job of articulating and inculcating social and moral norms as defined by the middle classes, who largely created and disseminated it. In the hands of lesser writers this could be done so crudely that the project rebounded on itself. More successful writers, however, succeeded in contributing to the drive to acculturate readers by conveying their messages more subtly. In boys' fiction, this was largely achieved through the agency of plot: exotic settings and frenzied action disguised the fact that boys were being asked to conform to a rigidly defined version of patriotic, dutiful, Christian boyhood. Girls' fiction for the most part lacked such distractions. Writers such as A.L.O.E., 'Brenda' and Hesba Stretton influenced their readers by providing stories that were emotionally charged rather than action packed, and which clearly set out the benefits of behaving virtuously. Although books such as Stretton's *Little Meg's Children* (1868) or 'Brenda's' *Froggy's Little Brother* provide detailed pictures of the hardships endured by the poor and agitate for social reform, ultimately they do not offer a critique of Victorian society. Readers were encouraged to admire the courage and generosity of the poor and to give generously to improve their living conditions, but these books offer no radical agenda for social change. They uphold the need for social division, presenting it as part of the divine plan for humankind. Similarly, they never question the authority of the governing classes. Their conservative message is driven home in securely closed plots that reward the good in little ways – Stretton's Meg, for instance, is reunited with her widower father, who stops drinking and relieves her of the burden of caring for his young family. They leave the garret in which Meg's mother and baby sister died, to begin a new life overseas, confident that they have God's blessing. This is attested

---

44 Humphries, *Hooligans or Rebels*, p. 35.
45 Salmon, *Juvenile Literature As It Is*, p. 237.

by Meg, who understands all the events in her young life as being divinely ordained; she concludes the book by repeating her favourite biblical passage: 'If ye then, being evil, know how to give good gifts unto your children: how much more shall your Father which is in heaven give good things to them that ask Him?'[46]

They Fell by the Way: A Story of Limited Gain and Revised Expectations

Reward fiction was created to support the educational system and supplant popular street literature. It became a distinct and active area of commercial as well as religious publishing, and established a tradition of equating prize-giving and books that continues to this day. It is doubtful, however, whether the majority of books written to be advertised, sold, and given and received as rewards, ever became genuinely popular with their readers. At around the time of the 1870 Education Act, enthusiasts for education and wholesome publishing argued that the impact of increasingly available schooling would result in 'a greatly increased demand for books ... of a solid and instructive character ... so that, if we did not become a nation of students, at the least a considerable proportion of the population would develop studious habits'. But by 1894, despite steadily increasing school attendance, juvenile reading was in decline in all areas except precisely those which reward fiction had been designed to combat: cheaply produced papers and sensational stories.[47] Reward books were hugely important to the development of children's literature in economic terms. They were popular with publishers and with those who gave them away. If we define popularity in terms of the attitudes of the recipients of reward books, though, we hear a different story. With very few exceptions, the history of books which were popular with children, and the history of the reward book industry, do not overlap.

---

46 Hesba Stretton, *Little Meg's Children and Alone in London* (London: Religious Tract Society, n.d.), p. 129.

47 J. Ackland, 'Elementary Education and the Decay of Literature', *Nineteenth Century* 2 (1894), 412–23 (pp. 413 and 419–21).

Chapter 11

Tracts, Classics and Brands: Science for Children in the Nineteenth Century[1]

Aileen Fyfe

If we are to believe William Makepeace Thackeray, science books for children were not popular. He claimed that in his younger days, 'Abominable attempts were made ... to make useful books for children, and cram science down their throats as calomel used to be administered under the pretence of a spoonful of currant-jelly.'[2] We get a similar impression from Charles Kingsley, writing the preface to his own children's science book 25 years later, and remembering that the books he read as a child were 'few and dull, and the pictures in them ugly and mean'.[3] Nevertheless, Kingsley went on to mention one story, which, even though it was an 'old-fashioned, prim, sententious story', had made an impact on him.[4] Writer and critic John Ruskin, botanist Jane Loudon, geologist Gideon Mantell and doctor's wife Phoebe Lankester, as well as religious leaders F.D. Maurice and Benjamin Gregory, all remembered the same story.[5] Here, at least, is one story which left a positive impression. It was called 'Eyes and No Eyes; or, The Art of Seeing', and was one of many stories contained in *Evenings at Home; or The Juvenile Budget Opened* (1792–96).

Written by John Aikin and his sister Anna Laetitia Barbauld, *Evenings at Home* contained a large proportion of conversations and stories about natural history,

---

1 Parts of this chapter originally appeared in my introduction to *Science for Children*, (7 vols, Bristol: Thoemmes Press, 2003).

2 William Makepeace Thackeray, 'On Some Illustrated Children's Books' (1846), quoted in Marjorie Moon, *John Harris's Books for Youth 1801–1843: A Checklist*, rev. edn (Folkestone: Dawson, 1992), p. 182.

3 Charles Kingsley, *Madam How and Lady Why* (London: Bell & Daldy, 1870), pp. viii–ix.

4 Kingsley, *Madam How*, p. ix.

5 John Ruskin, *The Works of John Ruskin on CD-ROM* (Cambridge: Cambridge University Press, 1996), vol. 26, p. 114; Jane Loudon, *Glimpses of Nature, and Objects of Interest Described, during a Visit to the Isle of Wight* (London: Grant & Griffith, 1844), p. vi; Dennis R. Dean, *Gideon Mantell and the Discovery of the Dinosaurs* (Cambridge: Cambridge University Press, 1999), p. 19; Mrs Lankester, 'For the Young of the Household: In Cozy Nook: Eyes and No Eyes', *St James's Magazine* 2 (1861), 121–7; Frederick Maurice, *The Life of Frederick Denison Maurice, Chiefly Told in His Own Letters* (2 vols, London: Macmillan, 1884), vol. I, p. 16; Richard D. Altick, *The English Common Reader: A Social History of the Mass Reading Public, 1800–1900* (London: University of Chicago Press, 1957), pp. 117–18. I would like to thank Anne Secord, Jim Secord and Bernie Lightman for these references.

chemistry and astronomy, alongside moral tales and the occasional poem. 'Eyes and No Eyes' was one of Aikin's contributions.[6] It describes two boys recounting a walk through the countryside. Andrew had been bored stiff, but William had enjoyed the walk and found plenty to interest him in the flora, fauna, people and places that he passed. The moral pointed out by their tutor was to 'learn that eyes were given you to use'.[7] We can see why this story might be especially remembered by those who, in later life, practised the art of observation, whether as naturalists or art critics. Assessing the popularity of children's books from these sorts of actual reading experiences is, however, made problematic both by the scarcity of such material and by the likelihood that adult recollections may have been coloured by the experiences of the intervening years. Equally, evidence of sales figures is no clear indication of popularity with children, as most sales were made to parents or guardians, whose charges may or may not have read, let alone enjoyed, the books.

Popularity with children, however, is only one aspect of the issue of popular children's books, and this chapter will concentrate on two alternative definitions of popularity. The first is the prevailing early nineteenth-century usage of 'popular', meaning a work which was intended for 'the people', and which would therefore be low in price and high in circulation.[8] The second concerns what was popular with publishers, rather than with children. For the first definition, I will take the example of the Religious Tract Society (RTS), a publishing organisation dedicated to low prices and high (often very high) circulations. Its evangelical mission to convert the industrial working classes to Christianity meant that – unlike most publishers – it was committed to getting its publications to the people who needed them, and not simply to the first paying customer. Its children's science publications were often not books, but much cheaper sewn pamphlets which would have had circulations far in excess of most books. Due to the RTS's habit of not dating its works, it is very difficult to know how long its works remained in print. We can be sure they sold in high numbers initially, but long-term influence is difficult to gauge. To consider my second definition, of works which were popular with publishers, I will examine two sorts of successful works, those which are kept in print for a long time, and those which are frequently imitated. Examples here will be the 120-year publishing history of *Evenings at Home*, and the vogue for books entitled 'Conversations on ...' in the 1820s.

These two approaches to the issue of popular children's books have the advantage of being linked more closely to publishers than to readers, and thus supply more

---

6   There is a list of the stories written by Barbauld in Lucy Aikin (ed.) *The Works of Anna Laetitia Barbauld, With a Memoir* (2 vols, London: Longman, 1825), note to pp. xxxvi–xxxvii.

7   John Aikin and Anna Laetitia Barbauld, *Evenings at Home; or the Juvenile Budget Opened: Consisting of a Variety of Miscellaneous Pieces for the Instruction and Amusement of Youth* (6 vols, London: Johnson, repr. as 6 vols in 2, Bristol: Thoemmes Press, 2003), vol. IV, p. 112.

8   On the meanings of 'popular', see Morag Shiach, *Discourse on Popular Culture: Class, Gender and History in Cultural Analysis, 1730 To the Present* (Cambridge: Polity Press, 1989), 'Introduction' and ch. 3. On the meanings of 'the people', see Patrick Joyce, *Visions of the People: Industrial England and the Question of Class, 1848–1918* (Cambridge: Cambridge University Press, 1991), 'Introduction'.

evidence for the historian. A recurring question in this chapter will be whether popularity with publishers can ultimately tell us anything about popularity with readers, particularly child readers. Before beginning, however, we need an overview of the state of children's science literature in the first half of the nineteenth century.

Early Science Books for Children

By the mid eighteenth century, the sciences had become part of a 'public culture', entering an increasingly commercial marketplace in the form of lectures, demonstrations, books and periodicals.[9] Among other new commodities were products aimed specifically at children, such as books, games and puzzles.[10] It was in this context that the first science books appeared which can be identified as written specifically for children. The first is usually said to be the pseudonymous Tom Telescope's *Newtonian System of Philosophy, Adapted to the Capacities of Young Gentlemen and Ladies* (1761), published and probably written by John Newbery, the man generally credited with the creation of the children's book genre in the 1740s.[11] In the *Newtonian System*, a group of budding young natural philosophers, the Lilliputian Society, attend lectures and demonstrations delivered by a youthful 'Tom Telescope'. Many of the features which would become typical of children's non-fiction for the next 70 years were already present: the inclusion of moral lessons alongside the natural philosophy; the recourse to easy-to-understand examples from everyday life; and the use of a conversational format, in which the information is conveyed in the form of a dialogue between two or more characters, with only limited narration to set the scene.

The combination of instruction and amusement blossomed in the late eighteenth century, and the sciences were regarded as particularly good subject matter.[12] Such books were expected to appeal to young children's innate curiosity about the natural world, and it was not too difficult for writers to move from nature to its Creator, thus introducing the almost compulsory moral lesson. In the first decades of the

---

9   Larry Stewart, *The Rise of Public Science: Rhetoric, Technology and Natural Philosophy in Newtonian Britain, 1660–1750* (Cambridge: Cambridge University Press, 1992); Jan Golinski, *Science as Public Culture: Chemistry and Enlightenment in Britain, 1760–1820* (Cambridge: Cambridge University Press, 1992).

10   J.H. Plumb, 'The New World of Children', in N. McKendrick, J. Brewer and J.H. Plumb (eds), *The Birth of a Consumer Society: The Commercialization of Eighteenth-Century England* (Bloomington: Indiana University Press, 1982), pp. 286–315.

11   On Telescope, see James A. Secord, 'Newton in the Nursery: Tom Telescope and the Philosophy of Tops and Balls, 1761–1838', *History of Science* 23 (1985), 127–51. On Newbery, see F.J. Harvey Darton, *Children's Books in England: Five Centuries of Social Life*, 3rd edn, rev. Brian Alderson (Cambridge: Cambridge University Press, 1982), ch. 8.

12   Darton, *Children's Books in England*, ch. 10; M.V. Jackson, *Engines of Instruction, Mischief and Magic: Children's Literature in England from its Beginnings to 1839* (Aldershot: Scolar Press, 1989); Alan Richardson, *Literature, Education, and Romanticism: Reading as Social Practice, 1780–1832* (Cambridge: Cambridge University Press, 1994); Aileen Fyfe, 'Young Readers and the Sciences', in Marina Frasca-Spada and Nicholas Jardine (eds), *Books and the Sciences in History* (Cambridge: Cambridge University Press, 2000), pp. 276–90.

nineteenth century, a myriad of 'conversations', 'dialogues', 'letters' and 'catechisms' flowed from the publishers' houses. Jeremiah Joyce's *Scientific Dialogues* (1800–5) claimed to follow on from *Evenings at Home*, and covered a range of sciences, but most books of this type were more restricted in subject matter. Samuel Parkes and Jane Marcet, for instance, both focused on chemistry, with his *Chemical Catechism* (1806) and her *Conversations on Chemistry* (1806). Marcet was just one of the many women to whom the conversation genre appealed. The frequent representation of girls learning from women within these books could help legitimate the authority of the female writer on the sciences.[13]

The regular publication of children's science books by the early nineteenth century indicates that the sciences were not merely acceptable in the nursery, but had become a standard part of education. Some form of natural history was particularly common, as discussions of plants or animals could be easily related to everyday life. Astronomy was another favourite, but subjects like natural philosophy or chemistry, which dealt with less tangible concepts, tended to be kept for older children. Around 30 or 40 children's science books were being published each decade in the early years of the century, and by the middle years, that had risen to around 90 books per decade.[14] There was clearly a growing market for such works, and middle-class parents were being offered an ever-increasing range of books to choose from. The now traditional 'instructive and amusing' style dominated during the first half of the century, although alternatives were beginning to emerge by mid century.

Fictional conversations such as Marcet's or Aikin and Barbauld's were supposed to mimic the real conversations that ideal parents would have with their children. Conversation was widely regarded as a good way for a young child to learn, even about complicated subjects. As Richard and Maria Edgeworth had put it in their *Practical Education* (1797), 'We have found, from experience, that an early knowledge of the first principles of science may be given in conversation, and may be insensibly acquired from the usual incidents of life.'[15] Reading fictional conversations mimicked the experience of a real conversation, allowing the child-reader to learn alongside the fictional child. It was generally accepted that children learned more effectively

---

13 Ann B. Shteir, *Cultivating Women, Cultivating Science: Flora's Daughters and Botany in England 1760–1860* (London: Johns Hopkins University Press, 1996), ch. 4.

14 These figures are based on searches of *the Nineteenth-Century Short Title Catalogue, series I–III* on CD-ROM (NSTC), Newcastle: Avero Publications, 1996–2002. I have followed the methodology set out in Simon Eliot's '*Patterns and Trends* and the *NSTC*: Some Initial Observations, Part I', *Publishing History* 42 (1997), 79–104. The same caveats apply. These figures are estimated from results for searches combining Dewey class 500 ('pure science') with titles containing 'youth', 'young', 'child' and 'children', and for a search combining Dewey class 500 with class 828.3 ('children's literature'). The resulting sets overlap but not as much as might have been expected, so my figures are merely estimates. The growth of children's science books was actually less rapid than that of science books in general. According to Eliot, the output of works of science almost quintupled between the first and sixth decades of the century: see Simon Eliot, '*Patterns and Trends* and the *NSTC*: Some Initial Observations, Part II', *Publishing History* 43 (1998), 71–112.

15 Maria Edgeworth, and Richard Lovell Edgeworth, *Essays on Practical Education* (2 vols, London: Hunter, 1815), vol. I, p. v ('Preface'). See also vol. II, p. 471.

when they were interested in the subject. Again, conversations were a useful form because they allowed authors to dramatise their works, with action either implied from the dialogue, or described in the accompanying narrative. Instruction was thus conveyed within a story, which helped to make learning fun.

In contrast to other non-fiction writers, science writers had some advantages when trying to be entertaining. Children's curiosity about the things they could see around them provided an obvious starting point. At its most basic, this could mean paying close attention to the behaviour of toys in the nursery, such as the spinning top used in Tom Telescope's *Newtonian System*. Similarly, John Ayrton Paris's *Philosophy in Sport Made Science in Earnest* (1827) used childhood toys and games to teach natural philosophy. Indeed, by the 1840s, a whole genre developed of the 'science of common things' or 'things familiar', including Charles Williams's *Philosophy of Common Things* (*c*.1845)[16] and Ebeneezer Cobham Brewer's *Guide to the Scientific Knowledge of Things Familiar* (1847). The latter was reputed to have sold 160,000 copies by 1874.[17] The sciences also offered opportunities for practical activities. Fictional children were frequently going places, collecting things or trying simple experiments, which might inspire their readers at home. For natural history, this might mean a walk in the garden or the nearby fields, observing the local wildlife or collecting plants, as the tutor frequently recommends Harry and George to do in Aikin and Barbauld's *Evenings at Home*. Astronomical knowledge could be imparted by looking at the stars, as Henry and his father do while walking home at the beginning of Sarah Tomlinson's *Starry Heavens* (undated, 1847), which formed the first part of the 'First Steps in General Knowledge' series issued by the Society for Promoting Christian Knowledge. Readers of *Evenings at Home* might even have been tempted to try the simple experiments with oyster shells and vinegar discussed by George and his tutor during a conversation on chemistry.[18] Learning through practical involvement would be even more effective (because interesting and exciting) than learning from a book. Although Greg Myers has noted the irony of books which encourage learning through practical activities while themselves imparting knowledge through the printed word, some writers did make strenuous efforts to encourage their readers to really go and do things, rather than simply read.[19]

The general trend in children's literature towards more realistic representations of children, and more complex modes of narration, was also reflected in science books.[20] Children in instructive conversations had routinely been given adult voices, and forced to behave in a way that suited the narrator's proposed scheme of instruction. Thus, the wording of their questions sounded unlikely, while the topic

16 The second series of Williams's work appeared in 1845.

17   According to the title page of the edition issued that year.

18 Aikin and Barbauld, *Evenings at Home*, vol. V, p. 8.

19 Greg Myers, 'Science for Women and Children: The Dialogue of Popular Science in the Nineteenth Century', in John Christie and Sally Shuttleworth (eds), *Nature Transfigured: Science and Literature, 1700–1900* (Manchester: Manchester University Press, 1989), pp. 171–200 (p. 179).

20 On the representation of children, see Darton, *Children's Books in England*, p. 220; Anne Scott MacLeod, 'From Rational to Romantic: The Children of Children's Literature in the Nineteenth Century', *Poetics Today* 13 (1992), 141–53.

of their questions appeared suspiciously suitable for their adult interlocutors' next point. For example, 12-year old Cecilia, in Priscilla Wakefield's *Mental Improvement* (1794–97), comments: 'I observed you named sponge among the zoophytes; surely that cannot be the habitation of insects. I have often wondered what it is, but have never been able to satisfy my curiosity.'[21] This tendency was exacerbated by the relatively small amount of surrounding narration in which most early nineteenth-century conversations were set, so that the reader's impression of the characters had to be gained almost entirely from their speeches. By the middle of the nineteenth century, authors who continued to use the conversational form strove to make their children sound more realistic. A good example of this can be seen in Eliza W. Payne's *Peeps at Nature: or, God's Works and Man's Wants* (1850), which will be discussed in more detail later. Here Alexander is full of ideas and questions that sound as if they actually came from a child, rather than a parent. By mid century, however, third-person narrative was beginning to overtake conversation as the dominant style for children's science books. Early efforts tried to create a sense of excitement by focusing on wonders and marvels, perhaps even using the conceit in their titles, as in Samuel Clark's *Peter Parley's Wonders of Earth, Sea and Sky* (undated but 1837), or Charles Williams's *Wonders of the Waters* (undated but 1842). The narrators of such works were often given a strong persona as the favourite, well-travelled and knowledgeable uncle. So, although no longer written as conversations, they still mimicked the form of oral storytelling.

One thing that did not change during the first half of the nineteenth century was that it remained utterly standard for children's authors to present the sciences as the study of God's creation. The study of nature could promote feelings of awe and devotion in young children, and could help to make real the God of Scripture. For some authors, particularly in the late eighteenth and early nineteenth centuries, this religious utility seemed to be the main justification for writing about the sciences, as is suggested by the title of Sarah Trimmer's *An Easy Introduction to the Knowledge of Nature and Reading the Holy Scriptures* (1780).[22] A clear religious framework was particularly crucial in the turbulent decades after the French Revolution. Secular, let alone atheistic, science had revolutionary overtones, and the radical associations were continued into the 1830s by working-class champions of political change who found support for their arguments in French scientific theories.[23] French chemistry, transmutation or celestial physics were therefore not the sorts of things which would be found in British children's books, and even the absence of explicit religion could raise suspicions. Supposedly the most delicate members of society, children had to be carefully protected from dangerous ideas. Although books on the sciences for

---

21 Priscilla Wakefield, *Mental Improvement: or, The Beauties and Wonders of Nature and Art* (London, 1794–97, repr. East Lancing, MI, 1995), p. 58.

22 On religion in Sarah Trimmer's *An Easy Introduction*, see Aileen Fyfe, 'Reading Children's Books in Eighteenth-Century Dissenting Families', *Historical Journal* 43 (2000), 453–74.

23 The classic exposition is Adrian Desmond, 'Artisan Resistance and Evolution in Britain 1819–1848', *Osiris*, n.s. 3 (1987), 72–110. See also Colin A. Russell, *Science and Social Change, 1700–1900* (London: Macmillan, 1983), ch. 8.

adults written in a secular manner began to be available from the 1840s, it was much later in the century before that became possible within children's books.

The Religious Tract Society

When mid nineteenth-century commentators talked about 'popular literature' they usually meant literature which was widely read outside the typical educated middle-class book-reading circles. It might mean literature which was cheap enough for at least some of the working classes, or it might additionally mean literature which was generally accepted and liked by them.[24] This no longer meant just chapbooks and ballads, but included the products of steam-powered printing, from penny periodicals to railway novels.[25] The place of children's books in such discussions of the popular is uncertain, since children's books were generally much cheaper than their adult counterparts. Each volume of *Evenings at Home* cost just one shilling and sixpence because they were small duodecimos, and only 150 pages long. A typical adult volume at the time would have been about 300 pages octavo, and would have cost around 10 shillings. This meant that science books intended for middle-class children might have appealed to working-class adults in the first half of the century because of their low cost and simple language, at a time when there was only a limited range of popular science books for adults. However, many of the canonical children's science books were not really that cheap. *Evenings at Home* ran to six volumes, and the complete work was being sold for 10 shillings and sixpence in the 1820s. Similarly, Marcet's *Conversations* cost 14 shillings, and Joyce's *Dialogues* 15 shillings.[26] These prices confined them solidly to the middle classes.

The Religious Tract Society, on the other hand, issued works on the sciences ranging in price from two shillings down to a farthing.[27] Its cheapest publications took the same form as its tracts, being unbound, and only 16 or 32 pages long. This

---

24 The various meanings of 'popular' are discussed in Mrs. Percy Sinnett, 'What is Popular Literature?' *People's Journal*, 5 (1848), 7–8 (p. 7), and, more recently, in Shiach, *Discourse*, 'Introduction'.

25 See, for instance, the usage of 'popular' in 'New and Cheap Forms of Popular Literature', *Eclectic Review* 22 (1845), 74–84 and [Coventry Patmore], 'Popular Serial Literature', *North British Review* 7 (1847), 110–36. See also Victor E. Neuburg, *Popular Literature: A History and a Guide* (Harmondsworth: Penguin, 1977).

26 Price for the 1806 edition of Marcet, 2 vols, 12mo and for the 1809 edition of Joyce, 6 vols, 18mo. See entries in Sampson Low (ed.), *The English Catalogue of Books* (London: Low, 1864–1914).

27 On the history of the RTS, see William Jones, *The Jubilee Memorial of the Religious Tract Society: Containing a Record of its Origin, Proceedings, and Results. AD 1799 to AD 1849* (London: Religious Tract Society, 1850); Samuel G. Green, *The Story of the Religious Tract Society for One Hundred Years* (London: Religious Tract Society, 1899). On the RTS and children's books, see Brian Alderson's 'Appendix I' to Darton, *Children's Books in England*, pp. 317–18. Also, Brian Alderson, and Pat Garrett (eds), *The Religious Tract Society as a Publisher of Children's Books: Catalogue of an Exhibition Prepared to Celebrate the 200th Anniversary of the Foundation of the RTS Presented at a Conference at the University of East Anglia, Norwich, 28 July to 1 August 1999* (Hoddesdon: Children's Book History Society,

format was printed in tens of thousands, at low unit prices, either for individual sale or bulk distribution. The Society's 1850 catalogue of children's books makes clear the variety of works it produced.[28] There were several series of short tracts specifically for children learning to read, and the authors of these sometimes took natural history as their theme. The 'New Series of Children's books, easy words and large print, 32mo with engravings' launched in 1845 included farthing tracts on *The Wren's Nest* by Mrs Wright of Croydon and *The Eagle's Nest* by J.B. Maynard, Esq., of Holmewood near Ryde, as well as Esther Copley (1786–1851) on *The Acorn* and George Mogridge (1787–1854) on *The Bamboo*, for one penny each. All four of these writers were RTS regulars, and none specialised in writing on the sciences. The ephemeral nature of works like these makes them difficult to locate in academic libraries, but it is probable that such works used the natural world as a setting for their story (with its religious moral), rather than specifically trying to convey instruction about nature. That a wide audience was intended is indicated by the note in the catalogue which claims these would all be suitable for 'Sunday, national, British and common day schools' as well as 'families and boarding schools'. Although these particular tracts were priced individually, it was common for the Society to price tracts, including children's tracts, by the hundred. The series which had preceded this 'New Series' had included a *History of Beasts* costing two shillings and eight pence per hundred (equivalent to a third of a penny each). This method of pricing encouraged philanthropically-minded members of the Society to buy in bulk, and give the tracts away to local school children. In this way, RTS children's works probably reached a far wider audience than most of the other books in this chapter.

The works intended for older children had a greater scientific content, although it varied with the expected age and social class of the audience. The RTS editor, the Rev. Charles Williams (1796–1866), wrote seven 'Penny Books on Natural Objects' in 1845–46. These were tiny 32-page tracts, discussing topics such as the nettle, the rose-leaf, the cherry and the hazel-nut, with an illustration of the relevant plant on the first page (that is to say, the cover). These were written as conversations between 'Uncle William' and his young friends, with narrative to set the scene. Thus, the discussion of hazel-nuts appears in the context of a 'nutting' expedition, while another tract opens with Uncle William meeting a boy who has been stung by a nettle. Uncle William applies the necessary dock leaf, and tries to convince the sceptical Henry that nettles really are fascinating.[29] Five of these tracts were reissued as a six-penny volume in 1846 under the title *Uncle William's Talkings with Children About Plants*, with gilt edging, and an orange paper cover.

1999) and Dennis Butts and Pat Garrett (eds), *From the Dairyman's Daughter to Worrals of the WAAF* (Lutterworth: Lutterworth Press, 2006).

28 Catalogue C, appended to RTS Annual Report (1850). RTS works were typically undated, and frequently anonymous. The publications dates and authors' names in the following discussion have been identified from marginalia on the Society's archive copies of its monthly publications lists (RTS/USCL archives, School of Oriental and African Studies, London). I am currently compiling a check-list of publications from these lists, which cover the years 1842–59.

29 [Charles Williams], *Uncle William's Talkings with Children about Plants* (London: RTS, 1846), 'The Hazel-Nut', pp. 1–16; 'The Nettle', pp. 6–7 (numbering restarts for each section).

Williams also wrote a series of four penny 'square books' for slightly older children, again focusing on natural history. As before, these initially appeared as tracts before being collected into groups of five. This time, the volume was bound in cloth boards with gilt decoration, and had been given a new, illustrated, title page. There were at least seven of these two-shilling volumes, including *Remarkable Insects* (1842), *Wonders of the Waters* (1842) and *The Face of the Earth* (1846). Unlike *Talkings*, they were not written as conversations, but used continuous third-person narrative. In an effort to hold his reader's attention, the narrator made a point of stressing the wonders of creatures from starfish to electric eels. This also enabled him to introduce devotional thoughts on the objects of Creation. Even the lobster, which has rarely 'awakened the admiration which it ought to call forth ... shows as clearly that God made it, as any creature that can be taken from the surface of the earth, or from the midst of the waters'.[30] All RTS works had a devotional cast, but they also had to have a statement of the route to salvation through faith in the atonement, which was more difficult to introduce. In *Wonders of the Waters*, it appeared in the chapter on the fish, when the narrator introduced the Redemption by reminding his readers that, 'In thus referring to the provision made for inferior creatures, it is of great importance that the mind should dwell also on the provision made for ourselves.'[31]

Williams was dismissed as an RTS editor in 1849, for spending too much time on his own writing, instead of overseeing the running of the Society's publishing operations. There was also concern that he had not subjected his own books to the usual reports of readers before publication.[32] Assuming they stayed within approved limits, however, it was quite usual for the Society's editors to engage in authorship, and the new children's editor, John Henry Cross, certainly did so.[33] Unlike Williams, he did not write on the sciences very often, but he did write the text for *A Book About Animals* (1852, two shillings). The showpiece of this book was the six Kronheim colour plates to which the large-print text provided commentary. Although some of the animals, such as the elephant, were not stunningly realistic representations, the very presence of colour plates would have been eye-catching enough. The book was bound in white cloth, embellished with blue and pink ink, and gilt, resulting in something far more elaborate than the Society's usual self-coloured paper with black printing, or drab cloth boards with just a hint of gilt. This work and its predecessor, Mrs Wright's *A Book About Birds* (1850), must be among the earliest fruits of the Society's connection with Kronheim.[34]

A Book About Animals was clearly not intended for children at National or Sunday schools. For different reasons, the same was true of the Society's more advanced

30 [Charles Williams], *Wonders of the Waters* (London: Religious Tract Society, 1842, repr. Bristol: Thoemmes Press, 2003), pp. 99–100.

31 [Williams], *Wonders of the Waters*, p. 147.

32 See Aileen Fyfe, *Science and Salvation: Evangelicals and Popular Science Publishing in Victorian Britain* (Chicago: University of Chicago Press, 2004), pp. 142–4.

33 After Williams's departure, the editorship was divided between two people, one as general editor, one as children's editor (Fyfe, *Science and Salvation*, p. 143).

34 The first reference to Kronheim that I noted in the RTS archives was from 1854.

books on the sciences. Most of those that appeared as books (rather than tracts) were more expensive – several shillings, instead of several pennies – and tended to use more complicated language. One of the many women writers who were first published with the RTS was Eliza W. Payne, of Plymouth and later Edgbaston. The fact that her husband, Alfred, was a technical chemist may explain her decision to write about the sciences.[35] Her first attempts were published as penny and three-halfpenny tracts from 1848, beginning with 'How are People Kept on the Earth? or, The Law of Attraction' and 'The Invisible Fluid; or, Our Own Atmosphere'. Unlike works which described the wonders of the natural world, Payne's works described less visible scientific concepts, such as gravity, the atmosphere and the causes of tides and rainbows. The Society's catalogue suggested that these works would be suitable only for 'families and boarding schools', indicating the need for a higher level of education than could be found in Sunday scholars, and perhaps also the need for educated parents to explain the difficult parts. Payne's 14 tracts were issued in a bound volume as *Peeps at Nature: or, God's Works and Man's Wants* (1850, one shilling and sixpence), and her subsequent works for the Society went straight into book format, including *Nature's Wonders; or, God's Care over All his Works* (1850, two shillings) and *Village Science; or, The Laws of Nature Explained* (1851, two shillings).

Despite, or perhaps because of, the more complicated nature of her subjects, Payne made particular efforts to ensure that the conversations between Alexander and his mamma were lively. It is tempting to imagine that they were based on her own conversations with her eldest sons, but (unless they were astonishingly precocious) it is unlikely. The real Alexander was about four years old when she was writing her first tracts, and his brother Richard was only a year older. The Alexander of the book seems to be a few years older than his namesake. Nonetheless, her experience with very young children might have inspired her declaration, in the preface to *Peeps at Nature*, that she would try to follow, 'the actual workings of a child's mind'.[36] And indeed, in the book, Alexander not only asks child-like questions, but his questions dart around and go off at tangents in a manner most unlike those of earlier nineteenth-century conversations. In the third chapter, on gravitation, Alexander has been thinking over a previous conversation in which he had learned that the earth was spinning. There is 'one thing that has puzzled me very much, mamma ... How is it that we do not fall off when it is our turn to be upside down as it were?' Mamma explains that God has provided an attractive force that keeps people on the earth. Whereas some fictional children would then have urged their parent to tell them more about this attractive force, Alexander asks, 'Is this the reason that a fly can walk on the under side of my book as well as on the top?' Mamma then has to explain about the 'sticky sponges' on the feet of insects before she can continue

---

35 Some of Eliza Payne's addresses are given in the RTS archives, which makes it possible to identify the family in those Census returns which have been computerised. They reveal that she was probably born *c.*1815 and that Alfred was a widower by 1881. Her last book was published in 1872. My thanks to Morag Fyfe for assistance with the census returns.

36 [Eliza W. Payne], *Peeps at Nature: or, God's Works and Man's Wants* (London: Religious Tract Society, 1850), p. [3].

with the story of gravity.[37] There are more interruptions and tangents, as Alexander connects what she is telling him to things he already knows, and tries to come up with his own explanations of how things work. This mode of writing means that the instructive element is much less logical and ordered than in other books, but it makes Alexander seem more like a real child, and more sympathetic, and interesting, to a child-reader.

Unfortunately, the RTS archives do not give any details about the print runs (or sales) of these works. The Society's *Jubilee Memorial* did give bestseller lists for children's works up to 1850, but the books discussed here were all too recent to be able to compete with the cumulative sales of older works. Most of the works listed had been published in the early 1830s: six had sold more than 100,000, and nine more had sold over 25,000. Compared with the Society's adult tracts, these were relatively small figures (successful adult tracts of similar age had sold 200,000 or 300,000 copies), but compared with the runs of most books at the time, these numbers are impressive.[38] Books such as Payne's *Village Science* or the *Book About Animals* would not have reached such high circulations, but the works which appeared first in tract format would certainly have been printed in several thousands, because that was how the Society operated. Few other works of science for children were as cheap as these farthing and penny tracts, and few others can have had (at least the potential for) such a wide readership.

Classics and Brands

This section will consider some better-known children's science books, and ask what we know about their popularity. For most books, all we have to go on is sales figures, if publishers' archives survive, or, more likely, numbers of editions. Two different sorts of successful book will be considered. 'Classic' books are those which continue to be reprinted (and, we assume, read) over a prolonged period of time. They are books which continue to speak to later generations, and in which later readers can find something of relevance to their lives.[39] They may or may not have been bestsellers at the time of their initial publication.[40] The other sort of books is those that form 'brands' – groups of books which share many features, and trade on each other's success. A very few might legitimately be called brands in the full modern

---

37 [Payne], *Peeps at Nature*, p. 27.

38 Jones, *Jubilee Memorial*, 'Appendix V'.

39 T.S. Eliot, *What is a Classic?* (London: Faber, 1944); Frank Kermode, *The Classic* (London: Faber, 1975); Italo Calvino, *Why Read the Classics?* trans. Martin McLaughlin (London: Jonathan Cape, 1999). My discussion of the role of publishers in creating classics is to be found in Aileen Fyfe, 'Publishing and the Classics: Paley's *Natural Theology* and the Nineteenth-century Scientific Canon', *Studies in History and Philosophy of the Sciences* 33 (2002), 733–55.

40 On bestsellers, see the list appended to Altick, *The English Common Reader*, and the follow-ups, Richard D. Altick, 'Nineteenth-Century Bestsellers: A Further List', *Studies in Bibliography* 22 (1969), 197–206 and 'Nineteenth-Century Bestsellers: A Third List', *Studies in Bibliography,* 39 (1986), 235–41.

sense, such as Pinnock's Catechisms, whose contents were (initially) controlled by William Pinnock, but most were less formal groupings, such as the Peter Parley phenomenon. With these, membership was less controlled, but there was still the possibility of trading off other members' successes.[41]

One of the best examples of a classic children's science book is Aikin and Barbauld's *Evenings at Home* (1792–96). Its six volumes of natural history, moral stories, poems and conversations on chemistry remained in print until 1915, and until the 1880s, was regularly reprinted by several different publishers. By that time, its status as a classic helped to ensure its continued sales, but we need to consider how it became so established. Its initial reception gave little indication that it would have such a long and successful career. Critics were divided on its merits because of the problematic absence of religion. In contrast to most children's writers of the 1780s and 1790s, Aikin and Barbauld did not regard religion as the main reason for writing about the sciences. They believed that the sciences were becoming such an important part of industrialising British culture that a child could not grow up to be a responsible member of society without a basic understanding of the natural (and social) world. For them, the sciences were useful subjects in their own right, not just as handmaidens to religion. Furthermore, as Unitarians, they disapproved of sectarianism, and kept their religious references to a minimum to avoid pressing one particular view upon their readers. As a consequence, critics who shared Aikin and Barbauld's viewpoint – Maria Edgeworth, for example – were enthusiastic about their work, while those who regarded religion as crucial were more damning.[42] The Anglican and self-appointed 'Guardian of Education', Sarah Trimmer, recommended that children should only read it 'under the care of a judicious parent, or teacher', for if they were left to read it on their own, 'to *ruminate* upon *all its contents*, without discrimination, it may prove very injurious'.[43] Unsurprisingly, most of the evidence for actual readings of *Evenings at Home* in its first 20 years is from liberal nonconformist families.[44]

This restricted audience did not augur well for long-term success, but publisher Joseph Johnson (also a Unitarian) had issued ten editions by 1814, indicating steady sales. And by the 1810s, there is evidence that it was beginning to be read more widely, including children from Anglican and Methodist families. Its volumes came out of copyright between 1820 and 1824, and the publisher (now a group of

---

41 On Pinnock, see Jonathan R. Topham, 'Publishing "Popular Science" in Early Nineteenth-Century Britain', in Aileen Fyfe and Bernard Lightman (eds), *Science in the Marketplace: Nineteenth-Century Sites and Experiences* (Chicago: University of Chicago Press, 2007). On the Parleys, see Darton, *Children's Books in England*, pp. 221–8. On Samuel Clark, and the natural history he wrote as Peter Parley, see James A. Secord's 'Introduction' to Samuel Clark, *Peter Parley's Wonders of the Earth, Sea and Sky* (1837, repr. Bristol: Thoemmes Press, 2003).

42 Edgeworth, and Edgeworth, *Practical Education*, vol. I, pp. 434–5.

43 Sarah Trimmer, 'Review of Evenings at Home', *Guardian of Education* 2 (1803), 304–11, 343–53 (p. 353).

44 Evidence for reading is discussed in Fyfe, 'Reading Children's Books'.

shareholders) produced a revised edition, thus renewing the copyright protection.[45] Not only were 10,000 copies of the revised edition printed in the 1820s and 1830s, but other publishers (usually provincial publishers, such as William Milner of Halifax, and Robert Griffin of Glasgow) began to reprint the original text.[46] This interest from publishers suggests that it was no longer regarded as a specifically Unitarian book, but had broader appeal.

Yet, by the 1840s, it seemed to be declining in popularity. The shareholders' print runs were getting smaller, and the 3,000 copies printed in 1836 had not sold out by 1846. Longman were selling only around 30 copies a year.[47] Its demise at this point would have been in keeping with the history of other books of a similar age. Tom Telescope's last edition had been in 1838, while Marcet's *Conversations on Chemistry* had its final edition in 1853. Yet, incredibly, *Evenings at Home* survived, and went on to sell far more copies in the second half of the nineteenth century than it had done in the first.[48] This was due to the intervention of George Routledge, and demonstrates the active role of publishers, not merely in responding to, but in shaping public demand. *Evenings at Home* had been a respected, but out-of-date work. Routledge established it as a classic, which deserved to be on every list of gift or reward books, and in so doing, he revived its fortunes for another 50 years.

As an entrepreneurial newcomer to the publishing trade, Routledge was looking for a quick way to make money. He made his name by producing cheap editions of out-of-copyright works, perhaps most famously with his 'Railway Library' of shilling volumes, from 1848.[49] His two main sources were old British works and American works, neither of which were protected by British copyright law. *Evenings at Home* appeared on page 1 of the Publication Book for 1851, the year in which Routledge and Co. was founded. Thomas Day's *Sandford and Merton* (1783–89) was on page 2, followed by *Swiss Family Robinson* (1814).[50] For *Evenings at Home*, Routledge commissioned a new set of revisions. Although they were less meticulous than the 1820s revisions, Routledge was able to claim copyright protection for

---

45 On these and other revisions, see Aileen Fyfe, 'How the Squirrel became a Squgg: The Long History of a Children's Book', *Paradigm* 27 (1999), 25–37.

46 Longman Archives, H10 214; H12 221. The Longman Archives are held at the University of Reading Library, and are also available on microfilm from Chadwyck-Healey. The guide to the microfilm edition is Alison Ingram (ed.) *Index to the Archives of the House of Longman, 1794–1914* (Cambridge: Chadwyck-Healey, 1981).

47 1846 sales figures are from Longman Archive, H1 11.

48 The full publishing history is discussed in Aileen Fyfe, 'Copyrights and Competition: Producing and Protecting Children's Books in the Nineteenth Century', *Publishing History* 45 (1999), 35–59.

49 F.A. Mumby, *The House of Routledge, 1834–1934, with a History of Kegan Paul, Trench, Trubner and Other Associated Firms* (London: Routledge, 1934). See also the 'Routledge' entry in Patricia J. Anderson, and Jonathan Rose, *British Literary Publishing Houses, 1820–1880* (Detroit, MI: Gale Research, 1991).

50 Routledge Publication Book (1850–58), 1–3. The Routledge Archive is kept at University College London, and is described in Gillian Furlong, *Handlist to the Archives of George Routledge & Co., 1853–1973* (London: University College London Library, 1973).

what appeared to be the most up-to-date edition on the market.[51] The shareholders' editions had been selling at ten shillings and sixpence, although leftover copies were reduced to five shillings in 1846.[52] In contrast, Routledge brought out his copies at three shillings and sixpence, and printed runs of 2,000 every two or three years. In 1866, he was printing runs of 4,000 copies of a one shilling and sixpence edition. The shareholders printed just 3,000 copies in the 1850s, compared to Routledge's 10,000 in the same decade.[53] Routledge clearly showed that by publishing the work more cheaply, he could sell far more copies of it. By 1900, he had sold a stunning 59,000 copies.[54] Furthermore, competing publishers (including Ward, Lock and Co. and Routledge's brother-in-law, Frederick Warne) also jumped on the bandwagon, issuing at least 14 reprint editions of the old, unrevised text. As well as issuing it in cheap editions, these publishers presented it as a reward book, in decorative covers, and added colour plates to the wood engravings which had been standard since the 1840s.[55] In this format, it became the reliable and well-loved classic which every child should own.

Publishers like classics because their past success holds out the promise of continued sales into the future. During the period of copyright protection, however, only one publisher is entitled to reprint a successful work. Other publishers could attempt to cash in on its success either by waiting for the end of copyright, or by issuing imitations. If there was a particular style, format or subject matter that seemed especially successful, publishers could hope that it would be again. Such imitations tell us something about the success of a work as judged by contemporary publishers and writers. The most commonly-imitated form for children's science books in the early nineteenth century was a variation on the conversation or the dialogue. Late eighteenth-century books had used the style (including Tom Telescope, and *Evenings at Home*) but if the word 'conversation' appeared in the title, it did so in the depths of the subtitle, as in Priscilla Wakefield's *Mental Improvement; or, The Beauties and Wonders of Nature and Art, in a Series of Instructive Conversations* (1797).[56]

In the early nineteenth century, works which used 'conversations' prominently in their titles were usually manuals for learning a foreign language, or religious tracts.[57] However, two books on the sciences used the style: Charlotte Smith's *Conversations Introducing Poetry, Chiefly on Subjects of Natural History* (1804), and Jane Marcet's *Conversations on Chemistry* (1806). There followed a great enthusiasm for science books called 'Conversations on...', which had its heyday in the 1820s, when (on average) two science books with such titles were published each year. The more successful of these were reprinted throughout the 1830s, but

---

51 On the revisions, see Fyfe, 'Squirrel'.

52 Longman Archive, H14 20.

53 Routledge Publication Book (1850–58), 1; (1855–58), 211; (1858–81), 645. Longman Archive H15 3; H1 11.

54 Routledge Publication Book (1866–84), 391; (1881–89), 254; (1889–1902), 386.

55 The first shareholder edition to be illustrated appears to be that of 1846.

56 Priscilla Wakefield, *Mental Improvement: or, The Beauties and Wonders of Nature and Art* (1797; repr. East Lancing, MI, 1995).

57 Results of searching NSTC title index for 1800–20.

the trend was in decline by the 1840s. By the 1860s, only two science books called themselves 'Conversations'.

Marcet is frequently placed in the canon of children's science books, not least because of her influence on Michael Faraday, and there is an implicit claim that her *Conversations on Chemistry* was the originator of the subsequent flood of 'Conversations on...'[58] However, there is a difficulty with this argument. The boom in 'Conversations on...' actually began in the late 1810s, and was at its peak in the 1820s. It included Sarah and Elizabeth Fitton's *Conversations on Botany* (1817), William Cole's *Conversations on Algebra* (1818), Marcet's *Conversations on Natural Philosophy* (1819), Delvalle Lowry's *Conversations on Mineralogy* (1822), the *Astronomical Conversations for Children* (1822) by 'Cantabrigiensis', the anonymous *Conversations on Geology* (1828) and Marcet's *Conversations on Vegetable Physiology* (1829). *Conversations on Chemistry* itself benefited from the boom, selling (on average) just over 600 copies a year in the 1820s, compared with around 490 copies a year in the 1810s.[59] If Marcet deserves the credit for this flood, her *Conversations on Political Economy* (1816) would be a more convincing contender.[60]

'Conversations on...' were not the only popular brands of the 1820s, as titles using 'Dialogues' and 'Catechisms' were also common ('catechism' more so, 'dialogue' less so). The 'dialogue' may well have originated with Joyce's *Scientific Dialogues*, but the enthusiasm for 'catechisms' cannot be ascribed to Parke's *Chemical Catechism*. Rather, William Pinnock's series of catechisms accounts for the majority of all the catechisms published in this period. Like 'dialogues' and 'conversations', the 'catechism' had almost died out by mid century, though it left traces in other forms, such as Brewer's catechetical *Guide to the Scientific Knowledge of Things Familiar*.

The existence of 'brands' such as these does not mean that every publication of the sort was a great success, but it strongly suggests that many of them (particularly the earlier ones) were. Other authors hoped that their works would be successful if framed in the same way, and publishers must have hoped so too, given their willingness to publish so many of them. Of the group of 'Conversations on...' mentioned above, the most reprinted works were Fitton's *Conversations on Botany*, and Marcet's works on chemistry and natural philosophy. By 1840, the botany and natural philosophy had reached their ninth editions, while chemistry was on its thirteenth. All of these were published by Longman and Co., as were Lowry's *Conversations on Mineralogy* and Marcet's other five books of 'Conversations'. Indeed, Longman was the dominant publisher of 'Conversations on...' in the 1820s,

---

58 On Marcet and her *Chemistry*, see M. Susan Lindee, 'The American Career of Jane Marcet's *Conversations on Chemistry*, 1806–1853', *Isis* 82 (1991), 8–23; Greg Myers, 'Fictionality, Demonstration, and a Forum for Popular Science: Jane Marcet's *Conversations on Chemistry*', in Barbara T. Gates and Ann B. Shteir (eds), *Natural Eloquence: Women Reinscribe Science* (Madison: University of Wisconsin Press, 1997), pp. 43–60.

59 Longman Archive, A1 285; A2 87–8, 105; A3 87, 285, 289.

60 Greg Myers refers to the political economy work as being very widely read, Myers, 'Fictionality and Demonstration', p. 43.

also using the style for subjects such as Christianity (1826), mythology (1827), the English Constitution (1828) and chronology and history (1830).[61]

Longman printed 1,000 copies of *Conversations on Chemistry*, in December 1805. By the third (1809) edition, the runs were increased to 1,500 copies, and there were even two editions of 2,000 copies in the 1820s. By 1840, it had sold 18,000 copies. Marcet had a half profits agreement, and received her first payment of £92.3s.11d in March 1807. By 1840, she had received just over £2,000 from *Conversations on Chemistry*, as, of course, had Longman. The conversations on natural philosophy and botany appear to have similar publishing histories and finances, which makes clear why Longman became so keen on the format in the mid 1820s. By the late 1820s, however, it was beginning to run out of steam. Longman printed 1,000 copies of *Conversations upon Chronology and History* by Jane Webb (later Loudon) in 1830, but remaindered the last 353 copies in 1836, leaving the work with a loss of £36. Just over 300 copies of the *Conversations on Animal Economy, by a Physician* (1827) were also remaindered in 1836, but it had at least been in profit (just) since 1830.[62] Marcet's name on the title page clearly helped, and her *Conversations on Vegetable Physiology* (1829) managed to sell three editions, but even Marcet was beginning to move away from the format, and was increasingly writing books specifically for young children.

So far, we have considered books which were popular with publishers, but we also need to examine what, if anything, this tells us about their readers. Sales of children's books are not an obvious indication of popularity among readers, since most children's books are bought by their parents or guardians. Continuing sales of children's books do not tell us whether children would have chosen to read those books. However, they do tell us that certain adults chose the books (admittedly, from the selection offered by publishers), and wanted their children to read them. Presumably, the adults must have acquired a positive impression of the book, whether from reviews, from personal recommendations or from memories of their own childhood reading. Continuing sales of classic children's books in the 1870s might indicate not so much popularity with the children of the 1870s as popularity with their parents, the children of the 1840s.

Thus the decline in sales of *Evenings at Home* in the 1880s and 1890s could indicate a decline in favour among children 30 years earlier, when the book-buying parents of the 1880s and 1890s had been child readers themselves. Their subsequent unwillingness to buy *Evenings at Home* for their own children suggests that it had not made such a strong impression on them as it had on their parents. Given the new developments in children's books that were happening at this time, this is hardly surprising. By the 1850s, there were more children's science books available, they looked more attractive, they were more precisely targeted at their readers, and they made greater efforts to be entertaining. Even in a recently revised edition, a work like *Evenings at Home* was up against stiff competition. By the time the children of the 1850s had children of their own, this was even more the case, and any adult who

---

61 See the listing for the title 'Conversations...' in the relevant volume of Low (ed.), *The English Catalogue of Books*.

62 Longman division ledgers, A1 285; A1 285; A4 63; and A4 65. Longman Archives.

was conscious of the rapid contemporary developments in the sciences would have realised that a 1790s book would now be extremely old-fashioned. This suggests that Routledge's success with *Evenings at Home* in the 1850s and 1860s was assisted by parents' fond memories from the 1820s and 1830s outweighing the temptations of newer books (and not just his lower prices).[63]

The Later Nineteenth Century

Few other children's science books lasted as long as *Evenings at Home*. Joyce's *Scientific Dialogues* was in print for at least 68 years.[64] Marcet's *Conversations on Chemistry* remained in print for 47 years, and her *Conversations on Natural Philosophy* for 39 years. Arabella Buckley's *Fairy-land of Science* (1879) is usually regarded as a late nineteenth-century classic, but it too managed no more than 40 years. It was increasingly difficult for any children's science book published in the second half of the century to achieve long-running sales, due to growing competition and the rapid pace of change in the sciences. This final section considers the changes which affected children's science books in the later nineteenth century, and the extent to which they were related to broader changes happening in children's literature in general.

Among the most obvious of the later developments were the new techniques for decorative bindings and colour printing. Like all children's books, science books benefited from a more attractive appearance.[65] It is less clear whether such improvements affected the instructional quality of science books, partly because line diagrams could already be adequately reproduced using wood engravings, but more importantly because colour plates were still expensive enough to be used sparingly, and thus tended to be seen as decorative extras, rather than as providing crucial explanations. Routledge's reward book editions of *Evenings at Home* had colour plates, but they were used to illustrate the activities of the characters in the conversation, not, for example, to elucidate the features of the particular flower under discussion.

The heyday of the conversational format was over by the mid century. It was still used occasionally, as in Agnes Giberne's *Among the Stars* (1885), but it was accompanied by a much more convincing fictional story. Third-person narrative had become the standard, but the avuncular narrator, who recounted all the wonders he had seen in Peter Parley style, was also passé. Writers still had to deal with the issue of creating excitement and staving off boredom, and one possible solution can be seen in Buckley's conceit of explaining the laws of nature in the language of fairies in her *Fairy-land of Science* (1879), an enterprise which indicates the imaginative effort that was being put into ensuring that instruction was entertaining. Equally, John

---

63   This also fits with the fact that much of the surviving evidence of reading for *Evenings at Home* comes from accounts of those who were children in the 1820s.

64   The last edition appears to be from 1868.

65   On technological developments, see Philip Gaskell, *A New Introduction to Bibliography* (Oxford: Clarendon, 1972); Michael Twyman, *Printing 1770–1970: An Illustrated History of its Development and Uses in England* (London: British Library, 1999).

Henry Pepper's use of exciting experiments in his *Boy's Playbook of Science* (1860) was part of an effort to keep his readers interested, as well as continuing the old emphasis on learning through practical involvement. His book included experiments with household objects such as glass jars or umbrellas to explain basic principles of science. Admittedly, it also included plenty of experiments which would have been more difficult to carry out in the home, but the emphasis on learning through practical demonstration was clear.

Children's books became more differentiated in the late nineteenth century, and this happened to science books as well. The majority were still intended for the children of middle-class families, for such families had disposable income to spend on their children, and the children had the literacy, educational background and leisure time to read such books. However, there was greater differentiation by age, particularly from the mid century onwards, as writers produced books with differing levels of language skills, technical difficulty and, importantly, numbers of pages. *Evenings at Home* had been aimed at seven to ten year olds, but its language would seem advanced for a modern ten year old. Pepper's *Boy's Playbook* was clearly aimed at teenagers, while the RTS continued to produce works for those just learning to read. The majority of early children's science books seem to have been aimed at readers of both sexes, but Pepper's title makes clear that he was aiming at a male audience, as did the Rev. John George Wood with his *Boy's Own Book of Natural History* (1861). This is in keeping with the generally increased gendering of children's literature that resulted in different school stories for girls and boys, as well as family stories for girls and adventure stories for boys. Yet, there were few girls' books of science, which is presumably a reflection of the increasingly masculine image of contemporary experimental science.

A particular problem for children's science writers was that the language of science was becoming increasingly complex by the second half of the century. This was the problem which Buckley's fairies were intended to solve. The various disciplines were becoming more specialised, and each was developing its own vocabulary of technical terms. One consequence was that it was more difficult for writers to be knowledgeable on the latest thinking across a full range of the sciences. This might not matter in books for five year olds, but it would in books for teenagers. Another issue arising was that science books were growing out of date more quickly: there were new discoveries to be added (such as the discovery of Neptune, and the many tiny 'planets' of the asteroid belt, which had to be inserted into astronomy books in the late 1840s and 1850s), and there were also new words to be used for existing knowledge. Fortunately, the demand for popular science books – for adults and children – had produced a horde of writers, making it far easier to get new books on the sciences written than it had been at the start of the century.[66] The importance attached to children's books may be gauged from the fact that several writers who usually wrote for adults turned their hand, at least occasionally, to children's books;

---

66 On late nineteenth-century popular science, see Bernard Lightman, *Victorian Popularizers of Science: Designing Nature for New Audiences* (Chicago: University of Chicago Press, 2007).

the astronomer Robert S. Ball, for instance, wrote *Star-land: Being Talks with Young People About the Wonders of the Heavens* (1889).

Although the writings of scientific experts became increasingly secularised over the course of the nineteenth century, popular writings – for children and adults – generally continued to operate within a religious framework.[67] The way in which religion was introduced, however, became more subtle, as in Margaret Gatty's *Parables from Nature* (1855).[68] For older children, it might even be acceptable to limit the discussion of religion to the preface, as did the Rev. John George Wood's *Boy's Own Book of Natural History* (1861), and Mary and Elizabeth Kirby's *Stories About Birds of Land and Water* (1873). Nevertheless, while fears of secular science bringing down the establishment had diminished, parents clearly remained concerned for the eternal future of their children. Religious publishing organisations such as the Religious Tract Society and the Society for Promoting Christian Knowledge continued to produce children's books on a wide range of subjects, including the sciences, and received solid support from parents and schools. The imprints of these organisations offered guardians a guarantee of safe, trustworthy knowledge, at a time when the literary marketplace was expanding, and it was virtually impossible to check the religious credentials of all the writers of books on the sciences. Their success, like that of Gatty's five series of *Parables from Nature*, shows that religion was far from dead in children's science books.

Conclusions: What Was 'Popular'?

It is much easier to find evidence about publishers than about actual readers. Publishers' catalogues and archives reveal a great deal about the works which were intended to reach wide audiences, and sometimes provide the opportunity for quantitative comparisons about total numbers of sales. We do not have that quantitative element for the RTS works, yet from their format and from the Society's typical mode of operation, we can be sure that some of those works reached audiences in the tens of thousands. The works which were printed and reprinted – the classics and the brands – also tell us a great deal about the sorts of projects which publishers were willing to take on, and which they thought would sell. Thus we have a different idea of 'popularity', as the works which publishers themselves wanted to reprint or imitate.

It is much more difficult to move from this sort of analysis to a discussion of actual child readers. The fact that publishers kept reprinting implies that someone was buying all these copies, but we have to assume that these were adults. Extrapolating from these to the experiences of their children is difficult, but we may learn something about their own experiences as children, 20 or 30 years earlier, although we must remember that their recollections may have become rose-tinted over the years, and that their choices may be more about what they think their children ought to read, than what they might enjoy. Without more evidence from childhood letters

---

67 On religion in adult works, see Bernard Lightman, 'The Visual Theology of Victorian Popularizers of Science: From Reverent Eye to Chemical Retina', *Isis* 91 (2000), 651–80.

68 Suzanne LeMay-Sheffield, 'Introduction' to Margaret Gatty, *Parables from Nature* (London: Bell, 1855, repr. Bristol: Thoemmes Press, 2003).

or diaries, it is extremely difficult to decide whether Thackeray was right to claim that children's science books were regarded as hateful medicine. We can, however, be confident that some of them were very widely read.

Chapter 12

Popular Education and Big Money: Mee, Hammerton and Northcliffe

Gillian Avery

'Both Arthur Mee and I', wrote Sir John Hammerton, 'have given the best of our lives, and I should hope without a shadow of regret, to the service of Alfred Harmsworth.'[1] Better known as Lord Northcliffe, the title he acquired in 1905, Harmsworth was the most frenetic of all press lords, a man who 'lived at a speed bewildering and, on the whole repugnant to most people'.[2] Even Lord Copper, the fictional press baron from Evelyn Waugh's *Scoop* (1938), was pallid in comparison. In his frequent accounts of his and Mee's careers at Carmelite House, Harmsworth's headquarters, Hammerton was always restrained about Northcliffe. It was only in his own memoirs that he admitted that both he and Mee, when they were still provincial journalists in Nottingham, had shared 'a strong anti-Harmsworth bias', and swore they would never work for him. Such scruples somehow evaporated. In 1905 first Mee and then Hammerton joined the vast staff of the Amalgamated Press, presided over by 'the Chief'. Hammerton was to stay for 17 years; Mee until his death in 1943.

They must have been the best investments Northcliffe ever made, star performers who reaped record-breaking profits for the firm. Mee's greatest contribution was the *Children's Encyclopedia*, which Hammerton called an inexhaustible source of income for the firm, though he also compiled and edited other notable Harmsworth ventures in popular education. Hammerton, described in the *Oxford Dictionary of National Biography* as 'The most successful creator of large-scale works of reference that Britain has known', was proudest of his *Harmsworth's Universal Encyclopedia.*[3] Issued in fortnightly parts from 1920 until 1922, it sold 12 million copies throughout the English-speaking world and was translated into six languages. He also edited compilations of 'wonders' in most subjects (a very popular selling line in the early decades of the twentieth century), other encyclopedias, war books, memoirs and gazetteers – one of his few commercial failures was *The World's Great Books in Outline*, in which, with Mee, he reduced about a thousand books to six volumes, published in fortnightly parts. In addition, Hammerton's memoir of Mee, *Child of Wonder* (1946), is almost the only firsthand account that we have of his life and work.

---

1 John A. Hammerton, *With Northcliffe in Fleet Street* (London: Hutchinson, 1932), p. 117.

2 A.P. Ryan, *Lord Northcliffe* (London: Collins, 1953), p. 7.

3 Bridget Hadaway, 'Hammerton, Sir John Alexander (1871–1949)', in *Oxford Dictionary of National Biography*, Oxford University Press, 2004, <http://www.oxforddnb.com/view/article/37505> (accessed 1 June 2007).

The extraordinary success of both men stemmed from Northcliffe's flair for spotting talent and finding the right use for it. In the obituary of his chief in the *Children's Newspaper* on 26 August 1922, Mee said, thinking of his own beginnings:

> He would give a man a thousand a year [roughly equivalent to £40,000 in modern money] to sit and wait until something turned up, and if the man grew tired of drawing his thousand for nothing, he would smile and say 'What is a thousand a year compared with what you are going to do some day?' He waited his time, and in the end began that long run of educational journalism which brings in the Children's Encyclopedia and the Children's Newspaper, two of the supreme successes of the journalism he had brought to life and being.

Though discreetly in the third person, it was one of Mee's very rare personal recollections, as was, in the same obituary, his memory of Northcliffe coming into a room and finding 'an editor upset by a sad mistake', and fretting that his paper was doomed because of it. '"I have made many mistakes, and shall make some more," [Northcliffe] would say, giving his little editor a hug to comfort him.' This is a genial glimpse of a man of whom Hammerton doubted 'if any spectres of those weaker individuals who broke under his criticisms ever haunted his memory', and of whom the old *Dictionary of National Biography* said, 'The driving-power which he displayed in his own business was better adapted to dictatorship than to team-work'.[4] This was written by Geoffrey Dawson, who had resigned as editor of *The Times* because he felt that Northcliffe's interference had threatened the paper's independence. Mee in his obituary confirmed that there were millions of people who never agreed with Northcliffe, and very few who always agreed with him.

Hammerton, if we are to believe his various accounts of life with Northcliffe, would face up to the man and answer back. Mee left no recollections; all we know of his personal life is from Hammerton's very sketchy biography. He was small and frail, but indomitable when it came to defending his ideas. The battle that he had with the Harmsworth brothers over the *Children's Encyclopedia* is sufficient proof of that. Otherwise we must gauge his personality from his educational writing. Many of his enthusiasms, particularly those shown in the *Children's Newspaper*, were the same as Northcliffe's – the belief in the British Empire, the passionate excitement about modern inventions, the love of the English countryside (which the young Alfred Harmsworth had explored on marathon bicycle journeys). It was unlikely that the latter exerted much control over the contents of the paper, which was founded only three years before his death. It is much more likely that Mee, in the years that he worked for Northcliffe, had – perhaps unconsciously – made "the Chief's" interests his own.

Harmsworth's career, as it affected the two others, should be briefly summarised. Alfred Harmsworth (1865–1922) had left school at 15 to help support his mother and nine younger siblings. He was a few years older than Hammerton (born 1871) and Mee (born 1875). All three were self-made, self-educated men. Mee, the second son of a Nottingham railway worker's ten children, went to work on the *Nottingham Evening Post* when he was 14, and educated himself from the books at the Nottingham

---

4 Hammerton, *With Northcliffe*, p. 48.

Mechanics' Institute. 'Sandy' Hammerton's father had died when he was three. He too left school at 14, and, always hungry for education, went to evening classes, read voraciously, and taught himself shorthand. From a more prosperous background, Harmsworth, like the other two, had at an early age settled on journalism as a career. He rejected opportunities of further formal education, and by 1882 was supporting himself and the family with freelance writing. One of the firms for whom he wrote was Cassell, and Cassell's famous *Popular Educator*, published in penny parts during 1852 (and from which Hammerton acquired much of his learning), was to influence many Harmsworth educational publications, including the *Children's Encyclopedia*. In 1887 he set up his own publishing company, issuing periodicals of which the most famous was *Answers*, a 16-page penny weekly, founded in 1888, which aimed to compete with the Newnes *Tit-bits*, and from which the *Children's Newspaper* (1919–65) was to inherit certain characteristics. It was a spectacular success, and within five years achieved a circulation of a million copies a week. *Answers* was followed by *Comic Cuts*, and papers for girls, for boys, for women, for Sunday reading, and many more. All of these, then, catered for lower middle-class readers. By 1894 he had secured control of the *Evening News*; 1896 saw the first number of the *Daily Mail* and the move to Carmelite House in Carmelite Street, London, EC4, just south of Fleet Street. In 1900 the Amalgamated Press was formed with capital of £1,300,000. Hammerton described the Amalgamated Press thus:

> Far more romantic in its growth and development than even the *Daily Mail*, associated with all his earlier and dearest successes it had become the greatest publishing concern in the world, in whose works a different periodical went to press every twenty minutes of the working day, their aggregate weekly circulations being something like ten million copies.[5]

Lord Salisbury maintained that Harmsworth's papers were written by office boys for office boys, but A.J. Spender, editor of the *Westminster Gazette*, said that he and his imitators influenced the common man more than all the education ministers put together. Northcliffe founded the *Daily Mirror* in 1903, and received a peerage in 1905. (It was averred by some of his staff that he chose the title Northcliffe so that he could emboss a Napoleonic N on his china and silver.) He became chief proprietor of the *Times* in 1908. In 1921 he celebrated the silver jubilee of the *Daily Mail* with a lunch party for 7,000 of his staff – in Olympia, the only building in London large enough to hold them. He died insane in 1922 – one of his last actions was to take a revolver from under his pillow and, shouting 'One of Lloyd George's bloody knights!' he tried to shoot the physician sent to him by that Prime Minister. Lord Beaverbrook (who recorded this finale) said that the Northcliffe domination of newspaper sales was unparalleled, and that at the time of his death he controlled half the daily papers sold in London.[6] There was an imposing funeral service in Westminster Abbey.

---

5 Ibid., p. 178.
6 Lord Beaverbrook (William Maxwell Aitken), *Men and Power, 1917–1918* (London: Hutchinson, 1956), p. 59.

The careers of Mee and Hammerton would have been impossible without the backing of the Harmsworth empire – a fact which Hammerton perhaps did not sufficiently realise. It was a symbiotic relationship in which all made big money but inevitably the Amalgamated Press made the most. Hammerton ruefully regretted his and Mee's naivety in money matters. He recalled that in 1905, when they came back from the interview which had resulted in a job for Hammerton, Mrs Hammerton was gleefully told that they had been 'making Sandy's fortune'. 'Perhaps it will illustrate how little adapted to the mentality of "big business" either Arthur Mee or I was [that] he and I looked on a modest £10,000 as a fortune.' A few pages later he remarked that while neither of them had any regrets, they had lost 'perhaps half a million of money, which might easily have been amassed had we cared jointly to capitalise our brains and our energies by turning these into a commercial concern'.[7]

There was a fourth man who at about this time could also have made a fortune from educational writing, but whose gentlemanly instincts forbade him to discuss money. This was Robert Stephenson Baden-Powell, who, dismayed by the 'loafers' and 'wasters' among working-class youth, had launched his Boy Scout Movement in 1908, seeking 'to turn the rising generation on the right road for good citizenship'.[8] *Scouting for Boys*, first published in fortnightly parts, and then in book form in 1908 by Northcliffe's rival, Arthur Pearson (who Joseph Chamberlain claimed was the greatest hustler he had ever known), was reprinted four times during its first year, and has been described by a Baden-Powell biographer as 'one of the steadiest best-sellers in the history of publishing'.[9] This romantic effort to regenerate urban youth through woodcraft, camping and open-air life, now a historical curiosity, was obligatory reading for scouts and guides for at least half a century. Baden-Powell hesitated to benefit financially from something that he felt was a patriotic duty, but Pearson had no such scruples, and *Scouting for Boys* and the official periodical of the movement, the *Scout*, were among his greatest business successes.

Harmsworth secured the best and brightest talent by paying his journalists phenomenally high wages. Whatever Hammerton's afterthoughts may have been, £10,000 was, for a man still in his early thirties, indeed a fortune in 1905. The day he signed on at Carmelite House he met a friend who said 'My dear Hammerton, believe me these salaries are chimerical . . . They can't go on paying them.' Mee, in his first year with the firm, aged 30, bought a large house in Kent with five acres of garden, including croquet lawn, tennis court, vinery, peach house, conservatory, palm house and stabling for five horses. He added a lake and an aviary for 200 birds. He was in no way a pretentious man, but he enjoyed living in style, and Harmsworth provided him with the means of doing so. Hammerton recalled that there was boundless scope then under the Harmsworth shield for people with ideas and the capacity to give them form. 'It was the most ordinary occurrence for a sub-editor earning three or four pounds a week suddenly to find his weekly income swollen to £20 or more as

---

7   John A. Hammerton, *Books and Myself* (London: MacDonald, 1944), p. 175.

8   R.S. Baden-Powell, 'Boy Scouts: A Suggestion', quoted in Tim Jeal, *Baden-Powell* (London: Hutchinson, 1989), p. 382.

9   Jeal, *Baden-Powell*, p. 396.

the editor of a new and successful penny paper on which he was paid one shilling for every thousand copies sold.'[10]

What one must marvel at now is the sheer output in words of both Hammerton and Mee. Other writers were of course employed in the big reference works, but certainly in all that bear Mee's name, the style is so homogeneous in its radiant idealism and so inimitably his that he must have reshaped most contributions, and at a conservative estimate may have written 50 million words by the end of his life. (John Derry, his first editor at Nottingham, reckoned that in his pre-Harmsworth days on the *Black and White* he set up a Fleet Street record by writing a million words a year. Added to speed, Derry said, was the advantage of 'a memory without leakages'.)[11] They were not only highly skilled editors; they had the ideas that brought in the money. Northcliffe indeed told Hammerton that Mee's 'fecundity in new ideas amounted almost to genius'.[12] But Hammerton considered that he himself had the more practical mind: 'I was constantly . . . turning quite attractive but barely workable ideas into practical possibilities', he boasted.[13]

The two men had been close friends since 1895, when they were both working for the *Nottingham Express*. Hammerton described how Mee could get through the editing while writing articles for *Tit-bits* or some other London journal – often making £20 a week from this moonlighting. Mee was also accumulating the press cuttings on which so many of his educational publications were to be based. As Hammerton was later to put it:

> Arthur had little use for the purely literary subjects, but unlimited need for every scrap of general information his daily examination of the press might yield. His collection, begun in Nottingham, eventually grew to such dimensions that a huge cabinet of many drawers had to be made to accommodate his hundreds of thousands of press cuttings, all neatly arranged in many thousands of specially designed envelopes. His ever-ready cabinet of information on every conceivable subject was insured for years at a thousand pounds, which was a gross undervaluation of its worth to him. With this, even in its earlier state, he could meet any demand made upon him as a free-lance, and no wonder was it that he never failed to impress with the universality of his knowledge.[14]

In 1896, Mee left the provinces to work in London, first with *Tit-bits*, then moving to the *Morning Herald*, and then to editing *Black and White*, a pictorial magazine notorious for its rapid turnover in editors. Mee stayed for two years – held to be a record – before he was finally turned out. By this stage Hammerton had joined him in London, and it was he who suggested the next idea – a weekly to be called *Who's Who This Week*, to compete with a similar paper published by C. Arthur Pearson's firm. Unfortunately the friend who had offered to help market the dummy

---

10 Hammerton, *Books and Myself*, p. 175.

11 Obituary by John Derry, *Children's Newspaper*, 12 June 1943.

12 Hammerton, *With Northcliffe*, p. 164. Northcliffe also called him, according to Hammerton, 'a narrow-minded little Nottingham nonconformist', and soon after hiring him sent him on a six-week holiday to Egypt to extend his horizons.

13 Ibid., p. 176.

14 John A. Hammerton, *Child of Wonder* (London: MacDonald, 1946), p. 83.

prepared by Mee took it to Pearson, who naturally rejected it. There was no one else to send it to but Harmsworth. 'Thus began an association', wrote Hammerton, 'which was to prove highly profitable to the "Napoleon of the Press", to Arthur, and not unprofitable to myself.'[15] That particular project never in fact materialised. Harmsworth only used it as an excuse for getting an extraordinarily bright young journalist onto his staff; he made Mee literary editor of the *Daily Mail*. 'It was thus', said Hammerton, whose prose style could be as lush as Mee's, 'that he was caught up in the Harmsworth web in which he has ever since remained a more or less willing prisoner.'[16] A month later Hammerton also took the Carmelite vows, as he termed it, renouncing past scruples.

The fact that it was Mee and not Hammerton who was to gravitate towards writing for the young seems to have been a fluke. He once said 'I know nothing about children', which did not surprise Hammerton, who saw him as a perpetual child. Hammerton, on the other hand, had been involved with several children's periodicals when he was working for the firm of S.W. Partridge in his early months in London. In fact in 1903 W.T. Stead had proposed a journal to be called the 'Children's Weekly', which would have had some of the same features as Mee's *Children's Newspaper* was to adopt 16 years later. But Hammerton had shown no enthusiasm, nor had Partridge, who was expected to publish it, and the project was dropped.

In 1905 neither Mee nor Hammerton was thinking of children. But 'the Chief' was into encyclopedias, as Hammerton remembered when Harmsworth first interviewed him:

> 'Do you realize', said Alfred . . . 'that Hooper and Jackson have spent about a hundred thousand pounds in making the British public conscious of one word, and that word is encyclopedia?' [This was the *Encyclopaedia Britannica*, bought in 1901 by Horace Hooper, an American bookseller and promoted by Walter Jackson.] I did. 'Well, I want you to cash in on that one word by producing a monthly magazine to be called The Monthly Encyclopedia. You see the idea: every encyclopedia must be kept up to date, and this monthly encyclopedia will do the trick.'[17]

This *Scoop*-like exchange apparently really took place. It is not surprising that the burlesques by C.L. Graves and E.V. Lucas appearing in *Punch* at this time were held by Carmelite House employees to be eerily near the truth. Hammerton quoted one of them, which had presumably been inspired by the appearance of the first instalment of *The World's Great Books in Outline*:

> *H.L.* [His Lordship]. Oh, Arthur Mee. Aren't you one of my editors?
> *A.E.* [Amalgamated Editor]. I hope so.
> *H.L.* Listen then. I've got a really good idea for you. Something really novel. ...
>   What do you say to a new periodical in which we give a brief concentrated
>   version of the 1,000 best books? There are 1,000, aren't there?

---

15 Hammerton, *Books and Myself*, p. 171.
16 Hammerton, *With Northcliffe*, p. 124.
17 Hammerton, *Books and Myself*, p. 174.

A.E. Of course. I'll get Hammerton to make a list of them.

H.L. Who's Hammerton?

A.E. He's in the office too.

H.L. Dear me, is he? I really must keep a 'Where is it.' Well, you boil them down and bring the whole thing out in periodical parts, and there you are.

A.E. Splendid. But will the public like it?

H.L. They will if we tell them often enough that full length is a bore, and that they can get a reputation for culture on our tabloids. I'll see to that: you get on with the boiling.[18]

Though Hammerton admitted that *The World's Great Books*, conscientiously reduced by himself and Mee, was a dismal flop, it did leave the drawing-board, and came out in some 50 fortnightly parts. But the 'Monthly Encyclopedia' came to nothing, a most impracticable scheme, he said, which would have been a dire failure if ever it got as far as the bookstalls.

Perhaps this was why he was so doubtful about Mee's idea in 1907 for a children's encyclopedia. As editor, Mee had been largely responsible for the great success of the *Harmsworth Self-Educator*, published in parts the previous year. 'The way in which the public of 1906 removed the Educator from the bookstalls as quickly as a new pile appeared was even more remarkable than their appetite had been for the Encyclopedia,' wrote Hammerton. 'The name of Arthur Mee was now made familiar to millions on the huge posters which were used to advertise the work.'[19] This had been the Chief's own idea, but it was followed up with one of Arthur Mee's – an adaptation of Hans Ferdinand Helmolt's *World History*, a translation of which had been brought out by Heinemann 1901–7. Mee visualised it as the *Harmsworth History of the World*, the original text augmented with articles by English scholars, and enhanced with an unprecedented number of pictures. It was to be brought out in fortnightly parts at a price of seven pence, from which Heinemann would be paid half a penny per copy. Only Mee's persistence and enthusiasm carried this through: the Chief and his brother Harold both had cold feet, and Heinemann was very dubious. The toss of a coin, said Hammerton, eventually decided their going ahead. But Heinemann made £20,000 out of it, and Hammerton supposed that the Amalgamated Press's profits were 'little short of £80,000'.[20]

After the *Harmsworth History* came the *Children's Encyclopedia*. Hammerton, as has been said, was discouraging: 'I could not see the children of England clamouring at their parents' knee for anything with so forbidding a name.' Besides, it was not going to be an encyclopedia as was generally understood; more a collection of books for children, arbitrarily grouped and published in parts. But, recalled Hammerton, Mee 'was so obsessed by the idea of providing for the young people of his time a book which would bring to them all the essentials of useful, scientific, and practical

---

18 'On the Telephone', quoted in Hammerton, *With Northcliffe*, p. 186.

19 Hammerton, *Child of Wonder*, p. 98.

20 Hammerton, *With Northcliffe*, p. 168.

knowledge, and also the endless entertainment that books would convey, that he would listen to nobody's criticism'.[21]

The urgent need at Carmelite house at that time was something large-scale to use the huge infrastructure set up to produce and market the *Harmsworth History*. But, like Hammerton, the Harmsworth brothers (Harold was the firm's financial advisor) had grave doubts about a children's encyclopedia. However Mee produced his own compelling advertising copy, argued, persisted and won. The first fortnightly part, priced at seven pence, came out on 17 March 1908, the last on 1 February 1910. Well before that, though, the Educational Book Company (EBC), a subsidiary of the Amalgamated Press, began issuing it in volume form. By the time Hammerton was writing his life of Mee in 1946, 26 large editions had been published and for over 20 years the EBC sold few other works. 'I calculate that their total sales to date throughout the Empire in terms of volumes amount to 5,380,000,' wrote Hammerton, 'and this, considering that each volume is sold at an average price of about fifteen shillings, means business beyond the dreams of most book-publishing firms in Britain.'[22] Even in 1910 Northcliffe had realised what a goldmine the work was, and wrote from Paris to warn Mee, who had expressed an interest in playing a part in local government, to keep his eye on the ball. 'Few men in England have such power in their hands as you . . . The fact that you are part of a vast machine hardly ever affects your surroundings. Yet you must remember that, for good or ill, you are part of that machine . . . With much affection, Your devoted Chief.'[23]

There were also substantial foreign sales. Walter M. Jackson, the astute American publisher who, with Horace Hooper, had turned the *Encyclopaedia Britannica* into a bestseller, in 1910 produced an American edition, renamed *The Book of Knowledge*. Thirty-five years later, he claimed that three and a half million sets had been sold. Branch offices were set up in all the chief American cities, with three separate printing and binding plants employed solely on this one work. There were French, Spanish, Portuguese and Italian editions, and it was also translated into Chinese and Arabic.

Arthur Mee addressed 'Boys and Girls Everywhere' in the preface to the first issue. It was, he told them, 'A Big Book for Little People, and it has come into the world to make your life happy and wise and good' (p. 1). It seems to have been the first time he had written for children, and the style that he evolved then was carried into his editorials for the *Children's Newspaper* 11 years later. He told his readers how the encyclopedia had come into being. There was once a lonely little girl (his daughter Marjorie, in fact) who 'would talk to the fairies in the trees, or beg Robin Redbreast to come down and be friends'. As she grew older, he continued,

> there came into her mind the great wonder of the Earth. What does the world mean? And why am I here? Where are all the people who have been and gone? Where does the rose come from? Who holds the stars up there? What is it that seems to talk to me when the world is dark and still? So the questions would come until the mother of the little maid

---

21 Hammerton, *Child of Wonder*, p. 112.

22 Ibid., p. 124.

23 Reginald Pound and Geoffrey Harmsworth, *Northcliffe* (London: Cassell, 1959), p. 398.

was more puzzled than the little maid herself. And as the questions came, when the mother had thought and thought, and answered this and answered that until she could answer no more, she cried out for a book: 'Oh for a book that will answer all the questions!' And this is the book she cried for. (p. 1)

'It is not an Alphabet of Facts,' said Mee, two pages further on. 'Admirable as that is for a busy man, it is useless torture for a child.' The book presented instead a simple scheme of universal knowledge. 'It seeks to stir the mind and awaken the sense of wonder born in every child' (p. 3). Wonder played a very large part in it; so did optimism, the history section being subtitled 'The March of Man from the Age of Barbarism to the League of Nations'. The opening preamble that launched the publication epitomises the Mee described by Hammerton in his obituary as 'a child of wonder moving through a world of endless surprise to his questing mind, the keen edge of his interest and joy in life never blunted'.[24] 'I give you the beauty of the Earth in the golden hour of dawn,' it begins, and so on through three ecstatic pages with a toast in every paragraph to the glories of nature, the passing of the seasons, the joys of life, rising to a climax when he evokes 'the Past with its heritage of good and ill, the Present with the opportunity that knows no bound, the Future with the years that never end and know no sorrow ... I give you the yearning and craving that make life sweet.' (Overwhelmed by his own rhetoric at moments like these, he was apt to lose the sense of what he was saying.)

Each part contained 19 different chapters – designated as 'groups': Earth and its Neighbours ('the story of the boundless universe and all its wondrous worlds'), Men and Women ('the story of immortal folk whose work will never die'), Stories, Animal Life, History, Familiar Things ('the story of the things we see about us every day'), Wonder ('plain answers to the questions of the children of the world'), Art, Ourselves ('the wonderful house we live in, and our place in the world'), Plant Life, Countries, Picture Atlas, Power ('the story of where power comes from, what it does, and how it works'), Literature, Ideas, The Bible, Things to Make and Do, and School Lessons. This last section, subtitled 'simple learning made easy for very little people', which gave kindergarten instruction in reading, writing, arithmetic, music, drawing and French, has echoes of *Cassell's Popular Educator* of 66 years before, from which Thomas Hardy had taught himself German, and other Victorians had learnt English grammar, French and Latin. It always seemed out of place, and these elementary lessons were dropped halfway through publication; only conversational French was retained.

The encyclopedia was lavishly illustrated. In the Art section, all jumbled up side by side, were reproductions of the great buildings of the world, sculpture (decently veiled when it came to the naked torso), paintings, the Bayeux tapestry (all of it), ivories, illuminated manuscripts, Byzantine mosaics, so that it was hard for any encyclopedia owner to escape knowing what the Victory of Samothrace looked like, or the Taj Mahal, or the Primavera, or Santa Sophia. (Mee's collection of photographs of the art of all nations was thought by John Derry to have been one of the best in

---

24 *Children's Newspaper* (12 June 1943). Hammerton had said elsewhere that great tracts of Mee's writing, with the occasional alteration of a word of two, could be shaped into sermons (Hammerton, *Child of Wonder*, p. 25).

the world.) Besides these were the unforgettable pictorial recreations of history –
Shakespeare reading to Anne Hathaway, Sir Philip Sidney giving up his water bottle
at Zutphen, William Harvey explaining the circulation of the blood to Charles I, the
child Handel discovered playing his clavichord in a garret. There were also picture
maps, which might show things as various as how the word 'mother' was spoken
in different countries, the distribution of animals and crops or 'the stirring past
of Palestine'.

The poems jostled each other in a random way, so that you might find William
Blake beside a ballad such as 'Annie Laurie', and Felicia Hemans beside Christopher
Marlowe, but good predominated, and the literature section ('the imperishable
thoughts of men enshrined in the books of the world') did not baulk at quoting long
passages from the *Canterbury Tales* in its original Middle English, or following an
account of Shakespeare's sonnets by printing 12 of them. There were also nursery
rhymes for the youngest. The story section was wide-ranging, with retellings of
legends and heroic deeds from many countries.[25] There was a lot about heroes –
Joan of Arc was a particular favourite – and about inventors and explorers, though
writers, artists and musicians all had their place. The Wonder section gave answers
to 'What is the deepest hole in the earth?', 'Why is Granny's hair grey?' and 'Why
can we not fly like birds?' 'Things to Make and Do' was one of the mostly fondly-
remembered sections. It not only gave instructions on how to be a ventriloquist,
how to make a telephone using two beef bladders and how to find your way in a
forest, but also girls could make sweets, 'a dainty blotter', 'a hair tidy for next to
nothing', or were instructed in how to make a fiddle from a cigar box. It included
useful tips on the right way to clean things, to dry wet boots (you fill them with oats),
to get out a splinter (with a pen nib), as well as tricks and jokes and problems in
mental arithmetic.

Though the last volume had an index, the work as a whole was not for reference
but for reading, and the young reader who grazed through its pages unconsciously
absorbed a vast amount of information and culture – as well as Mee's personal ethic.
This was largely lost when it was reissued as *The Children's Treasure-House* in 1926,
with the text re-arranged so that each subject had a separate volume. No children's
encyclopedia has been so loved, or indeed has had such a long life. Writing in 1946,
three years after Mee's death, Hammerton regarded it as imperishable:

> To designate the Children's Encyclopedia as the wonder-book of the twentieth century in
> the history of book-publishing would be no exaggeration . . . It is beyond all computation
> the modern classic of the children's world: a quarry in which his numerous imitators have
> dug for ideas. And as it is almost forty years since it began publication and has been selling
> almost continuously ever since, despite two world wars . . . its life force would seem to be
> strong enough to withstand whatever shocks of circumstance are in store for it . . . It has
> been the greatest force in all the world for enlightening the children of two generations,
> and it will continue to exercise that function for some generations to come.[26]

---

25 Mee was probably not involved in the choice of these; Hammerton said that he viewed
fiction with contempt. Hammerton, *Child of Wonder*, p. 33.

26 Ibid., pp. 121–2.

In this he was overoptimistic; even in the 1940s the Mee approach was beginning to seem old-fashioned, and by 1949 a very different sort of encyclopedia began publication, clearly designed as a corrective. This was the *Oxford Junior Encyclopaedia*, edited by Laura Salt and Robert Sinclair and published by the Oxford University Press. The first volume, *Mankind*, was followed by 11 more volumes, each devoted to a different subject. Unlike Mee's encyclopedia, it was entirely factual. The *Children's Encyclopedia*, revamped, was reissued in 1953 and 1964, but its day was over. The critics gave the Oxford production a warm welcome for its scholarship – the articles had all been commissioned from experts – but it was a highbrow venture, and readers never took it to their hearts like the Mee encyclopedia. Its dispassionate approach may have had less appeal for young readers. The illustrations, all chosen with fastidious care by an art historian, lacked the glorious kaleidoscopic randomness of the older work. And of course the editors were careful never to express a point of view.

Mee's personal convictions always stood out – his Christian values, his love of England and devotion to the Empire, his veneration for heroes – from Bede to Beethoven, from Joan of Arc to Kossuth – his humanitarianism, and above all, his enjoyment of the world about him and his excitement about technical progress, which it seemed to him could only better mankind. There was also the great advantage that his encyclopedia did not aim so much at scholarship as at awakening curiosity and interest, at conveying some of his own excitement in the discoveries he had made by himself. For he had little regard for formal education, and in his journalism there are frequent disparaging remarks about the uselessness of what was taught in schools – dates and suchlike. (In the *Children's Newspaper* of 10 April 1926 he was to announce with glee that '1200 men of distinguished scholastic careers are today among life's most complete failures'.) No doubt Mee would have been reassured to know that the life of the Oxford encyclopedia was less than half that of his own creation; after 1971 it was not reissued.

Much of the *Children's Encyclopedia* contents were recycled and reappear in other Mee publications, in for instance his anthologies of one thousand beautiful things, and the same number of famous things, everlasting things and heroes. Like so much of his work, they had a universal appeal, and must have been owned and read by as many adults as children. This could also be said of his series of enthusiastic accounts of the English counties – 'The King's England' – and must surely account for the huge popularity and long life of the *Children's Newspaper*.

This last had its origins in the encyclopedia, which from 1910 had an accompanying monthly periodical. After various experiments with its title it became *My Magazine*, under which name it continued until its demise in 1933. The *Children's Newspaper* described itself as its sister, 'the weekly companion of the best-loved magazine in the world'. Its ancestor was the *Little Paper*, which formed part of the contents of the Wonder-Box, 'an ill-considered idea which Mee said was Northcliffe's, and the latter said was Mee's'.[27] This box, about an inch deep and the dimensions of the *Children's Encyclopedia*, was designed to hold little toys and booklets, and also a miniature eight-page newspaper. It was never a practical proposition, and production

27 Ibid., p. 113.

difficulties ended it after two or three issues in 1910. Just over eight years later the
Children's Newspaper took its place. Published from Fleetway House in Farringdon
street, to which the Amalgamated Press had moved in 1912 (its many departments
housed for the first time under the same roof), the first issue, priced at a penny
halfpenny, appeared on 22 March 1919, designed to 'make goodness news'. As in
the editorial preamble to the *Encyclopedia*, the mood was a rhapsodic one. 'What
a world this is!' exclaimed Mee on the front page of the second issue of 29 March
(the very words of Dickens's Mr Toots, whose own view was that it was a great deal
worse even than Dr Blimber's school).[28] Not so Mee:

> The world is changing fast. Bliss is it in these days, as Wordsworth would have said, to be
> alive, and to be young is very heaven. The Children's Newspaper is young and it will live
> to see and tell the story of wonders yet undreamed. What do these pages tell?

They told that a Channel Tunnel was coming, which would take trains not only all
over Europe, but to Calcutta and beyond. There would be engines that would 'take us
through the clouds, or anywhere we want to go'; there would be radio telephone by
which we could talk to people anywhere. 'It is coming, all this and more. Those who
read the thousandth number of this paper will see it all, with wonders greater yet.' It
was a success from the start. In the second number of 29 March, Mee said proudly:

> Somebody who knows has been working out some figures. It seems that if you took all the
> lines of type in all the copies of the first number of the Children's Newspaper, they would
> reach from London round the world and back to Australia once more; and if you took the
> paper on which it was printed and laid it out flat, a million children could stand on it.

But this was apparently a gross underestimate which he had to correct in the seventh
issue (3 May): the lines of type would go *three* times round the world, and *three*
million children could stand on the paper.

Its huge popularity gave great hopes for 'a new well-informed generation' for the
future, and on 12 April Mee printed the John Addington Symonds hymn which begins,

> These things shall be! A loftier race
> Than e'er the world hath known shall rise
> With flame of freedom in their souls
> And light of knowledge in their eyes.

The contents of the paper changed very little during Mee's editorship, which
ended only with his death in 1943. There were 12 pages, later to be expanded to
16, featuring news items with swiftly moving focuses of interest in the style of
that early Harmsworth paper, *Answers*. There were accounts of remarkable human
achievements, like the 'Red Indian Boy, Houston T. Teehee, Whose Name Appears
on Every American Liberty Bond,' or 'How a Signalman Saved a Train'. And
there were animal stories: 'Snake and Lizard Race: Exciting Chase in a Museum',
or 'Caribou of Canada: Can they be Hunted by Aeroplane?' (for all this Mee's

---

28 See Charles Dickens, *Dombey and Son* (1847–48), ch. 32.

collection of press cuttings was invaluable). The sixth page was a medley which included Mee's editorial. In the second number, its theme was the hardship suffered by miners and their families, who were also featured in an eloquent article on another page, entitled 'The Children of the Cheerless Home and the Men of the Sunless Mine'. Indeed, the paper often spoke up for the underpaid, the deprived and exploited. The editorial page also included Peter Puck wanting to know such things as 'If the Everest Expedition Will Ever Rest', and, tucked in a corner, a prayer. There were many punning jokes and riddles in the *Answers* style ('Housewives are now asking moths what they camphor'). Other pages had nature notes, reviews of books of information (not necessarily written for children), a picture map showing times and seasons and harvests around the world, a serial (usually a boys' adventure story), a page of puzzles, anecdotes and more jokes, with a picture story about 'Jacko', an accident-prone chimpanzee who was still there in the closing number. The last page was pictures, usually of children or animals.

Up until the outbreak of war, Mee had unwavering faith in the League of Nations. It was something, he said in his editorial of 17 May 1919, 'against which pessimism cannot stand'. 'It is the triumph of the man who believes in noble things,' he trumpeted, 'It is the scientific proof that man moves on to a better world.' Indeed, in the first issue he begged for a 'Children's League of Nations', in which children would be educated for peace. They 'should not be taught that a nation's greatest heroes are its soldiers', but should be shown the links that bind one country to another (22 March 1919).

The commentaries on foreign affairs, shrewd and perceptive and always unsigned, were often at odds with the hopes expressed on the editorial page. As early as 5 April 1919, the possible result of the heavy reparations forced upon Germany was foreseen. The rise of Fascism was recorded – the Black Shirt march on Rome in 1922, the Heimwehr march on Vienna in 1929. The front page headline on 1 April 1933, when Hitler had been in power for a little over two months was 'The World in Shadow. Passing Clouds of War', and succeeding articles denounced Hitler's 'malignant and murderous attacks on the Jews' and his suppression of all opposition: 'Mankind is Confronted with the Greatest Tragedy since the Crucifixion', declared the issue of 15 April. Tragedies followed fast after that. 1935 saw Mussolini's invasion of Abyssinia; 1936 the beginning of the Spanish Civil War. In Russia the Bolsheviks were suppressing religion, and the nature of Stalin – about whom the paper had been hopeful in 1926 – was better understood. On 2 April 1938 the paper quoted the Bishop of Chelmsford: Europe had become a more savage place than it had been for a thousand years.

In the light of this it was hard for Mee to be in the celebratory mood that he had so triumphantly forecast for the paper's thousandth number. On 21 May 1938 all he felt able to promise was that there was no dark hour that did not pass away. In 'The Thousand Weeks to Come' he tried to recapture the mood of 1919 by predicting marvellous new inventions – better television, wireless communications, hot water – but 'The Editor's Judgment Day' conceded that it was harder and harder for good to hold its own against the powers of evil, and against inertia. When war finally came, the paper, like all the others, cheered its readers with accounts of the dauntless spirit of the British people, but as he said in his editorial of 3 April 1943 in the last weeks of his life, they were 'years of unutterable strain'. When he died on 27 May the tide had begun to turn and he had been able to write in his 15 May editorial 'we hear in the tramping feet of a victorious army the quickening of the hopes of free men everywhere'. On 22 May, the paper was able to report that it was 'All clear in Africa. One of the five continents is clean again, free from Nazi filth', The posthumous editorial of 29 May was about Empire Day, so much a feature of 1930s and 1940s childhood:

> Look at it, this flag that is three in one, so arranged that all three have equal shares. They stand for a Slave [St Patrick], a Soldier [St George] and an Apostle [St Andrew]. The slave reminds us that we set them free, the soldier that we fight for right, the apostle that we seek a different world from this.

Mee's last editorial was published 15 June. It spoke of the horrors of bombing, but suggested that perhaps it could in the end sweep away war because nothing could endure against it. The same issue contained a tribute to him by Hammerton. The *Children's Encyclopedia*, he said, had been the book of Mee's heart, but 'above all his satisfactions in life was the founding of the *Children's Newspaper*, which he wished to be his monument'.

By the time the paper came to a close on 1 May 1965 its appearance had completely changed. The format was skimpy, there was little information in it, far less text, more pictures. It was now wholly secular, with no mission to educate, trying to boost circulation with a page called Pop Spot (the only good thing Mee had found to say about Hitler was that he had banned 'jazz, swing, hot-numbers' (14 May 1938)). The sports page featured soccer stars. All that remained from 1919 was Jacko the chimpanzee, ever frolicsome. This last issue carried a cursory few lines about Mee by the 1953–61 editor. Hammerton had died in 1949 and there was probably no one left in Fleetway House who remembered the paper's founder. All that the writer could find to say about him was that he had been a brilliant journalist, whose talents and energies were dedicated to children. It was announced that *Look and Learn* was taking over; that too expired in 1982.

The popularity and long life of the *Children's Newspaper* are puzzling. At least one other paper, the *Boys' and Girls' Picture Newspaper*, was started in competition. Launched by Cassell in 1923, it only achieved 63 issues before it folded. It looked remarkably like the older paper, carried the same sort of contents, but with more pictures, and yet it failed. One can only suppose that Mee was the driving force that was missing. But who read the *Children's Newspaper*? Those of us for whom it was bought in the 1930s and 1940s were mostly bored by it, though we loved the *Children's Encyclopedia*. We did not bother to read the news, found the marvels of nature tedious and the jokes even more so. Most of us wanted fiction. Parents no doubt bought it hoping that it would deflect their children from comics. Private schools would have taken it for their pupils. Unlike the original Harmsworth periodicals it was decidedly an upmarket publication, with its photographs of public school boys, and little girls on ponies. Its sports coverage was restricted to cricket, the Boat Race and Wimbledon, and it offered reviews of piano recitals by Paderewski and Pachmann, and concerts of early music given by the Dolmetsch family. The adult now can appreciate the well-informed comments on foreign affairs, and feel great sympathy for an editor who so fervently wanted the world to behave itself properly and enjoy the good things God had provided. In the supplement issue with the thousandth number Mee had lamented,

> If all the world read the CN and believed in it there would be no hate in the world, no cruelty, no superstitions, no ugly things, no greed or selfishness, no bad neighbours, no slums, no poverty, no great country keeping another down, no nation seeking its own advantage. (21 May 1938)

This was not just rhetoric; it was something he genuinely believed. He never quite grew up, Hammerton said; 'But what was more exceptional was his capacity for communicating to the young minds around him, in that world where he seemed not to grow old, the marvel, the splendour, the beauty of it, even under the dense cloud of war.'[29]

---

29 Hammerton, *Child of Wonder*, p. 18.

PART IV
The Famous Three:
Blyton, Dahl and Rowling

Introduction

Julia Briggs

Over the last 60 years or so, three writers have dominated the sales of British children's fiction, and, if only in terms of popularity, they form a sort of 'apostolic succession'. Each of them created a market for their particular way of writing, and there are several links between them. Roald Dahl figures significantly among the many influences that J.K. Rowling has assimilated: Charlie Bucket (of *Charlie and the Chocolate Factory*) is a precursor of Harry Potter, while Harry's persecution at the hands of the dreadful Dursleys recalls James's experiences in *James and the Giant Peach*. Like Blyton, Dahl appealed directly to child readers, often over the heads of parents, teachers and librarians. His work aroused a certain amount of criticism, though it hardly compared with the much-publicised banning of Blyton's work by school libraries, the BBC and other upholders of middle-class 'values'. As David Rudd's essay points out, Blyton had learned the art of appealing to children partly from Arthur Mee, whose aims are discussed by Gillian Avery at the end of the previous section.

During the twentieth century, children's reading habits, the role of reading in child culture and the degree of independent choice exercised by the child reader have been steadily changing, but do children today enjoy greater freedom to select their reading for themselves, or is it merely that the forces acting upon their choices have changed? Now that children's paperbacks are as cheap and readily available as penny tracts were to the Victorians, books are in competition with radio and television, videos, DVDs and computer games for their users' attention.

A small number of children's books establish themselves as 'classics', and are regularly given to children to read, but what constitutes a 'children's classic', and how long does that status last? Aileen Fyfe's essay (in the previous section) on science books for children has shown how Aikin and Barbauld's *Evenings at Home*, though outmoded in terms of content, was marketed by Routledge as a 'children's classic' during the nineteenth century. In addition to old nursery tales, folk tales and fairy tales, a number of books originally intended for adults have been regularly rewritten as 'classics' for children, most notably two eighteenth-century fictions, Daniel Defoe's *Robinson Crusoe* and Jonathan Swift's *Gulliver's Travels*. Since then, a number of children's books have also achieved 'classic' status – animal stories such as *The Wind in the Willows*, *Peter Rabbit* and *Winnie-the-Pooh*, adventure stories such as *Treasure Island* and a growing number of fantasies that include Lewis Carroll's Alice books, Tolkien's *The Hobbit* and James Barrie's *Peter Pan*. Jacqueline Rose has discussed *Peter Pan* as a work published in a variety of forms, but with no single textual point of origin, in *The Case of Peter Pan, or the Impossibility of Children's Fiction*. But this problem is more widespread since children's classics are typically reproduced in a variety of formats to suit different age groups and reading contexts.

C.S. Lewis identified 'Three Ways of Writing for Children': the first consisted of telling a story 'to a particular child with the living voice and perhaps *ex tempore*', a method used by many of the classics listed above, although such narratives of origin are themselves intended for young readers and soon become part of that work's mythology (as Eccleshare's account of the writing of *Harry Potter and the Philosopher's Stone* illustrates). For Lewis himself, the second way of writing for children, and the only one that he could manage, 'consists in writing a children's story because a children's story is the best art-form for something you have to say'. Both of these methods had his approval, but he condemned the third way – '"giving the public what it wants". Children are, of course, a special public and you find out what they want and give them that.'[1]

Yet despite Lewis's condemnation, this book shows just how many writers for children, from John Newbery onwards, have consciously set out to write for the market. Such an approach can be seen as a 'sell out', a vulgarisation or betrayal of higher ideals, but although a good deal of commercial writing is quickly consumed and forgotten, commercial motives are not inherently at odds with serious achievement. As David Rudd points out, Enid Blyton deliberately aimed her work at particular age groups or markets, addressing the adventures of Noddy and Mary Mouse to younger readers, and the Famous Five to an older cohort. Her speed of writing and huge output recall those of the Victorian writer for boys, G.A. Henty (discussed earlier by Dennis Butts); both of them mingled excitement with repetitive narrative structures that provided a counterbalancing element of reassurance. Yet Blyton could also shock and startle her child readers, appealing over their parents' heads to less inhibited feelings – a technique Roald Dahl would develop and make his own.

Such tactics prompt further questions as to how far, and in what ways today's children differ from their predecessors, not merely in their tastes, but also in enjoying greater economic independence and possibly greater independence from adult influence – in particular that of parents or teachers, librarians or publishers. In her account of the launching of Harry Potter, Julia Eccleshare emphasises the importance of the Smarties Gold Award, because it demonstrated Rowling's appeal to children, who read her first book in competition with other titles. But how far does reader response determine the popularity of children's books? Obviously shrewd marketing, merchandising and extensive advertising play their part, and Rudd shows us how much Blyton enjoyed employing such devices. The closed communities and 'secret societies' of the playground may have their own contribution to make to the creation and maintenance of literary popularity and, thanks to the pioneering work of the Opies, cultural historians have become increasingly interested in the secret games, codes, rules and language of childhood. Such secret societies themselves figure significantly in popular fiction for children, from Maria Charlesworth's *Ministering Children* (1854) to the 'Harry Potter' series. J.K. Rowling dramatises the secret world of witchcraft and the exclusive nature of school gangs, refashioning what in reality can be oppressive aspects of home or school experience. Belonging to a particular group confers one kind of strength and energy, but exclusion may confer

---

1   C.S. Lewis, *Of This and Other Worlds*, ed. Walter Hooper (London: Collins, 1982), p. 57.

another: Lewis Carroll's Alice remains the outsider, and this characterises her vision, contributing to its subversiveness.

Blyton, Dahl and Rowling have, in their different ways, helped to reshape what popularity means in terms of child readers. It is a truism that Rowling has written challengingly long books whose value lies partly in the substantial demands they make on reading skills; yet at the same time they have been repackaged as films, tapes, games and websites, something that Stacy Gillis considers in her essay. Any assessment of the popularity of children's books must now widen its remit to take in such additional forms.

Chapter 13

From Froebel Teacher to English Disney: The Phenomenal Success of Enid Blyton

David Rudd

In his book *The Beauty of Inflections*, Jerome McGann argues for the importance of 'performative' aspects of texts: 'The price of a book, its place of publication, even its physical form and the institutional structures by which it is distributed and received, all bear upon the production of literary meaning, and hence all must be critically analyzed and explained.'[1] He is dealing with works of recognised literary merit, but it can be argued that when we look at more popular literature, these 'performative' issues are of even greater importance. Blyton herself spoke openly of the significance of such material concerns: 'I take a great interest in … the production and selling side of my job as well as in the creative side … I would not dream of having a book published unless I had co-operated in the production – advised on illustraions [*sic*], jacket, size of type, – yes, and on selling price and size of edition!'[2] This is confirmed in her autobiography for children, *The Story of My Life*, in which she includes two fairly technical pages entitled, 'How One of Your Books was Made', commenting, 'I and the publishers, the artist and the photographers, the printers and the binders, have all worked together as a team to make this book for you.'[3] In this chapter I shall argue that much of Blyton's success was due to her attention to these performative aspects of writing, and to the importance of a good team in achieving this. However, as we shall also see, Blyton – as Pied Piper – always called the tune.

Blyton, despite her productivity, should not be thought of as an instant success. Unlike, say, the popular author A.J. Cronin, she did not dash off her first book, then pick out a publisher at random, going on to achieve instant success. Like other writers in this volume, she was a 'jobbing' writer for many years, serving a typical apprenticeship. She received, she says, over 500 rejection slips 'before making any headway'.[4] In her early published work we find her experimenting with a variety of forms – verse, humour, newspaper advertisements and greetings cards:

---

1   Jerome McGann, *The Beauty of Inflections: Literary Investigations in Historical Method and Theory* (Oxford: Clarendon Press, 1985), p. 4.
2   Letter to Robert A. Holbrow, 29 May 1955, reproduced in *Green Hedges Magazine* 20 (November 1997), 20–24.
3   *The Story of My Life* (1952), pp. 92–3. All Enid Blyton publications cited here are listed with full bibliographical details at the end of the chapter.
4   'On Writing for Children' (1951), p. 4.

The fairy folk at Christmas time,
They ride with dear old Santa Claus,
And bring his gifts to you.
I hope they'll visit your house first,
And fill your stocking fit to burst.[5]

She also wrote a number of adult short stories, such as 'The Making of Merriden Major' (1921) and 'Aunt Jerusha's Earwig' (1922) which, though awkward in many respects, especially in their pretentious language, do show an unerring sense of narrative control and story shape. By the time Blyton found her métier as a children's writer she was already a qualified, Froebel-trained teacher, testing out her creations on her charges in a fairly crude form of market research. In Blyton's preface to her first published volume – *Child Whispers* (1922), a book of poems – she confirms this, her lifelong practice: 'As I found a lack of suitable poems of the types I wanted, I began to write them myself for the children under my supervision, taking, in many cases, the ideas, humorous or whimsical, of the children themselves' (pp. 7–8). Certainly, she gave the children what they wanted, but with an awareness of contemporary market trends. Thus, her early tales of fairies were designed to appeal to the public mood, drawing on Rose Fyleman's horticultural notions of fairies at the bottom of the garden and Conan Doyle's more 'scientific' accounts of the Cottingley fairies in Yorkshire.[6]

In the early part of her career, Blyton had been seen as an educational writer. She established this base through her writings in *The Schoolmistress* and, most famously, in *Teachers World* (15 February 1922 until 1945).[7] Here she could develop her teaching skills in a variety of directions: with poems, stories, plays, nature notes, illustrations, miscellaneous articles and reviews (she even reviewed Professor Thirring's *The Ideas of Einstein's Theory*!). The educational slant is apparent, too, in many of her early books, written for three main publishers: J. Saville, Thomas Nelson and George Newnes. Some of these were explicitly educational, such as Saville's *Responsive Singing Games* (1923), Nelson's 'Reading Practice' series (1925) and Newnes' *The Teachers' Treasury* (1926) – a three-volume work edited by Blyton, and substantially written by her, amounting to almost a National Curriculum in itself. The introduction, by T.P. Nunn, a professor of education at London University, helped consolidate her position as a reputable authority.

But Blyton did not want to be seen solely as an educationalist. She wanted to write more directly for children – as Arthur Mee, an important influence on her, had done – and to have more control over the finished product; that is, over the 'performative' aspects of her work. This would seem to be the reason that Blyton stopped publishing with both Saville and Nelson. For instance, though Saville improved the appearance of *Child Whispers* between the first and second editions

5 Verse from an undated Christmas card written by Blyton, in the Enid Blyton Society Archive held by Tony Summerfield for the Enid Blyton Society (hereafter Enid Blyton Society Archive), contactable at 93 Milford Hill, Salisbury, Wiltshire, SP1 2QL, UK.

6 Joe Cooper, *The Case of the Cottingley Fairies* (London: Robert Hale, 1990).

7 'Teachers' appears on the periodical without apostrophe.

(from an ephemeral-looking, dull, landscape booklet – typically suited for school use – to a colourful, dust-wrapped hardback, in portrait format, obviously aimed at a wider, more child-centred audience), they still had not created a work that stood out amongst contemporary children's works. Something similar seems to have occurred with Nelson. In 1924 she had agreed to produce 36 books for them in a series called 'Reading Practice'. The first six were readily accepted, with her payment being increased from ten to twelve guineas, and she prepared five of the next half-dozen. However, only eight of the eleven she prepared were ever published (between 1925 and 1927) and her relationship with Nelson apparently came to an end in 1927.[8] A letter written to Robert Holborrow some 25 years later, hints at the problem: 'Nelson's are good publishers, even though they don't happen to be mine. (They used to be, but alas, didn't believe in my ideas as my other publishers did! I was too go-ahead for their canny Scottish minds!)'[9] They, like Saville, obviously responded to some of Blyton's suggestions, issuing a much more attractive edition of *Silver and Gold* two years after its initial appearance in 1925. However, by 1927, her relation with Nelson had cooled, so that this, and the manuscript of *Let's Pretend* (1927), which appeared as a most attractive book the following year, came too late.

Blyton, I would suggest, was more influenced by her other publisher from those early years, Birn Brothers, whose part in Blyton's development remains obscure. Their books, unlike the rest, were definitely not recognised for their educational merit. They are generally of poor quality, often lacking copy-editing, but do have a raw child appeal, with attractive covers and internal illustration. Perhaps because of this, their books have proved remarkably difficult to find. At that time, Birn did not deposit their works in any copyright library, nor produce catalogues. These books were so ephemeral that, in some cases, they have now vanished without trace. Tony Summerfield, the leading Blyton bibliographer, has seen 24 of her Birn books, but believes there could be a further 30 waiting to be discovered.[10] And Birn material does continue to appear, to the surprise and delight of Blyton collectors. Indeed one title, *Sports and Games*, hit the national headlines in the British press when its owner, Mason Willey, claimed that it could be the earliest Blyton book, possibly 1918–19,[11] though it was subsequently found to have first appeared in 1924.

The Birn Brothers were crucial to Blyton's development because they gave her more room to experiment – something she was also doing in magazine form with *Sunny Stories*. A recent Birn Brothers find, *The Wonderful Adventure* (1927), demonstrates this. It predates what was previously thought to be Blyton's first,

---

8   Tony Summerfield, 'A Detailed Look At: The Nelson Books', *Enid Blyton Literary Society Journal* 1 (1996), 11–13.

9   Letter to Robert A. Holbrow, 12 August 1953, reproduced in *Green Hedges Magazine* 24 (Autumn 1998), unpaged.

10 See Tony Summerfield's *Enid Blyton – An Illustrated Bibliography, Part 1: 1922–1942* and *Part 2: 1943–1952* (Salisbury: Tony Summerfield, 2001), for details and illustrations of known Birn books, plus the *Enid Blyton Society Journal* for subsequent finds, for instance in volume 25 (2004), p. 47. Thanks are due to Tony Summerfield for his generosity, his bibliographical wizardry and for granting me access to his fabulous collection.

11 Mason Willey, 'Sports and Games', *Enid Blyton Book and Ephemera Collectors Society* 20 (1995), unpaginated.

full-length adventure story, *The Secret Island* (1938), by over a decade. Like *Let's Pretend*, and some other stories from around this time, it is told in the first person, and shows Blyton toying with what would later be one of her trademarks: a group of related children – boys and girls – involved in hunting for lost family treasure, finding sliding-panels, secret passages and a smuggler's cave. If Blyton had had more enterprising guidance at this time, she might have honed her characteristic adventure story formula earlier than she did. Interestingly, *The Wonderful Adventure* also challenges the notion that Arthur Ransome wrote 'the first modern story of holiday adventure' with *Swallows and Amazons* (1930), which it was thought Blyton had emulated.[12] Though *The Wonderful Adventure* clearly predates Ransome, its obscurity means that it was probably not very influential.

In these stories Blyton can be seen trying to find a narrative voice in which she can talk directly to children. A first person narrative might seem to offer this opportunity, as in E. Nesbit's Bastable stories (from 1898), which also, of course, feature the adventures of a group of children. However, Blyton obviously came to the realisation that, for her, the first person was limiting. Besides restricting reader identification, it also limited the narration to the viewpoint of a single character, whereas, writing in the third person, omnisciently, she could recreate something more akin to her oral storytelling in the classroom. She could also more easily reconcile entertainment with instruction, and Blyton always saw herself as a firm moralist.

In these early years we can already see Blyton taking control of the performative aspects of her work. This might seem a bold thing for a young woman in her twenties to do but in 1924 she had married Hugh Pollock, a worldly-wise editor at Newnes, who no doubt contributed both to her confidence and her business acumen. This is not to say, as some have suggested, that Blyton would not have been a success but for him. It would simply have taken longer. Pollock was clearly instrumental in the founding, in July 1926, of *Sunny Stories for Little Folks* (see Figure 13.1). Issues were not initially conceived as parts of a serial but, as the advertisements stated, 'cheap books for Newnes', so that a number of titles – each self-contained – would be simultaneously available from newsagents, priced two old pence each. And this is how they were published: two appearing each month, undated. Like the contents, the title was probably Blyton's invention, though with a nod to Cassell's long-established magazine, *Little Folks* (1871–1930).

Although Blyton wrote the entire thing, the cover only credited her as editor. As with her other publications, *Sunny Stories* began with retellings of traditional tales. The first issue, for example, featured versions of fairy tales, the second had 'Brer Rabbit', the third, 'Robin Hood and his Merry Men', and the fourth, 'Gulliver in Lilliput'. Later Blyton would move on to her own original works. The format was also to change, again in line with Blyton's wishes. From November 1928 she introduced each issue with a letter and began to include verse, making it closer, in fact, to what she was already doing in *Teachers World*, where she had steadily moved

---

12 Sheila Ray, *The Blyton Phenomenon* (London: André Deutsch, 1982), p. 15; Robert Druce, *This Day Our Daily Fictions: An Enquiry into the Multi-Million Bestseller Status of Enid Blyton and Ian Fleming* (Amsterdam; Atlanta, GA: Rudopi BV, 1992), p. 125.

away from speaking to teachers to speaking directly to children (and from 2 October 1929 her work was relocated in the 'Junior Edition' of the journal). Later still, Blyton introduced serials and picture strips. Further innovations were saved for her own *Enid Blyton's Magazine*, which she started when she left *Sunny Stories* in 1953.

Figure 13.1   Advertisement for Enid Blyton's *Sunny Stories* (no date but from the late 1930s). Reproduced by kind permission of Tony Summerfield of the Enid Blyton Society.

There has been speculation as to why Blyton abandoned *Sunny Stories* when it had become so closely and successfully associated with her name. After all, from 1937, it was no longer billed as simply 'edited by' her; rather, it was retitled *Enid Blyton's Sunny Stories* (in 1942 it had reverted to *Sunny Stories*, but was then clearly identified as 'by Enid Blyton'). What she lacked with *Sunny Stories* was full control, despite her increasing say over the content. It still belonged to Newnes, who would not allow other publishers' products to be advertised within its covers. But if we take 1952 only, the year prior to her move, Blyton was publishing books under 24 other imprints. And, though primarily a writer, she had an ever-growing number of non-book products that would benefit from promotion – particularly at this time, when many of her characters were generating spin-offs, above all her relatively recent creation, Noddy (1949). In fact, a 'Noddy Licensing Co.' had been formed especially to deal with his merchandising. Indeed, an anonymous piece of promotional material called *Focus on Enid Blyton* reveals that by 1958, there were 52 separate companies dealing with her non-book merchandising.[13] In the new *Enid Blyton's Magazine*, all of these products could be advertised. They included soap, china figures, pyjamas, jigsaws, cards, games, puzzles, 'sculptorcraft', lamps and much more.

There was clearly a battle over sales between the two magazines as a result of Blyton's move. Though *Sunny Stories* had been appearing fortnightly since wartime restrictions on paper had been imposed (since 27 March 1942, in fact, though it took 'Bimbo's Weekly [*sic*] Letter' a while to adjust!), it reverted to a weekly as soon as Blyton's new magazine appeared. However, Blyton and her publishers, Evans Brothers, clearly knew what they were doing when they brought out their new magazine on a Wednesday, earlier in the week than *Sunny Stories*. Newnes responded by moving *Sunny Stories* back to a Tuesday. Newnes also declined to announce Blyton's departure, hence her explicit disclaimer, 'the only magazine I write for', on her later venture. Even so, it seems that notions of her association with *Sunny Stories* persisted in the public mind, for in a 1958 letter Blyton is still addressing these: 'I have nothing whatever to do with *Sunny Stories*, which I relinquished about six years ago, in order to have a magazine of my own which I could control completely'.[14] The magazine sold well, though it declined from an initial sale of around 330,000 copies to about 250,000 in its second year. It was estimated that one in seven children in London bought a copy, and this was despite the fact that some 14 per cent of its sales (40,000 copies) went overseas, demonstrating her extensive commonwealth appeal in the 1950s.[15]

I have concentrated on Blyton's magazines at some length because, together with her *Teachers World* column which ran for 23 years, they constitute the backbone of Blyton's writing career. Indeed, by the time she came to write her own magazine,

---

13 Anon., *Focus on Enid Blyton: Supplement to Games and Toys* (May 1958), Enid Blyton Society Archive.

14 Blyton says 'six years' and explicitly refers to 1952. She was not simply mistaken, however, for this was when she first explored an alternative journal, a mock-up of which is dated 5 November 1952, and unimaginatively titled the *Junior Magazine*.

15 Minutes of meetings for *Enid Blyton's Magazine*, 9 June 1953 and 12 January 1954, held in the Enid Blyton Society Archive.

all her major characters and series had been created. The brief history given above also reveals her as being well versed in the world of publishing. From very early on she had the experience of working with a number of different publishers, besides gaining an insider's view of the process: through her husband's work, through her own, largely educational, editorial work and from her personal experience of publishing (she had a number of works about her dog 'Bobs' privately printed – for instance, *Letters from Bobs* (1933) – which she designed). One work that was not published, *Country Letters from Old Thatch*, still exists in Blyton's mock-up, where she decides upon such details as size of font and general layout. Not only was she capable of working productively with publishers (and we shall see further evidence of this below) but she was also quite capable of relinquishing any publishers that did not appreciate her ideas – such as Nelson. For this reason, we find several of her books appearing under a number of different imprints, for Blyton would chase up any publisher that allowed one of her books to go out of print, and seek a reversion of rights if they did not wish to reprint it. *The Happy House Children*, for example, was published by Blackwell, Latimer, Collins and Dean.

It was precisely because she had worked with such a wide range of publishers that she could play one off against another, insisting on competitive terms. It seems incredible today that she did all this without an agent until she asked George Greenfield to act for her in that role in 1954. He first met her in 1948 when he was working for Werner Laurie, 'her *seventeenth* regular publisher' as he put it.[16] He also describes his amazement that she kept details of all her correspondence with publishers in her head. According to Greenfield, she demanded four things of her publishers:

> 1. She would not take an advance but 2. the publisher had to guarantee a first printing of at least 25,000 copies; 3. she was to receive a straight 15 per cent royalty on the published price of all home sales ... [the norm was 7.5 per cent]. And her fourth stipulation was that she had to approve the dustjacket design and lettering.[17]

In particular, Blyton had informed views on fonts (she particularly liked Garamond), quality of paper, width of margins and layout – all of which were to come together in the production of Noddy. But before discussing this, something must be said about Blyton's awareness of her audience. Much to her critics' displeasure, she was determined to give the children what they wanted.

Her magazines certainly allowed her close contact with her readers. 'I do like the way you are telling me exactly what you want in our magazine', she told readers of *Enid Blyton's Magazine* in 1953 (p. 2). She was adept at conducting her own market research, always asking her readers to tell her which series they liked, which characters, and so forth. Many of her well-known works were, after the first volume, conceived in series of 6: this gave readers time to get to know the characters, she said. But she was also willing to be swayed by readers' comments. The 'Famous

---

16 George Greenfield, *A Smattering of Monsters: A Kind of Memoir* (London: Little, Brown, 1995), p. 111. Counting Blyton's 'irregular' publishers as well, Werner Laurie was actually the thirty-first.

17 Ibid.

Five, for example, was notably extended to 12 books in response to demand, and thence to a more-or-less open-ended annual ritual, so that ultimately there were 21 in all. Had her health not failed her, there would have been more; and the same applies to the 'Secret Seven' and 'Mystery' series (15 each).

Children, in turn, sent Blyton their own stories for comment, or suggested ideas to her, to which, as she herself has said, she was always receptive. In an article called 'Talk to the Children' (1953), she advises other writers to do just this, quoting examples of children's anecdotes that she had refashioned, with comments like, 'Wonderful material, this!' (p. 5). But this point should not be overstated; though the children helped shape and inform Blyton's writing, she had very clear ideas of her own about its general direction.

To illustrate this, let me use the famous story of how the 'Secret Seven' was said to have originated. Ewart Wharmby of Brockhampton Press, her Leicester publisher, related to Blyton the story of how his children had formed a secret society, complete with password, in the garden shed. Blyton pursued this, writing to the eldest son for more details and, after his informative response, sent them some money 'to defray expenses'.[18] However, good as this story is, it did not really launch the Seven (though it might have charmed Wharmby), for all this took place in 1949, a year after Blyton had published a story about the 'Secret Society of Seven' who meet in an Old Mill (1948). And even this was the second story about the main characters, who had already appeared the year before in *At Seaside Cottage*. One isolated idea is seldom responsible for a writer's work. The process is far more organic and extended – even if it furnishes a less satisfactory anecdote.

Not only did Blyton conduct market research, she was also adept at promoting the resultant products. The Sampson Low 'Noddy' series is a good example, one of its main themes being, precisely, consumerism. The books were mainly written in the fifties, a period of market expansion after the rigours of the war years, with television, car and house ownership all increasing dramatically, and hire-purchase buying becoming acceptable for the first time. This consumerism is heavily reflected in the books, both in their format – with their bookplates, 'This book belongs to', at the beginning, and the 'Look out for the next Noddy book' message at the end – and in the content, with much of the action occurring around Toyland marketplace. Stress was laid on the importance of having a job in order to be a consumer: 'You will have to work soon, then you can get money to buy heaps of things', Big-Ears explains to Noddy in the opening book (1949, p. 23). This is most blatant in *Noddy Meets Father Christmas* (1955), where the two of them tour the villages examining the stock that will fill children's stockings. Eventually they come to 'N. & B. Works' where some dolls are being made:

> 'N. & B. Works – of course, Noddy and Big-Ears Works!' said Father Christmas. 'I see that the children have asked for Noddy and Big-Ears toys, Noddy. I wonder why.'
>
> 'Well, there are lots of books about me,' said Noddy. 'Perhaps they have read them. Oh, Father Christmas – OH, Father Christmas – when I see all these little toys just like me I feel Very Very Important!'

---

18 Barbara Stoney, *Enid Blyton: A Biography* (London: Hodder and Stoughton, 1974), p. 154.

'Now don't you be grand and important or you won't be the dear little Noddy that children love,' said Father Christmas. He looked closely at the tiny figures running excitedly round the car. 'Yes, I like them. Pity the Noddies haven't little cars like yours, Noddy. I'll have to make a note of that.' (pp. 51–2)

Later, to consolidate this promotion, Father Christmas comments, 'one of the nicest, kindest little toys I've ever met' (pp. 58–9). It is quite a coup to have Father Christmas officially endorse one's products! Moreover, this book appeared at the very moment that *The Adventures of Noddy* were first broadcast on British commercial television, and when merchandising, following the play *Noddy in Toyland*, was rife. It is at its most blatant here, but such promotion occurs in other books, too. For example, in the short story 'Peter's Pencil Box' (1972), we are told that it 'was made of yellow polished wood, and had Little Noddy and Big-Ears on it' (p. 20). In *Secret Seven Win Through* (1955), a character has some of his Famous Five books stolen, one of the then most recently published Fives, *Five Go Down to the Sea*, being specifically named.

Such 'total product merchandising' seems to have been perfected by Blyton long before the concept had a name. It is apparent in her magazines, too, which carry many full-page advertisements from the publishers of her books. But the tie-ins go further than this. For instance, in the eighth *Enid Blyton's Magazine* (1953), there is a painting competition which explicitly asks for postcard entry, 'NOT ... an envelope!' (p. 35). The reason becomes apparent later, when we come across this advertisement: 'Children! Use Bateman's rubber paste to mount your entry for the Painting Competition and mend your books and toys too!' (p. 47). On another page, there is an advert for 'Reeves' Paint Box', bearing the heading, 'Painting competitions ... you'll have a better chance with REEVES' colours' (p. 37). This thematic use of advertising was to become common with commercial television, but Blyton was an inventive pioneer. A committee meeting minute records her view: 'if Mr. Osborne could let her know all the advertisers in advance, then she could probably tie-up with her newsletter'.[19]

Before leaving the issue of marketing, it is worth commenting on the prominence of Blyton's name in her titles. This occurs from very early on – in her first collection of stories in fact, *The Enid Blyton Book of Fairies* (1924), when she was relatively unknown. And she continued to foreground her name in somewhere between 100 and 200 more titles – probably following the example of Arthur Mee, an author who influenced her greatly in her early years.[20] As a promotional device it was even more successful when used in conjunction with her personal signature as a logo. Though this had appeared in *Teachers World* since the 1920s, it was only used on her books from 1942 onwards, beginning with her Macmillan *Enid Blyton's Readers*. Obviously the logo was a great help to those young fans who couldn't yet read her name.

---

19 Minutes of Meeting of the 'Enid Blyton's Magazine' committee, 28 April 1953 (unpublished).

20 Unfortunately, Tony Summerfield's otherwise excellent *Enid Blyton: A Comprehensive Bibliography* deliberately omits her name from such titles, unless it is an intrinsic part of them, as in *A Picnic Party with Enid Blyton* (1951).

Apart from the total product merchandising, all the elements of Blyton's success were in place by the Second World War. It was around this time that she created her key full-length serials, having served her apprenticeship retelling the tales of others, then writing her own short stories, drawing on many stock characters from popular culture. Here I shall mention just her most popular series: the 'Wishing Chair' (beginning in 1937) and 'Faraway Tree' books, the latter starting with *The Enchanted Wood* (1939); the 'Famous Fives', commencing with *Five on a Treasure Island* (1942); the 'Find-Outers' (starting in 1943) and 'Adventure' series (from 1944). This period also saw her become involved in the schoolgirl story genre, with the 'Naughtiest Girl' (from 1940), 'St. Clare's' (from 1941) and 'Malory Towers' (from 1946) series. Her other main series all started in 1949, with 'Noddy', and the 'Secret Seven' and 'Barney' mysteries (commencing with *The Rockingdown Mystery*).

The very popular 'Mary Mouse' books, starting with *Mary Mouse and the Dolls' House* (1942), also deserve mention. These were original in both size and concept: little strip books measuring 2 x 5 inches, developed as a result of paper shortages during the War. E.A. Roker of Brockhampton Press had the excellent idea of using *Picture Post*'s discarded off-cuts, hence the size and shape of these books. He asked Blyton to write the first, and she suggested – most appositely given their miniature dimensions – the character of a mouse. These were small books for small people, as Beatrix Potter had always insisted that hers should be.[21] This appealing size of book had not existed before, the nearest being the Stump Books for Children (2 x 6 inches), produced by Treherne at the turn of the century (for example, Mary Tourtel's *The Rabbit Book*, 1904). The format was to prove very successful.[22]

Though there was a paper shortage during and after the War, Blyton did not seem to suffer greatly, partly because she employed such a range of publishers, but also because publishers knew that her books would be bought and extensively read. Certainly this situation gave her a massive commercial advantage, but the strength of her 'brand' should not be seen as the sole reason for her popularity, as some critics have suggested.[23] The six books that were published under her married name, Mary Pollock, attest to this. Commercially these were also very successful, all being reissued under the Pollock pseudonym (two of the titles being separately reprinted as well) before eventually appearing under Blyton's own name.

In all these various series Blyton showed herself able to rework tales in a range of fictional genres: fairy and folk tales, school stories, animal and nature stories, family tales, religious and moral tales, and, most popularly, adventure tales – that ragbag category that includes mysteries, treasure tales, detective tales, island stories, holiday and circus stories. Though she produced separate tales in each of these genres, she also blurred the boundaries, often including a range of genres in any one short story

---

21 There is also a hint of Potter's *The Tale of Two Bad Mice* (1904), though 'Goldilocks' is a more obvious precursor. Needless to say, Blyton did not come up with Mary Mouse on the spot. It too had developed more organically, an earlier incarnation appearing in *Enid Blyton's Sunny Stories* (15 April 1938) as 'Miss Mary Ann Mouse'.

22 My thanks to Tessa Chester (former curator of the Children's Book Collections at the Victoria and Albert Museum, London) for this information.

23 Edward Blishen, 'Who's Afraid of Enid Blyton?' *Where* 32 (1967), 28–9 (p. 29).

collection. She seemed to think more comfortably in terms of age ranges, frequently dividing children into four stages. The first comprised very young children, to whom adults would read, and for whom she advocated short simple stories, with 'many pictures, preferably in colour'. The second stage was the seven year old, for whom 'Short stories, or books of about 10,000 words are suitable'. Adults should only be peripheral in these as children liked to read about their peers. For eight or nine year olds she recommended adventure stories, 'unlike in the earlier books, something they haven't experienced themselves'. At the last stage, nine years old and above, 'Girls begin to develop different tastes from boys ... and for them I write the School stories ... But although boys seldom read these girls' books, a girl will always read a boy's book.'[24] Yet she did allow for children reading outside their allotted 'stage'.

On the other hand, Blyton seemed to be against targeting child audiences too precisely, preferring to write about a group of children that spanned a reasonable age range – and included both sexes. As she put it in a review of Stephen Mogridge's *New Forest Adventure*, 'Why do the publishers (Nelson's) limit the book's public by saying this book is for boys? Girls will enjoy it every bit as much as boys ... It is a mistake to limit a writer's juvenile public unnecessarily, either as regards sex or age.'[25] Obviously this is a sensible approach to marketing, as her earlier comments note, but it also shows a dislike of pigeonholing children unnecessarily. Certainly the content of her own magazines demonstrates this, as do such series as the 'Famous Five', the first few volumes of which are explicitly subtitled, 'An Adventure Story for Boys and Girls'. But she was challenging standard publishing assumptions.

Besides breaking down barriers of genre, age and sex, Blyton was also keen to extend the boundaries of the book itself. Again, this reveals her astute eye for a new market, but also her sense of the fun in seeing stories appear in new formats and new places. One of the earliest is the Birn Brothers' *The Book Around Europe* (1929), which features a revolving disk on the front, from which a particular country can be selected. The 'Mary Mouse' strip books have already been mentioned; there were also the Evans' 'Little Books' (5 x 4 inches: 1942) and the even tinier 'Birthday Time' books from Brent Press (2 x 3 inches: 1954), which came attached to birthday cards. Also innovative were several series of Noddy 'Tiny Books' (3 x 3 inches), beginning with *Noddy's House of Books* (1951), which comprised five (or in this case six) volumes, held in a container in the shape of the eponymous object (house, ark, garage, castle, station and shop). At the other extreme were the 'John Jolly' books (8 x 2 inches: 1943) and Noddy 'Tall Books' (10 x 3 inches: 1960). Of course, much of the merchandising takes us right out of the book world, but there are many items that bridge the gap, like *The Enid Blyton Handkerchief Book*,[26] the obscure Martin Lucas 'film-books', with fold-out pages and accompanying filmstrips (1952) and *Enid Blyton's Christmas Story* (1953), combining the story with an advent calendar

---

24 Adam Sykes, 'The Books that Children Love' [an interview with Enid Blyton], *Time and Tide* 43, 47 (22–29 December 1962), 21–3.

25 Enid Blyton, 'A Book that Children will Like and Lend!' (1953), p. 18. Note that Blyton is evidently keen that we see that the book is one of Nelson's.

26 John Beck, '*The Enid Blyton Handkerchief Book*', *Green Hedges Magazine* 9 (1993), 21–2.

– besides the more standard cut-out, colouring, painting, pop-up, mounted card and rag books.

Obviously Blyton simply responded to many of the ideas put to her, but she would agree to them only if things were done the way she wanted, and her own ideas were taken into consideration. Thus, for example, at Lutterworth's request she wrote books with a more overtly Christian emphasis. However, when it came to American publishers pressurizing her to produce something with which she didn't agree, she was immovable. As she proclaimed, 'No murders. No ghosts. No horror. No blood.'[27]

This is an interesting comment for, after the War, Blyton began to be seen as something more than a children's writer: she became an ambassador for Great Britain, her books being disseminated worldwide. They were published not only in European languages, but in 'Tamil, Swahili, Hebrew, Indonesian, Fijian' amongst others.[28] Furthermore, not only was Blyton regarded as useful for the promotion of Britain abroad at this time, but she was congratulated as standing against the encroachment of American popular culture – a general fear of the time.[29] Blyton fought against this encroachment on two fronts: first, she stood out against the influx of American horror comics – hence her comment, above. In launching her *Enid Blyton's Magazine*, she drew on teachers as allies, 'many of whom', she said, 'had urged me to publish a magazine which should be a part answer to the "American-style comics"'. She even wrote a poem on the matter, 'American Comics (and Those Like Them)', seeing them as Satanic creations (1955). On the second front, there was a fear of 'Disneyfication', to be combated by Britain retaliating with its own home-grown product – Noddy!

Noddy, of course, became Blyton's most celebrated and lucrative creation, so his origins deserve attention. There is the oft-told story of David White, of Sampson Low, Marston and Co., publishers of some of Blyton's earlier work, looking for an artist to do justice to a new series, 'dependent upon strong, central characters of a "Disney-like" type'. J.C. Gibbs of Purnell, which owned Sampson Low, claimed that he was responsible for sending White the work of a Dutch artist, Harmsen van der Beek, which turned out to be exactly right. When Blyton and the artist met, according to Barbara Stoney, she 'immediately described the central character she had "seen" emerging from a background that she felt "*must* be Toyland"', which Beek then sketched 'exactly, Enid claimed, as she had visualised'. Four days later, on 21 March, Lewis received typescripts 'for the first two Noddy books with a covering letter in which Blyton showed just how well she had absorbed the notion of a series concept:

---

27 Enid Blyton, 'How I Regard Writing for Children', p. 138, Enid Blyton Society Archive.

28 This claim comes from an anonymous, undated document entitled *Publicity Matter Concerning Enid Blyton Children's Author (For Use either Abroad or At Home)*, Enid Blyton Society Archive.

29 Dick Hebdidge, 'Towards a Cartography of Taste, 1935–62', in Barry Waites, Tony Bennett and Graham Martin (eds), *Popular Culture – Past and Present: A Reader* (London: Croom Helm, 1982), pp. 194–218.

Now about the general title – at the moment this is 'All Aboard for Toyland', and I imagine we might have as a 'motif' a toy train rushing along crowded with passengers – going all round the jacket top, sides and bottom or something like that – to give the books a 'series' look. The specific titles ... will each contain the name 'Noddy'. In the end, if they are very successful, they'll probably be referred to and ordered as the 'Noddy' books.[30]

The rest, as they say, is history. The first book appeared eight months later, in November 1949, and vastly exceeded expected sales. By the end of the 1950s, the books had sold an astonishing 20 million copies in the UK alone. However, Blyton's seemingly instant conceptualisation of the character and series, just like the Secret Seven and Mary Mouse, has a history, which can be salvaged from the many 'myths' that have grown up around the character.

Blyton was certainly responding to requests for a Disney-style production, the character having similarities to Disney's *Pinocchio*, especially given that Noddy had been created by 'Old Man Carver'. There is also the presence of a cat – not in Collodi's original – but very like Figaro in Disney's animated version. But Blyton was not only exploiting contemporary influences, she was also reaching back to her own earlier work, and in particular to 'Tales of Toyland', with its adventures of a sailor doll (Jolly) who lives in a nursery together with a fairy-doll, Tiptoe.[31] Unwanted, they run away to Toyland, to which they are directed by 'a brownie who lives in the wood' (p. 21). He shows them a train to Toyland, where they journey in a crowded carriage, only to be refused entry on arrival because Tiptoe is not a toy. Adopting disguises, they manage to get in, but still have nowhere to live. Then a policeman advises them to build a house of their own, from bricks – and they come to live next to a teddy bear. For anyone who knows the first Noddy book, the above will be very familiar; and there are other familiar characters, too, like a Skittle Family, a Wobbly Man, a Clockwork Clown and a 'fat clockwork policeman'. Here, substantially, is the first Noddy book, some seven years before its more thoughtful – corporate – realisation.[32]

Blyton's conception of a story that '*must* be Toyland', then, did not appear out of nothing. Yet this prior point of origin is not the end of the matter. As I noted earlier, Blyton's intertextuality is generally diffuse and extended. She had in fact written earlier stories using the same characters' names as she later employed in the Noddy books. There are several featuring 'Noddy', himself in different incarnations. One, for example, 'Noddy the Gnome' (1931), includes a helper called 'Big-Eyes', a frog. 'Big-Ears' himself also appears in different guises. There is one other possible source for Blyton's Noddy: an undated, movable book and series of cards, not by Blyton,

---

30 Stoney, *Enid Blyton*, pp. 157–8.

31 This was serialised in *Sunny Stories* in 1942, appearing in book form in 1944.

32 *Tales of Toyland* (1944) also includes episodes that were to become major parts of Noddy books 11 (1955) and 18 (1959). Blyton had tested the waters for Noddy in a newspaper serialisation in *The Sunday Graphic* six months before his book appearance. In this, the order of the first two books is reversed, so that *Hurrah for Little Noddy* appears before the book *Noddy in Toyland*, about Noddy's arrival in 'Toytown' (see David Chambers 'Blyton in Periodicals No. 9: *The Sunday Graphic*', *Enid Blyton Society Journal* 21 (2003), 30–33).

featuring a character called Nickleby Noddy.[33] This character wears a bell on his hat, has pointy ears (such as a gnome might have) and a nodding head. On one particular card in which he is pictured with his dog called, coincidentally, Timmy, there is a tab to pull which makes his head nod. He also wears a blue hat with a yellow bell, yellow cowl, red jacket and shoes and blue trousers – exactly Noddy's colours, in fact.

The 'Noddy' series was, of course, more successful than anyone had anticipated, and Blyton's name has almost become synonymous with that of her creation. As Peter Hunt suggests, once Blyton had popularised the term 'noddy', it quickly 'entered the English language as a dismissive phrase for idiotic simplicity'.[34] But in fact the word has a far longer history appearing, coincidentally, in the story of Nickleby Noddy's near-namesake, *Nicholas Nickleby* (1838) – 'To think that I should be such a noddy!'[35] – and in the closely contemporary poem 'The Pied Piper of Hamelin' by Robert Browning (1842), where the mayor is called 'a noddy'. 'Plod', as a slang term for a policeman, is similarly wrongly assumed to derive from Blyton's Noddy books. In fact, she does not actually name this corpulent policeman till the fifth book, and in any case, she had used the name in earlier stories featuring the police, picking up on what was, in the 1930s, already a slang term.[36]

The key point of all this is to demonstrate how adept Blyton was at using names and characters that were already part of popular culture, and reworking them – just as she had used fairies, Robin Hood and Brer Rabbit at the very beginning of her career. She has been wrongly credited with inventing some of these names simply because of her extraordinary popularity. A related point is that all these figures have a prehistory, often having appeared in less successful formats. The 'Noddy' books show a mature writer drawing on earlier material, having teamed up with a gifted artist and a market-wise editor. All these, though, would be nothing without the substantial backing of her publisher. Though the tail should not be seen to wag the dog, it was certainly the case that Purnell had been looking out for a Disney-style figure, whose print demand would help fuel the vast presses they had established in Paulton, Somerset – one of the earliest outside America to handle photo-offset lithography.[37]

Blyton's publicity explicitly picks up on Noddy's ideological purpose: 'this little, essentially British character is now gradually ousting the American creations of Walt

---

33 My thanks to Geoff Phillips for this information. He has two of these cards and the book, entitled *Over the Hill with Nickleby Noddy*, published by Candlelight. One of the book's poems is attributed to Noel, so it is possible that he was responsible for the whole work. Candlelight, it seems, were active in the 1940s and 1950s.

34 Peter Hunt, 'Enid Blyton', in Donald Hettinga and Gary D. Schmidt (eds), *British Children's Writers, 1914–1960*, Dictionary of Literary Biography 160 (Detroit, MI: Gale Research, 1996), pp. 50–71 (p. 69).

35 *Oxford English Dictionary*, 2nd edn (Oxford: Clarendon Press, 1989), vol. 10, p. 459.

36 See Anne Valery, *Talking About the War… [1939–1945: A Personal View of the War in Britain]* (London: Michael Joseph, 1991), who refers to 'the slow-witted Constable Plod of the comics [who] popped up in many a guise' (p. 148).

37 My thanks to Robert Tyndall, the illustrator who anonymously took over from Beek, for this information.

Disney from our nurseries and homes'.[38] Fortunately for her, the Disney empire had not spotted an earlier story she'd written for *Sunny Stories*, 'Mickey Mouse's Key', the title of which was sensibly changed to 'Joey's Lost Key' when it was collected in book form (1946). Blyton was less lucky with what she no doubt thought of as another stock character, Brer Rabbit, receiving a writ for infringement of copyright in 1953; however, in the event, no extant copyright in Joel Chandler Harris's work was found to exist in the UK at the time. As far as Noddy was concerned, despite his Disney-like success, neither Blyton nor her many business advisers were able to realise the full commercial potential of their golden goose. What Disney had achieved was almost complete 'vertical integration' in regard to its products, making the efforts of Darrell Waters Ltd look amateur in comparison (something which the new owners of Blyton's works, Trocadero – now Chorion – have struggled to reverse). But in the 1950s all we find are such small-time deals as that granted to Bob Cotton, who for £800 a year was given two years' rights to merchandise Blyton characters in cereal packets, a franchise that he sold on to Kellogg's for £6,000.[39]

Even so, the huge commercial success of Noddy should not be underestimated – it was to prove too much for its initial illustrator, van der Beek, who died after producing the first seven Sampson Low books, besides much other Noddy artwork. It also had a profound effect on the rest of Blyton's career, blighting it to some extent, for it was thanks to Noddy that she came to be seen as a rather twee, 'noddy' character herself. Noddy's market penetration, too, helped in the process of redefining Blyton as an over-productive hack – a view captured most famously in Colin Welch's *Encounter* article, where Noddy is described as an 'unnaturally priggish ... sanctimonious ... witless, spiritless, snivelling, sneaking doll'.[40] Through Noddy, Blyton became not just a popular children's writer, but a household name. There were countless spin-offs: aside from the 125 or so books featuring him (up to 1970), there were comics, a Christmas play (and film), a television puppet series, and extensive product merchandising. But, probably as a result of this, Noddy was the last really popular character that Blyton created; only Bom (1956) made any other significant impression – though today he is generally forgotten.

After Noddy, Blyton also lowered the age range for which she wrote, though some of her best series had been at the top end of a child's reading: that is, the school stories, the 'Adventure' and 'Barney' series. But these were not extended, nor were their equivalents begun. Again, there might have been other factors at work. Commercially, there was the recognition that older children soon stopped being child readers. In fact, Blyton once observed 'that there was bound to be a certain amount of wastage at the top age range'.[41] Another reason might have been Blyton's health: the books for older children were generally longer, and therefore required

---

38 *Publicity Matter Concerning Enid Blyton.*

39 Rufus Segar, 'Will the Real Noddy Please Stand Up: Enid Blyton and her Noddy Artists', *Illustrators* 22 (1978), 20–22 (p. 21).

40 Colin Welch, 'Dear Little Noddy: A Parent's Lament', *Encounter* 10 (1958), 18–23 (pp. 21–2).

41 Minutes of Meeting of the 'Enid Blyton's Magazine' committee, 18 November 1954 (unpublished).

more effort to produce. She does show a general tailing off in production from an incredible average of over 50 publications a year in the first half of the 1950s (in 1955 there were 69!), to 21 by 1959, the year that she gave up her magazine.

We need also to look at the other side of the coin. It was in the 1950s, again largely as a result of Noddy, that more negative views of Blyton began to be voiced (like Welch's, quoted above). These had unintentional repercussions that were to work in Blyton's favour, though at some personal cost. For example, there was an indirect promotional effect from the actions of 'quality' publishers (or those seeking to be seen in this light). Thus Barbara Ker Wilson recalled her dismay when she discovered 'five early Blyton titles on the Bodley Head list, and set about selling them off'.[42] Eleanor Graham, in similar terms, always celebrated the fact that Puffin books were a Blyton-free zone: 'I was, of course, frequently urged to get some Blyton on our list but I never did. It was not intended for that kind of public.'[43] The impact of such decisions helped concentrate Blyton's works in precisely those imprints such as Dean, Purnell and World Distributors that were more readily available outside the book world: in newsagents, kiosks and supermarkets.

Librarians were also party to this discrimination. They got rid of the one author who had helped so many reluctant readers over the library threshold in the first place. Even though much of 'the banning of Blyton' was hyped, the effect was the same. This action by the cultural gatekeepers also helped the publishers of new paperback imprints who were then eyeing up the market. Noting that children's pocket money averaged half-a-crown (12½ new pence) a week, they saw a lucrative market in encouraging children to purchase their own books, pitched at exactly this price, rather than have the choices of others thrust on them. It was natural, then, that these publishers would turn to Blyton to help promote their wares while promoting her own. Thus Sidney Bernstein, the brains behind Messrs William Collins's Armada, the first of these paperback imprints, treated Blyton's agent, George Greenfield, to lunch, saying to him, 'I must have Enid. I start off with a batch of her titles, there's no stopping me.'[44] He launched his flotilla in 1962, armed with *The Adventurous Four* (1962) and *The Naughtiest Girl in the School* (1962); three years later, one-third of his list was by Blyton. So, inadvertently, by creating exclusive notions of 'quality' versus 'non-quality' writing (categories used by Frank Whitehead *et al* in their extensive Schools Council survey),[45] such gatekeepers made it more likely that many young readers would stumble across huge caches of Blyton, and little else.

The more general criticisms by commentators such as Colin Welch also played their part. For Blyton's close links with her child audience, and the nature of her subject matter – often explicitly about empowering children against a myopic adult world – led to that very audience defending her all the more vigorously and, of course, reading her books in more covert and exciting ways, under bedclothes, at

---

42 Barbara Ker Wilson, 'Grace Abounding', *Signal* 26 (1995), 151–65 (p. 162).

43 Quoted in Ray, *The Blyton Phenomenon*, p. 28.

44 Greenfield, *Smattering of Monsters*, p. 122.

45 Frank Whitehead, A.C. Capey, Wendy Maddren and Alan Wellings, *Children and Their Books: School Council Research Project into Children's Reading Habits, 10–15*, (Basingstoke: Macmillan Education, 1977).

friends' houses and the like. Her child readers had discovered a buried treasure they could only share in their own exclusive world.

Blyton, then, though an extraordinarily gifted and dedicated writer, could not have achieved her success without, as she herself put it, working as part of a 'team' – even though she was the key player.[46] She had learnt her craft early on, paying particular attention to her readers' predilections – not only considering a book's content, but its whole character: its appeal in terms of shape, design, and address. Her early years, working with a wide variety of publishers, permitted her to establish her credentials and build up a following. From there, the 'Matthew effect' ('Unto every one that hath shall be given') paid off, with publishers and others actively seeking her out. As we have seen, any that did not share her vision of 'good' children's books – and many, as the years went on, did not – were forsaken (or forsook her). However, when she was 'believed in' (as she put it in a foreword to *A Complete List of Books by Enid Blyton* (1950), p. 4), her imagination and marketing sense were galvanised. I have illustrated this most extensively with 'Noddy', though other series have also been mentioned, like the 'Secret Seven' and 'Mary Mouse' books. These, together with her more mature books, like the 'Famous Fives', show Blyton's success in writing 'for every age-group' of children (p. 2), though she relinquished the oldest age-group in her later years. At the same time, Blyton preferred to blur specific genre and age categories, writing in as inclusive a manner as she could – something that her magazines gave her most licence to do. In today's terms her approach might seem naïve, but for her time, she was way ahead of all her competitors.

Works by Enid Blyton cited in this chapter (listed chronologically)

'Aunt Jerusha's Earwig' (1921), *Londoner* (22 October).
'The Making of Merriden Major' (1922), *Teachers World* (12 April), 88 and 122.
Child Whispers (1922, revised 1923), London: John Saville.
Real Fairies (1923), London: John Saville.
Responsive Singing Games (1923), London: John Saville.
Sports and Games (1924), London: Birn Brothers.
The Enid Blyton Book of Fairies (1924), London: George Newnes.
Silver and Gold (1925), London: Thomas Nelson.
The Teachers' Treasury (1926), London: George Newnes.
Let's Pretend (1927), London: Thomas Nelson.
The Wonderful Adventure (1927), London: Birn Brothers.
'The Adventures of Bobs' (1927), *Sunny Stories for Little Folks* 19 (April).

---

46 The focus of this chapter has been on Blyton's place in the market, so her skills and appeal as a writer have largely been ignored – vital ingredients though they are. I have dealt with these elsewhere: see David Rudd, 'Why the "Ephemeral" Blyton Won't Go Away', and 'The Paradox of Enid Blyton and Children's Literature', in Nicholas Tucker and Kimberley Reynolds (eds), *Enid Blyton: A Celebration and Reappraisal* (London: National Centre for Research in Children's Literature, Roehampton Institute, 1997), pp. 36–50 and 17–29; and *Enid Blyton and the Mystery of Children's Literature* (London: Macmillan, 2000).

'Gulliver in the Land of Giants' (1927), *Sunny Stories for Little Folks* 20 (April).

'Tibby's Adventures' (1927), *Sunny Stories for Little Folks* 28 (August).

The Book around Europe (1929), London: Birn Brothers.

'Noddy the Gnome' (1931), *Teachers World* 1485 (11 November), 222.

Letters from Bobs (1933), privately printed.

Adventures of the Wishing Chair (1937), London: George Newnes.

The Secret Island (1938), Oxford: Basil Blackwell.

Mr. Galliano's Circus (1938), London: George Newnes.

The Enchanted Wood (1939), London: George Newnes.

The Naughtiest Girl in the School (1940), London: George Newnes.

The Twins at St. Clare's (1941), London: Methuen.

Shadow, the Sheep-Dog (1942), London: George Newnes.

Five on a Treasure Island (1942), London: Hodder and Stoughton.

Mary Mouse and the Dolls' House (1942), Leicester: Brockhampton Press.

Brer Rabbit (1942), London: Evans Brothers.

The Mystery of the Burnt Cottage (1943), London: Methuen.

John Jolly by the Sea (1943), London: Evans Brothers.

The Island of Adventure (1944), London: Macmillan.

Tales of Toyland (1944), London: George Newnes.

The Enid Blyton Holiday Book 1 (1946), London: Sampson Low, Marston and Co.

At Seaside Cottage (1947), Leicester: Brockhampton Press.

Secret of the Old Mill (1948), Leicester: Brockhampton Press.

Noddy in Toyland (1949), London: Sampson Low, Marston and Co.

The Secret Seven (1949), Leicester: Brockhampton Press.

The Rockingdown Mystery (1949), London: William Collins.

'A Foreword from Enid Blyton' (1950), in *A Complete List of Books by Enid Blyton*, London: John Menzies, pp. 1–4.

'On Writing for Children' (1951), *Writer* (December), 4–5.

A Picnic Party with Enid Blyton (1951), London: Hodder and Stoughton.

Noddy's House of Books (1951), London: Sampson Low, Marston and Co.

The Story of My Life (1952), London: Pitkins.

Snow White (1952), Manchester: Martin Lucas.

Enid Blyton's Magazine (1953) 1, iv (29 April).

'Talk to the Children' (1953), *Writer* 12, v, 4–5.

Five Go Down to the Sea (1953), London: Hodder and Stoughton.

Enid Blyton's Magazine (1953), 8 (24 June).

'A Book that Children will Like and Lend!' (1953), *Newsagents and Booksellers Review* (5 September), 18.

Enid Blyton's Christmas Story (1953), London: Hamish Hamilton.

A Surprise for Mary (1954), London: Brent Press.

Noddy Meets Father Christmas (1955), London: Sampson Low, Marston and Co.

Secret Seven Win Through (1955), Leicester: Brockhampton Press.

'American Comics (and Those Like Them)' (1955), *Writer* (May), 132.

Bom the Little Drummer Boy (1956), Leicester: Brockhampton Press.

'Comics' (1958), *Economist* (29 November), 781.

Noddy Goes to Sea (1959), London: Sampson Low, Marston and Co.

Noddy's Tall Red Book (1960), London: Sampson Low, Marston and Co.

The Adventurous Four (1962), London: Armada [originally published George Newnes, 1941].

The Naughtiest Girl in the School (1962), London: Armada [originally published George Newnes, 1940].

'Peter's Pencil Case' (1972), in *Goodnight Stories*, London: Purnell, pp. 17–26.

Chapter 14

'And Children Swarmed to Him Like Settlers. He Became a Land.' The Outrageous Success of Roald Dahl[1]

Peter Hollindale

In 1990, the year of Roald Dahl's death, a scene in the BBC comedy television series *Smith and Jones* showed the actor Griff Rhys Jones reading a story book at bedtime to his (real-life) daughter, then aged about three. The story became steadily more and more violent, nauseating and destructive of cherished sentimental stereotypes such as the loving grandmother. Jones the father appeared increasingly taken aback, uncertain, concerned, and his voice trailed off into worried puzzlement. Finally he looked at the book's cover, and instantly his face changed to a beaming smile of understanding and reassured pleasure. 'Oh, it's by *Roald Dahl*!' he said. It was a striking comment on the power of this name to create its own rules of engagement, and vindicate its own ostensible transgressions.

The popular achievement of Roald Dahl is a complex phenomenon. His commercial success has been so huge that mere figures are of small interest compared with the reasons behind them and the controversies they arouse. Dahl's dubious public status and ambivalent reception as a children's writer were evident from the start of his career, if we discount his very earliest work, *The Gremlins* (1942), and are perhaps best exemplified by his second major children's book, *Charlie and the Chocolate Factory* (first published in America in 1964 and in Britain in 1967).[2] Chris Powling, in his children's biography of Dahl, charts the progress of the book's popularity in America, where in the first year after publication it sold 5,000 copies in hardback, and then '6,000, 8,000, 35,000, 85,000 and 125,000 for each of the following five years'. In the early 1980s, Powling noted, the book 'still sells in paperback at the rate of more than 100,000 copies annually'.[3] Yet in Britain Dahl had great difficulty in finding a publisher. Despite its accelerating American success, *Charlie and the Chocolate Factory* did not appear in Britain until 1967, the same year as *James and the Giant Peach*, which had been published in America as early as 1961. Since then, of course, *Charlie* has enjoyed a phenomenal worldwide success. Dahl's obituary in the *Daily Telegraph*, for example, noted that the book 'went down well even in China, where it enjoyed an initial print run of two million'.[4] Yet the

---

1   This quotation is the closing line from W.H. Auden's sonnet, 'Edward Lear', in *Collected Shorter Poems 1927–1957* (London: Faber and Faber, 1966), p. 127.

2   Full bibliographical details of Dahl's works are given at the end of this chapter.

3   Chris Powling, *Roald Dahl* (London: Hamish Hamilton, 1983), p. 47.

4   *Daily Telegraph*, 24 November 1990.

book's subsequent chequered history confirms the mixed reactions that marked its initial appearance. Always immensely popular with children, it has continued to divide adult readers, both on ethical grounds (it has been condemned on grounds of racism, sadism and various other political and psychological transgressions) and in judgements of its literary quality.

Precise estimates of sales vary from source to source. Jeremy Treglown, in his unofficial biography of Dahl, puts a higher figure on the initial sales, but confirms the initial reaction (and the subsequent ethical retreat) which makes the resistance of British publishers still harder to understand:

> In September 1966 *Charlie and the Chocolate Factory* appeared in the USA, to general acclaim. The allegations of racism did not come until later. Even the sober *Library Journal*, which had dismissed *James and the Giant Peach* as crude and exaggerated, was enthusiastic. Within a month, the first printing of 10,000 copies had sold out.[5]

By March 1968, only a few months after its first printing in Britain, *Charlie* had sold 607,240 copies in America. Eventually Britain caught on and caught up. Treglown reports that by 1975, Dahl's books 'were becoming bestsellers in Britain as well as the USA. *Charlie* had sold 225,000 copies here in paperback, 60,000 in hardback; *James* [*and the Giant Peach*] 115,000 and 45,000; *Fantastic Mr Fox* 74,000 and 15,000.'[6]

What was true of the early books was, of course, still more true of the later ones. Three of Dahl's greatest popular triumphs, *The BFG* (1982), *The Witches* (1983) and *Matilda* (1988) were produced in the last decade of his life, and their success was spectacular: in Britain, *Matilda* achieved paperback sales figures of half a million within six months of publication.

The two most striking things about Dahl's stories have been their ability to retain their dominance and the extent of the margin over their competitors for so long. For example, a list of bestsellers for the 6–11 age group published in the *Sunday Telegraph* in 1991 showed *Matilda* in first place with estimated weekly sales of 5,445. The book in second place, *Pongwiffy* by Kay Umansky, had an estimated figure of 1,685.[7] Dahl continued (at any rate up to the publication of J.K. Rowling's *Harry Potter* stories) to retain his dominance in terms of sales and children's expressed preferences. In January 1998 the journal *Books for Keeps* reported the results of a poll conducted shortly before its demise by the BBC Radio 4 programme 'Treasure Islands', in search of the nation's favourite modern children's author. Dahl received 1,957 votes. The remainder of the top ten consisted of R.L. Stine (the author of many 'Goosebumps' and 'Point Horror' titles), with 1,052 votes, Dick King-Smith (412), Jacqueline Wilson (340), Terry Pratchett (168), Judy Blume (154), Anne Fine (121), Animal Ark's 'Lucy Daniels' (103), Shirley Hughes (103) and Robert Westall (63). The article's slightly weary headline was 'Dahl's Top (Again)'.[8] Early in 1998 no one suspected that Dahl was about to be dislodged from pride of place by

---

5 Jeremy Treglown, *Roald Dahl* (London: Faber and Faber, 1994), p. 144.
6 Ibid., p. 186.
7 *Sunday Telegraph*, 14 April 1991.
8 *Books for Keeps* 108 (January 1998), 7.

J.K Rowling. Dahl might, though, have taken consolation from the fact that Rowling's work has often been said to have drawn on his own, or at least to have been heavily influenced by it.

Rowling's *Harry Potter and the Philosopher's Stone* was first published in 1997, and after a gentle commercial start it has famously become a publishing phenomenon which in sheer volume of sales and spin-off marketing eclipses not only Roald Dahl, and the rest of children's literature, but virtually all bestseller history, whether for child or adult. Not surprisingly, Dahl's sales have declined in consequence, the Harry Potter effect probably accentuating the customary short-term fall in popularity which follows an author's death. Although it is possible that Dahl's former massive popularity will continue to decline, the example of Enid Blyton (whose relationship to Dahl I discuss below) suggests that more probably it will level off and then recover, though never regaining its former eminence. By most criteria he still sells very well.

Hugely popular as Rowling presently is, it is of course impossible to predict her own commercial future. The completed 'Harry Potter' series may retain supremacy for many years, or it may prove to depend on a happy but evanescent cultural coincidence, and vaporise as quickly as it first ignited. What can be confidently foreseen, however, is that the fashion element of Rowling's success will not last indefinitely, and her books will have to fight for their place on their merits as reworked traditional stories rather than as newly minted commercial products. Because the Potter cycle creates incremental complexities, with each successive book posing ever-greater narrative and technical challenges to the author, its fate – whatever that proves to be – will add a permanent chapter to the history of popularity .

Meanwhile, not even Rowling at the height of her success can colonise the whole of children's storytime, and Dahl is unobtrusively surviving the phenomenon of Rowling just as Enid Blyton has survived the phenomenon of Dahl. Unless Rowling has permanently altered the culture of childhood, which is possible but very unlikely, both Dahl and Blyton are still excellent actuarial risks.

Enid Blyton, though, had been a notable absentee from the 'Treasure Islands' top ten list. This indicated not so much a belated collapse in her popularity as that by 1998 she could scarcely be classed as a 'modern children's author'. But since the 1970s the names of Dahl and Blyton have repeatedly been linked, because together they long outshone all other children's writers in terms of the sheer volume of their sales. This was true of both sexes. For example, a survey conducted by the *English Magazine* and entitled 'What Do 170 Boys Read?' investigated the reading habits of boys in two London schools. Under the subheading 'Roald Dahl and Enid Blyton', it concluded that 'Roald Dahl and Enid Blyton maintain an impressive supremacy in both first-year classes. Between them, they have as many readers from the two lists as all other authors put together', provided that annuals and 'other collated books' were excluded from the count.[9]

An unfortunate consequence of this joint success has been the temptation to treat Dahl and Blyton as if they were also readily comparable by the measures of literary quality. The confusion is helpfully pointed out by Aidan Chambers, yet his

---

9   John Richmond, 'What Do 170 Boys Read?' *English Magazine* 5 (1980), 26.

discussion inadvertently perpetuates it. There is 'confusion about books as units of commerce, the success of which is determined by volume of sales', he wrote:

> By this standard, Enid Blyton, Roald Dahl, Barbara Cartland and Jeffrey Archer are judged more successful than Jan Mark, Alan Garner, Brigid Brophy and William Trevor. But this is a misjudgement about what books are for … To judge success by large quantity sales is to confuse the book's easy reproducibility for its main purpose and to encourage the belief that those that sell a great many copies are better than those that sell only a few.[10]

Although his general point is valid, there is a difficulty here with both the argument and the examples. Massive sales are not a proof of merit, but they are not a proof of inferiority either; some recognised great works have been bestsellers at their first appearance. Concerning the particular authors cited, it is arguably unfair to both Blyton and Dahl to pair them as the children's equivalent of Cartland and Archer. These two 'adult' writers were chosen from many possible blockbuster authors because they typify popular success devoid of literary merit, whereas Blyton and Dahl are self-selecting examples of commercial success because they shared an overwhelming dominance of the children's market, but each can be plausibly credited with literary gifts. This may seem much harder in the case of Blyton than of Dahl, but Blyton could write extremely well at her best, especially about natural history and the countryside. All the same, the automatic pairing of the two in so many discussions does a serious disservice to Dahl, whose work consistently displays an inventive joy in language. He does not use his medium inertly, as Cartland and Archer do and as Blyton undoubtedly often does. Elsewhere Chambers said of Dahl's writing that he 'aims to achieve – and does – a tone of voice which is clear, uncluttered, unobtrusive, not very demanding linguistically'.[11] This comment was made about *Danny the Champion of the World*, an untypical Dahl novel, and it may be inexact as a description of Dahl's work in general. His tone of voice could not usually be characterised as 'unobtrusive', and he is quite capable of being 'linguistically demanding'. But in any case, Chambers's comment certainly implies a more generous judgement than the standard lumping together with Blyton (let alone the parallel with Cartland and Archer) would suggest.

Blyton and Dahl are in fact radically different writers. Blyton was astonishingly prolific, whereas Dahl wrote sparingly; Blyton is a patchily gifted and linguistically unselfconscious writer, whereas Dahl is a highly conscious and deliberate linguistic craftsman; in Blyton's work, the story is detachable from the style, but in Dahl it never is; Blyton is conformist and does not interrogate her values, while Dahl is both conservative and subversive; Blyton contentedly inhabits the storytelling stereotypes of her own day, whereas Dahl is both the conscious inheritor of a tradition and a respectful iconoclast in his dealings with it. Ironically, in view of their current reputations, when histories of children's literature are written a century from now, it

---

10 Aidan Chambers, 'The Difference of Literature: Writing Now for the Future of Young Readers', in Geoff Fox (ed.), *Celebrating Children's Literature* (London: Hodder and Stoughton, 1995), p. 256.

11 Aidan Chambers, 'The Reader in the Book', in Nancy Chambers (ed.), *The Signal Approach to Children's Books* (London: Kestrel, 1980), p. 256.

may be much easier to locate Dahl than Blyton in the mainstream of Anglo-American children's writing.

In short, the very concept of 'popularity' is problematised by the accidental and incongruous pairing of Dahl and Blyton. They are popular with children for very different reasons, and arguably at opposite ends of a spectrum. Although Blyton is present in her own work as a distinct and audible voice, it is essentially a simple, monotone presence, ingenuously aunt-like in its complacent assumption of straightforward readerly acquiescence. She seeks the 'invisibility' of uncontroversial teacherliness, and her language is 'invisible' to match. Dahl's voice, by contrast, is loudly audible everywhere, speaking directly to the reader, and constantly using a typographical notation that derives from an oral storytelling technique. He is always stirring the pot, complicating the oppositional and confrontational dialogue between child and adult, conspiring overtly with the child reader but also needling the child with indirect and discomfiting exposures of childhood shortcomings and support for chosen adult values. He is a humorously aggressive and slightly unpredictable ally in the dynamic interaction between child and story.

In the last resort, 'popularity' possesses an extra element of credit when the reader is a child, and this is a credit that Dahl and Blyton share. Children who read willingly and enthusiastically are more likely to develop a 'reading habit' which is an essential part of educational development. Adult professionals and concerned parents would usually prefer children to read 'quality' writers, as provisionally defined at any one time. In 1977 Dahl himself was included in the list of 'Juvenile Quality Narrative Books' in the Schools Council research report *Children and their Books*.[12] This is a little surprising, in fact, because by 1977 his growing popularity was acquiring elements of shadiness that might well have consigned him to the 'non-quality' basement of this morally severe report, and attracted the kind of vituperative attack which it directed at Blyton, but strangely he received no attention apart from a complimentary listing. But in any case, most people accept that where children are concerned, popularity is its own badge of merit, because it makes readers. There may be scepticism as to whether children progress to a later taste for more demanding fictions, but mere habituation to the needs of a print culture is often considered merit enough.

Perhaps it is risky in any case to disparage what children like. Dahl certainly thought so. Treglown reports that after Dahl's brief and disastrous membership of Professor Brian Cox's committee on English in the National Curriculum, to which he was appointed in 1988, Dahl 'publicly disagreed with the panel about Enid Blyton, whose books the majority wanted to exclude from a list of approved texts, but which he backed because children liked them'.[13] Yet the very fact that Dahl was in a position to assert this view as he did, the very fact that he was included in the Cox Committee, no matter how short-lived his cantankerous membership of it, demonstrates the difference between his status and Blyton's; had she still been alive, no one would have dreamed of appointing her to such a body. Dahl was taken

---

12 Frank Whitehead *et al.*, *Children and Their Books* (London: Macmillan Education, 1977), p. 330.

13 Treglown, *Roald Dahl*, p. 248.

seriously as a proponent of reading and of literacy, not only because he was a popular author but because he had acquired an authoritative if controversial persona over and above his actual writing, and this is the phenomenon which I wish to explore and illustrate in this chapter. The point is that repeated comparisons with Blyton, based on sales alone, have been deeply unfortunate for Dahl's reputation and the just appraisal of his work. The jump which Chambers makes from parity of commercial success to parity of literary achievement is widespread and widely taken for granted.[14] In order to identify Dahl's peculiar achievement, it is necessary to divorce them, and moreover to suggest that there are no other writers 'like' Dahl; for a unique blend of literary and extra-literary reasons, he is *sui generis*.

In his children's biography of Dahl, Chris Powling noted that for millions of children 'Roald Dahl himself is the Big Friendly Giant'.[15] He describes how easy it is to identify Sophie in *The BFG* with Dahl's own granddaughter, since she also wore glasses with 'steel rims and very thick lenses'. Sophie Dahl, now an adult and a person well known herself as model and actress, has confirmed the accuracy of the connection and the link between the story and real life:

> I stayed with him a lot as a child. When I was about five, he told me and a friend about the big friendly giant who came to children's windows. [This was before *The BFG* was written.] Then in the middle of the night there was a big bang bang bang at the window and a loud 'oooooh, wooooo, oooooh', and round the curtains came this old tortured face. It was my grandfather on a ladder, with a trumpet pretending to be the BFG. Mum was standing at the bottom going, 'Christ, Dad. You're going to fall off.'[16]

This is a small example of something which is writ large in Dahl's life and work. It is a commonplace that many of children's literature's famous texts were originally told or written for and about particular children in the author's life, and also that writers, not surprisingly, draw extensively on their own childhood experiences, lived and imagined, as material for stories. Sometimes news of these particulars is transmitted to the distant child reader of the published book, so that Christopher Robin, for instance, becomes a character in other children's lives. But most information of this kind, such as the identity and later lives of Alice Liddell or Alastair Grahame, or Arthur Ransome's boyhood holidays in the Lake District, or Lucy Boston's discovery

---

14 Barbara Wall, for example, refers to 'fine modern writers such as Mary Norton, Lucy Boston and Philippa Pearce on the one hand, and much read though less substantial writers such as Enid Blyton and Roald Dahl on the other' (*The Narrator's Voice* (London: Macmillan, 1991), p. 178). For his part, Charles Sarland asks 'What was it about the work of popular authors like [James] Herbert, or at a younger age, Blyton and Dahl, that could unite young readers across the ability levels where more "respectable" authors of supposedly greater literary worth succeeded in dividing them?' (*Young People Reading: Culture and Response* (Milton Keynes: Open University Press, 1991), p. 3). There is a welcome hint of reservation in Sarland's phrasing about the automatic sheep-and-goats separation of 'quality' from 'non-quality' achievement, but the 'Blyton and Dahl' marriage persists intact.

15 Powling, *Roald Dahl* (1983), p. 62.

16 Interview with Sophie Dahl by Eleanor Mills, *Sunday Times*, 25 October 1998.

and renovation of 'Green Knowe', is 'marketed' in biographical or autobiographical work for adult readers. Children as a rule are not expected to be interested in it.

Dahl, by contrast, has a public biography for children, in which certain edited highlights have gained quasi-mythic status. He is himself the 'Big Friendly Giant' because children know a great deal more about him than they do about most authors, and the 'life' that they know hovers uncertainly between reality and invention. There is an unusual reciprocity between fiction and fiction-maker: pleasure in Dahl's books arouses children's interest in his life, while the life (eventful enough in itself, but selectively presented and opportunistically fictionalised) creates yet more interest in the stories. If the process of reading used to be regarded, in electrical terms, as a direct current from text to child, but is now thought of as closer to alternating current, Dahl's unique achievement was to adjust the wiring so that the alternating current passed through himself and his life. In some respects he reinvented children's authorship, an appropriate achievement for someone whose vocation as inventor extended beyond the boundaries of literature.

Dahl himself wrote two volumes of autobiography for children, *Boy* (1984) and *Going Solo* (1986). A shorter piece, 'Lucky Break : How I became a Writer', was included in his book for older children, *The Wonderful Story of Henry Sugar* (1977). In form and address these works are virtually indistinguishable from the stories. *Henry Sugar* is itself a compilation of fiction and non-fiction. These are key texts in establishing features of Dahl's popularity. Chris Powling has written two biographical works on Dahl for children, both entitled *Roald Dahl*. The first, intended for Dahl's older readers, was first published in 1983. The second, which is very short and is directed at the youngest Dahl enthusiasts, those still busy with *The Enormous Crocodile* and *The Magic Finger*, appeared in the 'Tell Me About: Writers' series in 1997. Both are conspicuously free of criticism and reinforce both the general personality cult of Dahl and the particular episodes on which it mainly rests (the 1983 book describes its subject somewhat implausibly as 'modest'). In addition there have been radio and television programmes, including one in the series about six key children's writers called 'An Awfully Big Adventure', which reiterate a number of the famous incidents in Dahl's life.[17] Biographical publicity has been disseminated through the various institutions and charities with which he was, or remains, or posthumously has become, connected. Collectively this is a formidable biographical output for the child reader, and I am not aware of any precedent or parallel in the case of any other writer.

Certain incidents in Dahl's life are now legendary. Because they form part of a composite myth for children, Dahl may have fallen into a trap of his own vigorous making and produced a self-created life which is almost indistinguishable from story. However, the 'almost' is important. Young readers have been invited with great skill, both by Dahl himself, promoters such as Powling and latterly those in charge of his estate, to enjoy his life as an exciting story but retain a consciousness of factuality which makes it different. In life, the Dahl of biography for children was a heroic magician, and his stories become a part of a more general magic. Moreover,

---

17 'An Awfully Big Adventure': television programme on Roald Dahl transmitted on BBC2, 7 March 1998.

his magic was born from suffering and pain, and represents a positive, imaginative, improvisatory, defiant response to it. As such, the story behind the stories has a moral, and all the controversial, seemingly anarchic, subversive and salacious material which has repeatedly provoked the adult world to protest, is framed by a metanarrative of the author's life, and justified by it.[18] My account of this process does not imply denigration of it, and the collective achievement (collective in that other people have greatly expanded it since Dahl died) seems to me on balance admirable. Precisely because the curriculum vitae of Dahl's public persona is now inevitably trapped in its own quasi-fictionality, it is important to affirm the painful realities which underwrite the legend.

The key events concern Dahl's childhood, his war service in the RAF, and his adult family life. Pain, illness or loss in one form or another are common to them all. Dahl was born in Wales of Norwegian parents in 1916. His early experience of bereavement, and its tragic repetition in his own adult life, are baldly sketched for the child reader in *Boy* (1984):

> In 1920, when I was still only three, my mother's eldest child, [Dahl's father was a widower who had re-married, and had two children by his first wife] my own sister Astri, died from appendicitis. She was seven years old when she died, which was also the age of my own eldest daughter, Olivia, when she died from measles forty-two years later. (p. 20)

Dahl's father, grief-stricken by Astri's death, himself died two months afterwards, leaving the boy's mother to supervise his upbringing and education. After kindergarten, he was sent first to Llandaff Cathedral School (where he was beaten), then as a boarder to St Peter's preparatory school in Weston-super-Mare (where he was regularly beaten) and then to Repton (where he was beaten by prefects, and where according to Dahl the headmaster was a sadistic flogger). Corporal punishment comes over from his writings as Dahl's dominant memory of his schooldays. It later became an event in his self-created biography, but whatever its later narrative attractions for him, the experience was an actual, not an invented, horror.

In the Second World War Dahl was a fighter pilot. This period of his life also became significant material for writing; indeed, it started his literary career. His first supposedly factual accounts of his experiences, and a set of flying stories which are different in nature from anything he wrote afterwards, were followed many years later by the war chapters in his second autobiography for children, *Going Solo*. These dangerous and heady days were also to feature prominently in Dahl's self-created biographical myth. Dahl had a cavalier and less than modest attitude both to flying and the narratives he later made from it, but even Treglown, who is a sceptical biographer, concedes that 'Dahl had a right to boast, and his having been a war hero was to be important to him for the rest of his life'.[19] In 1940 he flew a Gloster

---

18 *Sunday Times*, 20 August 1995, reported an attempt by a woman in Stafford County, Virginia, to ban six Dahl titles, most notably *George's Marvellous Medicine*. She was reported as saying: 'My children have been taught to love and cherish their grandparents, and they have also been taught that household cleaning products are poisonous. When the teacher read that book, she undermined those basic values.'

19 Treglown, *Roald Dahl*, p. 44.

Gladiator, a type of aircraft with which he was not familiar, under orders to join his squadron in western Egypt. Problems of navigation meant that, having almost run out of fuel, he was obliged to make a forced landing in the desert, and he crashed the plane, sustaining serious injuries. The crash probably saved his life, because he was out of action for several months, and although he recovered well enough to take part in a significant period of active service, the after-effects of his injuries eventually caused him to be invalided out of service as a pilot. He constructed a heroic romance, eventually for children, out of these experiences, but the reality at the heart of them meant that he was in pain for the rest of his life.

In 1953 Dahl married the American actress Patricia Neal, and three traumatic events from that marriage make up the other major events in the Dahl legend. In 1960 his baby son, Theo, only four months old, was desperately injured when his pram was hit by a cab in New York while being wheeled across the road by a nanny who was escorting his elder sister Tessa home for lunch. One consequence was that the family came to live in England, at Gipsy House, Great Missenden in Buckinghamshire, which was Dahl's permanent home thereafter. Here, in the autumn of 1962, his eldest daughter Olivia died of complications following measles. Then, early in 1965, his wife Patricia suffered a catastrophic stroke which, but for Dahl's instant prompt action, would undoubtedly have been fatal, and which left her disabled. Patricia went on to make a remarkable recovery, in part thanks to Dahl, making more films and building a rehabilitation centre in Knoxville.

What unites this appalling series of events is the fact that Dahl's child readers know about them. The earlier ones he narrated himself in *Boy* and *Going Solo*. The later ones feature prominently in various kinds of publicity aimed at children. For example, Theo's accident, Olivia's death and Patricia's stroke are all given coverage (backed by photographs) in Powling's mini-biography for the youngest readers.[20] Dahl put his own life on the table as part of the contract with his young readers, and over and above the intrinsic appeal of the stories it is the extra element of conspiratorial trust, the sense that Dahl is placing his adult self within reach of children, breaking the rules of adult–child decorum, disclosing secrets and saying the unsayable, that largely explains his enormous popularity with children and discomfiture for adults. The life events are an essential element in this contract, which changed and deepened its nature over time. (Hints of what might come can already be seen in the intimate narrative voice, the mediation of ruthlessness through comedy, the hilarious but shocking exposure of sudden, unforeseen life-chasms, in the first page of *James and the Giant Peach*, but Dahl's self-focused success is nevertheless an evolutionary process.)

These life events affect Dahl's work in different ways. The deaths of Astri and Olivia naturalised child death for the modern reader. Nineteenth-century conditions, in which high child mortality would be expected, have long gone, having given place – against the evidence – to a myth of total childhood safety. Dahl's fictions, biographically reinforced by his own known losses, deal ruthlessly with this cosiness. He does not actually exterminate children in his stories, except under cover of the farcical-grotesque, as in *Charlie and the Chocolate Factory*, but he encompasses

---

20 Chris Powling, *Roald Dahl* (London: Evans, 1997), pp. 14–15.

death in the strange and moving blend of disquiet and comfort at the end of *The Witches*, and almost always shows up life as unsafe ground. Critiques of Dahl make too little allowance for children's recognition that, behind all the showmanship, behind the comic, fantastic, grotesque and bizarre, they are being admitted to 'adult' truths.

The war reminiscences are rather different, and simpler. These are buccaneering experiences, with Dahl cast as the boyish adventurer in a war game, undercut by reminders that the game is real and deadly. They are also tales of authority mocked, in which powers-that-be are depicted as fallible, incompetent, amusing, but also – precisely because of the power invested in them and their superior incompetence – life-threatening. These episodes are consistent with a pattern widely discernible in Dahl's work, of adult authority falling contemptibly short of the good and necessary reasons why authority exists. In the stories this is variously true of parents, grandparents, teachers and those with power over animals. It is a pattern that children recognise. In seeming to pander to it Dahl incurs the charge of subversiveness, but the framing narrative of anger against tyranny, and conformist support for well-used authority, provides a context which children are just as quick to accept, and which grew steadily clearer as his own life became inextricable from his work. Dahl was a very conformist anarchist. Treglown reports an incident at the time of Dahl's brush with the Cox Committee:

> even in the English-teaching debate, he wasn't unequivocally on the same side as the Conservative powers-that-were. True, Dahl told the *Daily Mail* that he was a firm believer in the necessity of teaching 'proper parsing and proper grammar'. Yet *Matilda*, which was published in the same year as Dahl's resignation from the Baker–Cox Committee, is among other things an onslaught on Gradgrindian teaching methods. Soon afterwards, the cultural commentator Bryan Appleyard suggested that in his authoritarian guise, Dahl 'should disapprove of his own books' because they were subversive. The author admitted to Appleyard that he had no answer to this. 'It's a tightrope act and you've got me in a bit of a corner.'[21]

But Appleyard had not really got him in a corner. What Dahl repeatedly showed was a need (because of adult human shortcomings) for subversion, but a need (for reasons of civilised order) to subvert the subversion once it has destroyed the tyrants, such as Trunchbull or the Twits. The subversive narratives exist within a conformist metanarrative. And this is a scenario perceived and approved by children who, like so many, have welcomed the reassertion of classroom discipline in the wake of a disorder they have thoroughly enjoyed. Even Matilda, having saved Miss Honey, needs her.

Dahl in fact had a triple position which he himself (as his response to Appleyard shows) imperfectly understood. It consisted of belief in 'civilisation', anger with generalised adult defection from it, and an attitude to children compounded of sympathetic alliance and dislike (which is how most children view children). Among Dahl's life experiences, nothing reflects his unresolved ambivalence more clearly than the question of corporal punishment. Dahl certainly suffered beatings at three

---

21 Treglown, *Roald Dahl*, p. 249.

schools, and *Boy* is obsessed with them – so much so that by the time he gets to the Repton chapters he feels obliged to explain himself:

> By now I am sure you will be wondering why I lay so much emphasis upon school beatings in these pages. The answer is that I cannot help it. All through my school life I was appalled by the fact that masters and senior boys were allowed literally to wound other boys, and sometimes quite severely. I couldn't get over it. I never have got over it. It would, of course, be unfair to suggest that *all* masters were constantly beating the daylights out of *all* boys in those days. They weren't. Only a few did so, but that was quite enough to leave a lasting impression of horror upon me. (1986, pp. 144–5).

It certainly seems that Dahl could not help it. The beating of small boys by seniors is the subject of his adult short story 'Galloping Foxley', which appeared in the collection *Someone Like You*. In the essay 'Lucky Break', he recounts three of the four beating episodes which later appeared in *Boy*, including the accusation that the Headmaster of Repton in Dahl's time, Geoffrey Fisher, who subsequently became Archbishop of Canterbury, was a sadistic flogger. This lurid anecdote resurfaced for a third telling in yet another autobiographical work for children, the posthumous *My Year* (1993), which had first appeared in *The Dahl Diary* (1992). There is also a beating in *Danny the Champion of the World*, which redeploys a number of details from the first-hand experiences. There is the appalled disbelief ('It was almost impossible to believe that this man was about to injure me physically and in cold blood'); the struggle not to cry out but the impossibility of holding back tears; and Danny's horror when his father threatens to go to the school and counter-attack the teacher, which echoes the young Dahl's unsuccessful effort to prevent his mother from confronting the Headmaster of Llandaff Cathedral School.

Dahl's attitude to these atrocities is ostensibly one of humanitarian outrage. In fact it is more complex, as indeed was the attitude of many children, and provides a better argument against corporal punishment than simple indignation. Dahl's writing reveals a voyeuristic fascination with the ritual of beating, even when he himself is the sufferer. He shows Danny almost able to stand outside himself, observing his own role in the enactment of a ritual, and that is how he represents his own experience. The child reader is invited to share the appalled excitement, from a standpoint of precarious immunity. The obsessive memory is unhealthy but also highly marketable, to children who are readily fascinated by the punishment of other children.[22] But once again Dahl transmits a mixed signal. The *ritual* of beating arouses in Dahl, and expects of the child reader, an enthralled repugnance. The brute fact of violence inflicted by large men on small boys – the abuse of children and abuse of power – makes him angry. But the still small voice of authority is not silenced, though contained by jocularity of tone: 'There is nothing wrong with a few quick sharp tickles on the rump', wrote Dahl in *Boy*, immediately after his

---

22 An apposite comment is that of Edwin Muir, on the effect of witnessing corporal punishment as a boy in Orkney: 'Certain boys were punished day after day as part of the routine: a brutal ceremony which we watched in a silent fascination and dread which might easily have implanted in us a taste for sadism and insidiously corrupted us.' Edwin Muir, *An Autobiography* (London: Hogarth Press, 1954), p. 70.

burst of indignation: 'They probably do a naughty boy a lot of good' (1986, p. 145). In an interview shown in the television programme 'An Awfully Big Adventure', he spontaneously invented a 'beating-machine', which would administer beatings automatically, 'without the human element of the beater', and this reveals his standpoint clearly. It is not physical punishment that he opposes, but 'the human element'; not the principle of authority, but its abuse by fallen adult humankind. Again there is a narrative within a biographical metanarrative. Its attractions for children are far from simple but extremely strong.

Boy and *Going Solo* are popular and important books, largely original in kind. They supply essential clues for readers of Dahl's stories, but are in no sense ancillary. They lie at the centre of Dahl's reinvention of children's authorship, as junction points between the books and the persona which collectively comprise the Dahl phenomenon. The literary precedent for *Boy* is surely Dylan Thomas's *Portrait of the Artist as a Young Dog* (1940). Dahl greatly admired Thomas. They were almost exact contemporaries (Thomas was born in 1914, Dahl in 1916), and because Dahl was an anglicised Norwegian it is often forgotten that he was born and spent his earliest years in South Wales. The culture which made Thomas had its share in Dahl. Some lines by Thomas are quoted by Miss Honey in *Matilda* (1988), and described by the narrator as 'great romantic poetry' (p. 185). In Thomas's book of loosely linked and freely autobiographical short stories, especially the early ones with their child's-eye-view of adult absurdity, Dahl surely found the ideal model for his own books, which he was able to convert to a form expressly for children. What Dahl did with these two books is essentially what he did with his life: an experiment in self-creation which is highly original and seductive for child readers.

The two remaining life events important to Dahl's legendary status are his son Theo's accident and his wife Patricia's stroke. Dahl did not write about these events for children, but children know about them. They are part of the means by which others have incorporated Dahl himself in his world of story. His response to both events shows Dahl at his most practical and determined, a polymath for emergencies, an inventor of ways and means who could write the storyteller's continuities into every aspect of life.

The events themselves are well known and can therefore be briefly described. One consequence of Theo's head injuries, sustained in the New York street accident, was that 'he developed hydrocephalus, – a build-up of cerebrospinal fluid which puts pressure on the brain.'[23] The fluid must be drained, and at the time this was done through a tube controlled by a one-way valve. The valve kept clogging, causing major problems, and each time this happened an operation was necessary to renew the tube and valve. Dahl set out to investigate Theo's problem and to see if a better valve could be designed. Cutting a long and extraordinary story short, he did so with the aid of a hydraulic engineer called Stanley Wade and a neurological consultant called Kenneth Till. The result was the Wade–Dahl–Till Valve, a device which was generally marketed and widely used for many years. The details of the story are absorbing in themselves, but what concerns us most here is its potency as an element of the Dahl persona for children. Faced with an urgent difficulty which is quite outside

---

23 Treglown, *Roald Dahl*, p. 127.

your usual field, you do not genuflect in deference to experts and do nothing – you invent a solution. Dahl's patent beating-machine may be a mere facetious whim, but the cast of mind behind it is impressive and effective when it turns to serious things. Both his stories and the selective examples of his life convey to children the virtues of a fundamental educational positive, that of motivated curiosity; and the positive underlies even its most gleefully anarchic and irresponsible expression in the stories, notably in *George's Marvellous Medicine* and *The Twits*.

The final biographical event which is now part of the Dahl legend for children is his dedicated and ruthless (and successful) programme of rehabilitation for his wife Patricia, after her stroke. This episode is well known, complex and controversial, and no doubt reaches children in a very simplified and anodyne form, but it forms part of an appealing story-and-life unity in which the principle of action is to cut away norms of convention, restraint and probability in order to improvise solutions to a crisis.

Although the 'life events' occurred many years ago, and Dahl's first children's book was published in 1961, the bulk of his best work was written and published in the final decade of his life, and it was also at this late stage that he became a 'public figure', associated with educational and philanthropic causes. Jeremy Treglown helpfully summarises these activities, while sceptically suggesting that much of the impetus behind them came from Dahl's hopes of a knighthood. Far more importantly, much of his activity was connected, sometimes closely, with his family experiences, and this appears to have been the real driving force behind it. Treglown sets out some of his enterprises:

> He gave the £3000 proceeds of the Whitbread prize [which he won for *The Witches*] to an Oxford hospice for terminally ill children. He bought equipment for disabled children and for research programmes into neurological disorders, supported hospital fund-raising schemes (on behalf of the Great Ormond Street Hospital, for example). He gave time and money to organizations concerned with learning difficulties, particularly the Dyslexia Institute, and backed anyone he heard of who was doing anything to encourage children to read.[24]

Where literacy and reading were concerned, Dahl was tireless, and one of his inspired enterprises was the Readathon, with its simple concept that children would undertake sponsored reading or other literacy-based activities in support of charities caring for sick children, one of them the Malcolm Sargent fund for children suffering from cancer. As chairman of Readathon for the last two years of his life, he said to teachers: 'Please join Readathon. Not only will your pupils be encouraged to read good books, they will help sick children at the same time.'

Another such story-based benevolent enterprise was *The Vicar of Nibbleswicke* (1991), written at the very end of his life with proceeds donated to the Dyslexia Institute. It is typical of Dahl to give his aid to this excellent cause by writing a story built on jokes about dyslexia, not least the lavatorial humour which many children find hilarious. It is a miniature example of Dahl's transgressive orthodoxy. Even the Communion service is recruited to the joke. The Reverend Lee, a vicar who

---

24 Ibid., p. 248.

suffers from 'a very rare disease called "Back-to-Front Dyslexia"', is explaining the administration of Communion wine to Mrs Purgative, who wants to know whether she should take 'a good gulp or just a little sip'.

> 'Dear lady,' cried the vicar, 'you must never plug it! If everyone were to plug it the cup would be empty after about four goes and the rest of them wouldn't get any at all! What you must do is pis. Pis gently. All of you, all the way along the rail must pis, pis, pis. Do you understand what I mean? (pp. 15–16)

Dahl loved this kind of joke.[25] For children Dahl could foster constructive real-life sympathies out of scatological comedy, and *The Vicar of Nibbleswicke*, like *Boy* and *Going Solo* though less obviously, links his writing with his total extra-literary persona as a children's author.

Nowhere is this more 'officially' done than in another small late work, *Roald Dahl's Guide to Railway Safety* (1991), which he wrote at the request of the British Railways Board. Like his membership of the Cox Committee, this splendid pamphlet is an indication of his status. Dahl was chosen for his popularity, for the 'Oh, it's by *Roald Dahl*!' factor with which we began. Here was someone whose mere name on a pamphlet would capture children. Yet the message was clearly to be didactic: the children's ally and entertainer would use that part of himself which stood for Authority. Dahl does this with great skill, in a miniature version of his contract with the child as I have tried to describe it. First he places himself on the child's side, with the last of his many variations on the theme of physical size.[26] The grown-ups are shown (literally shown, with the customary marvellous aid of Quentin Blake's illustrations), as tyrannous giants, who are pesky monsters incessantly ordering children about. Then comes the avuncular diktat implied in so many earlier stories:

> What the child does not understand is that unfortunately the GIANTS *have* to do this. It is the only way to bring up a child properly. When you are born you are an uncivilised little savage with bad habits and no manners and it is the job of the GIANTS (your parents and your teachers) to train you and discipline you. The child hates this and resists it fiercely. Yet it has to be done. (p. 3)

The aggressive rudeness of this, with its mix of humour and real-life matter-of-factness, keeps enough of Dahl's child-to-child contract to sanction the adult voice and attitude – only a little more explicitly than usual. Dahl then takes the reader into his confidence about the fame and appeal of *Matilda*: 'In it there are a pair of perfectly revolting parents and a foul tyrant of a teacher. The young reader is invited to hate them all and he does.' Only after this careful renewal of his contract does Dahl

---

25 It is a repeat performance of the story *Esio Trot*, in which backwards language is used by tortoises. ('Tortoises are very backward creatures. Therefore they can only understand words that are written backwards'.) Mr Hoppy shows Mrs Silver an example of it. '"WORG PU, FFUP PU, TOOHS PU!"' Mrs Silver says: '"How clever. But there's an awful lot of poos in it. Are they something special? " "Poo is a very strong word in any language," Mr Hoppy said.'

26 Jokes about size, which in some respects replicate the motif from *Alice's Adventures in Wonderland*, are to be found in Dahl's *Boy*, *George's Marvellous Medicine*, *The Twits* and *The Witches*.

proceed to the lessons on railway safety, first defensively asserting that 'I have been careful never to preach, never to be moralistic and never to convey any message to the reader.' But this is completely untrue. Dahl's matchless prestidigitation is that his works *seem* to repudiate moral norms and intentions, while his known biographical persona, indivisible from the stories, acceptably embodies them. In his books, even here in this brilliant little manual, Dahl offers the child both the excitement of anarchy and an authorial charm against it.

Since Dahl died his educational and philanthropic enterprises have been expanded by others. Most important, his widow, Felicity Dahl, established the Roald Dahl Foundation, which gives grants in three major causes – literacy, because Dahl so passionately believed in it; neurology, because the family had such painful first-hand experience of brain damage and brain disease; and haematology, because Dahl himself died of leukaemia. Just as the Readathon showed Dahl's own ability to recruit one good cause in the service of another, so Mrs Dahl has fostered children's orchestral music, both to enrich the limited repertoire and to benefit the Foundation from the royalties accrued. In ways such as these, Dahl's life and personality are even more deeply implicated in the popularity of his texts than they were in his own lifetime. Even Dahl's ambivalences are alive and well. His hatred of greed and love of food (both evident at the start in *James* and *Charlie*) have won posthumous life in *Roald Dahl's Revolting Recipes. The Roald Dahl Diary* annually renews awareness of the Foundation and the Roald Dahl Club. In Aylesbury, Buckinghamshire County Museum has opened the Roald Dahl Gallery, a hands-on museum experience which is partly an actualisation of the stories, partly an education in problem-solving and invention, partly a celebration of Dahl's life and its legendary highlights. For children, the work is the man; the books are the life.

The 'real' Roald Dahl was clearly a very difficult man who was not, to put it mildly, universally loved. He was undoubtedly a misanthrope, of whom at one level it is true to say 'He hates people; adults and children', and that the books have 'covert, anti-child (and perhaps anti-human) purposes'.[27] There may also be some validity in John Rowe Townsend's list of charges laid against him, which 'include sadism (as in the ghastly punishments inflicted on the horrid children in *Charlie and the Chocolate Factory*), misogyny (the dreadful aunts in *James and the Giant Peach*), the identification of women with villainous magic (*The Witches*), obsession with the excremental ... and the encouragement of children's vengeful and aggressive impulses'.[28] Both man and work, considered separately, have some unappealing features. I have argued that they were usurped by a complex phenomenon which included both but is unlike either. And it is this charismatic presence which children recognise as a much-loved entertainer, truthteller and ally. Beginning with the marketing of children's texts in the 1960s, Dahl's success gathered pace in the 1970s and especially the 1980s, as it evolved into the marketing of an authorial persona.

---

27 Cedric Cullingford, *Children's Literature and Its Effects: The Formative Years* (London: Cassell, 1998), p. 158; Peter Hunt, *Criticism, Theory and Children's Literature* (Oxford: Basil Blackwell, 1991), p. 191.

28 *Times Educational Supplement*, 30 November 1990.

Before his death this had taken specific form as a composite embracing children's literature, literacy and philanthropy. This Superdahl figure has prospered since he died, meticulously served and tended by his legatees and inheritors. The subversive maverick became a public institution.

Works by Roald Dahl cited in this chapter (listed chronologically)

James and the Giant Peach (1961), New York: Knopf; (1967), London: Allen and Unwin.

Charlie and the Chocolate Factory (1964), New York: Knopf; (1967), London: Allen and Unwin.

The Magic Finger (1966), New York: Harper; (1968), London: Allen and Unwin.

Fantastic Mr Fox (1970), London: Allen and Unwin; New York: Knopf.

Danny the Champion of the World (1975), London: Cape; New York: Knopf.

The Wonderful Story of Henry Sugar and Six More (1977), London: Cape; New York: Knopf.

The Enormous Crocodile (1978), London: Cape; New York: Knopf.

The Twits (1980), London: Cape; (1981), New York: Knopf.

George's Marvellous Medicine (1981), London: Cape; (1982), New York: Knopf.

The BFG (1982), London: Cape; New York: Farrar Straus.

The Witches (1983), London: Cape; New York: Farrar Straus.

Boy: Tales of Childhood (1984), London: Cape; New York: Farrar Straus; (1986), London: Penguin.

Going Solo (1986), London: Cape; New York: Farrar Straus.

Matilda (1988), London: Cape; New York: Viking Kestrel.

Esio Trot (1990), London: Cape.

Roald Dahl's Guide to Railway Safety (1991), London: British Railways Board.

'Galloping Foxley', in *The Collected Short Stories of Roald Dahl* (1991), London: Michael Joseph.

The Vicar of Nibbleswicke (1991), London: Random Century.

My Year (1993), London: Cape.

Chapter 15

'Most Popular Ever':
The Launching of Harry Potter[1]

Julia Eccleshare

On 26 June 2003, 4,000 school children filled the Albert Hall in London. From ceiling to floor they were divided into the four Hogwarts houses of Hufflepuff, Ravenclaw, Slytherin and Gryffindor by presiding 'prefects' decked out in gowns and school ties. They were already in a frenzy of expectation as they awaited the arrival of 'the world's best selling and most famous author' as her host, actor Stephen Fry, described her. In a blaze of spotlights and with a heralding fanfare J.K. Rowling stepped onto the stage. The applause was tumultuous. No one but Rowling herself could have heard the involuntary 'wow' which could be seen to pass her lips.

Unparalleled in literary history, J.K. Rowling's Albert Hall appearance is just one of numerous 'firsts' created by the 'Harry Potter' novels. Rowling's celebrity now reaches far beyond the world of books. She is reputedly one of the richest women in the world, having amassed rather more than £280 million from the sales of the books and all the related material, including film rights and the controversial merchandising deal with Coca-Cola. So unusual is this degree of commercial and non-book media success that it is sometimes hard to remember that she is an author, and a children's author at that.

The same could be said of the books themselves. In general, children's books do not usually figure importantly in the world of the media, and when they do achieve celebrity status, the process of finding the right publisher and audience may well have taken several years – but the almost instant success of the 'Harry Potter' series has stood such received wisdom on its head. For children and adults alike, these books are now read not only for the enjoyment they give but also because reading them has itself become culturally significant. The force of their cultural impact can be measured by the fact that, in the weekend following the publication of the fifth volume in the series, *Harry Potter and the Order of the Phoenix*, published throughout the world at midnight on 21 June 2003, it accounted for 44 per cent of total book sales. It is that impact, rather than critical judgements on Rowling's developing writing style or the relative merits of individual volumes as the series evolves, that has become the standard method of evaluating her achievement.

The extent of that achievement, both qualitatively (because the books have been so widely read and enjoyed), and quantitatively (because of their quite exceptional commercial success), gives the series an inarguable and exceptional place in popular culture. More surprisingly, the books may also be seen to claim their place within

---

1 Some of the material in this chapter has appeared previously in *A Guide to the Harry Potter Novels* by Julia Eccleshare (London: Continuum, 2002).

high culture, since they look set to enter the permanent canon of children's literature, worldwide.

As with comparable cultural phenomena, the reasons for the overwhelming success of the 'Harry Potter' titles are entirely explicable, though they can be represented in different ways. Unlike other art forms, even other forms of fiction, children's fiction tends to rely on familiar and traditional elements as much or even more than on original elements to make its mark. The popularity of children's fiction is necessarily different from that of adult fiction because, according to current views of child development, children enjoy and are reassured by the predictable. Even Roald Dahl's stories, though often thought of as subversive, are predictable in that his child heroes overcome adversity – and the reader knows that they will. Thus, almost by definition, fiction for children makes less of an impact on the public at large than that written for adults, where there is a higher premium on originality. A further nudge towards the conventional derives from the 'moral' dimension present in almost all children's fiction. Such conformity to convention, the hallmark of the 'Harry Potter' books, is often regarded as a strength in this particular context. And there may be further, and more fundamental reasons for Rowling's success: Lisa Damour has argued that, 'The astounding popularity of the 'Harry Potter' series may derive, in part, from the fidelity with which these stories speak to the dynamic and unconscious conflicts, fears and wishes that arise when children set their sights on becoming adults.'[2]

Analysis of the books as 'fiction' with their 'action' storylines, the heroic figure of Harry himself and their firm emotional underpinning suggests obvious reasons for their success as stories for the young. But nothing within them explains how they became so popular with a far wider and more adult readership. It is often argued that their popularity derives only partly from the books themselves. Undoubtedly, the unparalleled scale of their success is largely due to their adoption or exploitation by a range of other media, and in particular to the film versions. Philip Nel examines the case for this view in his article, '"Is There a Text in This Advertising Campaign?": Literature, Marketing and Harry Potter', although in the final analysis, he attributes the success of the series to J.K. Rowling's literary skills.[3]

Nel ultimately disagrees with those who argue that Harry Potter's place in popular culture has little to do with the textual qualities of the books, their place within the canon of children's fiction or their celebration of morally, socially and culturally approved messages. Questioning their dominant position, Jack Zipes has claimed that, 'Phenomena such as the 'Harry Potter' books are driven by commodity consumption that at the same time sets the parameters of reading and aesthetic taste.'[4] 'What's so special about the Harry Potter books?' and 'Are they deserving

---

2   Lisa Damour, 'Harry Potter and the Magical Looking Glass: Reading the Secret Life of the Preadolescent', in Giselle Liza Anatol (ed.), *Reading 'Harry Potter': Critical Essays*, (Westport, CN and London: Praeger, 2003), p. 15.

3   Philip Nel, '"Is There a Text in This Advertising Campaign?": Literature, Marketing and Harry Potter', *Lion and the Unicorn* 29 (2005), 236–67.

4   Jack Zipes, *Sticks and Stones: The Troublesome Success of Children's Literature from Slovenly Peter to Harry Potter* (London and New York: Routledge, 2001), p. 172.

of such a heralded place in our culture?' are questions asked by Elizabeth Heilman in the introduction to her collection of essays on the subject.[5] Zipes is certainly not alone in believing that, far from benefiting children by offering them an imaginative and stimulating world, Harry Potter is an aesthetically 'failed fantasy', containing dangerously conservative ideology and including messages that are subliminally sexist and racist. According to this view, it is the underpinning of the stories with such subliminal messages that has made the books so readily and eagerly exploitable by the rapidly growing cultural industries that shape our attitudes and expectations through the practice of global and multi-national capitalism.

On the face of it, much that Rowling espouses – and certainly the core concept of a selective boarding school – cuts across the current daily reality of the lives of young readers across the world. In providing her stories with such a setting, Rowling was adopting a long-standing British tradition that, despite its evident distance from children's actual experience, had found popularity in fiction at least since the nineteenth century. In his essay on the appeal of school stories, George Orwell linked it to the British preoccupation with social status, defining the real function of such stories as allowing 'the boy who goes to a cheap private school (*not* a Council school) to imagine that his school is just as "posh" in the sight of God as Winchester or Eton.'[6] While the terms of reference have changed, Orwell's reasoning may still hold good. Central to the Rowling phenomenon is Hogwarts Academy, which offers a version of an élitist ideal that struck a chord in the highly conventional 1990s, and such élitism may still play a part in middle-class fantasies. Tammy Turner-Vorbeck has argued that, 'The Harry Potter books participate in cultural hegemony by featuring socially normative messages and middle-class cultural hierarchies.'[7]

Whatever impact Harry Potter may have had on cultural expectations, his origins are quite as traditional, familiar, predictable and heroic as the books themselves. The moment J.K. Rowling embarked on her sequence of 'Harry Potter' stories was not a propitious one for children's books. In the first half of the 1990s reading among children, even as a functional tool, had become a problem for which the British government had devised a special National Literacy Strategy. It was hoped that by returning to the basics of grammar, spelling and punctuation, this strategy would produce more and better readers. For a number of reasons, in part linked to the appeal of other available media, many children were neither proficient at reading nor interested in being so. While literary authors such as Anne Fine, Peter Dickinson, Berlie Doherty and Philip Pullman (then far less well known, and certainly not the high-profile 'crossover' author he would later become) were quietly keeping their readers entertained, too many young people found reading children's books boring and irrelevant. Publishers in the UK were desperately searching for a formula that

---

5   Elizabeth E. Heilman in her introduction, 'Fostering Critical Insight through Multidisciplinary Perspectives', to her edited collection, *Harry Potter's World: Multidisciplinary Critical Perspectives* (New York and London: RoutledgeFalmer, 2003), p. 23.

6   George Orwell, 'Boys' Weeklies' (1940), in *Critical Essays* (London: Secker and Warburg, 1946), p. 77.

7   Tammy Turner-Vorbeck, 'Pottermania: Good, Clean Fun or Cultural Hegemony?' in Heilman, *Harry Potter's World*, pp. 13–24 (p. 13).

would help to stem the tide running against reading. Established authors and safe, formulaic writing were most in demand. In particular, knowing that, in choosing their next book, children are mainly guided by the author's name and the series in which it appears, publishers were eagerly searching for a home-grown series that might rival the two big American imports – Ann M. Martin's 'The Baby-Sitter's Club' series (begun in 1986) and R.L. Stine's 'Goosebumps' (from 1992).

The lack of serious literary or academic interest in children's books in the public sphere during the 1990s further contributed to their low status. In the post-war decades, children's reading had been regarded as crucial in order to establish a strong and committed adult readership. The *Times Literary Supplement* had devoted four substantial issues a year to children's book reviews, while at the *Times* and the *Guardian* respectively Brian Alderson and John Rowe Townsend had regularly reviewed the books produced by a strong band of 1960s and 1970s authors that included Jill Paton Walsh, Nina Bawden, Robert Westall and Jan Mark. But by the 1990s, this regular and properly critical coverage had to some extent been abandoned. Instead, children's books were increasingly seen as an adjunct of education. Now they were defined by their readership, and often addressed to a specific need – suitable books for 'reluctant' boy readers were particularly in demand.

It was against this background that Joanne Rowling began to plan her books. A keen reader herself as a child, with favourites ranging from the obvious Enid Blyton to less familiar works such as Elizabeth Goudge's *The Little White Horse* (1946), she knew rather less of the contemporary children's book scene. In fact, she wasn't even certain that she was writing a children's book at all, although, with its strong school setting, it must always have had an obvious and direct link with children. Rowling's story of the invention of Harry Potter has, in turn, become part of the Potter mythology: according to her account, the idea for the stories came to her on a train, as she travelled from Manchester to London. Without pen or pencil to hand, she invented the central character, Harry, and some of his entourage – Harry's best friend Ron Weasley, Hagrid and the ghost 'Almost Headless Nick'. Their names were often developed later, from Rowling's knowledge of classical literature (she had a degree in French and classical studies), or from *Brewer's Dictionary of Phrase and Fable*.[8] The school setting was conceived from the beginning, and became the centrepiece of the stories: 'I was thinking of a place of great order, but immense danger, with children who had skills with which they could overwhelm their teachers.'[9]

Rowling spent five years planning the books – she knew that there were to be seven of them, one for each of Harry's years at Hogwarts – and she filled up a number of cheap notebooks with names of people and places. All were grounded in a detailed background of facts which the reader need not know, but they explain how the characters can be developed to fit into a particular story as it unfolds.

The actual writing was carried out at the end of five years during which Rowling had held a series of office jobs before moving to Oporto in Portugal and getting married there. The first three chapters almost in their final form, along with a rough

---

8   See Jessy Randall, 'Wizard Words: The Literary, Latin, and Lexical Origins of Harry Potter's Vocabulary', *Verbatim: The Language Quarterly* 26 (2001), 3–7.

9   Interview with J.K. Rowling by Lindsey Fraser, *Scotsman*, Saturday 9 November 2002.

draft of the rest, were written in the months before Rowling's 28th birthday and the birth of her daughter. According to the legend, Rowling left her husband and moved to Edinburgh, writing in a café with the baby beside her, asleep in its buggy. This story of how the first book, *Harry Potter and the Philosopher's Stone,* was written, eking out a cup of coffee, which was all she could afford on her single-parent benefit payment, is now almost as well known as the book itself.

While Rowling found writing a positive pleasure, getting her book published was more difficult, but a Scottish Arts Council Bursary paid for a typewriter and gave her the confidence to finish *Harry Potter and the Philosopher's Stone*. Consulting the *Writers' and Artists' Year Book*, she realised that, at 90,000 words, her book was more than twice the optimum length that children's publishers were looking for. The current crisis of confidence in children's books meant that they were becoming shorter and shorter, in the hope of appealing to reluctant readers. Rowling accordingly tried to make her manuscript look shorter by typing it in long lines and with single spacing, but it remained a very long book by the standards of the day.

Following the advice of the *Writers' and Artists' Year Book*, Rowling sent a synopsis and the first three chapters to an agent and then to a publisher, both of whom returned them. In a second attempt to find an agent, she sent the manuscript to Christopher Little, since his name amused her. But she had failed to notice that Christopher Little didn't handle children's books, believing that there was no money in them, and her typescript would have been automatically rejected if Little's 25-year-old assistant had not read it and enjoyed the opening, especially the character of Mrs Dursley. She asked to see the rest.

Once they had read the whole manuscript, Christopher Little and his team were still enthusiastic about *Harry Potter and the Philosopher's Stone* and agreed to take it on the terms of their standard agreement, which included the control of all literary rights and the exploitation of any merchandising rights. Little then spent a year sending the manuscript to different publishers, all of whom rejected it on the grounds that it was too long. A comparable fate had attended Richard Adams's *Watership Down*, turned down by all the major publishing houses because it was too long. Finally Rex Collings, a tiny independent publisher, accepted it, and it went on to become an international bestseller. Little persevered, however, and the book was sold for the reputed figure of £1,500, along with six other titles in the series, to Barry Cunningham, then editorial director of Bloomsbury Children's Books.

Rowling was duly invited to London to meet the Bloomsbury publishing team. Cunningham thought

> she was shy about herself but very confident and intense about the book and, most importantly, very confident that children would like Harry. I knew she had had a tough time since coming from Portugal so I was very impressed with her dedication to the story. She just so understood about growing up.[10]

Cunningham, an experienced and enthusiastic editor with a strong marketing background, was assembling a small list of carefully chosen and distinctive books, each of which was strongly promoted as widely as possible. He believed in

10 Sean Smith, *J.K. Rowling* (London: Michael O'Mara, 2001), p. 138.

publishing 'books that children would respond to', and was always optimistic that, because Bloomsbury was small and its children's list so new, they could do things differently. But he was realistic as well, and, knowing how hard it was to break into the children's book market, he warned Rowling at the end of their first meeting, 'You'll never make any money out of children's books, Jo.'[11]

As a small, new publisher, Bloomsbury was seldom offered the well-established, big-name authors since these were mostly tied by contract to larger and older children's publishers such as Puffin, Reed Children's Books (now Egmont), HarperCollins Children's Books and Transworld. This suited Cunningham well as he liked to take on new authors and illustrators, despite the fact that they were considered hard to sell or get noticed. He published picture books and fiction, and his early lists were experimental, both visually and in terms of the kind of fiction he was prepared to take a chance on. His own preference was for fantasy. By the time he was offered *Harry Potter and the Philosopher's Stone*, he had already published – with some success – Carol Hughes's *Toots and the Upside Down House* (1996), the first in a series set in a strange world where trendy latter-day fairies walk upside down on the ceiling.

Like other publishers of children's books, Cunningham knew that a sequence or series of titles by the same author was far more marketable than a one-off. As the first in a projected seven book series, *Harry Potter and the Philosopher's Stone* promised to be the kind of long-running publishing project that, once established, might take over from 'The Baby-Sitters Club' series or 'Goosebumps'. It was not only the concept that was marketable, though. The story itself was exactly the kind of entertaining, child-centred book that Cunningham was looking for. Like many of the best fantasies (L. Frank Baum's *Wizard of Oz*, for example), it created a fully realised alternate world. And like J.R.R. Tolkien's Middle Earth or C.S. Lewis's Narnia, this was a world to which Rowling had given a wholehearted, long-term commitment, returning Harry to it for the central action of each of her books. Full of references to mythology, folk and fairy stories, the book portrays an unhappy orphan, a classic male-version of Cinderella, brought up by unwilling and ill-intentioned relatives who lock him up in the cupboard under the stairs, steal his post and dress him in rags. Bullied by his overweight cousin, Harry has much to escape from but no obvious means of doing so.

On the point of being sent to Stonewall High School in home-dyed, cast-off clothes belonging to his cousin, Harry's life is revolutionised on his eleventh birthday, discovering his real history and his magical destiny when he is invited to study at Hogwarts School of Witchcraft and Wizardry, the magical boarding school for children with special powers. His first official taste of magic comes when he is whisked away by Rubeus Hagrid, the school's giant Keeper of the Keys and Grounds, on a pre-school visit to Diagon Alley, a Dickensian shopping street in the alternative world. Its archaic nature is reinforced by the school outfitters – a bespoke tailor, a specialist bookshop and a wand-maker, all of whom might have come out of

---

11 Ibid.

Thomas Hughes's *Tom Brown's Schooldays* (1857) – a book that the 'Harry Potter' novels recall at more than one point.[12]

As Harry stocks up on his school kit, Rowling's gift for pastiche is much in evidence. His school uniform list includes, 'Three sets of plain work robes (black). One plain pointed hat (black) for day wear. One pair of protective gloves (dragon hide or similar). One winter clock (black, silver fastenings)', while an equipment list requires '1 wand, 1 cauldron (pewter, standard size 2), 1 set glass or crystal phials, 1 telescope, 1 set brass scales'.[13] This blend of the familiar and the magical, set out without any obvious indication of its humour, allows its readers to discover the joke for themselves.

On the Hogwarts' Express – the school train – Harry begins his magical education, while still quite ignorant of the wizarding world in general and the school in particular. Here he meets Ron Weasley and Hermione Granger, who will become his closest friends, and encounters for a second time his immediate and implacable enemy Draco Malfoy, with his equally unattractive sidekicks Crabbe and Goyle.

Rowling quickly establishes her child characters, sharply delineating one from another, and making each represent a clear 'type'. The use of threesomes, such as Rudyard Kipling's Stalky, Beetle and M'Turk in *Stalky and Co.* (1899) or even Athos, Porthos and Aramis in Alexandre Dumas's *The Three Musketeers* (1844), is a familiar fictional device which permits a variety of responses to any situation. Harry, with superior powers but greater ignorance of the world he now inhabits, is the innocent abroad; Hermione is the most knowledgeable and scholarly of the three; and Ron, the youngest brother in a family of wizards, is the most familiar with anything magical. As a team, they provide a range of responses to different challenges.

The 'Harry Potter' novels have assimilated much that is familiar from the mainstream of nineteenth- and twentieth-century children's literature. Harry's initial awareness that he is not the person the Dursleys think he is, recalls many previous children's classics (and reflects the longing to escape from the family that Freud termed 'the family romance'). So too is his conviction that the life that his real identity might entitle him to live is better than the life he is actually living. Also familiar is the nostalgia for the boarding school setting, a world where the pupils commonly run rings around their adult teachers. Indeed, it might be said that the 'Harry Potter' series has a Dahlesque beginning, with later overtones of Tolkien, and several Narnian fantasy sequences (as in Rowling's Forbidden Forest, for instance). A number of critics have pointed out more precise points of correspondence between Rowling's world and those of earlier children's books: a comparable school for wizards in which the pupil discovers his own powers was imagined by Ursula Le Guin in her 'Earthsea' trilogy (from 1968), while a very successful version was provided for younger readers by Jill Murphy in her series of schoolgirl witch stories, starting with *The Worst Witch* (1974). In Anthony Horowitz's *Groosham Grange* (1988), a

---

12 See David K. Steege, 'Harry Potter, Tom Brown, and the British School Story: Lost in Transit?' in Lana A. Whited (ed.), *The Ivory Tower and Harry Potter: Perspectives on a Literary Phenomenon* (Columbia, MO; London: University of Missouri Press, 2002), pp. 140–56.

13 *Harry Potter and the Philosopher's Stone* (London: Bloomsbury, 1997), pp. 52 and 53.

mysterious boarding school turns out to be a legendary Academy of Witchcraft, while an orphaned wizard finds his true destiny in Diana Wynne Jones's *Charmed Life* (1977), first of the 'Crestomanci' series (1977–88), when Gwendolen's downtrodden younger brother Cat discovers the truth about his magical powers (though here in a domestic rather than a school setting).

Originality has certainly never been Rowling's forte, but innovation is no guarantee of success in the field of children's books, and may not even be an advantage. Classic themes continue to be unashamedly popular, and both adults and children seem to enjoy the reassurance they bring. The distinction of the 'Harry Potter' books lies rather in Rowling's ability to assimilate so many different sources, and in her skill in retelling familiar stories in a fresh and engaging way. Her talent for manipulating a complex plot and gradually revealing it with a careful sense of timing is particularly notable, and so is her attention to detail, her inventive sense of humour and her power to transform the familiar into the spectacular through the addition of some fizzing magic. For Barry Cunningham of Bloomsbury Books, these qualities more than made up for any lack of originality. In her essay 'The Perils of Harry Potter', Alison Lurie observed,

> As with most first-rate children's books, there is something here for everyone. Pico Iyer, in *The New York Times Book Review,* sees the stories as only half-fantastic accounts of life in an English public school (in his case, Eton), 'designed to train the élite in a system that other mortals cannot follow'. There, as at Hogwarts, he claims, 'we were in an alternate reality where none of the usual rules applied'. A.O. Scott, on the other hand, thinks that 'being a wizard is very much like being gay: you grow up in a hostile world governed by codes and norms that seems nonsensical to you, and you discover at a certain age that there are people like you'.[14]

The length of the first 'Harry Potter' book did not worry Cunningham. His main concern about his new author was her name. Its title, *Harry Potter and the Philosopher's Stone,* sounded like that of a book for boys, and Cunningham knew that boys prefer books by male authors, so Joanne became 'J.K.' Rowling and the process of establishing the new author and her books began. Since it is notoriously difficult for a new author to gain attention, Bloomsbury followed the usual practice of sending bound proofs with an accompanying letter to selected authors, critics and booksellers in the field of children's books in order to elicit quotations to be used for future publicity. Some replied. 'Splendid stuff!' wrote David Morton of 'Daisy & Tom', the chain of one-stop children's shops. 'It's got just the right mix of normal life versus magic to make it extra-ordinary and hugely readable.' Fiona Waters concurred, also praising the book's readability, and its humour: 'I just loved this book, it is full of pace and interest and so very funny. There is something about Harry Potter that reminds me of Charlie Bucket in *Charlie and the Chocolate Factory.*' Lindsey Fraser of Book Trust Scotland found it 'a bold and confident debut from a splendid writer and storyteller'. The front of the first edition carried Wendy Cooling's opinion that this was 'A terrific read and a stunning first novel', a high compliment

---

14 Alison Lurie, *Boys and Girls Forever: Children's Classics from Cinderella to Harry Potter* (London: Penguin, 2003), p. 118.

snipped from a much fuller and more telling response. Cooling went on to say that 'Joanne Rowling clearly has a remarkable imagination and this splendid first novel leaves me full of anticipation of what she might do next.'

Cunningham had found the support he needed. Enough of the feel of the book was conveyed through the enthusiasm of its first readers, even though much of it was no more than the bland and interchangeable puffing produced by pre-publicity. Cunningham then selected the little-known artist Thomas Taylor for the cover illustration, selecting a cover as simple and old-fashioned as the story itself. Avoiding the glossy airbrushed style so popular for bestselling children's titles, Taylor produced an old-fashioned image of the schoolboy Harry, against the background of the scarlet Hogwarts Express. Random stars hint at magic. The portrait of Dumbledore on the back exposed Taylor's too hasty reading of the story: his initial image of Dumbledore shows a young-looking wizard, smoking a pipe and clutching a book that might contain spells. His beard and whiskers, like his hair, are brown, although the text describes Dumbledore's hair as silver, the only thing to shine as brightly as the ghosts when Harry sees him for the first time in the Great Hall. Dumbledore's hair and jacket were altered in later editions (see Figures 15.1 and 15.2).

In June 1997 *Harry Potter and the Philosopher's Stone* was published as a paperback original with the endorsements quoted above. Though Rowling had not envisaged the book as specifically for children, she came to see it as such, and it was originally published entirely for children, with no attempt to attract the kind of 'cross-over' market sometimes achieved by children's books, particularly in the USA. The print run was small, in line with the standard quantity for a first novel, and Cunningham and Bloomsbury hoped, as with all their books and especially their new authors, that booksellers would read it, get behind it and interest their customers in it.

Having done what they could to promote *Harry Potter and the Philosopher's Stone* before publication, Bloomsbury waited. Typically, there was no immediate response or review coverage on publication, but living in Edinburgh, Rowling was lucky to have the support of a thriving and committed book community: Waterstone's Edinburgh bookshops promoted the book strongly and Rowling herself as a local author. There was an excellent review in the *Scotsman* (quoted on many subsequent dustjackets), claiming that the book 'has all the makings of a classic'. The reviewer continued, 'Rowling uses classic narrative devices with flair and originality and delivers a complex and demanding plot in the form of a hugely entertaining thriller. She is a first-rate writer for children.'[15]

Further reviews followed. Reviews of children's books in the UK are seldom anything but positive, so their mere existence is quite as important as what they actually say. The *Glasgow Herald* pinpointed Harry Potter's immediate appeal to children: 'I have yet to find a child who can put it down. Magic stuff.' The London papers picked it up later: 'A richly textured first novel given lift-off by an inventive wit', wrote the *Guardian*. The specialist children's book magazine, *Books for Keeps*, also endorsed this new writer. Editor Rosemary Stones selected *Harry Potter and the Philosopher's Stone* for her 'New Talent' column in the September 1997 issue,

---

15 Quoted by Philip Nel, *The Harry Potter Novels: A Reader's Guide* (London and New York: Continuum, 2001), p. 53.

Harry Potter thinks he
is an ordinary boy –
until he is rescued by an
owl, taken to Hogwarts
School of Witchcraft and
Wizardry, learns to play
Quidditch and does
battle in a deadly duel.
The Reason…

HARRY POTTER IS
A WIZARD!

ISBN 0-7475-3269-9

9 780747 532699

http://www.bloomsbury.com

Figure 15.1   Outside back cover (first version) of J.K. Rowling, *Harry Potter and the Philosopher's Stone*, illustrated by Thomas Taylor (London: Bloomsbury Books, 1997). Collection of Julia Briggs. Reproduced with kind permission of Bloomsbury Publishing and the Christopher Little Literary Agency.

Figure 15.2   Outside back cover (revised version) of J.K. Rowling, *Harry Potter and the Philosopher's Stone*, illustrated by Thomas Taylor (1997; London: Bloomsbury Books, 2000). Collection of Julia Briggs. Reproduced with kind permission of Bloomsbury Publishing and the Christopher Little Literary Agency.

awarding it four out of a possible five stars: 'A school story for young wizards and witches has been done before', she wrote, 'but in this ambitious, many-layered, overlong first novel, Rowling creates a fresh and amusing school of magic.' She praised its use of the 'everyday friendships and rivalries of school life' to 'give a realistic base to the plot', and congratulated the author for convincingly developing 'the themes of bravery and the need to understand the "desperate desires of our hearts"'.[16]

Other critics compared it with Roald Dahl: 'a story full of surprises and jokes;' wrote the *Sunday Times*, so that 'comparisons with Dahl are, this time, justified'. For the *Mail on Sunday* this was 'the most imaginative debut since Roald Dahl'. Indeed, its resemblance to some of Dahl's fiction was so marked that it was difficult to overcome the feeling that Rowling had borrowed some of the basic elements of her story directly from his work. Harry's subjection and treatment as a servant at the hands of the Dursleys at the beginning of *Harry Potter and the Philosopher's Stone* closely echoes James's experiences in Dahl's *James and the Giant Peach* (1961), while Vernon and Petunia Dursley recall James's fat Aunt Sponge and thin Aunt Spiker: he has hardly any neck and a large moustache, while she is thin and blonde and has a long neck for spying on her neighbours; they are also reminiscent of Mr and Mrs Wormwood in *Matilda* (1988).

But the originality of Rowling's invention lay in the fact that Harry Potter is a boy hero who can take on adults by adopting adult responsibilities, while still remaining essentially child-like. She has a kinder eye than Dahl, and her characters are less brutal in their treatments of one another. She avoids the humiliation that Dahl revelled in. When retribution comes in *Harry Potter and the Philosopher's Stone*, it is tempered by salvation, rather than endorsed with glee (except perhaps where the odious Dudley Dursley is concerned). The actual similarity between Dahl and Rowling lies in their ability to speak directly to children without condescension or artifice – a crucial skill for writers for children.

An heir to Dahl had long been sought for. All quirky or imaginative writers since the 1970s had been hailed as 'the next Roald Dahl', but none had come anywhere near him in terms of popularity with readers, though some, like Andrew Davies with his *Marmalade Atkins* titles (1979–84) or Philip Ridley with his grim urban fairy stories such as *Krindlekrax* (1990), *Scribbleboy* (1991) and *Kasper in the Glitter* (1993), had attracted a certain amount of enthusiasm and a dedicated, if limited, readership. Dahl had died in 1990, but his books continued to dominate bestseller lists. In the months that followed the publication of *Harry Potter and the Philosopher's Stone* in 1997, Waterstone's Bookshops and the BBC ran a poll for the Nation's Favourite Children's Book. It was won by Dahl's last major novel, *Matilda* (1988), and out of the top ten, a further six were Dahl titles: *Charlie and the Chocolate Factory* (1964), *The BFG* (1982), *James and the Giant Peach* (1961), *The Witches* (1983), *The Twits* (1980) and *George's Marvellous Medicine* (1981). Indeed, only one book published during the nineties made it into the top ten – the tenth entry, Jacqueline Wilson's *Double Act* (1996).

---

16 Philip Nel, in ibid., lists a number of major early reviews of the 'Harry Potter' books, pp. 89–93.

Ultimately, new books would be needed to fill the gap left by Dahl's death. The British publishing industry may have hoped that a living British author would challenge the only other current multi-volume seller, the American writer R.L. Stine. That hope may have contributed to Rowling being selected as one of the three authors shortlisted for the 9–11 years category of the 1997 Nestlé's Smarties Book Prize. A panel of adult judges made up of an author, an illustrator, a publicist and a critic selected *Harry Potter and the Philosopher's Stone* along with Philip Pullman's *Clockwork* and Henrietta Branford's *Fire, Bed and Bone* to be ranked in order of gold, silver or bronze by the schoolchildren who acted as judges for the prize. First novels hardly ever hit prize shortlists, but *Harry Potter and the Philosopher's Stone* had enough original sparks to make it stand out. Once on the shortlist, Rowling stood a chance of winning the prestigious Smarties Gold Award. Voted for by children all over the country, this is a much coveted prize, since it is awarded by the young readers themselves. The unknown Rowling won the Gold Award by a healthy margin. Not only did this bring her considerable media attention but, more importantly, it was an early indication of what was to become increasingly evident: that children loved the book. Comparatively unaffected by the reputation of its author, they had voted for the book they liked the best. Harry was an ideal schoolboy hero in an entertaining magical world.

Favourable adult responses to *Harry Potter and the Philosopher's Stone* had placed it in children's hands, but winning the Smarties Gold Award marked it out as a book that aroused passionate enthusiasm in its readers. This gave it a high profile within the first six months of publication, by contrast with most children's books, which can take years to establish themselves. The following year, 1998, *Harry Potter and the Philosopher's Stone* won all the major children's book awards allocated by children. It was the overall winner of the Federation of Children's Book Groups Awards, winner of the *Young Telegraph* Paperback of the Year Award, winner of the Birmingham Cable Children's Book Award, and winner of the Sheffield Children's Book Award. It was also shortlisted for prizes awarded by adults, such as the Carnegie Medal and the Guardian Children's Fiction Prize. It did not win these, but Rowling collected two awards given by the publishing industry itself for unusual and considerable success in terms of sales and profile, rather than for literary merit: the British Book Awards Children's Book of the Year for the book, and the Booksellers Association/The *Bookseller* Author of the Year for J.K. Rowling. While it is often claimed that *Harry Potter* was created by media hype, these awards confirm that its initial success in the UK lay in its adoption by child readers, as a book that they genuinely enjoyed.

When *Harry Potter and the Philosopher's Stone* was published in the USA, now retitled *Harry Potter and the Sorcerer's Stone*, it became an overnight sensation. An early indication of its future success occurred at the Bologna Book Fair in April 1997, when Scholastic Inc. bought the rights to the US edition for an initially undisclosed six-figure sum (later revealed to be $105,000), an exceptionally large amount for a first children's book. The stir this caused led to the first news stories of Rowling as a struggling single parent, writing in a café to keep warm, while her baby slept beside her.[17]

In 1998, within months of its US publication, *Harry Potter and the Sorcerer's Stone* won the School Library Journal Best Book of the Year, the American Library Association Notable Book and Best Book for Young Adults, *Publishers Weekly*'s Best Book of the Year and *Parenting Magazine*'s Book of the Year Award, and also hit the bestseller list in the *New York Times*, the first children's book to do so since E.B. White's *Charlotte's Web* more than half a century earlier.

The enormous transatlantic success of the first 'Harry Potter' book established Rowling as a major new author for children. Across two continents, children had found a writer they actually wanted to read. The pattern was repeated all over the globe. With the US publication, adults, too – at least those professionally involved with children's books and reading – strongly endorsed Harry Potter. Rowling now began to scoop up the prizes awarded by adults, as well as those decided by children.

Harry Potter had become a phenomenon, and the success of the already-planned sequels was all but guaranteed. Although the first of the series had been released into a tough and inattentive marketplace, its successors would be published for a world queuing for them outside bookshops on the eve of their publication. But for *Harry Potter and the Philosopher's Stone* it was not so much shrewd marketing as the enthusiasm of its first young readers that launched it to fame.

---

17   See, for example, Dan Glaister, 'Debut Author and Single Mother Sells Children's Book for 100,000 Pounds', *Guardian*, 8 July 1997, p. 4.

Chapter 16

The Brand, the Intertext and the Reader: Reading Desires in the 'Harry Potter' Series

Stacy Gillis

Harold Bloom claims that J.K. Rowling's 'Harry Potter' novels are bland and lack 'an authentic imaginative vision'. Along the same lines, Jack Zipes regards them as 'formulaic and sexist', while John Pennington argues that the series does 'not have a firm footing in fantasy' and is 'never certain about fantasy content, structure, theme and how these components are essential to the reader's response to the fantastic'.[1] Despite these opinions – and numerous other similar responses – the 'Harry Potter' novels have gone from strength to strength with a global fanbase and substantial commercial success. In late 2005, it was announced that the series had sold over 300 million copies worldwide. Rowling is now only outsold by the Bible and Shakespeare.[2] Her novels have been translated into 63 languages, a number which is matched by such other international bestsellers as Agatha Christie. As the result, Rowling has become one of the top five wealthiest women in the United Kingdom. The novels have, of course, also been adapted for the screen and each of the films has achieved ticket sales which has put them at the top of the global box office. It is difficult to comprehend the vastness of Harry Potter's popularity. No other fictive character – whether in adult or children's literature or film – has generated so much interest. Sumon Gupta makes several points about the novels' popularity, stating that they 'are *economically* the most successful of all literary books published in recent years', that they 'have apparently transcended cultural boundaries more effortlessly than any other fictional work of recent years' and, subsequently, that they 'are the most challenged … and banned books of our time'.[3] It is difficult, if not impossible, to deny the overwhelming global presence of Harry Potter.

---

1   Harold Bloom, 'Can 35 Million Book Buyers Be Wrong? Yes', *Wall Street Journal*, 11 July 2000, p. A26; Jack Zipes, *Sticks and Stones: The Troublesome Success of Children's Literature from Slovenly Peter to Harry Potter* (London: Routledge, 2001), p. 171; John Pennington, 'From Elfland to Hogwarts, or the Aesthetic Trouble with Harry Potter', *Lion and the Unicorn*, 26, i (2002), 78–97 (pp. 82–83).

2   For example, *Harry Potter and the Half-Blood Prince* (2005) sold 6.9 million copies in the US over the space of 24 hours or almost 300,000 books per hour. At that point, it was the fastest-selling book in history. It generated book sales revenue over the opening weekend which outperformed the top movies at the box office.

3   Suman Gupta, *Re-Reading Harry Potter* (Basingstoke: Palgrave Macmillan, 2003), pp. 15 and 18.

Andrew Blake, Pennington and Zipes have all argued that Harry Potter or the Potter phenomenon is a prime example of contemporary capitalism.[4] As Philip Nel puts it, 'the novels and the hype become intertwined' and 'Harry Potter is both a marketing phenomenon and a literary phenomenon'.[5] The conflation, however, of these two categories can never fully answer the question of why precisely these novels are so popular. The marketing surrounding Harry Potter is certainly part and parcel of the series' popularity, just as the popularity of the series has become part and parcel of the marketing. In other words, the novels sell in such numbers partly because they are advertised as already having sold in high numbers. To elide these differences is to ignore the complexities of contemporary reading practices, markets and desires. This chapter is not, however, an account of the marketing or literary phenomenon that is Harry Potter. Other critics, already mentioned, have provided analyses of the impact of the novels on the global book market and of the Potter phenomenon, while recent collections have provided readings of the series which have touched upon such issues as fantasy, gender and class.[6] This chapter is more broadly concerned with the implications of this popularity on the field of children's literature criticism. Colin Manlove makes the point that children's literature is 'written at a distance, by people who have to try to remember what it feels like to be a child, or try to construct a childhood to write at', echoing Jacqueline Rose's argument that children's literature 'sets up a world in which the adult comes first (author, maker, giver) and the child comes after (reader, product, receiver), but where neither of them enter the space in between'.[7] It is the distance or space between with which this chapter is concerned: with the critical discussions of the 'Harry Potter' series which attempt to bridge this space. This chapter will discuss the growing pile of work which could be loosely grouped under the title of 'Harry Potter Studies', pointing up the ways in which this field exemplifies the popularity and the problems of children's literature criticism.

The Brand, the Intertext and the Reader

The 'Harry Potter' novels have been synergistically sold by a horizontally-integrated company. The series was able to move into the global market in such an overwhelming way primarily because of its initial popularity with its target reading audience of

---

4   Andrew Blake, *The Irresistible Rise of Harry Potter* (London: Verso, 2002); Pennington, 'From Elfland to Hogwarts'; Zipes, *Sticks and Stones*.

5   Philip Nel, 'Is There a Text in This Advertising Campaign?: Literature, Marketing and Harry Potter', *Lion and the Unicorn* 29, ii (2005), 236–67 (p. 236).

6   Several collections of essays have recently been published on the Potter phenomenon: Lana A. Whited (ed.), *The Ivory Tower and Harry Potter: Perspectives on a Literary Phenomenon* (Columbia: Missouri University Press, 2002); Giselle Liza Anatol (ed.), *Reading Harry Potter: Critical Essays* (Westport, CN: Praeger, 2003); Elizabeth E. Heilman (ed.), *Harry Potter's World: Multidisciplinary Critical Perspectives* (New York: RoutledgeFalmer, 2003).

7   Colin Manlove, *From Alice to Harry Potter: Children's Fantasy in England* (Christchurch: Cybereditions, 2003), p. 8; Jacqueline Rose, *The Case of Peter Pan or The Impossibility of Children's Literature* (Basingstoke: Macmillan, 1984), pp. 1–2.

children. Julia Eccleshare likens the novels' popularity to that experienced by Blyton and Dahl.[8] Manlove similarly compares the success of the books to the other

> smash hits with children last century – the *William* stories, Enid Blyton's books, and the fantasies of Roald Dahl. All of them can be enjoyed by children aged about 7–11 … Further, they often require thought and sophistication to understand – in short, a certain amount of work, which most younger children do not often feel should be required of their amusements.[9]

As with the works of Blyton and Dahl, the early popular reception of the 'Harry Potter' novels was largely contingent upon word-of-mouth recommendations between children, backed up by a reasonably positive reception in the reviews. While the increased communication possibilities of the internet certainly enabled an informal – and unquantifiable – reviewing to take place in a more accelerated fashion than had occurred with earlier popular children's texts, the success of the first novel in the series – *Harry Potter and the Philosopher's Stone* (1997) – was largely the result of children liking it and subsequently telling their friends that they should read it, and request it from libraries. This series of events has occurred with many other popular works for children. However, the conditions under which these works are consumed have changed, as Zipes has noted: 'the conditions under which literature for the young have been transformed through institutional corporate conglomerates controlling the mass media, and market demands. Phenomena such as the 'Harry Potter' books are driven by commodity consumption that at the same time sets the parameters of reading and aesthetic taste'.[10] The 'Harry Potter' novels became a force in the global marketplace because children *liked* the books: it is now, however, irrelevant whether children still like the individual books because of the strength of the Harry Potter brand.

Harry Potter is an instantly recognizable global brand, able to move between different cultural contexts. The novels

> are about something that appears not to be confined to the text or its 'implied readers' or, for that matter, actual readers or even the 'interpretative strategies' or 'interpretive communities'. It [is] more to do with images and the production of images and the place of images in producing, advertising and marketing books.[11]

Blake similarly identifies the success of the series as the result of the burgeoning strength of children's consumer identity and corporations capitalising thereon.[12] It is undeniable that the Potter brand has been an extremely lucrative one. The cross-media manifestations of the intertext that is the Potter brand – books (both in the series and spin-offs), toys, games (board, card, computer and so on), websites,

---

8   Julia Eccleshare, *A Guide to the Harry Potter Novels* (London: Continuum, 2002), pp. 11–12, 33–37.
9   Manlove, *From Alice to Harry Potter*, p. 186.
10   Zipes, *Sticks and Stones*, p. 172.
11   Gupta, *Re-Reading Harry Potter*, pp. 6–7.
12   Blake, *Irresistible Rise of Harry Potter*, pp. 76–80.

clothing and, of course, the movies – foregrounds Harry Potter as a global brand.[13] Indeed, Stephen Brown, in a review of the series in the *Journal of Marketing*, argues that

> Harry Potter is particularly pertinent to the contemporary marketing condition. The books, after all, are as much about marketing as the outcome of marketing. They deal with marketing matters, they are replete with marketing artefacts, they contain analyses of marketplace phenomena, and they hold the solution to an ancient marketing mystery. The books are not merely a marketing masterpiece, they are a marketing master class.[14]

Brown is here concerned with the narrative structures of the books but also with the ways in which the series has been embedded within consumer culture. In her work on *Batman* (1989), Eileen R. Meehan argues the film 'becomes only one component in a product line that extends beyond the theater, even beyond our contact with mass media, to penetrate the markets for toys, bedding, trinkets, cups and the other minutiae comprising one's everyday life inside a commoditized, consumerized culture'.[15] That is, the selling of an intertext rather than a single media product means the interconnection of multiple sites of production and consumption which are not normally connected with one another. The publication of these novels in a global market, which is becoming increasingly integrated horizontally, means that it is the Harry Potter brand which has penetrated multiple markets.

A key marker of the Harry Potter phenomenon has been the way in which adult readers have bought and read the texts. Adult readers of children's texts are not uncommon: for example, Lucy Maud Montgomery is a children's author who has remained popular with readers once they move beyond childhood. However, the readers of the 'Harry Potter' novels are not returning to texts read as children; rather, these novels are being purchased as fiction *for* adults. The 'Harry Potter' novels – as the alternative covers for children and adult readers make evident – have been marketed specifically to target a new audience for children's literature.[16] The distinctness of these markets was evidenced by a £1 price difference. There is a crucial distinction here between different *kinds* of children's literature. There are those books which are written for children and the form and tone of which make them appropriate for children: Enid Blyton's works, for example, would fall into this category with their child-orientated narratives and reliance upon an adventure

---

13 J.K. Rowling has contributed to the horizontal integration of this commercial intertext through the movie rights and the licensing agreements and also through writing such spin-off books as *Fantastic Beasts and Where to Find Them* (2001), by 'Newt Scamander', and *Quidditch Through the Ages* (2001), by 'Kennilworthy Whisp'.

14 Stephen Brown, 'Harry Potter and the Marketing Mystery: A Review and Critical Assessment of the Harry Potter Books', *Journal of Marketing* 66 (2002), 126–30 (p. 127).

15 Eileen R. Meehan, '"Holy Commodity Fetish, Batman!" The Political Economy of a Commercial Intertext', in Roberta Pearson and William Uricchio (eds), *The Many Lives of Batman* (New York: Routledge, 1991), pp. 47–65 (p. 50).

16 The economic viability of the adult covers was very quickly perceived, Bloomsbury recognising the crossover appeal of *Harry Potter and the Philosopher's Stone* as early as October 1998. See Philip Nel, *J.K. Rowling's Harry Potter Novels: A Reader's Guide* (London: Continuum, 2001), p. 67.

formula common in children's literature. There is another category of children's fiction which consists of those novels written for children   and which also contain child-orientated narratives – but which are comfortably read by adults (sometimes, but not usually, as first-time readers of the texts): Roald Dahl's *Danny the Champion of the World* (1975) is an example of this sort of children's literature. While the 'Harry Potter' novels fit into this latter category as well, there is a crucial difference because of the power of their brand. The novels have experienced horizontal market integration of a level previously not seen as possible for novels, enabling them to reach markets previously closed to children's literature. Whereas there was an existing body of children's literature which was read widely by adult readers before the arrival of Harry Potter, the Harry Potter adult market is a function of the deliberate targeting of markets not previously open to children's literature.

The ubiquity of the brand makes it easier for adults to become consumers of it: in the first place, they cannot be unaware of its existence and, in the second place, its pre-eminent place in contemporary popular culture means that to *not* read the 'Harry Potter' novels or watch the 'Harry Potter' films is to make a conscious decision to not participate in a global popular activity. Returning to Meehan's argument about *Batman*, she makes the case that in order to understand how these texts and intertexts move through popular culture – whether Batman or Harry Potter – requires an engagement with the economics of market structures: 'conditions of production select, frame, and shape both *Batman* as a commercial text and the product line that constitutes its commercial intertext'.[17] Children's books such as the 'Harry Potter' novels which are positioned within a horizontally integrated market can never be solely 'for' children. That is, as a result of horizontal integration, the 'Harry Potter' novels *had* to become novels for adults as well. Adults were able to view themselves as possible consumers of the novels – and of the intermedial products all bearing the Harry Potter brand – because of the ways in which the brand was embedded within popular culture. They became a commercial publication which targeted adults. Gupta makes the related point that 'Irrespective of actual readership, adult interest in, contribution to an engagement with the Harry Potter phenomenon has certainly been substantial.'[18] The film adaptations, for example, have been so closely tied to the novels that, certainly in respect of the first three shorter novels, a novel reader could substitute watching a film for reading one of the novels. So while adults may not be reading the 'Harry Potter' novels, they are unable to not be aware of them and of the intertext that is Harry Potter. Quite simply, while there have been phenomenally successful children's books before – commercially, critically and culturally – never before have so many adults been so involved in the commerce, criticism and cultural reception of a children's book.

One facet of this particular popularity of the 'Harry Potter' novels with adult readers has been its immediate and occasionally fervent discussion within academic contexts. There have been numerous panels and conferences devoted to Harry Potter, and the number of academic publications which emerged in the decade after the publication of *Harry Potter and the Philosopher's Stone* is substantially higher than

---

17 Meehan, '"Holy Commodity Fetish, Batman!"' p. 50.

18 Gupta, *Re-Reading Harry Potter*, p. 9.

usually accrues to other texts in a similar length of time. The marketing of Harry Potter to adult readers has resulted in scholars taking it up as an object of study not because they study children's literature but because of the overwhelming popularity of the 'Harry Potter' novels. In other words, they are part of the target market of adult readers and are now discussing and justifying their choice of reading matter through the means of scholarly debate. While scholarly engagement with extremely popular texts is a common feature of late twentieth and early twenty-first century academia – another example of this would be the work on the television series *Buffy the Vampire Slayer* (1997–2003) – the sheer amount of work on the 'Harry Potter' novels indicates its popularity. While Zipes points to a 'split between a minority of professional critics, who have misgivings about the 'Harry Potter' books, and the great majority of readers, old and young, who are mesmerized by the young magician's adventures', the ubiquity of the Potter brand has allowed for a substantial amount of critical work to be produced which does not always approach the subject with the scholarly rigour appropriate to academic debate.[19] Considering the criticism of the 'Harry Potter' novels as merely a function of the Harry Potter intertext, I want to identify the ways in which the popularity of the 'Harry Potter' novels with the adult reader has resulted in a particular form of children's literature criticism.

Readerly Comfort

The popularity of the 'Harry Potter' novels owes a great deal to the ways in which it references recognizable and long-familiar genres: the school story, the fantasy epic, the boy-wizard tale, the bildungsroman. Others have discussed in great detail the range of references within the novels; what I am interested in here is how the familiarity of the Harry Potter novels engenders a comfortable reading audience.[20] While children may recognise the similarities with other texts they have read recently – whether the school from Jill Murphy's *The Worst Witch* (1974) or the boy-wizard in Ursula Le Guin's *A Wizard of Earthsea* (1968) – adult readers of the novels experience the familiarity at a distance. It is a rare adult reader who will be reading children's literature regularly. I would argue that the multiple references in the 'Harry Potter' novels to other texts, genres and kinds of reading experiences provide a feeling of comfort, of returning to something once known well. There are echoes of this in Harry's experience of a physical desire for Hogwarts:

> He missed Hogwarts so much it was like having a constant stomach ache. He missed the castle, with its secret passageways, and ghosts, his lessons (though perhaps not Snape, the potions master), the post arriving by owl, eating banquets in the Great Hall, sleeping in his four-poster bed in the tower dormitory, visiting the gamekeeper Hagrid, in his cabin,

---

19 Zipes, *Sticks and Stones*, p. 171.

20 Gupta comments on the echoes of the 'faintly familiar' in the 'Harry Potter' novels: 'The names of magical characters, the motifs and rituals of magic, the stories and histories that give body to the Magic world appear often to refer back to a shimmering vista of folklore, fairy tale and myth drawn indiscriminately from a range of sources and contexts.' *Re-Reading Harry Potter*, p. 97.

in the grounds next to the forbidden forest and, especially, Quidditch, the most popular sport in the wizarding world.[21]

The desire for this world is certainly part of Potter's negotiation of the loss of his parents, but this passage also foregrounds many of those points in the text which are vaguely familiar to the adult reader from years of reading school stories (banquets in the Great Hall, sleeping in the dormitory), the fantasy epic (the castle with its secret passageways) and the magical adventure of the boy-wizard tale (post arriving by owl, Quidditch). The 'Harry Potter' novels have a relationship with other texts which moves beyond intertextual references to specific texts; rather, they have resonance with tropes and themes which are embedded in the genres which populate children's literature.

More so than the fantasy epic and the boy-wizard tale, however, it is the school story which controls the narrative in the 'Harry Potter' novels and also renders so much of what happens comfortingly recognizable to the adult reader: that is, we already know what is going to happen because we have been here before, albeit with other writers and in other series.[22] When Potter arrives at the magical Platform Nine and Three-Quarters in *Harry Potter and the Philosopher's Stone*, it is all very familiar and we know how the train journey will occur: families are saying goodbye, prefects are behaving in a way indicating their awareness of their position, trunks are being corded up and so on. This scene has been enacted in countless school stories with the train acting as a transitional space between home and school. Pat Pinsent points out that the school story 'encompasses three distinct domains of time and space: home (often also holiday), train journey and school' while Alice Jenkins notes that 'trains tend to have a peculiarly ambiguous status, negotiating between and blurring the boundaries of the home, "real" world and the utopian, dystopian or fantasy world'.[23] In the 'Harry Potter' novels, part of the excitement of the train journey to Hogwarts is the comfortable familiarity which readers feel with what will happen next: he must arrive at the school eventually for a series of (largely) school-based adventures. Pinsent goes on to note that, in the school story, the 'school itself often becomes a kind of additional character in the book, moulding its pupils almost in spite of themselves, or of the efforts of the staff, into its own ethos', a characteristic which can be traced back through the genre to Thomas Hughes's *Tom*

---

21 J.K. Rowling, *Harry Potter and the Chamber of Secrets* (London: Bloomsbury, 1998), p. 8.

22 I am not arguing that child readers do not experience this same sort of familiarity with these tropes and themes: the popularity of the series with child readers clearly indicates that they do. However, the adult reader is experiencing this familiarity at a distance, a nostalgia which imbues the series with a different level of reception and circulation than for the child reader.

23 Pat Pinsent, 'Theories of Genre and Gender: Change and Continuity in the School Story', in Kimberley Reynolds (ed.), *Modern Children's Literature: An Introduction* (Basingstoke: Palgrave Macmillan, 2005), pp. 8–22 (p. 13); Alice Jenkins, 'Getting to Utopia: Railways and Heterotopia in Children's Literature', in Carrie Hintz and Elaine Ostrey (eds), *Utopian and Dystopian Writing for Children and Young Adults* (London: Routledge, 2003), pp. 23–37 (p. 25).

Brown's School Days (1857).[24] Whether from having read school stories as a child or as the result of a wider cultural acquaintance with the genre, the adult reader of the 'Harry Potter' novels already knows what will happen: at the end of each novel, Potter must return home having completed another year of school.[25]

The novels thus have the problem common to much series fiction: how to keep things fresh for the reader if the reader already knows broadly what will happen?[26] We read detective fiction in part because of the anticipation of the narrative resolution: we *know* that Hercule Poirot will have to solve the crime precisely because he has to return, still successful as a detective, to solve the next crime. We know that Potter will survive the year precisely because he has to return to school the following year.[27] The tension then must be supplied from elsewhere in the narrative and is primarily achieved through the confrontations which Potter has with Voldemort. Pinsent notes this, arguing that 'The major difference between Rowling's work and the traditional "realist" school story lies in the fact that in each book Harry is presented with situations which pose a threat to his own life and, increasingly, to the future of the world.' For Pinsent, these 'life-and-death issues are more the province of fantasy'.[28] It is the fantastical fairy tale possibilities of the magic world which provide a frisson of the unexpected to the comfortable spaces of the school story. Yet it could also be argued that the references to the fantastic and to fairy tales also provide a level of familiar comfort for the reader. Joyce Thomas reminds us that the 'four most common settings in traditional fairy tales are the woods, the castle, the tower and the hut in the woods'[29]. These easily map onto Rowling's woods (and the Whomping

---

24 Pinsent, 'Theories of Genre and Gender', p. 13. For more on the school story in general, see Sue Sims and Hilary Clare, *The Encyclopaedia of Girls' School Stories* (Aldershot: Ashgate, 2000). For more on the school story and Harry Potter see Karen Manners Smith, 'Harry Potter's Schooldays: J.K. Rowling and the British Boarding School Novel', in Anatol (ed.), *Reading Harry Potter*, pp. 69–87.

25 The global popularity of the 'Harry Potter' novels with adult readers cannot be explained completely by reference to a wider cultural acquaintance with the genre; however, the novels do fetishise a particularly compelling account of British class politics which is certainly part of a wider cultural acquaintance with Britishness. See George Orwell, 'Boys' Weeklies' (1940), in *The Collected Essays, Journalism and Letters of George Orwell*, Volume I: An Age Like This, 1920–1940, ed. Sonia Orwell and Ian Angus (London: Secker & Warburg, 1968), pp. 460–85, for a compelling argument about the popularity of boarding school stories as related to the need for the working class to imagine themselves among the élite. The global popularity of the 'Harry Potter' novels can certainly be linked to the British imperialist tradition in literature.

26 For more on the problems and potentials of series fiction see Victor Watson, *Reading Series Fiction: From Arthur Ransome to Gene Kemp* (London: Routledge, 2000). For Watson, series fiction provides a 'series of profoundly satisfying narrative or thematic closures' (p. 7).

27 As Elizabeth D. Schafer summarises in *Exploring Harry Potter* (London: Ebury, 2000), the books offer 'a happy ending complete with a vanquished archenemy, restoration of the status quo, and recognition of Harry's prowess' (p. 6).

28 Pinsent, 'Theories of Genre and Gender', p. 20.

29 Joyce Thomas, 'Woods and Castles, Tower and Huts: Aspects of Setting in the Fairy Tale', in Sheila Egoff *et al.* (eds), *Only Connect: Readings on Children's Literature*, 3rd edn (Oxford: Oxford University Press, 1996), pp. 122–29 (p. 133). See Elaine Ostry, 'Accepting

Willow), Hogwarts, the various towers in Hogwarts (including the dormitory) and Hagrid's house. The 'Harry Potter' novels thus draw upon a number of genres, evoking familiar tropes and images and providing a sense of readerly comfort.

The ways in which these novels are embedded within certain cultural narratives has played a strong role in the criticism. Much of the critical work on the series references the work of Carl Jung and Joseph Campbell, with particular attention paid to Jungian archetypes and Campbell's hero myth. So, for example, Jann Lacoss draws on Campbell to explain that the 'folktale structure allows Rowling to communicate her plots in a way that is familiar to both young and older readers', while Lucy Rollin argues that 'Rowling is working from ... the hero myth elaborated by Joseph Campbell'.[30] Similarly, Deborah Bice suggests 'that the success of this series clearly lies in its recognizable, recycled metaphysical representations and motifs' and that 'when Rowling manifests Hogwart's [*sic*], she is in fact recreating Camelot, for like Camelot, Hogwarts is a modern microcosm of formulaic bravery and loyalty'.[31] I do not disagree with these readings of the novels as it is evident that the 'Harry Potter' series is intertextually embedded within a wide range of other sources and genres. The series, however, more broadly also relies upon an expectation of readers' familiarity with at least some of these texts. My concern is that these sources and genres are being categorised as archetypal and, more broadly, with the ease with which many of those writing about the 'Harry Potter' novels draw upon the work of Jung and Campbell, sometimes by quoting from their work but more often by speaking generally of 'archetypes' and 'structures', without identifying precisely what is meant by these categories. The readings of how the 'Harry Potter' novels are embedded in the complex histories and intertextualities which make up the 'Harry Potter' series need to be carefully unpicked in order that we can more readily understand how these novels function, both on an individual reading level and also as a global brand. Recognisability, even before the consumer has any knowledge of specific connotations, is after all a function of the intertext.

Daniella Caselli makes the point that children's literature criticism, for a long time, has not been seen as 'a serious critical activity, because it focuses on what have been regarded as simple, easy, or not very valuable texts'. The same argument could, of course, be made about much genre fiction and popular culture in general. However, the expansion of the academy and the widespread embracing of theoretical models have led to a re-evaluation of what constitutes a possible object of study. With specific reference to the 'Harry Potter' novels, Caselli argues that the simultaneous positioning of originality and tradition in the series by children's literature critics demonstrates why work on fairy tale and myth is used so often in the field:

Mudbloods: The Ambivalent Social Vision of J.K. Rowling's Fairy Tales', in Anatol (ed.), *Reading Harry Potter*, pp. 89–101, for more on fairy tales and the 'Harry Potter' novels.

30 Jann Lacoss, 'Of Magicals and Muggles: Reversals and Revulsions at Hogwarts', in Whited (ed.), *The Ivory Tower and Harry Potter*, pp. 67–88 (p. 87); Lucy Rollin, 'Among School Children', *South Carolina Review* 34, i (2001), 198–208 (p. 202).

31 Deborah Bice, 'From Merlin to Muggles: The Magic of Harry Potter, The First Book', in Deborah Bice (ed.), *Elsewhere: Selected Essays from the '20th Century Fantasy Literature: From Beatrix to Harry' International Literary Conference*, (Lanham, MD: University Press of America, 2003), pp. 29–36 (pp. 31 and 35).

Harry Potter the book needs to be both spontaneous (original) and part of a tradition (legitimate). This tradition, however, is not envisioned as a legacy of texts to be interpreted, but is constituted as either experience, which is passed on orally (in the case of fairy tales), or are innate values that are rediscovered (in the case of myths and archetypes). The link between orality and the child is what explains the prominence in children's literature criticism of studies on myths and fairy tales.[32]

Much of the critical work on the 'Harry Potter' series provides evidence of Caselli's claim for the widespread use of myths and archetypes to explore children's literature. While there has been much work done on the history of the fairy tale, the tendency to draw upon the archetypal structures of the fairy tale to *explain* children's literature needs to be more widely questioned. Discussing her *The Case of Peter Pan: The Impossibility of Children's Literature* (1984), Rose argues that instead 'of asking what children want, or need, from literature, [my] book has asked what it is that adults, through literature, want or demand of the child'.[33] Just as the field of children's literature is now widely understood to be the product of the adult producer of that literature, so too does the field of children's literature criticism need to be understood as part of the same impulses and desires. This is not to say that children's literature and children's literature criticism as categories do not or should not exist – they most certainly do and should exist. However, the work that the children's literature scholar produces should always be located within wider literary, historical and theoretical landscapes, landscapes understood to articulate adult desires.[34]

Gothic Desires

For Sigmund Freud, the uncanny is a resurfacing of long familiar feelings, constituting a return of the repressed. Familiarity and comfort are replaced with estrangement and unease: 'this uncanny is in reality nothing new or foreign, but something familiar and old – established in the mind that has been estranged only by the process of repression'. For Freud, the potential for estrangement and unease has always resided within that which is familiar: 'This reference to the factor of repression enables us, furthermore, to understand [the] definition of the uncanny as something which ought to have been concealed but which has nevertheless come to light.'[35] The uncanny has long been acknowledged as a key component of the Gothic

---

32 Daniella Caselli, 'Reading Intertextuality. The Natural and the Legitimate: Intertextuality in "Harry Potter"', in Karín Lesnik-Oberstein (ed.), *Children's Literature: New Approaches* (Basingstoke: Palgrave Macmillan, 2004), pp. 168–88 (pp. 171 and 176).

33 Rose, *Case of Peter Pan*, p. 137.

34 As an example of how this might work, see Lucie Armitt on genre fictions: 'we can look at the fantastic as a form of writing which is about opening up subversive spaces within the mainstream rather than ghettoising fantasy by encasing it within genres. In the process it also retains its important subversive properties without capitulating to classification'. *Theorising the Fantastic* (London: Arnold, 1996), p. 3.

35 Sigmund Freud, 'The Uncanny', in *The Complete Psychological Works of Sigmund Freud*, Volume XVII (1917–1919), ed. James Strachey *et al.*, trans. James Strachey *et al.* (London: Hogarth, 1955), pp. 221–52 (p. 234).

and its presence in the 'Harry Potter' novels indicates how the Gothic informs these narratives. The uncanny is articulated in the novels is a number of ways, one of which is the conflation of the unfamiliar and the familiar, as demonstrated when Potter first discovers how to get on the Hogwarts train:

> Harry walked more quickly. He was going to smash right into that ticket box and then he'd be in trouble – leaning forward on his trolley he broke into a heavy run – the barrier was coming nearer and nearer – he wouldn't be able to stop – the trolley was out of control – he was a foot away – he closed his eyes ready for the crash –
> It didn't come ... he kept on running ... he opened his eyes.
> A scarlet steam engine was waiting next to a platform packed with people. A sign overhead said *Hogwarts Express, 11 o'clock*. Harry looked behind him and saw a wrought-iron archway where the ticket box had been, with the words *Platform Nine and Three-Quarters* on it.[36]

Potter is in the familiar territory of a British rail station and believes that he *knows* how to navigate it; however, he finds that what he believed to be the logic of the physical reality of the station is not true. In this sense, the magic world which punctuates the non-magic world at certain points articulates the uncanny – something which has been estranged by repression. It is not that Potter enters a magic world via a portal to another dimension; rather, the magic and the Muggle worlds are one and the same. It is just that the Muggles do not acknowledge the magical: 'The people hurrying by didn't glance at it. Their eyes slid from the big book shop on one side to the record shop on the other as if they couldn't see the Leaky Cauldron at all.'[37] Here the uncanny functions at a level of cultural repression, a repression which Potter must learn to overcome if he is to succeed in the magic world.

The uncanny also works within the 'Harry Potter' novels specifically in terms of familial repression, castration and the fear of the Father – tropes which wend their way throughout all the novels. The emergence of the literary Gothic in the second half of the eighteenth century in opposition to the neoclassical realist aesthetic has been defined as a 'darker undercurrent to the [latter] literary tradition'.[38] The counter-cultural positioning of the Gothic has historically rendered it a relevant site for challenging Enlightenment notions of a universalised, rational, male subject and the modes of its representation:

---

36 J.K. Rowling, *Harry Potter and the Philosopher's Stone* (London: Bloomsbury, 1997), p. 71.

37 Ibid., p. 68. Nel notes that as 'in E. Nesbit's novels, Rowling's Potter series offers a matter-of-fact fantasy; secondary and primary worlds exist side by side, frequently overlapping with each other' ('Is There a Text in This Advertising Campaign?', p. 251). Kate Behr identifies the Muggle world as 'the Signifier recognizable as everything apparent on the surface and also the controlling, defining language, but, below (and sometimes alongside) it is the signified wizard world, which exists largely in the gaps in Muggle perceptions'. '"Same-as-Difference": Narrative Transformation and Intersecting Cultures in Harry Potter', *Journal of Narrative Theory* 35, i (2005), 112–32 (p. 122).

38 Fred Botting, *Gothic* (London: Routledge, 1996), p. 15.

Gothic signifies a writing of excess. It appears in the awful obscurity that haunted eighteenth-century rationality and morality. It shadows the despairing ecstasies of Romantic idealism and individualism and the uncanny dualities of Victorian realism and decadence … In the twentieth century, in diverse and ambiguous ways, Gothic figures have continued to shadow the progress of modernity with counter-narratives displaying the underside of enlightenment and humanist values.[39]

The 'Harry Potter' novels are replete with Gothic excess – whether it be the literal excess of food on the tables at banquets or the narrative excesses of all the adventures which Potter and his friends experience. In considering contemporary versions of the Gothic, Steven Bruhm argues that we should consider 'the central concerns of the classical Gothic [as] not that different from those of the contemporary Gothic: the dynamics of family, the limits of rationality and passion, the definition of statehood and citizenship, the cultural effects of technology'.[40] I argue that it is the dynamic of familial structures within which Potter finds himself which marks these novels as participating in the contemporary Gothic.[41] The 'Harry Potter' novels are all concerned with Potter's quest for familial reassurance. The orphan who lives with emotionally and physically abusive family members is a staple of Gothic fictions and Potter's early childhood easily maps onto this tradition. Potter is actively seeking a father to endorse his place within these patriarchal structures. Rebeus Hagrid, Albert Albus Dumbledore, Severus Snape, Sirius Black, Arthur Weasley and Prongs all stand in at different points for Potter's desire for his natural father, James Potter.[42]

It is the result of the loss of this family that impels Potter into direct conflict with the ultimate father-replacement, Voldemort. This desire for the lost object of paternal authority wends its way throughout the series and is marked by violence and anger. Bruhm summarises these tensions in the contemporary Gothic in noting that 'we intensely desire the object that has been lost, or another object, person, or practice that might take its pace, but we are aware at some level that this object carries with it the threat of punishment: the anger of the father, the breaking up of the law, castration'.[43] The uncanny functions in the ways in which Voldemort and Potter

---

39 Ibid., pp. 1–2.

40 Steven Bruhm, 'Contemporary Gothic: Why We Need It', in Jerrold E. Hogle (ed.), *The Cambridge Companion to Gothic Fiction* (Cambridge: Cambridge University Press, 2002), pp. 259–76 (p. 259).

41 Other readings are possible. One critic has argued that the *Harry Potter* novels conform to the Gothic tradition because throughout the texts 'are multiple allusions to doublings, uncanny coincidences, peregrinations, and uncommon symptoms. These point to the young wizard's need to account for a traumatic secret that, while it compels him and effects his destiny, is too painful to be absorbed by his ego'. Judith P. Robertson, 'What Happens to our Wishes: Magical Thinking in Harry Potter', *Children's Literature Association Quarterly*, 26 (2002), 198–211 (p. 204).

42 Annette Wanamaker makes the point that the 'Harry Potter' novels are intrinsically concerned with haunting and the past: 'Harry learns who he is and finds his way in the world, only by coming to terms with specters, only by learning history, more specifically, by learning to *read* history'. 'Specters of Potters: Inheritance in the *Harry Potter* Series', in Deborah Bice (ed.), *Elsewhere*, p. 50.

43 Bruhm, 'Contemporary Gothic', p. 263.

mirror one another – the real mirror of Erised – in that neither are pureblood wizards, both speak to snakes, both have black hair and both have been raised by Muggles. Potter simultaneously struggles with his increasing identification with Voldemort and realises that his mourning for his father means that he must *become* his father:

> 'Come on,' he muttered, staring about. 'Where are you? Dad, come on –'
> And then it hit him – he understood. He hadn't seen his father – he had seen *himself* – Harry flung himself out from behind the bush and pulled out his wand.
> 'EXPECTO PATRONUM!' he yelled.[44]

In his wish to save yet another of his father-figures (Black), Potter's desire for his natural father leads him to uncannily not recognise himself. Once he does so, he is able to summon a Patronus, a figurative version of his natural father, to protect him, as Dumbledore explains: 'Harry, in a way, you did see your father last night … You found him inside yourself.'[45] Desire for patriarchal authority informs all of Potter's relationships with men as he looks to the paternal figures to police 'the boundaries of legitimacy, thereby constituting meaning, behavior, and identity'.[46] The death or loss of authority of the men to whom Potter turns is an indication, however, that ultimately he will find paternal and patriarchal legitimacy only with Voldemort.

It is in the physical structures of Hogwarts that the Gothic is the most physically identifiable in these novels. The Gothic castle has been vital to the Gothic *mise en scène* since its formulation by Horace Walpole in *The Castle of Otranto* (1764). With its subterranean vaults, labyrinthine passageways, concealed doors and hidden chambers, the imaginative currency of the architectural topology of Walpole's castle has been much replicated and Hogwarts is no exception: 'The narrow path had opened suddenly on to the edge of a great black lake. Perched atop a high mountain on the other side, its windows sparkling in the starry sky, was a vast castle with many turrets and towers.'[47] It is in Hogwarts that Potter finally feels at home after his life with the Dursleys, but this place of refuge is also one of danger: as Manlove points out, it is in the school that Voldemort most often operates, suggesting that Hogwarts is not the space of safety it might first appear to be.[48] The family romance of the Gothic, with its tropes of imprisonment, is echoed in *Harry Potter and the Chamber of Secrets* and *Harry Potter and the Prison of Azkaban*. But it is in the relationship between Potter and the castle where we find the Gothic to be at its most transgressive. The Gothic novel has traditionally been concerned with a young individual who is caught up in a mystery:

> Within an imprisoning structure, a protagonist, typically a young woman whose mother has died, is compelled to seek out the centre of a mystery, while vague and usually sexual

---

44 J.K. Rowling, *Harry Potter and the Prisoner of Azkaban* (London: Bloomsbury, 1999), p. 300.

45 Ibid., p. 428.

46 David Punter, 'Aftergothic: Consumption, Machines, and Black Holes', in Hogle (ed.), *Cambridge Companion to Gothic Fiction*, pp. 277–300 (p. 282).

47 Rowling, *Harry Potter and the Philosopher's Stone*, p. 83.

48 Manlove, *From Alice to Harry Potter*, p. 189.

threats to her person from some powerful male figure tower on the periphery of her consciousness. Following clues that pull her onward and inward – bloodstains, mysterious sounds – she penetrates the obscure recesses of a vast labyrinthean space and discovers a secret room sealed off by its association with death.[49]

That Potter is a young *man* whose parents have died and who is compelled to seek out a mystery, who has had threats made by a powerful male figure, and who must follow clues that pull him into penetrating both the secrets of Hogwarts but also secrets which threaten to disrupt how the magic world functions, indicates that we might understand Potter to be a feminised Gothic hero.[50]

Indeed, the Gothic has been traditionally associated with the feminine and it has been aligned with female literary culture. Gothic writers have been often 'criticised as dealing in trivialities or as being too emotional, charges frequently characterised as feminine'.[51] The Gothic *heroine* presses normative social and cultural boundaries by transgressing the physical and subjective borders of the Gothic castle, but the provisionality of her flight is most frequently marked by her redomestication within traditional familial frameworks, often via the 'happy ending' motif of marriage, at the end of the narrative. Potter is contained within the narrative of the Gothic hero(ine) and is feminised by his location within the text. While he is searching for his father and for patriarchal authority and uses masculine force to effect this quest, the texts repeatedly feminise him through their use of the Gothic tradition. In feminised spaces of secret chambers, hidden tunnels and in the lake, Potter seeks the solution to the mystery of what he is supposed to do. Ximena Gallardo-C. and C. Jason Smith argue that the

> opponents of the aggressive and power-hungry Lord Voldemort resist his ability to penetrate, wound, and kill by exhibiting kindness, selflessness, a desire for intimacy with other, and responsibility. Thus, whereas the series apparently favors characters of the *male sex*, this preference continually conflicts with a context of symbols and actions that are *gendered feminine*.[52]

In texts which are overtly concerned with patriarchal lineage and with the Law of the Father – texts which 'celebrate male dominance and blood rule' – there are implicit references to the valorization of the feminine, a further indication of the Gothic

---

49 Claire Kahane, 'The Gothic Mirror', in Shirley Nelson Garner, Claire Kahane and Madelon Sprengnether (eds), *The (M)other Tongue: Essays in Feminist Psychoanalytic Interpretation* (Ithaca: Cornell University Press, 1985), pp. 334–51 (p. 334).

50 Noel Chevalier notes that '[w]ithin the wizarding world, therefore, Harry must appear as a radical, since his defeat of Voldemort must depend in some way upon his first transcending the obstacles of regulation, hierarchy, and social order established by, and embodied in, authoritarian structures'. 'The Liberty Tree and the Whomping Willow: Political Justice, Magical Science and Harry Potter', *Lion and the Unicorn* 29, (2005), 397–415 (p. 400).

51 Juliann E. Fleenor, 'Introduction', in Juliann E. Fleenor (ed.), *The Female Gothic*, (Montréal: Eden Press, 1983), pp. 3–28 (p. 8).

52 Ximena Gallardo-C. and C. Jason Smith, 'Cinderfella: J.K. Rowling's Wily Web of Gender', in *Reading Harry Potter*, ed. Anatol, pp. 191–205 (p. 200).

tropes of the texts.[53] Indeed, Potter's relationship with Ginny Weasley, who used the feminine form of the diary to become one of the first students at Hogwarts to succumb to Voldemort, provides further evidence as to the ways in which the gender politics of the Gothic can be used to disrupt the traditional male quest narrative.

Reading Desires

I have provided this reading of the uncanny and the Gothic in the 'Harry Potter' novels as an example of how these texts might be located within broader cultural histories without succumbing to generalizations about archetypes. This reading also demonstrates the way in which adult desires are embedded within these texts. This is of particular relevance with texts as popular as the 'Harry Potter' series. As Hans Heino-Ewers notes, 'it has become a characteristic of great narratives to strive for more or less simultaneous presentation in as many media as possible'.[54] The brand of Harry Potter has moved far beyond the pages of the seven novels which make up the series and has become an intertext which draws together multiple sites of production and consumption. This new market for children's literature in which the brand reigns supreme is one which must be navigated carefully by children's literature scholars. Rose points out that there 'is no child behind the category "children's fiction", other than the one which the category itself sets in place, the one which it needs to believe is there for its own purposes'. Yet much work still rests on the notion that 'there is a child who is simply there to be addressed and that speaking to it might be simple'. As Rose goes on to argue, this 'is an idea whose innocent generality covers up a multitude of sins'.[55] The field of 'Harry Potter Studies' makes evident that children's literature criticism must police itself. It must reach out to other disciplines and explore those histories, theories and intertextualities which can deepen our understanding of how children's literature functions. The texts, in addition to the child readers – *and* the adult readers – deserve this level of critical interrogation.

---

53 Zipes, *Sticks and Stones*, p. 183.

54 Hans-Heino Ewers, 'A Mediation of Children's Literature in the Age of Multimedia', in Emer O'Sullivan, Kimberley Reynolds and Rolf Romøren (eds), *Children's Literature Global and Local: Social and Aesthetic Perspectives* (Oslo: Novus, 2005), pp. 255–67 (p. 256).

55 Rose, *The Case of Peter Pan*, p. 1.

Further Reading

The following list contains no primary material and is not a complete catalogue of all sources cited in the essays. For this information, please consult the lists and footnotes attached to individual chapters. What appears below is intended as a guide to further reading, set out according the section divisions that have been used in this volume.

Part I: Old Tales Retold

Adams, Gillian, 'Medieval Children's Literature: Its Possibility and Actuality', *Children's Literature* 26 (1998), 1–24.

Alderson, Brian and Felix de Marez Oyens, *Be Merry and Wise: Origins of Children's Book Publishing in England, 1650–1850*, London: The British Library; New Castle, DE: Oak Knoll Press, 2006.

Bolter, J.D. and R. Grusin, *Remediation: Understanding New Media*, Cambridge MA: MIT Press, 2000.

Bottigheimer, Ruth B., 'Misperceived Perceptions: Perrault's Fairy Tales and English Children's Literature', *Children's Literature* 30 (2002), 1–18.

Burke, Peter, *Popular Culture in Early Modern Europe*, 1978, repr. Aldershot, Scholar Press, 1994.

Carpenter, Kevin, *Penny Dreadfuls and Comics: English Periodicals for Children from Victorian Times to the Present Day*, London: Victoria & Albert Museum, 1983.

Darton, F.J. Harvey, *Children's Books in England*, 3rd edn, rev. Brian Alderson, Cambridge: Cambridge University Press, 1982.

Dipple, Sue, *Chapbooks: How They Be Collected by Sondrie Madde Persons, and Something of their Trew Historie*, Hoddesdon, Herts.: Children's Books History Society, 1996.

Duggan, Anne E., *Salonnieres, Furies, and Fairies: The Politics Of Gender and Cultural Change in Absolutist France*, Newark: University of Delaware Press, 2005.

Fergus, Jan, *Provincial Readers in Eighteenth-Century England*, Oxford: University Press, 2007.

Grenby, M.O, 'Chapbooks, Children and Children's Literature', *The Library. Transactions of the Bibliographical Society* 8 (2007), 277–303.

___, 'Tame Fairies Make Good Teachers: The Popularity of Early British Fairy Tales' *Lion and the Unicorn* 30, i (2006), 1–24.

Haining, Peter, *The Penny Dreadful,* London: Gollancz, 1975.

Hannon, Patricia, *Fabulous Identities: Women's Fairy Tales in Seventeenth-Century France*, Amsterdam; Atlanta, GA: Rodopi, 1998.

Harries, Elizabeth Wanning, *Twice Upon a Time: Women Writers and the History of the Fairy Tale*, Princeton, NJ: Princeton University Press, 2003.

Harris, Michael, 'A Few Shillings for Small Books: The Experience of a Flying Stationer in the Eighteenth Century', in Michael Harris and Robin Myers (eds), *Spreading the Word: The Distribution Networks of Print 1550–1850*, Winchester: St Paul's Bibliographies, 1990.

Harris, Tim, *Popular Culture in England, c.1500–1850*, London: Palgrave Macmillan, 1995.

Hearne, Betsy, *Beauty and the Beast: Visions and Revisions of an Old Tale*, Chicago: University of Chicago Press, 1989.

Hole, Robert, 'Hannah More on Literature and Propaganda, 1788–1799', *History. The Journal of the Historical Association* 85 (2000), 613–33.

Isaac, Peter and Barry McKay (eds), *Images and Texts, Their Production and Distribution in the Eighteenth and Nineteenth Centuries*, New Castle, DE: Oak Knoll Books, 1997.

Jackson, Mary V., *Engines of Instruction, Mischief and Magic*, Lincoln: University of Nebraska Press, 1989.

James, Louis, *Fiction for the Working Man*, 1963, repr. Harmondsworth: Penguin, 1974.

Kline, Daniel (ed.), *Medieval Literature for Children*, London; New York: Routledge, 2003.

Lewis, David, 'The Picture Book: A Form Awaiting its History', *Signal* 77 (1995), 99–112.

McKay, Barry, *An Introduction to Chapbooks*, Oldham: Incline Press, 2003.

Mellor, Anne K., *Mothers of the Nation*, Bloomington: Indiana University Press, 2000.

Moon, Marjorie, *Benjamin Tabart's Juvenile Library*, Winchester: St Paul's Bibliographies, 1990.

___, *John Harris's Book for Youth*, Winchester: St Paul's Bibliographies, 1987.

Mullan, John and Christopher Reid (eds), *Eighteenth-Century Popular Culture: A Selection*, Oxford: Oxford University Press, 2000.

Neuburg, Victor E., *The Penny Histories. A Study of Chapbooks for Young Readers Over Two Centuries*, London: Oxford University Press, 1968.

___, *Popular Literature*, London: Woburn Press, 1977.

O'Brien, John, *Harlequin Britain: Pantomime and Entertainment, 1690–1760*, Baltimore, MD: Johns Hopkins University Press, 2004.

O'Malley, Andrew, *The Making of the Modern Child: Children's Literature and Childhood in the Late Eighteenth Century*, New York; London: Routledge, 2003.

Opie, Iona and Peter, *Classic Fairy Stories*, Oxford: Oxford University Press, 1974.

Orme, Nicholas, *Medieval Children,* Newhaven, CT: Yale University Press, 2001.

Palmer, Melvin D., 'Madame d'Aulnoy in England', *Comparative Literature* 27 (1975), 237–53.

Palmer, Roy, *A Ballad History of England: From 1588 to the Present*, London: Batsford, 1979.

Pedersen, Susan, 'Hannah More Meets Simple Simon: Tracts, Chapbooks, and Popular Culture in Late Eighteenth Century England', *Journal of British Studies* 25 (1986), 84–113.

Reay, Barry, *Popular Cultures in England 1550–1750*, London: Longmans, 1998.

Reid-Walsh, Jacqueline, 'Pantomime, Harlequinades and Children in Late Eighteenth-Century Britain: Playing in the Text', *British Journal for Eighteenth-Century Studies*, special issue 'The Cultures of Childhood', ed. M.O. Grenby, 29 (2006), 413–25.

Rogers, Pat, *Literature and Popular Culture in Eighteenth-Century England*, Brighton: Harvester Wheatsheaf, 1985.

Salberg, Derek, *Once Upon a Pantomime*, Luton: Cortney, 1981.

Sarland, Charles, *Young People Reading: Culture and Response*, Milton Keynes: Open University Press, 1991.

Seifert, Lewis C., *Fairy Tales, Sexuality, and Gender in France, 1690–1715. Nostalgic Utopias*, Cambridge: Cambridge University Press, 1996.

Shepherd, Leslie, *The History of Street Literature*, London: David and Charles, 1973.

Springhall, John, *Youth, Popular Culture and Moral Panics: Penny Gaffs to Gangster-Rap, 1830–1996*, Basingstoke: Macmillan, 1998.

Spufford, Margaret, *Small Books and Pleasant Histories: Popular Fiction and its Readership in Seventeenth-Century England*, London: Routledge, 1981.

Stott, Anne, *Hannah More: The First Victorian*, Oxford: Oxford University Press, 2003.

Summerfield, Geoffrey, *Fantasy and Reason: Children's Literature in the Eighteenth Century*, London: Methuen and Co., 1984.

Tatar, Maria, *Off with their Heads! Fairy Tales and the Culture of Childhood*, Princeton, NJ: Princeton University Press, 1992.

Warner, Marina, *From the Beast to the Blonde: On Fairy Tales and Their Tellers*, London: Chatto and Windus, 1994.

___, *No Go the Bogeyman,* London: Chatto and Windus, 1998.

Watt, Tessa, *Cheap Print and Popular Piety 1550–1640*, Cambridge: Cambridge University Press, 1991.

Wilson, A.E., *Christmas Pantomime: The Story of an English Institution*, London: George Allen and Unwin, 1934.

Zipes, Jack, *Fairy Tales and the Art of Subversion*, London: Heinemann, 1983.

___, *The Trials and Tribulations of Little Red Riding Hood*, 2nd edn, London: Routledge, 1993.

Part II: Forgotten Favourites

Allen, W.O.B. and E. McClure, *200 Years: The History of the Society for Promoting Christian Knowledge 1698–1898*, London: SPCK, 1898.

Auchmuty, Rosemary, *The World of Girls: The Appeal of the Girls' School Story*, London: The Women's Press, 1992.

Avery, Gillian, *Childhood's Pattern: A Study of the Heroes and Heroines of Children's Fiction 1770–1950*, London: Hodder and Stoughton, 1975.

Boyd, Kelly, *Manliness and the Boys' Paper Story in Britain: A Cultural History, 1855–1940*, Basingstoke: Palgrave Macmillan, 2003.

Brantlinger, Patrick, *Rule of Darkness: British Literature and Imperialism 1830–1914*, Ithaca; London: Cornell University Press, 1988.

Bratton, J.S., *The Impact of Victorian Children's Fiction*, London: Croom Helm, 1981.

Briggs, Julia, 'Women Writers and Writing for Children: From Sarah Fielding to E. Nesbit', in Gillian Avery and Julia Briggs (eds), *Children and Their Books: A Celebration of the Work of Iona and Peter Opie*, Oxford: Clarendon Press, 1989, pp. 221–50.

Bristow, Joseph, *Empire Boys: Adventures in a Man's World*, London: HarperCollins, 1991.

Butts, Dennis and Pat Garrett (eds), *From the Dairyman's Daughter to Worrals of the WAAF: The RTS, Lutterworth Press and Children's Literature*, Lutterworth: Lutterworth Press, 2006.

___, 'Shaping Boyhood: British Empire Builders and Adventurers', in Peter Hunt, (ed.), *An International Companion Encyclopedia of Children's Literature*, 2 vols, London and New York: Routledge, 2004, vol. 1, pp. 340–51.

Cadogan, Mary and Patricia Craig, *You're a Brick, Angela: A New Look at Girls' Fiction 1839–1975*, London: Victor Gollancz, 1976.

Castle, Kathryn, *Britannia's Children: Reading Colonialism through Children's Books and Magazines*, Manchester: Manchester University Press, 1996.

Cecil, Mirabel, *Heroines in Love 1750–1974*, London: Michael Joseph, 1974.

Cockburn, Claud, *Bestseller: The Books that Everyone Read 1900–1939*, London: Sidgwick and Jackson, 1972.

Cutt, Margaret Nancy, *Ministering Angels: A Study of Nineteenth-Century Evangelical Writing for Children*, Wormley, Herts.: Five Owls Press, 1959.

Dalziel, Margaret, *Popular Fiction 100 Years Ago: An Unexplored Tract of Literary History*, London: Cohen and West, 1957.

Davis, Robert Murray, *Playing Cowboys: Low Culture and High Art in the Western*, Norman, OK; London: University of Oklahoma Press, 1992.

Foster, Shirley and Judy Simons, *What Katy Read: Feminist Re-Readings of 'Classic' Stories for Girls*, Basingstoke: Macmillan, 1995.

Green, Martin, *Dreams of Adventures, Deeds of Empire*, London: Routledge and Kegan Paul, 1980.

Green, Samuel G., *The Story of The Religious Tract Society for One Hundred Years*, London: The Religious Tract Society, 1899.

Howarth, Patrick, *Play Up and Play the Game: The Heroes of Popular Fiction*, London: Eyre Methuen, 1973.

Hunt, Leon, *British Low Culture: From Safari Suits to Sexploitation*, London and New York: Routledge, 1998.

Kirkpatrick, Robert J. (ed.), *Boys School Stories*, Aldershot: Ashgate, 2000.

Kutzer, Daphne M., *Empire's Children: Empire and Imperialism in Classic British Children's Books*, New York and London: Garland, 2000.

Mitchell, Sally, *The New Girl: Girls' Culture in England 1880–1915*, New York; Chichester: Columbia University Press, 1995.

Moorcock, Michael, *Wizardry and Wild Romance: A Study of Epic Fantasy*, London: Victor Gollancz, 1987.

Ousby, Ian, *Bloodhounds of Heaven: The Detective in English Fiction from Godwin to Doyle*, Cambridge, MA: Harvard University Press, 1976.

Quigley, Isobel, *The Heirs of Tom Brown: The English School Story*, London: Chatto and Windus, 1982.

Randall, Don, *Kipling's Imperial Boy: Adolescence and Cultural Hybridity*, Basingstoke: Palgrave, 2000.

Reynolds, Kimberley, *Girls Only? Gender and Popular Children's Fiction in Britain, 1880–1910*, Hemel Hempstead: Harvester, 1990.

Richards, Jeffrey (ed.), *Imperialism and Juvenile Literature*, Manchester: Manchester University Press, 1989.

Salway, Lance, *A Peculiar Gift: Nineteenth Century Writings on Books for Children*, London: Kestrel, 1976.

Sims, Sue and Hilary Clare (eds), *Girls' Schools Stories*, Aldershot: Ashgate, 2000.

Turner, E.S., *Boys Will Be Boys: The Story of Sweeney Todd, Deadwood Dick, Sexton Blake, Billy Bunter, Dick Barton et al.*, 1948, London: Penguin 1976.

Vallone, Lynne, *Disciplines of Virtue: Girls' Culture in the Eighteenth and Nineteenth Centuries*, New Haven, CT: Yale University Press, 1995.

Part III: Popular Instruction, Popularity Imposed

Ahier, John, *Industry, Empire and the Nation: An Analysis of National Identity in School Textbooks, 1880–1960*, London: Falmer Press, 1988.

Alderson, Brian, 'Tracts, Rewards and Fairies: The Victorian Contribution to Children's Literature' in Asa Briggs (ed.), *A History of Publishing in Celebration of the 250th Anniversary of the House of Longman 1724–1974*, London: Longman, 1974.

Austin, Frances and Christopher Stray (eds), 'The Teaching of English in the Eighteenth and Nineteenth Centuries: Essays for Ian Michael on his 88th Birthday', special issue of *Paradigm. The Journal of the Textbook Colloquium* 2, vii (2003), <http://faculty.ed.uiuc.edu/westbury/Paradigm/> (accessed 25 April 2007).

Avery, Gillian, *Childhood's Pattern: A Study of the Heroes and Heroines of Children's Fiction 1770–1950*, London: Hodder and Stoughton, 1975.

___, *Nineteenth-Century Children: Heroes and Heroines in English Children's Stories 1780–1900*, London: Hodder and Stoughton, 1965.

Boyd, Kelly, *Manliness and the Boys' Story Paper in Britain: A Cultural History, 1855–1940*, Basingstoke: Palgrave Macmillan, 2003.

Castle, Kathryn, *Britannia's Children, Reading Colonialism through Children's Books and Magazines*, Manchester: Manchester University Press, 1996.

Chancellor, Valerie E., *History for their Masters: Opinion in the English History Textbook 1800–1914*, Bath: Adams and Dart, 1970.

Demers, Patricia, *Heaven upon Earth: The Form of Moral and Religious Children's Literature to 1850*, Knoxville: University of Tennessee Press, 1993.

Drotner, Kirsten, *English Children and their Magazines, 1751–1945*, New Haven, CT: Yale University Pres, 1988.

Entwistle, Dorothy, 'Counteracting the Street Culture: Book Prizes in English Sunday Schools at the Turn of the Century', *History of Education Society Bulletin* 55 (1995), 26–34.

___, 'Embossed Gilt and Moral Tales: Reward Books in English Sunday Schools', *Journal of Popular Culture* 28 (1994), 81–96.

Fauvel, John, 'Platonic Rhetoric in Distance Learning: How Robert Record Taught the Home Learner', *For the Learning of Mathematics: An International Journal of Mathematics Education*, 9 (1989), 2–6.

___, 'Tone and the Teacher: Instruction and Complicity in Mathematics Textbooks, in D. Pimm and E. Lowe (eds), *The Teaching and Learning of School Mathematics*, London: Hodder and Staughton, 1991, pp. 111–21.

Fyfe, Aileen, *Science and Salvation: Evangelical Popular Science Publishing in Victorian Britain*, Chicago: University of Chicago Press, 2004.

___, 'Young Readers and the Sciences', in Marina Frasca-Spada and Nicholas Jardine (eds), *Books and the Sciences in History*, Cambridge: Cambridge University Press, 2000, pp. 276–90.

Gillespie, Joanna, 'An Almost Irresistible Enginery: Five Decades of Nineteenth Century Methodist Sunday School Library Books', *Phaedrus*, 7 (1980), 5–12.

___, 'Schooling through Fiction', *Children's Literature*, 14 (1986), 61–81.

Graves, Norman, *School Textbook Research. The Case of Geography 1800–2000*, London: Institute of Education, University of London, 2001.

Heathorn, Stephen, *For Home, Country and Race: Constructing Gender, Class and Englishness in the Elementary School, 1880–1914*, Toronto; London: University of Toronto Press, 2000.

Issitt, John, 'The Natural History of a Textbook', *Publishing History* 47 (2000), 1–30.

Johnson, Clifton, *Old-Time Schools and School-Books*, 1904, repr. New York: Dover Publications, 1963.

Lundgren, Anders and Bernadette Bensaude-Vincent (eds), *Communicating Chemistry Textbooks and their Audiences 1789–1939*, Canton, MA: Watson Publishing International, 2000.

Mangan, J.A. (ed.), *Benefits Bestowed? Education and British Imperialism*, Manchester: Manchester University Press, 1988.

Michael, Ian, *Early Textbooks of English*, Reading: Colloquium on Textbooks, Schools and Society, 1993.

___, *Literature in School: A Guide to the Early Sources, 1700–1830*, Swansea: Textbook Colloquium Series, 1999.

Mitchell, Rosemary, *Picturing the Past: English History in Text and Image 1830–1870*, Oxford: Clarendon Press, 2000.

Myers, Greg, 'Science for Women and Children: The Dialogue of Popular Science in the Nineteenth Century', in John Christie and Sally Shuttleworth (eds), *Nature Transfigured: Science and Literature, 1700–1900*, Manchester: Manchester University Press, 1989, pp. 171–200.

Myers, Mitzi, 'Impeccable Governesses, Rational Dames, and Moral Mothers: Mary Wollstonecraft and the Female Tradition in Georgian Children's Books', *Children's Literature* 14 (1986), 31–59.

___, 'Socialising Rosamund: Educational Ideology and Fictional Form', *Children's Literature Association Quarterly* 14 (1989), 52–8.

Richardson, Alan, *Literature, Education, and Romanticism: Reading as Social Practice, 1780–1832*, Cambridge: Cambridge University Press, 1994.

Ritvo, Harriet, 'Learning from Animals: Natural History for Children in the Eighteenth and Nineteenth Centuries', *Children's Literature*, 13 (1985), 72–93.

Secord, James A., 'Newton in the Nursery: Tom Telescope and the Philosophy of Tops and Balls, 1761–1838', *History of Science* 23 (1985), 127–51.

Shiach, Morag, *Discourse on Popular Culture: Class, Gender and History in Cultural Analysis, 1730 to the Present*, Cambridge: Polity Press, 1989.

Shteir, Ann B., *Cultivating Women, Cultivating Science: Flora's Daughters and Botany in England 1760–1860*, Baltimore, MD: Johns Hopkins University Press, 1996.

Smith, Johanna M., 'Constructing the Nation: Eighteenth-Century Geographies for Children', *Mosaic: A Journal for the Interdisciplinary Study of Literature*, 34 (2001), 133–48.

Townsend, John Rowe, 'John Newbery and Tom Telescope', *Signal* 78 (1995), 207–14.

Vincent, David, 'The Domestic and the Official Curriculum in Nineteenth-Century England', in Mary Hilton, Morag Styles and Victor Watson (eds), *Opening the Nursery Door: Reading, Writing and Childhood 1600–1900*, London: Routledge, 1997, pp. 161–79.

Weedon, Alexis, *Victorian Publishing: The Economics of Book Publishing for a Mass Market 1836–1916*, Aldershot and Burlington, VT: Ashgate, 2003.

Part IV: The Famous Three: Blyton, Dahl and Rowling

Beckett, Sandra (ed.), *Transcending Boundaries: Writing for a Dual Audience of Children and Adults*, New York: Garland, 1999.

Bennett, Tony, *Popular Fiction: Technology, Ideology, Production, Reading*, London: Routledge, 1990.

Blake, Andrew, The Irresistible Rise of Harry Potter, London: Verso, 2002.

Bloom, Clive, *Cult Fiction: Popular Reading and Pulp Theory*, Basingstoke: Macmillan, 1996.

Brown, Stephen, 'Harry Potter and the Marketing Mystery: A Review and Critical Assessment of the Harry Potter Books,' *Journal of Marketing* 66 (2002), 126–30.

Buckingham, David, *After the Death of Childhood: Growing Up in the Age of Electronic Media*, Cambridge: Polity Press, 2000.

Cullingford, Cedric, *Children's Literature and Its Effects: The Formative Years*, London: Cassell, 1998.

Donaldson, Eileen, 'Spell-Binding Dahl: Considering Roald Dahl's Fantasy', in Thomas Van der Walt (ed.), *Change and Renewal in Children's Literature*, Westport, CT; London: Praeger, 2004, pp. 131–40.

Druce, Robert, *This Day Our Daily Fictions: An Enquiry into the Multi-Million Bestseller Status of Enid Blyton and Ian Fleming*, Amsterdam; Atlanta, GA: Rudopi BV, 1992.

Golby, J.M. and A.W. Purdue, *The Civilisation of the Crowd. Popular Culture in England 1750–1900*, 1984, rev. 2nd edn, Stroud: Alan Sutton, 1999.

Gupta, Suman, *Re-Reading Harry Potter*, Basingstoke: Palgrave Macmillan, 2003.

Heilman, Elizabeth E. (ed.), *Harry Potter's World: Multidisciplinary Critical Perspectives*, New York: RoutledgeFalmer, 2003.

Hendrick, Harry, *Children, Childhood and English Society, 1880–1990*, Cambridge, Cambridge University Press, 1997.

Hettinga, Donald and Gary D. Schmidt (eds), *British Children's Writers, 1914–1960*, The Dictionary of Literary Biography 160, Detroit, MI: Gale Research, 1996.

Hodge, Robert and David Tripp, *Children and Television: A Semiotic Approach*, Cambridge: Polity Press, 1986.

Hollindale, Peter, 'Ideology and the Children's Book', *Signal* 55 (1988), 3–22.

James, Allison, *Childhood Identities: Self and Social Relationships in the Experience of the Child*, Edinburgh: Edinburgh University Press, 1993.

___, Chris Jenks and Alan Prout, *Theorizing Childhood*, Cambridge: Polity Press, 1998.

Jenkins, Henry (ed.), *The Children's Culture Reader*, New York; London: New York University Press, 1998.

Kehily, Mary and Joan Swann (eds), *Children's Cultural Worlds*, Chichester: John Wiley in association with the Open University Press, 2003.

Kenway, Jane and Elizabeth Bullen, *Consuming Children: Education, Entertainment, Advertising*, Maidenhead: Open University Press, 2001.

Kinder, Marsha (ed.), *Kids' Media Culture*, Durham, NC; London: Duke University Press, 1999.

Kline, Stephen, *Out of the Garden: Toys, TV and Children's Culture in the Age of Marketing*, London: Verso, 1993.

Lesnik-Oberstein, Karin (ed.), *Children in Culture: Approaches to Childhood*, Basingstoke: Macmillan, 1998.

Lurie, Alison, *Boys and Girls Forever: Children's Classics from Cinderella to Harry Potter*, London: Penguin, 2003.

Mackey, Margaret, *The Case of Peter Rabbit: Changing Conditions of Literature for Children*, New York: Garland, 1996.

Manlove, Colin, *From Alice to Harry Potter: Children's Fantasy in England*, Christchurch: Cybereditions, 2003.

McCracken, Scott, *Pulp: Reading Popular Fiction*, Manchester: Manchester University Press, 1998.

Mitchell, Claudia and Jacqueline Reid-Walsh, *Researching Children's Popular Culture: The Cultural Spaces of Childhood*, London: Routledge, 2002.

Nel, Philip, '"Is There a Text in This Advertising Campaign?": Literature, Marketing and Harry Potter', *Lion and the Unicorn*, 29, ii (2005), 236–67.

Nicholson, Catriona, 'Dahl, the Marvellous Boy', in Dudley Jones and Tony Watkins (eds), *A Necessary Fantasy? The Heroic Figure in Children's Popular Culture*, New York and London: Garland, 2000, pp. 309–26.

Oswell, David, *Television, Childhood and the Home: A History of the Making of the Child Television Audience in Britain*, Oxford: Clarendon Press, 2002.

Pawling, Christopher, *Popular Fiction and Social Change*, London: Macmillan, 1984.

Postman, Neil, *The Disappearance of Childhood*, New York: Delacorte, 1982.

Ray, Sheila, *The Blyton Phenomenon*, London: André Deutsch, 1982.

Reynolds, Kimberley, *Radical Children's Literature. Future Visions and Aesthetic Transformations in Juvenile Fiction*, Basingstoke: Palgrave Macmillan, 2007.

___, *Young People's Reading at the End of the Century*, London: The Book Trust, 1996.

___, and Nicholas Tucker (eds), *Children's Book Publishing in Britain since 1945*, Aldershot: Scolar Press, 1998.

Rose, Jacqueline, *The Case of Peter Pan, or the Impossibility of Children's Fiction*, 1984, repr. Basingstoke: Macmillan, 1994.

___, 'Peter Pan and the Commercialisation of the Child', in Tony Bennett, *Popular Fiction: Technology, Ideology, Production, Reading*, London: Routledge, 1990, pp. 413–24.

Rudd, David, 'Cultural Studies', in Charles Butler (ed.), *Teaching Children's Fiction*, Basingstoke: Palgrave Macmillan, 2006.

___, *Enid Blyton and the Mystery of Children's Literature*, Basingstoke: Palgrave, 2000.

Sarland, Charles, *Young People Reading: Culture and Response*, Milton Keynes: Open University Press, 1991.

Steinberg, Shirley R. and Joe L. Kincheloe, *Kinderculture: The Corporate Construction of Childhood*, Boulder, CO: Westview, 1997.

Stephens, John, *Language and Ideology in Children's Fiction*, London: Longman, 1992.

___, and Robyn McCallum, *Retelling Stories, Framing Cultures: Traditional Story and Metanarratives in Children's Literature*, London: Garland, 1998.

Waites, Barry, Tony Bennett and Graham Martin (eds), *Popular Culture: Past and Present: A Reader*, London: Croom Helm, 1982.

Warren, Alan, Dale Salwak and Daryl F. Mallett, *Roald Dahl: From the Gremlins to the Chocolate Factory*, San Bernardino, CA: Borgo Press, 1994.

West, Mark, *Roald Dahl*, New York: Twayne, 1992.

Whited, Lana A. (ed.), *The Ivory Tower and Harry Potter: Perspectives on a Literary Phenomenon*, Columbia: Missouri University Press, 2002.

Wolf, Shelby Anne and Shirley Brice Heath, *The Braid of Literature: Children's Worlds of Reading*, Cambridge, MA: Harvard University Press, 1992.

Zipes, Jack, *Sticks and Stones: The Troublesome Success of Children's Literature from Slovenly Peter to Harry Potter*, London; New York: Routledge, 2001.

Index

The definite and indefinite articles are ignored in the alphabetical sequence, but are not inverted. For example, *The Amulet* is under 'A'.

References to illustrations are in **bold**.